IN THE WAKE OF REICH

IN THE WAKE OF REICH

EDITED BY
David Boadella

Ashley Books, Inc.
Port Washington, N.Y. 11050

Published simultaneously in Canada by
George J. McLeod, Limited, 73 Bathurst Street,
Toronto, Ontario M5V 2P8

IN THE WAKE OF REICH © Copyright 1977
by Ashley Books, Inc., Edited by David Boadella
Library of Congress Number: 77-75314
ISBN: 0-87949-103-5

All rights reserved. No part of this book may be used or reproduced in any manner whatsoever without the express permission of the Publisher except in the case of brief quotations in articles and reviews.

Address information to Ashley Books, Inc.,
Box 768, Port Washington, New York 11050

Published by Ashley Books, Inc.
Manufactured in the United States of America
by special arrangement with Coventure, Ltd.,
London, England

First U.S. Edition

9 8 7 6 5 4 3 2 1

Contents

INTRODUCTION

PART I: LOVE-LIVE AND SOCIETY

Introduction	3
Wilhelm Reich and the bio-social revolution *Myron Sharaf*	5
The force of love *Tage Philipson*	28
Reich, sex, and orgasm *Alexander Lowen*	34
Sexual revolution and cultural transformation *George Frankl*	49
Life and religion *Ola Raknes*	66
The primary personality and its relationship to the streamings *Gerda Boyesen*	81

PART II: BIRTH, INFANCY AND CHILDHOOD

Introduction	101
The self-regulated child *A.S. Neill*	103
Self-regulation in birth *Paul and Jean Ritter*	113
The use of vegeto-therapy in childbirth *Peter Jones*	123
Some thoughts about breast-feeding and health: the role of information and support *Alice Ladas*	138
The needs of children *Herb Snitzer*	154
Youth and the meaning of growth *Ronald Rybacki*	158
On the creation of a masochist *Eric Edwards*	164

PART III: EMOTIONAL EXPRESSION AND THERAPEUTIC CONTACT

Introduction	179
Bio-energetic analysis *Alexander Lowen*	181
Bio-energetic concepts of grounding *Stanley Keleman*	192
A developmental view of bio-energetic therapy *Robert Lewis*	210
The role of affect expression and defense in the character *Carl Kirsch*	222
Why touch? *Jerome Liss*	236
Pulsation and feeling *Laura Dillon*	249
The kick of life *Nadine Scott*	261

The psycho-diagnosis of the body
    Nic Waal, Anne Grieg and Mogens Rasmussen   266
Muscular tonus and integrated respiration
    Lillemor Johnsen   282
The divided body *David Boadella*   302
The development of the schizoid character and the
    therapeutic process *Robert Hilton and Renato Monaco*   322

PART IV: BIO-ENERGY IN HEALTH AND DISEASE
Introduction   337
Sexual repression and individual pathology *Luigi de Marchi*   339
New techniques in vision improvement *Charles Kelley*   351
Bio-energy and cancer formation
    Bruno Bizzi and Georgio Chiurco   382
The treatment of a malignant melanoma with orgone
    energy *Walter Hoppe*   391
The case of the broken heart *John Pierrakos*   400

Introduction

Wilhelm Reich died in 1957, destroyed by the last in a series of persecutions which his dynamic work on the emotional life of the body attracted. In the first decade after his death it seemed that the fruits of much of his work had been successfully destroyed: his books had been burned by government order, his experimental work had been stopped, and his colleagues and students were fragmented and dismayed. The past five or six years have seen a strong resurgence of interest in Reich, first among young people on both sides of the Atlantic, who found in Reich's powerful critique of authoritarian society, much to which they were sympathetic; and increasingly now Reich is taken seriously in many quarters where previously he would have been attacked or ignored.

More than twenty books about Reich have appeared in the last few years, and more still will be written. I have set down in my own book on Reich (*Wilhelm Reich: The Evolution of His Work*, Vision Press, London 1973) a record of his achievements. The aim of the present book however is a different one. Reich's work was not destroyed by his death and the campaigns against it. Indeed it is alive and well, flourishing in many parts of the world, and putting out independent shoots of contact in many different directions.

IN THE WAKE OF REICH collects together in one volume a number of important papers by those of Reich's colleagues and students who wrote about their own work, either during the time Reich was alive, or in the twenty years since his death. These contributions span three generations of Reichian studies, since the oldest contributor, Ola Raknes, died last year at the age of eighty-six while the youngest are still in their twenties.

When a great pioneer of a new therapeutic and scientific approach has died, the work he has created suffers from two dangers: rigidification and fossilisation by those who seek to prevent his work from being diluted, on the one hand; and diversification with the risk of erosion of crucial concepts, on the other. Those who follow the first course will often remain in relative isolation from contact with other work that is relevant or related through fear of losing a separate identity; those who follow the second course are sometimes so eager to have their work meet with acceptance, that its distinctive character gets quickly absorbed and levelled down to what is generally current in the climate of thought; and the work of the pioneer gets sometimes forgotten.

All the people in this volume were influenced in a major way by the work of Reich, and have succeeded in developing their own style of working with the concepts, insights, and techniques that his work generated. For all but two of the contributions, this is the first time they have appeared in book form in English. They illustrate not only the richness and creativity of the common source from which they drew their original inspiration, but also the range and depth of continuing the work, both therapeutic and educational, that is possible if one is not afraid to confront directly the emotional life of the body.

David Boadella

Part One

Love-Life and Society

LOVE-LIFE AND SOCIETY : INTRODUCTION

When Reich began his work with the study of the orgasm, in Vienna of the nineteen twenties, it was an act of considerable courage. Today, studies of the orgasm are commonplace, and sexuality has come very much into the public eye. Reich's approach had a number of features which distinguished it from the many studies that followed it, from Kinsey to Masters and Johnson and beyond. Firstly, he was concerned with the quality of emotional experience, and not simply with the physiology of performance. Reich was interested in sexuality as a particularly clear expression of excitability as a basic life function in which people were able to experience a deeper sense of unity and contact than was possible in their routine lives. His studies of the pathology of sexuality went much further than most, because he showed how much that passes as 'normal' in sexual behaviour proves to be unsatisfying and stereotyped.

When people accused Reich of being over-preoccupied with sex, he would reply: if the circulation of water in your house is blocked up, it will become the centre of attention until the blockage is cleared. Reich saw the free flow of erotic feeling, libido, through the body, as the foundation of emotional and mental health. He stood for better and more decent conditions in people's love lives, so that they could enjoy loving contact without guilt, without tension, and without compulsion from externally imposed morality. He argued that people, moved by a clear stream of desire, behaved in a way that was naturally moral, that was both responsive and responsible. As strongly as he fought for basic sexual rights and freedoms, he fought against the commercialisation and trivialisation of sex which tends to dominate the pseudo-sexual revolution that has been coming about in western culture. The historical tendency to split sexuality from love, and to over-value one at the expense of the other, has not changed: the pendulum has swung the other way. Reich saw repressive moralism, and commercialised pornography as two sides of the same split. His entire work-effort was dedicated to exploring ways, whether therapeutic, educational, or social, of overcoming this basic split, and to helping people to lead more integrated lives in which the head and the body spoke the same language as the heart.

Wilhelm Reich and the Bio-Social Revolution

by Myron R. Sharaf, Ph.D.

Assistant Clinical Professor of Psychiatry
Tufts University School of Medicine, Boston, USA

Dr. Myron Sharaf studied under Reich for a period of ten years. He translated some of Reich's papers from German and contributed to Reich's journals, and to the Journal of Orgonomy. *He is at present writing his own book on Reich. This paper is the transcript of a lecture given at a Forum on Human Ecology for the Massachusetts Institute of Technology, March 1970. It appeared in Vol.3 of* Energy and Character, *in May and September of 1972.*

I've been involved for many years with Reich's work. I've also been involved in a number of other ways of thinking, including psychoanalysis and traditional sociology. But I keep coming back to Reich's work as a kind of nagging, unfulfilled kind of thing both at a personal level and at a scientific level because much of the work is simply non-examined. That is not to say people aren't interested — they are destructively interested, by and large — so vividly so that many of Reich's best books were burned in 1956. Reich was imprisoned around the same time and died in prison. And I don't mean that just the books on the orgone accumulator, which you may or may not have heard about, were burned; also many of his writings on human beings were burned, as 'advertisements' for the accumulator, a claim which was absurd. Also, the present ignorance is due in part to the fact that Reich's books weren't republished until the early sixties, when some of them began to appear in paperback. By and large, they still have not really been reviewed.

While I certainly don't agree with all that Reich has written or stands for, and while I am incompetent to say whether I agree or don't agree with much of it because I haven't studied it that closely, my thesis is that Reich has always been ignored concerning the essence of what he was talking about. What has been picked up are the less essential parts of Reich that can be assimilated into various traditional positions, e.g. psychoanalytic and sociological.

I have been currently concerned in thinking through Reich's relationships to the bio-social revolution of our time. One of the things that is often said about our time is that lots of things are happening socially and lots of things are changing, but that we lack a coherent theory of what's going on. It is my thesis that Reich provides such a theory. I won't define in any great detail what I mean by the 'bio-social revolution' but will merely suggest some of its connotations. It includes certainly the changes in sexual attitudes — which have been going on for a while, but which seem to be accelerating. There is even talk about repealing abortion laws in Massachusetts, which is pretty good. And the whole cultural tone of the mass media, particularly the movies, contains a much greater affirmation of sexuality. This serious look at what is involved in sexual relationships, in sexual feelings, in sexuality generally is something new under the sun. This is a profound and I think an exciting and also a very dangerous thing — dangerous because people who grew up under strongly sex-negative attitudes must be quite terrified by what is going on. And I feel I have enough of that in myself to know what they are going through. It's all over the place — miniskirts, movies, nudes in magazines, etc. From a certain perspective, it's terrible — i.e. from the perspective of an organism that has learned to control these feelings and to have a veneer of socialness, compulsive marriage, of getting along in life. I don't think that perspective of what Reich called the armored organism should be ridiculed. It takes an awful lot of course to keep going when you feel empty inside. Many people have to do that. They have to make great sacrifices to do it — internal sacrifices. And then they see young people coming along who are not making the same kind of sacrifices. Some of these young people are doing very positive things, but others are doing very negative, destructive things. And in most it is a mixture of positive and negative things. This is an era when, as you know, it can 'all hang out' — from the most genuine positive impulses to all kinds of distortions, destructiveness and so forth. The veneer is breaking down. It has been breaking down for some time. So that the anger of the average armored person, the person who is just 'getting along,' minding his own business, is directed toward both the *secondary*, destructive level and also toward the *primary*, healthy life forces. The average older person doesn't like either part of this breakthrough. Understandably, they dislike the breakthrough of destructive impulses, but they also dislike the emergence of the healthily spontaneous ones.

Let me arrive at this viewpoint a little more chronologically by reviewing the development of Reich's work. What I would like to do is clarify his relationship not only to contemporary pro- and anti-sexual attitudes but to other aspects of our culture such as the 'new politics'.

There is a growing awareness that something new is going on politically among young people. The young are unwilling to sacrifice the present for some revolutionary 'pie in the sky' — whether that pie is the withering away of the state fifty years from now, which never seems to wither away, or any other kind of ideological dream of something nice in the future while the present reality is very different. The discrepancy between rhetoric and reality I think is a very strong element in the young movement and it is also very strong in Reich's work.

One other aspect of the present 'cultural revolution' relates to the sexual question, but it is so widespread that it deserves separate comment. I am referring to a whole series of therapeutic and quasi-therapeutic activities which increasingly involve the body — as opposed to purely verbal forms of psychotherapy — which have been dominant since Freud. I am referring to therapy centers such as Esalen, where there is a great deal of emphasis on bodily expression; the living theater, Albert Pesso's psychomotor therapy, Paul Goodman's gestalt therapy, and the like. I could cite many other examples. The common denominator is awareness that neuroses — using that word to cover most of us in the sense of the term 'normal neuroses' — are anchored somatically in bodily rigidities as well as in a series of psychic complexes. I think it is a growing awareness and that it owes a great, often unacknowledged debt to Reich's work.

There has also been in the last few years a rediscovering of Reich's sociological work of the 1920's and 30's. There has been considerable enthusiasm for this aspect of Reich among college students and others. Reich's radical social perspective was stressed in Paul Robinson's book, *The Freudian Left*. The Women's Liberation movement also reflects this kind of trend in an important way.

In regard to Reich's own career, what is very fascinating is that he did not start out with a particularly social viewpoint at all. So that it has the quality, as you read it, of a discovery rather than a kind of preconceived notion of cultural change. He was not at all a political person in his early manhood and his early years as a psychoanalyst. One of the things that is also interesting is that his career spans a long, important, and recent period. He started very young — he was only about 22 years old when he first became a psychoanalyst in 1919. This was very close to the time of the Russian Revolution and its enormous impact on Europe. While he was an analyst in Vienna and Berlin during the 1920's and early 1930's, he experienced first-hand not only the influence of the Russian experience on the European radical parties, but also the rise of Nazism. Like so many of his generation, he was also a political refugee during the 1930's, moving from place to place in Europe and finally settling in the USA in 1939.

But, to return to our story, he started as an analyst much interested almost from the beginning in the question of what is the *goal* of psychoanalytic treatment. Now this was an important question because at that time the goal was rather narrowly conceived as relieving people from certain kinds of symptoms. People at that time came to psychoanalysis for fairly circumscribed symptoms — compulsions, and the like. Psychoanalysts, in the main, didn't treat psychotic patients at that time. There was a more clearly defined sense in those days of ill and normal. Ill were people with symptoms and the really crazy people, and the normal were the rest of us. If you drank too much and were not very happy, that was tough — that was life. As Freud said of psychoanalysis, we must be content to replace hysterical misery with ordinary unhappiness.

But Reich was not content with so modest a goal. He first became involved with the technical problem that you often couldn't replace 'hysterical misery' — or the symptom — without also altering the patient's total character structure. Furthermore, he noticed that the patients who were permanently relieved of their symptoms were also the patients who were able to achieve healthy sexual functioning. That kind of functioning increasingly became what he saw as the goal of therapy — namely, the establishing of the capacity for full genital experience. Now it is right here that we are at a fundamental misunderstanding concerning Reich because his therapeutic goal was never accepted by psychoanalysis. Much that I will discuss was accepted, but this wasn't.

The argument was made — and it still is made — that there are plenty of people who are sexually healthy but who also are very neurotic or even psychotic.

This kind of argument led Reich to give a much more detailed description, which still is not known very widely, of his concept of full genital functioning or 'orgastic potency.' To quote Reich's *The Function of the Orgasm*,

> 'The more exactly I had my patients describe their behavior and sensations in the sexual act, the firmer became my clinical conviction that all of them, without exception, suffered from a severe disturbance of this genitality. This was especially true of those men who bragged the loudest about their sexual conquests and about how many times a night they could do it. There was no doubt: they were erectively very potent, but ejaculation was accompanied by little or no pleasure, or even the opposite, by disgust and unpleasant sensations. An exact analysis of the fantasies accompanying the act revealed most sadistic or self-satisfied attitudes in the men, anxiety, reserve or masculinity in women. To the so-called potent man, the act had the significance of conquering, piercing or raping the woman. They wanted to

give proof of their potency, or to be admired for their erective endurance. This "potency" could easily be destroyed by laying bare its motives. It served to cover up serious disturbances of erection or ejaculation. In none of these cases was there as much as a trace of involuntary behavior or loss of alertness during the act.'

Without going into the full description, as important as it is, of what Reich meant by 'orgastic potency,' I would like to call attention to what he found invariably missing in patients, i.e. the capacity for involuntary contractions of the organism and the complete discharge of the accumulated excitation. This capacity for involuntary contraction and discharge of excitation equivalent to the buildup of the tension were the characteristics of human genitality that he was most concerned with and they were the characteristics that had been most neglected. To quote Reich again (*The Function of the Orgasm*):

'Clinical experience shows that man — as a result of the general sexual repression — has lost the capacity for ultimate vegetatively involuntary surrender. What I mean by "orgastic potency" is exactly this ultimate, hitherto unrecognized portion of the capacity for excitation and release of tension. Orgastic potency is the biological primal and basic function which man has in common with all living organisms. All feelings about nature derive from this function or from the longing for it.'

I would still maintain that in most summaries of Reich the concept of 'orgastic potency' has not emerged clearly. People usually just talk about some kind of 'sex prophet' but without making clear the nature of his prophecy. In terms of the technique that Reich evolved to get at the basic biological level of the human being, many are drawn to his technique initially not through an interest in the capacity for full genital experience but as an aid in helping patients with their problems, whatever they might be. What Reich found was that releasing the unconscious ideas behind a particular symptom was often insufficient to produce a change in the patient's behavior. In addition to particular unconscious ideas, the neurosis was also embedded in certain characteristic ways that the person defended himself against repressed feelings and ideas both psychologically in terms of rigid character traits and somatically in terms of bodily armoring. Reich's interest in the matrix, if you will, of the neurotic symptom — namely, the total character, became an important part of his therapeutic approach. And this is what has been incorporated in psychoanalysis — not the *goal* of character analysis in the sense of *orgastic potency*, but aspects of Reich's technique of character analysis. Many therapists became aware that you couldn't just deal with symptoms, you had to deal with the total personality. They also realized that Reich had a point when he stressed that there was a certain logic and order in how you should deal with the material that the patient brought up, if you wanted to influence the symptoms and other disturbing aspects of the patient's life. There came to be much more emphasis on what were called the 'defense mechanisms' and other character defenses first stressed by Reich.

This emphasis on defense arose from Reich's concern as to how the organism defends itself against feelings in general and genital excitation in particular. Nietzsche once said: 'All the regulations of mankind are turned to the end that the intense sensation of life may be lost in continual distraction.'

Well, the question is: how does the organism defend itself against intense sensations, and what function do those defenses serve? Taking the latter question first, the function is to protect against pain. When the intense sensations are connected with punishment, as they often are, or — and this Reich later put more emphasis on — *lack of response*, which also has a frustrating, punishing effect, the organism responds by 'armoring up' against strong feelings which lead or have led in the past to painful consequences. I may add parenthetically that this emphasis on the frustrating aspects of non-responsiveness was a very important distinction because in the early years of his work — the twenties and early thirties — Reich emphasized the more overt frustrations — a child masturbates, somebody slaps his hand and threatens to cut off his penis, *ergo* fear of genital sensation and an armoring against having to experience again the sensations and the fear and guilt that went with them. However, during the 1940's and 1950's he also emphasized the damaging effect of non-responsiveness. For example, the baby with its strong oral impulses encounters a preoccupied mother who is feeling empty and unalive. She may not be consciously hostile at all — she may believe in all the good things and even try very hard to respond in the 'right way'. But if she is not alive biologically, she cannot truly respond. Thus, there is no more mistaken idea than the common notion today that, well, we have had a lot of this permissiveness, and it doesn't work. True, there is much guilt-ridden permissiveness that doesn't work — but we haven't had permissiveness in the sense that Reich was talking about it. He was talking about affirmation of these deep biological impulses that you can't just permit indifferently — you must respond to them. And the capacity to respond to them has been severely damaged through people's own negative childhood experiences. So that we constantly just keep repeating this cycle of armoring, in spite of the best intentions. Now that can be altered. It is being altered to some degree. It isn't an absolute thing. There are quantitative differences which become qualitative. And there are important changes going on. But it isn't as though it just comes about that you take down some taboos and then there is permissiveness — and then if there are still problems, *ergo* permissiveness doesn't work. Or as many people say today — we have still got a lot of problems: it must be aggression. You know, supposedly sex is free now, and if we still have problems, then aggression must be the problem. We should now pay attention to aggression. But from Reich's point of view, sex has not been free at all in the deepest sense. The ground has been softened and much has been done that will permit more and more to be developed in terms of the deeper levels of biological functioning. But it isn't as though this has been freed and we can go on to other matters. It is nowhere near as mechanical as that.

I want to go back a bit to the character analysis part. I think Reich did a marvellous job on character analysis — the details and specifics of how character armor develops and its functions in warding off both pleasure and pain.

In discussing character development, Reich compares the layers in the character to:

> 'geological or archaeological strata which, similarly, are solidified history. A conflict which has been active at a certain period of life always leaves its traces in the character, in the form of a rigidity. It functions automatically and is difficult to eliminate. The patient does not feel it as something alien to him, but often feels it as something rigid and unyielding or as a loss or diminution of spontaneity. Each of these layers in the character structure is a piece of life history which is preserved in another form and is still active. It was shown that by loosening up these layers, the old conflicts could — more or less easily — be revived. If the layers were particularly numerous and functioning automatically, if they formed a compact unit which was difficult to penetrate, they seemed like an 'armor' surrounding the living organism. This armor may be superficial or deep-lying, soft as a sponge or hard as nails. In each case its function was to protect against unpleasure. However, the organism paid for this protection by losing a great deal of its capacity for pleasure. The latent content of this armor was the conflicts of the past. The energy that held the armor together consisted mostly in destructiveness which had become bound. This was shown by the fact that destructiveness would be set free as soon as the armor began to crack. Whence came this destructive and hateful aggression? What was its function? Was it primary, i.e. biological destructiveness? It has taken many years to solve such questions. I found that people reacted with intense hatred to any attempt to disturb the neurotic equilibrium which was maintained by their armor.'

So we should not be too surprised when Judge Hoffman gets very angry when people start talking about sex and begin to prance around. They are disturbing his armor. They don't often do it in a therapeutic fashion. They do not create an alliance with some part of him which wants to work with them on getting rid of his armor. If you don't have that relationship, all you do is provoke destructive hate which is not worked through.

To continue Reich's description of character armor:

> 'Gradually I began to comprehend the latent hatred which is never lacking in patients. If one did not let oneself be deceived by the patient giving associations without any affect, if one was not content with dream interpretation, if, instead, one approached the patient's character defense, he would inevitably get angry. At first this was puzzling. He would complain about the emptiness in his emotional life. If, however, one showed him the same emptiness in the manner of his communications, his coldness, his bombastic or artificial behavior, then he would get angry. A symptom such as a headache or a tic he felt as alien to himself. But his fundamental personality — that was himself. He felt disturbed and angry when it was pointed out to him.'

He goes on to talk about the hateful disruptiveness bound up in the character which is nothing but the

> 'anger about frustration in general and denial of sexual gratification in particular. If the analysis penetrated to a sufficient depth, every destructive tendency gave way to a sexual one.'

Now this is not to say there is no destructiveness in the human organism. Obviously, if it is confronted by threats, it will react destructively. If the organism is irrational, it will react destructively to imagined threats. But, therapeutically, it was found that beneath this destructiveness was a spontaneous substratum, if you will, which, in the absence of real threat, would react in a nondestructive way.

Let me go on and briefly mention that Reich also focused on the form the character took, not just what the person said. The patient's whole manner now became an object of scrutiny — whether he was, for example, aristocratic, sly, ingratiating, or whatever. One can look at a person and see what kind of dominant tone and configuration are emerging in his emotional expression. This emphasis on the form of emotional expression led in time to an enormously important discovery, i.e. the muscular armor. The resistances to deep emotional expression were seen as embodied not only in a character trait of shyness or meekness or bombasticness or what not, but also in a more literal armor, i.e. bodily rigidities. Thus, when we talk of somebody being stiff-necked, for example, this is not just a way of speaking; it denotes very often a real stiffening in the body, including the neck, which is the somatic side or anchoring of the characterological attitudes of stubbornness. In short, when pleasurable impulses are frustrated, anger results. When anger is punished, crying results. When crying is punished, one becomes anxious. To be anxious for a long time is also very painful. So you bind the anxiety in various character and bodily spasms that absorb this free-floating anxiety — making it temporarily, at least, less uncomfortable for the organism. You don't have to go around feeling so anxious, you can go around feeling dead. And, to repeat, this deadening process takes place not just in the character but in the body, in a whole series of particular kinds of rigidities that were later to be called muscular armoring. These 'armor rings' are cross-sectional, in contrast to the movement of energy in the body which flows longitudinally from the head to the toes. Thus, an impulse may start to go through the body and then be blocked — it may get caught in the throat, or in the eyes. There is a logic in the technique used to dissolve those blocks so that the energy can flow freely. With the successful dissolution of these characterological and muscular armorings, there is a free flow of energy, an experience which the organism subjectively perceives as a pleasurable sensation in connection with respiratory expiration. The person is then capable of surrendering to the most intense expression of these sensations in the act of love. In general, the person is capable of 'self-regulation' of a spontaneous sociality and a lack of need for rigid internal or external 'thou shalt nots'.

This is not to imply that, in Reich's view, discipline or constraint are unnecessary and that everybody can live in a continual orgy of self-indulgence. It is to say that discipline becomes a much more organic or self-regulative process than that which takes place in the presence of heavy armoring. The highly armored organism needs a central nervous system to dictate to him — 'now you will do this, now you will do that,' the kind of 'living machine' who gets his orders either from his own brain or from somebody else's brain. The latter is preferable because over time one gets tired of ordering oneself around; you prefer to have somebody else to order you. You just march in formation. Obviously, somebody who is encumbered by this load of armor will turn to a 'leader.' This takes us now to Reich's social concepts.

Reich first became interested in a more radical social perspective on the etiology, treatment, and prevention of emotional disturbances when he started working in a psychoanalytic clinic which saw working class patients instead of the usual upper class persons. Working in this setting he began to see several things very clearly. To quote the lessons Reich described from this experience:

'Neuroses are widely prevalent, like an epidemic; they are not a fad of pampered women, as was claimed in the fight against psychoanalysis.

Disturbances of genital function far outnumbered any other forms of disturbance as the reason for seeking help in the clinic.

If one was to make any headway, the establishment of prognostic criteria in the treatment of divers cases was indispensable. Previously, no attention had been paid to this important question.

Equally decisive was a clarification of the question as to why one achieved a cure in one case and not in another. This would give a means of better selection of patients. At the time, no theory of therapy had been formulated.

Neither in psychiatry nor in psychoanalysis was it customary to ask patients about their social conditions. That there was poverty and need, one knew; but somehow that did not seem to be relevant. In the clinic however, one was constantly confronted by these factors. Often enough, social help was the first thing necessary. Suddenly, the fundamental difference between private practice and clinic practice was evident. After some two years of clinic work it was clear that individual psychotherapy has a very limited scope. Only a small fraction of the physically sick could receive any treatment. Working with this fraction, one lost hundreds of hours' work because of failure due to unsolved technical problems. There remained a small group which repaid the efforts made. Psychoanalysis has never made a secret of this unfortunate state of affairs in therapy.'

Nowadays, everybody says we have got to get out of the private office and do something about preventing this epidemic of neuroses. Reich was saying 'Let's do something about it' over forty years ago when he worked in clinics and found such a high incidence of disorder. People would come with all kinds of inner and external difficulties. There were all kinds of social frustrations. Abortion was illegal, contraception you couldn't talk about. Housing was crowded, material conditions were very poor. And he became much more aware of the importance of material conditions — the lack of housing, worry about food — in addition to all the internal difficulties which were harassing the poor. Even with internal problems the wealthy could more or less plod along with all kinds of secondary satisfactions that would at least soften the blow of the internal pain. They did not have to worry about where the next meal was coming from. Thus through clinical work with the poor, he became much concerned with the social issues that were agitating Europe of the 1920's.

Another stimulus to this concern was the Russian Revolution. You may have no idea what hope the Russian Revolution aroused — of economic equality as well as a liberalization of social-sexual attitudes. When the Russian Revolution initially started, marriage laws were changed, marriage and divorce became very simple procedures. Provisions for day-care centers and other things that Women's Liberation is talking about now were in the original constitution of the Soviet Union. Initially, Reich was very hopeful that these kinds of social change would help prevent neurosis.

Reich and Freud quarrelled about the signficance of the

Russian Revolution as well as about the role of psychoanalysis in influencing social change. Freud was very sceptical about the whole idea of ever preventing neurosis. According to Freud, the whole logic of civilization worked against it. In his book, *Civilization and its Discontents*, Freud powerfully describes man's tragic condition in society. This book grew out of evening discussions with Reich and others.

Reich was arguing: let's get into the political parties, let's get rid of abortion and contraception laws, let's get rooms for the youth. If neurosis stems from sexual frustration, let us free sexuality. Freud wasn't prepared to get into all that. In addition, he thought that civilization depended upon sublimation, upon considerable sexual frustration. You don't hear much about that now, but you heard more about it at that time when psychoanalysis, initially under attack as an advocate of sexual chaos, argued that through knowing the unconscious one could better renounce the instincts and go on to 'higher things.'

Also Freud's later concept of the 'death instinct', a primary destructive force reflected in sadism and masochism, militated against a concern with social change. If there is a death instinct, and if further you need sublimation for civilization, then neurosis is not preventable. You could soften, dilute, manage, control to some extent its development, but basically it is built into the man-civilization dilemma. Reich argued that it wasn't built into the human condition. Sexual fulfilment and civilization were incompatible in some senses, but not in the important ones. On the contrary, according to Reich, orgastic potency, or the absence of neuroses, was the best characterological basis for healthy productive work and genuine sociality, two fundamental characteristics as associated with a 'civilized' person.

We come then to the profound question of where does the armoring come from? Why is there an armoring in man? Why did armoring arise only in the human species? Originally, Reich took a rather Marxist view on this question, namely, that armoring developed with exploitation when a patriarchal form of kinship replaced a matriarchal one. Matrilineal society had a much more permissive upbringing for children with considerable sexual freedom. Reich used Malinowski's work on the

Trobrianders very effectively, I think, to show their lack of much secondary behavior, e.g. sadism, homosexuality, severe neurosis. Matriarchy, lack of economic exploitation, sexual permissiveness, and relative psychic health were found among the Trobrianders, and according to Reich, this association of characteristics was not accidental.

Reich asked:

> 'What social function does it serve to stop children from masturbating, to stop adolescents from sleeping together, compel people into monogamous, life-long, compulsive forms of sexual relationships during adulthood? What functions does all this serve?'

And his answer as a good Marxist — but an answer he would maintain at least in part until the end — was that it served to keep people submissive — that if they were subdued in their vital energies, they would be less critical and more willing to go along with 'the system' — whatever the system might be. Now in the twenties, Reich made this sound quite political — almost a kind of conspiracy. The capitalists think, ' ... how can we keep them down on the farm? Aha now, we'll kill sexuality, they won't be critical, and they'll just go through work mechanically doing their job, and we can exploit them.' The trouble with that is that the capitalists were caught up in the system of armoring and sexual suppression as much as the workers. They were all the victims of a system that transcended any of them and that reproduced armoring from generation to generation. The family was the transmission belt which prepared the growing organism for authoritarian society.

Again influenced by Marxism, Reich emphasized that technological changes tend to break down this system. There was a lag between new technological forms and character attitudes developed at an earlier time which perpetuated themselves somewhat independently of the technological changes.

Without going into all the details of Reich's analysis of the relationship between the individual and society, we may summarize that he began to see the basic mechanism of repression particularly vividly in the suppression of childhood impulses, particularly genital impulses. He was concerned with such things as toilet training, the restrictions on natural forms of aggression — to be a good little girl and a good little boy — restrictions on masturbation and on childhood genitality, which as far as heterosexual play goes and even masturbation is still not affirmed, as he would put it. You can read Spock, who is supposedly the bible of the permissive generation, and if you read about masturbation, he still says, distract the child, get him a toy when he masturbates. It is unclear why you should, but you better do it, because otherwise he will become lonely or something. If you say, well, what about if it's heterosexual play where loneliness doesn't come into it, that question you can't even ask. He doesn't deal with the subject of heterosexual play which still is not talked about very much. And where it is talked about there is once again the recommendation to distract the children. But you can't distract children from heterosexual play without creating guilt, you can't distract them without making this play an unacceptable activity. Since children pick up our attitudes consciously or unconsciously, this is very important. It isn't just a question of 'accepting' or not 'accepting' the impulsive life of children. It is a question of a basic attitude toward the free expression of deep emotional mobility, which is most vividly expressed often in sexual life. And you can't change that attitude automatically. We all have our anxieties over instinctual life from our own upbringing, but at least one can be aware of this very important dimension that isn't even talked about very much.

So there was infantile sexuality which was prohibited, there was also adolescent sexuality which was prohibited, and still is but to a lesser extent today. Finally, as a third crucial area of sexual suppression, there was the whole question of compulsive marriage and compulsive family life. In connection with the latter, he very much stressed the need for independence in women so that they did not have this deep extrinsic, economic investment in marriage. Marriage should be separated from issues of economic dependence and the woman's lack of a life of her own. This living of the woman through the man that people are talking so much about today has been an added incentive toward life-long monogamous forms of marriage. Also, related to the issues of non-compulsive marriage was the question of collective forms for the upbringing of children. (One can readily see the similarities between what Reich was talking about regarding the implications of non-compulsive marriage and many of the emphases of the Women's Liberation Movement.)

Reich never worked out in detail the whole question of child upbringing and family life, and I frankly don't think it can be worked out in detail. It is impossible to say the kinds of social forms of living people will have who are not heavily armored. Our forms of living today reflect this armoring, and I don't think we should try to chart exactly how unarmored people will arrange things — will we have the kids in kibbutzes, will we do this, will we do that? We don't know. All we can do is try — and I think this was Reich's position — to see to it that the living is protected as much as we are able to protect it. Then we will see what will develop. In the 1920's and 30's, many people opposed Reich's concepts on the grounds that they would destroy 'cherished institutions' such as 'marriage and the family.' And in a sense they were right. If you don't have early frustration of sexuality, you are not likely to have people who are prepared to go through the marriage ceremony and remain monogamous 'until death do us part'. You have to have gone through a certain wringer to be able to accept that kind of concept, to accept it really and genuinely. And the wringer is the social sex suppression from age 0 on. But Reich would say that vital marriage is destroyed anyway by that very wringer because early sex suppression makes it impossible for people to enjoy happiness in marriage. Suppression is destroying it functionally, anyhow. Plus the breaking down of lifelong monogamy for many people in any case whether people read his books or not.

He himself was much concerned with changing these social forms — he thought we could at least eliminate what was obviously negative. And he took a lot of personal risks to do that. If you read *The Sexual Revolution*, written in 1933, it is still the clearest affirmation of adolescent sexual life that you can find. I should also briefly mention that around the time *The Sexual Revolution* was published, Reich was in a very difficult position.

He had been kicked out of the psychoanalysts' organization for stressing its social consequences. He had been kicked out of the Communist Party for stressing that economic revolution itself is not enough. Because the Communists were saying, 'Never mind all this sex business, first let's get people fed and then somehow sex will take care of itself.' It didn't And he was right in saying that it wouldn't and that a revolution which did not move to change human character structure, would end up as a repetition of what had been only a new guise. In the USSR all the old antisexual laws came back, with even more rigidity than before. True, certain important social changes had occurred, but the kind of Communism Marx and Engels had been talking about did not emerge in its human dimension.

Following the failure of the Russian Revolution and also many of Reich's own activities in terms of creating major change in human character through various short-term measures, Reich faced a difficult situation. He was adrift, as we have mentioned. But even more important were other disillusionments. He began to see that various changes, such as contraception for the young, while they were helpful, were insufficient. He had hoped, rather optimistically, that he could create massive changes in young people through very practical kinds of help. I think to some extent he was disillusioned on that score. It wasn't that he didn't remain committed to the affirmation of healthy adolescent sexuality. He did remain committed. But also he became much more aware of the difficulties, the problems, the early damage that had been created in many adolescents during their infancy and childhood. He became aware of how hard it was for many of them to change very much, very fast. And he saw how quickly youth could get into what he termed 'secondary', i.e. distorted, expressions of energy in diverse political forms. Nazism was the most dramatic example of how youth flocked to a kind of jazzed-up, emotion-laden political ideology which clearly appealed to certain instinctual needs while providing a moralistic guise for their distorted expression. However, his experiences also with leftist parties led him to become very suspicious of political organizations in general.

During this period of social upheavals and disillusionments, he continued to make progress in his technical therapeutic work on muscular and character armoring. However, he remained unshaken in his conviction that individual therapy could never be a socially effective measure because it is just impossible to reach many people with it. With 100,000 therapists one could still only treat a small fraction of those who need help. If individual therapy was socially ineffective, and if broad-scale political change was ineffective in terms of changing individual character structures, what do you do? He faced that question forty years ago. We all face it today.

His own answer was an increasing emphasis on organic, slow, individual and social development. People who knew what they were doing should quietly work and set an example so that life positive concepts and techniques would slowly, organically spread and influence others. This principle applied in education, psychiatry, sociology, and later in his biological and physical work. His point was: let work itself and the interconnections between workers dictate development. Let us eliminate the usual agitations in their usual political ideological forms.

I would like to mention one or two lines of thinking which are confusing in terms of understanding today's culture. I have already mentioned the simplistic notion that now since 'sex is free', and there are still problems we'd better go on to something else like aggression. Another unsatisfactory answer represents a palliative kind of psychoanalytic tradition: one is supposed to manage things so that people become a little less tense, a little more aware of certain things. I don't mean to minimize the value of this piecemeal approach. It has accomplished a great deal in many psychological directions. But it by no means gets at the obstacles in the way of biological impulses whose expression poses a real threat to many existing social institutions. Even worse, this way of looking at life is not aware, even in principle, that man and his social life could be radically different, radically better. In understanding today's welter of confusing images of man, Reich's three-layered concept of man is useful. The first layer represents a kind of facade — what Laing and others call the 'false self', compulsive morality, rigid politeness, restraint, and so forth. Beneath that first layer is a second anti-social layer — the incestuous wishes, sadism, hostility, guilt, and so forth and so on. These two levels are well-known. What is less known is the biological core of personality which according to Reich, is spontaneously social and capable of self-regulation. This third layer is not to be confused with a kind of wild LSD trip. It includes the capacity for sustained, pleasurable work and the capacity for lasting sexual relations. In this view, the Don Juan is as disturbed as the timid, fearful soul who stays in the marital strait jacket out of guilt and fear. Promiscuity, as well as compulsive morality, are two sides of the same coin. There exists a deeper level of sexuality which is qualitatively different from either compulsive morality or pornography. And the same thing applies to the passive and meek (the first layer) versus the wild and destructive (the second layer). There is a third unarmored style of aggression which can be destructive where it is appropriate, but in general is aggressive in the sense of outgoing, not sadistic and not caught up in self-aggrandizement and the like. What we are experiencing today is the need to distinguish among phenomena in terms of these three levels. Part of the current debate about much of youth's 'counter culture' relates to the question of whether one prefers the first or the second layer. The social facade level has its merits. At least it doesn't hit you over the head. It has been a magnificent way of making certain that we keep things going — half-dead, to be sure. The legal code is a marvellous instrument for restraining the second layer though at the same time it also often restrains the third level as well because neither the wild criminal nor the saint can manage within the average man's law. How much you are willing to take your chances on the wild criminal coming out along with the saint as the social facade level breaks down is often a value question. In his earlier years, Reich was more concerned with breaking down that facade, even at the risk of a lot of impulses coming out destructively, chaotically, as indeed they must when they erupt outside very controlled therapeutic conditions. But after one lives through Nazism, Stalinism, and the like, one is a little more respectful of just ordinary old-fashioned compulsive restraint, even at the cost of the considerable suffering that such restraint entails and even at the cost of the considerable suppression of the third level of biological functioning. All one can ask is that one knows what one is doing, that one at least tries to distinguish which of the expressions is appearing around what kinds of issues and how one and others order their priorities concerning expressions from the three levels.

A third relevant issue is the attitude of youth to science. Theodore Roszak in his book, *The Making of a Counter Culture*, well describes the negative attitude of many youths toward science. Some of their accusations are that science embodies a technocracy, exploited by the ruling class, which is killing us all. More basically, there is suspicion toward highly cognitive, mechanistic instrumental modes of thinking which science represents in contrast to emotive, affective, humanistic approaches of art and religion. Once again, Reich's distinctions are important. We recall that psychoanalysis gave a tremendous emphasis to the issue of control which was executed by the intellect or the ego. Knowledge of the irrational, which, incidentally, was equated with the emotional, was stressed the better to understand, the better to control 'the emotional.' This emphasis did an injustice to the non-cognitive forces because the non-cognitive is not necessarily irrational. There is nothing irrational about a baby reaching for the mother's breast. It is a very rational act. Thus, deep rational emotions became lumped together with the irrational in the sense of destructive, antisocial, 'senseless' feelings. The older generation still says down with the irrational, up with reason, thinking things through; many of the young at the other extreme say down with sterile thinking, up with feeling.

At this point we may be involved in Reich's final speculations, not long before his death, concerning the origin of human armoring — a question that had preoccupied him for several decades. When one is trying to counteract thousands of years of armored living, one is always close to the questions: maybe I am wrong? Perhaps armoring is necessary for some reason or other?

His final very tentative speculations had to do with the whole question of the cognitive process. He had, you will recall, never believed that sexual frustration helped thinking. On the contrary, he believed that it hindered it. One is preoccupied with sexual fantasies and thereby distracted from productive work and thought. For Reich, there is a clear alternation between genuine sexual gratification, on the one hand, and work and thought on objective problems, on the other. There is a conflict if you try to think and experience sexual pleasure at the same time. If one is thinking about sex during the embrace, it is going to interfere. Poetry, we recall, is emotion recollected in tranquillity. At the height of emotional experience, it can be very damaging to do a lot of thinking about what you are experiencing. But you can separate them temporally, and each can be added to by the intensity of the other. Thus he never split off thought and feeling, as so many do. Moreover, if you read his work carefully, you will find that while it contains much that is dogmatic, there is also love of good, hard thinking and objective argument integrated by an extraordinary capacity for conceptualizing empirical findings. Thus, he liked thought. And he did not see it as hostile to feeling or sexuality. But he also speculated that at some far-gone time when man started to think about what he was feeling, a sensation of being dazzled, a kind of self-consciousness emerged. Cogito ergo sum. I think, therefore I am. This awareness of being aware is, I believe, unique to man. (I don't know for sure since I have never talked with an animal but it's hard to think of a dog thinking to himself, 'I wonder who I am. What is the meaning of it all? This short life etc ...' you know?) Man alone seems to have developed this capacity, and Reich speculatively relates the origin of this capacity to the origin of the disposition toward armoring. If a centipede were to ask himself how he walks, he would get all mixed up. And when man began to think about his feelings, there may have been some tendency to split his awareness. One sees this most clearly in schizophrenics who get so caught up with the 'who am I' question that they are badly crippled in their functioning.

Today we may be getting to a point where we can be 'self conscious' in the good sense through knowledge without being 'self conscious' in the negative sense of alienation and armoring. This is the problem and we see it enacted in wild swings today: 'Oh thought is important, catharsis is terrible; no, feelings are important, in the Living Theater who needs thought? Down with discipline ...' We are surrounded by these clichés and oversimplifications. The solution is not either/or, but both/and. One must be aware that everybody — this is a point Reich made very early in his career — is right in some way, it is a question of finding out in what way they are right. Then the task is to incorporate that awareness into a deeper synthesis and a deeper way of being. I don't pretend that any of this is easy. My argument is that Reich's work, carefully studied, can help us to understand the truly chaotic and revolutionary situation we are in right now. And it can help us to clarify progressive and retrogressive directions confronting us, and the obstacles, internal and external, in the way of the development of a free man in a free society.

The Force of Love

by Tage Philipson, M.D.

Formerly Consultant Physician
Saltsjobaden Institute for Applied Psychology, Stockholm

Dr. Tage Philipson was the first psychotherapist to train with Reich in vegetotherapy, which he later practised in Copenhagen and Stockholm until his death in 1962. Tage Philipson edited a two-volume work Kaerlighedslivet: Natur Eller Unatur [*Love-Life: Natural or Unnatural) which was published in Copenhagen in 1952. His chapter 'The Force of Love' is based on extracts from that book, translated from the Danish by David Boadella.*

I will attempt to give some landmarks of the physical geography of an unexplored world which deserves a history in a hundred volumes. The first of these landmarks seems to be that love acts upon us with a force as powerful as that of a spring, or of sunlight, both of which promote growth and development. Those who are in the grip of this force feel happy and light-hearted; and sadness and heartache are made to disappear.

It is clear that in the struggle between pleasure and unpleasure, which governs all psychic life according to Freud, and which for Reich is even a basic principle of the living — in this struggle love is entirely on the side of pleasure.

How is it possible that love is able to banish sorrow and pain in this way? The reason is that love is able to pervade a person through and through and fulfil him entirely, in a way that no other feeling can. Not only can it do this, but it seems to be in the nature of love to strive after doing this, and to seek to overcome any forces which hinder it. Here then are two of the most important characteristics of love: it fills people with pleasure, happiness, life, and movement; and it reaches into the depths of a person, filling the whole of his body and the whole of his soul. A third characteristic is the expression of love through sexuality. Love, on the one hand, gives rise to a tendency between two people who have fallen in love with each other to unite with each other in sexual love-making which usually leads to a mutual fusion in the supreme pleasure of an orgasm. On the other hand, love can lead to the strongest possible sense of relatedness between the two lovers.

We have now mentioned the four most important characteristics of love: pleasure, the permeating of the whole personality, the fact that it nourishes personal relationships, and that it gives rise to sexuality. Love appears so nearly identical with life, that we can begin to understand the powerful role which love plays in each person's existence, where it is often the single most decisive factor affecting the inner prosperity and happiness of a person and of humanity as a whole.

Theories stressing the central significance of sexuality have had an historic mission: under the influence of christianity, and Victorian morality, sexuality had become so suppressed, and the whole understanding of love-life lay in such obscurity and confusion, that there had to be an extreme reaction to this heritage. There is still so much of this obscurity left, and so much sexual negation still active, that there is every reason to fight strongly for more clarity and understanding; but the position in recent years has altered so much that it is necessary now to react against the exaggeration, and in particular against the over-emphasis on sexuality at the expense of love. It was not surprising that when scientists began to study the nature of love, they had first to study the damage that the havoc in sexuality had produced. The social attitude to sexuality had been deeply imprinted in human beings. The result was the basic split between a spiritualised love associated with feelings of romanticism and purity, and a guilt-laden sexuality associated with a sense of sin. Before Reich there was scarcely a single scientific researcher who had understood that in sexuality it was the experience of pleasure, and the satisfaction of the desire for pleasure, which was of central significance.

The result of this split was a sick and damaged sexuality which in turn ruined the capacity for love. People whose sexuality has been damaged may be unable to really give themselves to each other, or to unite fully in a sexual embrace, and the disappointment which this brings with it inevitably undermines the love relationship.

It is a natural consequence of our view that in healthy people sexuality and love will always be associated together. Sex will come from the heart and return to the heart. The essential condition for the connection between heart, love and sexuality, is a free movement within the organism. Only under this condition can the force of love affect the whole organism, so that the centre of the organism is not only the anatomical centre, but also the functional centre of the whole body. We can also express it this way: that love will be able to stream out into the whole organism from the centre and will be able to pervade a person fully. This means that a fully healthy person is a person with unobstructed love feelings, which will be able to stream freely in all directions within him. Such a person will feel that his love feeling will be in everything: his heart, his eyes, his brain, and all the parts of his body. When this is so, other feelings will also be able to stream through the entire organism — anger, sorrow, anxiety, and so forth. For such a person also when orgasm occurs at the high point of his sexual contacts, it will affect him totally. Often the loving sexual feelings are experienced directly as a current running through the body. Reich called this 'vegetative streaming'.

This view of health and freedom in all the functions of the organism is completely in agreement with Reich's view of the vegetatively free movements in the organism. There is a difference of emphasis, in that Reich focused particularly on sexuality, while I feel that the force of love, which is basic to the sense of personality and the feeling of freedom, assumes such a central position, that it must provide the starting point for my viewpoint. People are often found who show the split that was mentioned earlier: they may have a good ability for immediate surrender, and even show an orgasm reflex in Reich's sense, but for whom it is a matter of sexuality by itself, with no feeling of love, or deeper personal involvement. Such people are not fully healthy emotionally.

The repression and destruction of a natural love-life by upbringing and social conditioning results in love-life being misunderstood and distorted in one of two ways: either the sexual side is given little significance, and the emotional side is overvalued, so that one has over-romantic love. Or the sexuality is regarded as the only important aspect, sometimes so strongly that love feelings fall entirely into the background. This view has been called 'sexualism' by the Norwegian professor Harald Schjelderup; more recently on Danish radio it has been called 'sexual functionalism' by Dr. Henck.

Over-romantic love does not play such a very great role in our time, though it was dominant in our grandparents' day. Perhaps its greatest significance for us is that it provides the historical background for the sexualism of our time. It is a matter of common observation that whereas previously a girl felt ashamed not to be a virgin, in our day she is ashamed if she remains a virgin. Sexualism has played a very dominant role in over-valuing the significance of sexuality at the present time. There are now very many people who believe that the last word on how to get their sexual life in order, or to be 'satisfied' sexually, is to have an orgasm. But for most people in general, and for many popular scientific writers, having an orgasm simply means reaching an acme. Many people have an acme without knowing what a real orgasm with complete surrender is like. There is so much talk of sexuality, of the drive to sexuality, the capacity for sexuality, sexual relations, sexual enlightenment and guidance, the significance of the sexual impulse, the force of the impulse, the necessity of satisfying the impulse, etc., and so on endlessly, that it has become sexuality in which we see the problem, and sexuality that has become the answer we seek. The result is that many people for whom everything has been reduced to a sexual problem, remain completely unaware that there can be a problem of love, and of happiness in love.

We have already mentioned what significance pleasure has for an individual organism. Pleasure which is part of sexual fusion is many times greater, and has correspondingly greater significance for the two organisms. It is better than any other pleasure in being able to provide an expression for the pleasure-tension which is held unreleased in the body, and which will impede the free and natural functioning of the organs in which it is dammed up. Thus far Reich is correct in his view of the orgasm as a basic function not only of pleasure, but also of health. At the same time I have already mentioned that the free movement of the whole organism and all its individual parts is the basis for a satisfactory release in a full orgasm, and that it is of great importance that the inner organs, not least the heart, fully participate in the experience, and the feelings that go with it. It is important to emphasise, even at the risk of repetition that many people are able to have a strong sexual discharge which they may not be able to distinguish from a full orgasm, even though sexual inhibitions to complete surrender may exist.

According to the conditions in the body, there may be either a capacity for genuine sexual gratification; or, alternatively, an over-emphatic dependence on sexual outlets. Sexuality can be used in such cases (or, if you like, misused) so as to hide unpleasant conditions and tensions of many kinds, particularly depression. Moreover, in a manner that has a striking similarity with the habituation to narcotic drugs, the habitual use of sexuality in this way may lead to a situation where the greater the inner strain becomes, the more a person clings to the pleasure source which he now makes use of in this kind of way.

It is in contrast to this pale and colourless picture of sexual compulsiveness that we can emphasise the role of genitality as the strongest possible pleasure experience, with the greatest possible significance for the health of the whole organism. When two people love each other, and experience together all the joy, all the passion, and all the ecstasy that they are able to feel, there are deep results in the basis of their lives, their relation to each other and in many other ways. The most important of these consequences of a rich love-life is that it refreshes life like nothing else. When sexuality is mainly the expression of love, then love in return is renewed by it and is strengthened, while feelings of mutual connection are deepened. There are few things that give such a solid basis for a natural self-respect and the self-possession that follows from this, as a deep and inner knowledge of the happiness one has given in one's sexual love to the person one shares it with.

In contrast to more casual or indifferent experiences this kind of contact puts an end to irresponsible unnaturalness and sexual superficiality, and gives an inner feeling of basic happiness, and a sense of meaningfulness and joy in life. The special function of genitality when it is in natural connection with love, is to awaken and satisfy the greatest possible pleasure feelings, and to bring about a natural balance (or sexual economy, if one prefers this term) in the pleasure processes of the organism.

Reich, Sex, and Orgasm

by Alexander Lowen, M.D.

Director of the Institute of Bio-Energetic Analysis,
New York

Alexander Lowen was one of the first to study character analysis and vegetotherapy with Reich in America. He took his M.D. in Geneva and on his return to America he founded the Institute of Bio-energetic Analysis, in 1956. He has developed many new concepts of diagnosis and treatment, and these are described in his many books: The Language of the Body, Love and Orgasm, Betrayal of the Body, Pleasure, *and* Bio-Energetics. *This paper is the transcript of a lecture given in the Community Church, New York, November 1974; it was first published in* Energy and Character, *Vol.6, No.3, September 1975.*

I Bio-energetics, as most of you know, is an extension and development of the therapeutic concepts of Wilhelm Reich. Briefly stated, these are:

1 The functional antithesis and identity of all psychic and somatic processes.

2 The importance of character analysis on both the psychological and physical levels. This implies an emphasis upon present behavior and attitudes and a corresponding attention to the muscular tensions that underlie and determine the behavior and attitudes.

3 An energetic point of view from which all problems are seen as disturbances in the basic functions of expansion and contraction or as blocks to the flow of excitation in the body.

4 The key role of sexuality in personality especially the nature

and function of the orgasm in the regulation of emotional health.

One of the modifications which bio-energetics made in the Reichian approach to the treatment of emotional problems was to defocus from orgastic potency as the immediate goal of therapy. For example, orgasm anxiety is a term rarely used in our analysis of a patient's reaction. I believe that it would be valuable at this time to compare the bio-energetic position on sex and orgasm with Reich's and to explain the modification referred to above. That will be the subject of this paper.

Let us start with Reich's understanding of the orgastic response in sex. Reich described the orgasm as a total involuntary or convulsive discharge of all the excess energy or excitation in the organism. Such a discharge is extremely pleasurable and satisfying; pleasurable because the discharge of excitation is pleasure-producing and satisfying, because of the total nature of the reaction. The key words are total, involuntary, and discharge. *Total* denotes that every part of the body participates in the *involuntary* movements that occur in the climax of the sexual act. Discharge occurs through the genital apparatus. If all the free energy of the body is committed to the discharge, one would have a full orgasm in the Reichian sense.

If the discharge is only partial, the undischarged energy would be experienced as anxiety unless it was 'bound' by neurotic attitudes or chronic muscular tension. By the same token, chronic tensions and neurotic attitudes prevent the commitment and surrender to a complete discharge and preclude the full orgasm. An individual who had the capacity to experience this orgastic response, that is, who was orgastically potent, would be free of any neurotic tendencies. Reich claimed to have discovered such persons in the German working class during the 1920's. To contrast with the neurotic character he labeled the personality of such persons as the 'genital character.' This label was a synonym for emotional health.

When a person achieved the full orgasm, he became free from his neurotic complexes. In the orgasm the person discharged the energy that had been used to maintain the neurotic structure and so that structure collapsed. And as long as he retained his orgastic potency he would remain free of any neurotic tendencies. This was Reich's experience in terms of his patients. Therefore, the goal of therapy for Reich became the development in the patient of orgastic potency, the capacity for full surrender and discharge in the sexual act.

In Reichian theory the economic factor in neurosis is the stasis of sexual energy, that is undischarged sexual excitation which should be distinguished from genital excitation. Reich saw neurosis as stemming from the fear of 'giving in' to the overwhelming excitation that leads to the full orgasm. He called this fear 'orgasm anxiety.' Every tension or neurotic manoeuvre was seen as a defense against orgasm anxiety. Of course, Reich recognized that there was also a psychic factor in every neurotic problem which represented an earlier traumatic experience. He was also well aware of the dynamic factor represented by the person's adjustment to his life situation. He paid some attention to the psychic and dynamic elements of the personality problem but his aim was to eliminate the stasis of sexual excitation which he believed was at the core of every problem.

When I was in therapy with Reich, the main thrust of the work was towards 'giving-in' to the body — to full deep and easy respiration, to the free flow of feeling and excitation, and to the spontaneous and involuntary movements of the body. One allowed the breathing to develop freely and fully, especially the expiration which is the phase of surrender or 'letting go.' Reich also worked on the muscular tensions to facilitate the letting-go or giving-in. In the course of my therapy many early memories surfaced and I experienced some very deep emotions in relation to the past and the present. At the end of about three years of therapeutic work broken by a year's leave of absence I was able to give in and allow the orgasm reflex to occur easily and consistently.

The orgasm reflex is an involuntary reaction to the wave of excitation that passes through the body with deep and relaxed expiration. When the person is lying on the bed, the head falls backward, the throat comes forward and as the wave reaches the pelvis, it, too, moves forward. With inspiration this movement is reversed. It is called an orgasm reflex because the same movement occurs during the sexual orgasm. I might add that the movement is identical in both men and women both as a reflex action and as a sexual response.

The essence of the movement is its involuntary, rhythmic and harmonious quality. Occurring in the therapy sessions it has a pleasurable, releasing and integrating effect. It is not an orgasm, however, since it is low-keyed and without any genital charge. (An orgasm is a high-keyed, highly intense release coming off from the build-up of intense sexual and genital excitation. In the orgasm there can be some clouding of consciousness which doesn't happen when the movement is purely reflexive.) The pelvic movements during orgasm are faster and stronger yet harmonious with the deeper and more rapid respiration.

Since the orgasm reflex is a natural reaction to deep and relaxed breathing, it can occur whenever such breathing takes place provided one can let go fully to the body. Normal functioning in daily living necessitates a degree of ego control which may vary with different individuals but is never absent. We are generally head oriented and we do not surrender this orientation except in special situations which allow us to defocus our consciousness from the world.

This last point needs some clarification. Defocusing consciousness from the world doesn't mean just shutting one's eyes to it. The world about us persists in our images and as long as these are consciously present in the mind one cannot fully give in to the body and its sensations. For the orgasm reflex to occur our consciousness must become fully identified with the body. This can happen in therapy or sex since both situations encourage the focusing of consciousness upon the body and its sensations.

The above pretty much defines Reich's views about sex and therapy. Before we examine the modifications that bio-energetics has introduced, let us look at Reich's ideas critically from the vantage point of hindsight.

II Let me say at the outset that Reich's position was logically sound as far as it went. Its weakness lay in its failure to comprehend the complex problems of people in our culture. These problems are so big that even if a patient develops the orgasm reflex in therapy, there is little likelihood that it will hold up after therapy or lead to orgasm in sex unless these problems are worked through. That was my personal experience and that of other patients.

By 1946 Reich had developed his therapeutic ability to where some patients were able to give in to the orgasm reflex after only a few months of work. This was possible because of Reich's charisma, authority and technical skills. Through his support and help these patients were able to 'give in' to the body's involuntary movements. However, they were not able to maintain this ability after their therapy ended and several consulted me afterwards because of their need for more therapeutic help. They could not 'make it' standing alone on their own feet. It became evident to me that there was no shortcut to emotional health even with the best of therapists. Each person had to work through his problems thoroughly both in his personality and in his life situation in order to be sure that his developing sexuality rested upon the firm foundation of self-possession.

We can easily understand why the orgasm reflex does not transfer automatically to the sexual act. The latter as compared with the therapeutic situation is much more highly charged energetically. The amount of energy or excitation involved in the sexual response is much greater than the excitation normally experienced in the therapeutic relationship. This quantitative factor is important to understand. The ability to 'give in' to a small degree of charge doesn't imply a similar ability when a larger charge is experienced. This statement is true of all life situations. For example learning to dive off a two-foot board doesn't mean that one can repeat the performance automatically on the high board. Another factor is also involved in this problem. The therapeutic situation is supportive whereas the sexual one is stressful in that one must deal with the feelings and expectations of another person. Still a certain amount of transference does occur between the two situations. One doesn't learn to dive off the high board without first learning how to handle the two-foot board. If a person cannot give in, therefore, to the body and its feelings in the secure and supportive therapeutic situation he will not be able to do so in the more stressful and exciting sexual situation.

A necessary aspect of therapy, therefore, is to help a person develop the ability to meet stress without blocking his energetic flow. This is the same as saying that a person has to be able to stand on his own feet, alone, and still function at an optimal level. Genital sexuality is an adult activity which requires for its fulfilment an adult attitude. Maturity, independence and responsibility are characteristics of this attitude and these qualities are not gained by a patient simply as a result of experiencing the orgasm reflex. This natural development in a person requires many years of growth; it would be naive to think that they could be acquired by any short-term therapeutic process. Only by working through the hang-ups and emotional conflicts of patients do these qualities develop in the personality. In view of the fact that so many people are so deeply disturbed we must be prepared for a long-term therapeutic undertaking in most cases in which the focus upon the specific problems of the person is never lost.

We must also recognise that our culture is neither life-positive, sexually affirmative, nor body oriented. It emphasises money and power, it recognises performance in all situations including sex, and it is concerned with ego values. In a competitive, dog-eat-dog economic climate people are in a constant state of tension and alertness because of the pressures and dangers to which they are constantly exposed. This makes it very difficult to defocus consciousness from the head and transfer it to the body. The result is that we come to sex with a head consciousness and seek through sex to get back to our bodies. Under these circumstances it is not likely that people can be orgastically potent. It seems to me that we need to change our style of life if we wish to have a richer fulfilment of our sexual lives.

Though sex is a relatively private and circumscribed activity, it does not take place in isolation. It is only one side of a person's existence and relationship to the world. The other side, the social, productive and spiritual one is equally important. Each side is dependent upon and influenced by the other. The two sides are like two legs; neither alone can support a person, each is necessary to the other and both are necessary for the on-going movement of a person's life. We cannot 'make it' through sex alone and yet we cannot 'make it' without sex.

Peter Marin expressed this idea nicely in his book *In a Man's Life*. 'The sexual and private realm cannot stand in isolation. Beyond them there must be some sense of deeper grounding and connection, a sense of further mystery. But it is also true, most true of all, that those mysteries in themselves are not enough. They must be present and felt in the world of things, rooted in flesh, in the ways we touch, for without that fleshed habitation they too corrode and go askew, and they do us as much damage then as we do to one another in their absence.'

Reich was not unaware of these relationships. Those of you acquainted with his writings know that he was a social as well as a sexual revolutionist. But though he saw the immensity of the problem of modern man he was impatient and determined to effect a change. He put his faith first in sexuality, then in orgone energy, and the result in his personal life was tragic. Reich did not fully foresee the destruction of the earth's environment by technology. He died in 1957 before the problem of pollution was widely recognised. He did not see the degree of man's estrangement from the natural world, and he did not take account of the post-war explosion of population and power.

To avoid these weaknesses in orgone therapy, bio-energetics started with a commitment to spend more time on character analysis and generalized body work. We endeavoured to understand the problems our patients presented and to work them through analytically and physically. We were not clear where the orgasm reflex and the orgasm fitted into our theory of personality.

III One of the big advances that bio-energetics made over Reichian therapy was the introduction of the concept of grounding. This concept proved so valuable in promoting our understanding of the problems patients presented and in furthering our therapeutic ability that the focus in bio-energetics was shifted from the orgasm reflex and orgastic potency to how well a person is grounded through his legs and feet.

Grounding, as the term is used in bio-energetics means having one's feet solidly planted on the ground or being fully in contact with the ground. It does not describe a mechanical process but an energetic one. To be grounded a person must *feel* his feet touching the ground. This is not possible unless there is an energetic charge in the feet and an energetic interchange between the feet and the ground.

Grounding is not a term that Reich ever used to my knowledge nor is it a concept that he worked with actively. Reichian therapy takes place with the patient lying on a bed and makes no attempt to explore with the patient the functions of standing, holding one's ground, moving forward and falling. Other therapies which also work with the patient in the prone position suffer from the same lack. Actually bio-energetics was born when I investigated these aspects of my own functioning seven years after my therapy with Reich had 'successfully' terminated. I felt that my therapy with Reich had left too many problems unresolved though I had reached the point where the orgasm reflex occurred consistently. I asked John Pierrakos to work with me and we began this therapy with me in the standing position rather than lying down. I sensed that I had to get more fully into my pelvis and into my legs.

The two positions, lying and standing, reflect two different ways of being in the world. In the lying down position one adopts by implication an infantile mode; being on one's back denotes helplessness. This position favors regression and facilitates the recall of early memories and experiences. Standing or being on one's feet denotes an adult posture and furthers the processes leading to maturity and responsibility. Its outlook is forward and progressive. Stanley Keleman in his last book, *Your Body Speaks Its Mind* has some interesting observations about the significance of man's upright posture. There must be some significance in the fact that while copulation is possible and done in the standing position, most people prefer to engage in sexual activity from the prone or lying down position.

Bio-energetics exploits all positions for their therapeutic value. It uses the lying down position to further the process of regression. It uses the standing position to help the patient face the world and learn to confront a situation or a person. Then, when discussion is in order, both therapist and patient are seated to promote the exchange of ideas. But it is in the use of standing positions and in the special exercises designed to improve one's standing and to further the sense of standing that bio-energetics is unique among therapies. However, I do not wish to give the impression that our understanding and work with standing is the only important contribution of bio-energetics to therapy.

Standing is, nevertheless, a key function of the human organism and as such it plays a major role in sexuality. I mentioned earlier that without the ability to *stand up* to the negative pressures in our culture it is impossible to maintain or support a healthy sexual functioning. But more specifically it is the ability to *stand* the excitement or stress of a high charge that determines whether the orgasm reflex will be translated into orgastic potency in the sexual act. In the broader area of personality the important questions to answer are how one *stands* in the world and whether one stands on one's own feet.

Standing, moving, rising and falling are functions of the lower part of the body which also includes sexuality. These are paired functions. The ability to stand is related to the ability to move, the ability to rise to the ability to fall. Insecurity in the standing position implies a fear of falling and generates what is known as falling anxiety. Falling anxiety is present in every individual who is not fully grounded. Where there is falling anxiety one *holds* on and finds it difficult to let go and give in to the body. Falling anxiety underlies what Reich called orgasm anxiety or to put it differently, I would say that orgasm anxiety is a form of falling anxiety. It is also the counterpart in the lower half of the body of breathing anxiety, an anxiety related to the feeling of 'choking in the marrows.' It is one of the assets of the bio-energetic approach that we can work with falling anxiety both analytically and through special exercises.

To appreciate the significance of being grounded one has to contrast it with its opposite — being hung-up. A person is hung-up when he doesn't have his feet on the ground and this implies that he is out of touch with reality. He is hung-up by an illusion. In order to ground a person, therefore, his illusions must be uncovered. This requires careful character analytic work. In addition the tensions and blocks in all segments of the body have to be significantly reduced so that there can be a fairly free and full flow of energy and excitation through the body and into the legs and feet. Disturbances in respiration have to be thoroughly worked out so that the person can feel the breathing movements down to his or her balls — the balls of the feet.

In effect, then, grounding means getting a person fully in touch with reality: first, the reality of the ground on which he stands; second, the reality of his body which is the condition of his being a person — a somebody; third, the reality of his sexual nature; and fourth, the reality of his life situation. This emphasis upon reality and grounding insures that whatever progress a person makes in therapy will be transferred to his life situation. It insures that whatever gains a person makes in opening up his sexuality will be transferred to his sexual life.

Our approach to sexuality is not only from the head down as Reich worked but also from the ground up. Reich, as I stated earlier, could open up a person's sexual feelings but his approach failed in my view to help the person develop the aggression to express these feelings in sexual situations. The reason for this failure is that aggression is a function of the legs. The word aggression as we use it means 'to move towards'. One can't move effectively unless one is grounded. Our patients report that this approach consistently results in improved sexual functioning. Few procedures offer the rich reward of positive personality change as the work with the legs in the function of grounding.

The shift of emphasis from orgasm reflex and orgastic potency to grounding was necessary so that we could fully explore the problems of the human personality. However, this shift of focus was by no means as complete as I have implied. Grounding cannot be divorced from sexuality. It is my purpose in this lecture to re-define the role of orgasm in personality in the light of twenty years of bio-energetic experience.

In these twenty years my colleagues and I have examined the depths of the emotional distress in people. We have seen the terror in their eyes, we looked at the face of death in their visage, and we recognized the stunned condition that horror produces in the mind. In my previous lectures I described these problems. We studied the different character types finally developing a hierarchy of structures which enabled me to draw up a bill of rights for an individual. Simply stated, these are:

1   The right to exist — its absence leads to the schizoid condition.
2   The right to need — its absence is associated with the oral personality.
3   The right to be independent (autonomous) which is missing in the psychopathic character.
4   The right of self-expression and self-assertion — its absence leads to masochism.
5   The right to freely pursue one's erotic desires — lacking in the rigid structure.

I have detailed these rights because it should be obvious that in working with the person whose right to exist is questionable, the issue of orgasm is largely irrelevant. The same is generally true of the oral character, the psychopathic personality and the masochistic individual. Only in the rigid structure is orgasm the immediate issue. This is what I meant by the severity of the problems that have forced us to defocus from orgastic potency. Certainly until these problems are fairly well resolved there seems little sense in talking about orgastic potency.

And yet, sexuality lurks in the background of all these character problems regardless of the degree of disturbance. It is the key factor in the etiology of the schizoid structure as I pointed out in *Betrayal of the Body*. It is sexual seductiveness which creates the psychopathic personality, and it is fear of sexual aggression that determines the rigid structure. Similarly a strong sexual element underlies both orality and masochism. The psychological sophisticate of today talks facilely about personality theory as if it had no connection with sexuality. This, I believe, is a grave mistake. A person is conceived in two sexual acts, one of the coupling of a male and female individual, and two, the fusion of male and female gametes. While it is true that an individual's sexuality cannot be understood except as an expression of his personality, it is equally true that one's individual personality cannot fully be comprehended except as the specific form of his sexual drive.

I refuse to surrender my vision of man even in the face of the reality I see about me. I would like to see people stand straight and tall with pride in their bearing and dignity in their manner as I believe they were meant to be. I would like to see them be straightforward in their expression and principled in their behavior, with a sense of humility and a feeling for the 'decent thing.' Above all, I would like to see people freed from their obsession with money, power and material things. Regardless of what they say most people put money ahead of health, power ahead of pleasure and things ahead of feelings. This is not surprising since it is the cultural pattern. Two millenia ago Jesus chased the money-lenders out of the temple. Today they have their own temples at which we all pay homage.

The situation doesn't call for rebellion. To be against is not the same thing as being for. Nor can one fight power with power. There is an old adage which says that if one fights the devil with the devil's weapons, one becomes a devil.

What do you stand for? If you tell me that, I can tell you how close you are to orgastic potency. Do you stand for body values — breathing, feeling, moving? Do you stand for animal values — freedom, independence, self-expression? But saying is not enough. It has to be manifested in your *standing*. How you stand and how well-grounded you are — are the criteria I apply. Not in your words but in your body the story is told. For your body is your sexuality and the life of your body is sexual.

All of our patients are sexual beings. I have never met a neuter. They are heterosexual, homosexual or bisexual but they are not neuters. They may be children on some levels of their personality but on another they are genitally oriented. Even the schizophrenic is not an asexual person. Their sexuality may be dissociated just as are their other emotional responses but it is not absent nor irrelevant. I am speaking of sexuality not orgastic potency. The therapeutic questions are — when and how does one deal with the patient's sexuality?

The answers to these questions will depend on the individual therapist. For my part I like to introduce the sexual theme early and keep it in the *near* background while I work with the personality problem. However, I bring the sexual question to the fore whenever I think it appropriate for I cannot avoid the conviction that it is the key to the personality. This conviction has become very strong lately. It includes the belief that the oedipal problem is the central or focal element in every character disturbance. Towards the end of therapy I return to the issue of orgastic potency.

In bio-energetics we use a number of exercises which are specifically designed to open up sexual feelings. Most of you are familiar with the use of the stool to deepen a person's breathing. Lying over the stool passively will accomplish this purpose. One can transform the position into an active exercise by having the person bounce his pelvis rhythmically up and down. If these movements become co-ordinated with the breathing, the whole body becomes excited and involuntary tremors develop which culminate in a vibration of the pelvis. When this happens, the lower half of the body feels very charged and alive. Positive pressure through the feet against the floor will maintain this charge for some time. I need not describe the positive effect upon a person of increased charge and feeling in the lower part of the body.

Unless one grounds a patient first, it is difficult to open up his sexuality. But the reverse is equally true. Unless a person's sexual anxiety is tackled directly, it is difficult to fully ground him. In all patients both male and female, this anxiety takes the form of a fear of castration or injury to the genital area. It is a more localized aspect of falling anxiety.

Actually, then, bio-energetics doesn't minimize the importance of sexuality or, for that matter, of orgastic potency. It doesn't claim that opening up a person's sexuality will make him into a 'mentch,' a Jewish term meaning to be fully a man or woman. But neither does it hold to the position that one can become such an individual without working through one's sexual problems psychologically and physically. The focus in bio-energetics is never upon a single aspect of the personality. It is always upon the polar aspects, emphasising both equally. The ego merits equal attention with the body. The work with the body doesn't minimise the need for careful analysis. Pleasure and reality though antithetical are not contradictory functions. A person needs two legs to stand on. In the same way, sexuality and grounding are interdependent. If one is to fly in orgasm, one has to take off from the ground. And in the end one returns to the ground.

IV Reich suggested that the act of sex involves the super-imposition of two energy systems replicating a process on the human scale that occurs on a cosmic scale in the formation of galaxies. For most individuals sex is as close as they come to experiencing themselves as part of the cosmic order. In the full orgasm, the boundaries of the self are dissolved and one feels as if one is participating in a cosmic event. Unfortunately for civilized man such experiences are rare, maybe once or several times in a life-time. But whether this experience does or does not happen to an individual, there is in all persons a subconscious awareness that the gateway to the cosmos is through sex. Sexuality is the basis of one's spirituality, as grounding is the foundation of one's sexuality. It is never the other way around. The flower grows out of the plant.

Reich had hoped that the lifting of sexual repression would free the personality. This hope has not materialised. Since Freud we have known the important role of sex in shaping personality. The other side of the relationship has been generally ignored. The question that needs further discussion is — what kind of a person is capable of orgastic potency? Reich claimed that he had discovered a high degree of orgastic potency among the German workers he studied in the 1920's, but he never described the qualities of the persons and their culture which were responsible for such a high degree of emotional health.

In this difficult study we have one guide-post. Sex is, perhaps, the most animal function of the human personality. What I mean by most animal is that it (the sexual act) has been least subject to cultural modification. Our patterns of sleeping, eating, excreting have been more influenced by cultural standards. Certainly, the sexual act is the function that most closely identifies us with our animal nature. It is the function that most expresses our animal nature.

The wild animal living in a state of nature lives the life of the body fully and is orgastically potent. To the degree that we lose touch with the life of the body and, therefore, with our animal nature we become disturbed, especially in our sexual functioning. Culture and nature are antithetical and may easily become antagonistic. Our culture particularly is detrimental to nature and the life of the body. The extensive destruction of the natural environment is evident of this attitude. Under the conditions of modern living it is impossible for most people to be orgastically potent. Some may have moments when they touch the ecstasy of cosmic union but that is exceptional. However, this ideal is not to be dismissed. Otherwise we must accept the neurotic state as our inevitable fate. Our task is to understand human nature and to influence cultural patterns so that they favor this nature.

I refuse to surrender my vision of man.

Sexual Revolution and Cultural Transformation

by George Frankl

Psychotherapist, London

George Frankl was born in Vienna. He turned from the study of philosophy to psychoanalysis and neurology, and was much impressed by Reich's writings, in particular The Mass Psychology of Fascism. *He emigrated from Austria when the Nazis came to power, studied in America and Canada, and has since settled in London. In addition to his work as a psychotherapist, George Frankl edits a philosophical journal, and was among the first to introduce the writings of Reich to a wider audience in Britain. This chapter first appeared in his book* The Failure of the Sexual Revolution, *published in 1974 by Kahn and Averill, and is reproduced here with their permission.*

In his book *The Sexual Revolution* Reich describes the initial stage in the treatment of neurosis: 'Character analytic treatment releases the vegetative energies from their fixations and their armour. The immediate result of this is an intensification of the anti-social and perverse impulses and with that of social anxiety'. In my own work with patients I also find that the liberation of libido energy initially releases aggressive and sadistic urges previously not conscious to the patient. If we consider the sexual revolution as a mass therapy then we must realise that it has got stuck in the first stage. Let us see how Reich explains the next stage of therapy:

'When one begins to dissolve the infantile fixations to the parental home, to the infantile traumata and the antisexual taboos, more and more energy finds its way to the genital system...'

'While previously the whole thinking and acting was determined by unconscious, irrational motives, the patient now becomes increasingly capable of acting and reacting rationally. In the course of this process, inclinations to mysticism, religiosity, infantile dependence, superstitious beliefs, etc., disappear more and more, without the exertion of any "educational" influence on the patient. While previously the patient was completely armoured, incapable of contact with himself and his environment, capable only of unnatural pseudocontacts, he now develops an increasing capacity for immediate, natural contact with his impulses as well as his environment. The result of this is a visible development of natural, spontaneous behaviour instead of the previous unnatural, artificial behaviour.'

The capacity for full orgastic gratification and the abolition of orgasm anxiety, the capacity for immediate natural contact free from personal distrust and tribal paranoia and the development of natural spontaneous behaviour was the aim of the sexual revolution seen as a mass therapy.

At the present time we are still very much in the first stage of the therapy and I am concerned to draw attention to this in order to prevent advocates of the sexual liberation from mistaking the phenomena of the initial stage for the cure. For if we forget the aims of therapy, i.e. the aims of the sexual revolution, then the released aggressive and perverse drives will acquire dominance and parade as freedom.

It would be disturbing if, for instance, a depressive patient in the early part of treatment were to consider his released sadistic impulses as a norm of health to be emulated by others. It is equally disturbing if a society undergoing the experience of sexual liberation were to become fixated upon the first stage, content with the release of hostility and perversion and with a mechanistic attitude to sex, declaring it as the cure, as the achievement of freedom. This would be an arrest in the development of liberation, a diversion from the quest for the wholeness of sexual experience and of being, and would be a kind of decadence before the liberation even got under way. The toleration of such a state of affairs would undermine the potentials inherent in human freedom. While the pioneers of the sexual revolution intended to overcome the root causes of the authoritarian structure of individuals and of society, i.e. sexual repression — the sexual liberation movement of our time has only removed the secondary repressions and left the primary repressions intact.

So we see a multitude of perversions which previously were held in check bursting to the surface and masquerading as freedom. Having removed the inhibitions against them we can act them out more freely but we are no more in contact with our primary libido than before. We are still alienated from ourselves.

We can see a similar situation in the socio-political sphere. With the breakdown of religious and state authority there occurs a release of pent-up aggression and violence. The superego no longer has the power to contain the anger against it by the traditional method of channelling it against other states or religions, partly because thermonuclear weapons have made major wars too risky.

There is no doubt that we are entering an era of civil violence and political guerilla warfare, and most striking is the notion that violence against authority is in itself a realisation of freedom. In the past freedom was seen as an alternative social condition and the revolutionary struggle a means for its establishment: now the struggle itself is elevated into a realisation of freedom. The arguments about ends and means which were central to the writings of Orwell and Koestler are ignored and means have become ends. There is nothing beyond. It is all here and now. And here and now is violence, the activism of hate in which a man's identity as a free being is supposed to be realised. Fight against the oppressors and you are already free!

The analogy between the socio-political liberation of secondary drives and the sexual liberation of secondary drives is all too obvious. Those who are concerned with freedom as an alternative to repression and hatred should recognise the real aim of freedom — the fulfilment of man's primary urges, his freedom to love and to be acknowledged as a whole person — and see the present liberation in its proper perspective. Alienated people who have no awareness of the process of becoming and of development, who cannot comprehend the aim of freedom, will mistake the freedom of aggression for freedom itself. Thus they will not only cause much misery but make the achievement of freedom impossible. They end up as reactionaries who are content with hate; they do not understand that love, work and knowledge (as Reich has put it) are the well-springs of life. They are reactionaries shutting the door to freedom, finding satisfaction in fighting, inviting other reactionaries to fight them and we have a battlefield of perverse gratifications.

It is, as I have said, necessary to have a theoretical understanding of the stages of liberation from sexual repression and social oppression and to encourage an understanding of freedom both in sexuality as well as in the socio-political field. These two are of course inter-related. They are two dimensions of one reality. To comprehend what freedom is gives significance to the means by which it is to be achieved.

In the individual treatment of the neuroses it is left to the therapist to have an understanding of what health means and to make an effort to direct his patient's attention to it, to make him aware of the significance of released aggression in relation to the sexual needs still repressed. While of course it is wrong to impose rigid concepts, the art of the therapist lies in his ability to gauge the authentic needs of his patient's libido and open his eyes to them. Thus the treatment is necessarily patient-orientated but it needs the help of the therapist to overcome the patient's alienation from himself. In the same way a definition of socio-political or sexual freedom must not be merely an effort to impose one's own idiosyncracies upon people and imagine that by doing so one liberates them. This has been the fate of many Utopias.

> 'But what is historically possible cannot be achieved simply by a straightforward progression of the immediately given (with its "laws"), but only by a consciousness of the whole of society acquired through manifold mediations, and by a clear aspira-

tion to realise the dialectical tendencies of history. And the
series of mediations may not conclude with unmediated contemplation: it must direct itself to the qualitatively new
factors arising from the dialectical contradictions: it must be
a movement of mediations advancing from the present to the
future'.*

The future becomes possible if the present is released from its
anchorings in the past. The next stage, therefore, is to become
conscious of our fixations upon infantile traumas and taboos and
on the social level to become aware of our fixations upon mystical
and irrational concepts which determine our society. If we can
make our individual and social fixations conscious and if we can
release our energies from their unconscious anchorings the ego
may find a new way to satisfy our primary needs for love and
acceptance; the capacity for choice can take over from the rein of
compulsion. While the determinants of our behaviour and our
thoughts remain unconscious we are obliged to act them out
compulsively and defeat all efforts for individual and social
sanity.

The central core and determinant of the taboos and inhibitions
which dominate patriarchy is the oedipus complex. From it stems
pleasure-anxiety, submissiveness to and glorification of authority,
fear of intellectual and emotional spontaneity, mistrust of oneself
and of others, social and individual paranoia, as well as the
processes of splitting, projection, alienation and reification which
we have discussed earlier. The oedipus complex is anchored in
the family and reproduced itself in society with its authoritarian
symbols of power and its hierarchic order. The oedipus complex
causes us to be in awe of authority, compelling us to adopt
submissive and sacrificial or aggressive attitudes which as we have
seen have made freedom impossible both on the social as well as
on the personal level. The most important project of the sexual
and social revolution must therefore be the abolition of the
oedipus complex. As the oedipus complex is the result of
patriarchy and in turn perpetuates it, its abolition means the

---

*Georg Lukacs: *History and Class-consciousness.*

abolition of patriarchy. This must be the long-term aim of true radicalism.

Let us first understand the size of the task. Let us understand that the abolition of patriarchy means nothing less than the creation of a new culture. It is not concerned merely with changes in institutions, for we have seen that new institutions will quickly absorb the compulsions of patriarchy. Radicalism now must be concerned with a fundamental cultural transformation. We know that the foundations of a culture are created in the infantile experiences shared by its members, and that the repression of the libido creates symbols and complexes which become the dominant orientations in society. This knowledge might make us despair of ever breaking through the fundamental psychic structures that operate in a culture or to wait for future generations of better brought-up people to create a culture without guilt and paranoia. In the hey-day of psychoanalytic hope there used to be a saying meant to be funny; if you really want to succeed in psychoanalysing a person you have to start with his grandparents. We cannot wait that long and in any case nothing ever happens by passively hoping for it.

I visualise two stages in the cultural transformation ahead of us. Firstly we must create a milieu, an ideology if you like, where people learn that the capacity of experiencing sexual pleasure, not only genitally but in all the bodily functions, is a virtue to be encouraged; while the negation of pleasure experiences both in ourselves as well as in others, and the spreading of guilt, is evil. At the same time we must help parents to realise that the communication of libido pleasures to their children is essential for their development into healthy and free persons.

Secondly, we must subject the life-negating characteristics of our culture to a critical analysis, relating them to the compulsions of patriarchy and then conceptualise a society which is free from patriarchal fixations and compulsions. If one learns to trace complex behaviour patterns in individuals to the oedipus complex and the destructive compulsions of societies to patriarchy, then one paves the way for the psychological and cultural transformation which will be necessary in the not-too-distant future.

While it is inevitable that the small child sees its parents as huge and all-powerful beings who, as Freud has pointed out, are later transformed into images of omnipotent deities, it is not necessary for these images to be frightening. It is the sexual conflicts of patriarchy which fundamentally transform the primal objects into symbols of anxiety and even terror, creating fixations and over-dependency and making the process of maturation and the achievement of freedom exceedingly difficult.

Let us look at some of the taboos which a child encounters in the family. This is not just a matter of inhibitions of sexual genitality, although these are of major importance. It firstly concerns the child's reactions towards it own polymorphous erotic sensations. We have mentioned that the mother who experiences pleasure at breast-feeding will communicate pleasure to the child's oral activities and furthermore a sense of pleasure in itself, a sense of being loved and wanted. But how can a mother communicate pleasure to the child if she herself is anxious, frustrated and inhibited? This does not only relate to breast-feeding but also to her communication of peripheral pleasure by cuddling and caressing and her attitudes to anal and urethral functions. If any of these processes arouse the mother's unconscious anxiety and evoke a forbidding or demanding attitude in her, then one can be quite sure that retentive, compulsive character attitudes or neuroses will appear in the child, influencing it as an adult and in turn reproducing similar reactions in her children.

One has to propagate the truth that breast-feeding, cuddling, caressing, urination, defaecation, eating and drinking are not merely physical activities to be pursued mechanically in the right quantities and at the right times but are sources of pleasure: that the libido component of all these functions is just as important, if not more so than their physical aspects. If we want a child to breast-feed correctly then the mother must allow herself the erotic sensations which arise during the sucking. It is worthwhile mentioning in this connection that sucking creates vaginal sensations in women which in turn arouses unconscious inhibitions of the libido component of suckling. One must be able to enjoy the pleasures of one's own biological activities and not dissociate oneself from one's own body as if it were an alien thing. If you can have pleasure in your natural activities then you can communicate them to the child and, all being well, the child will learn to consider itself as a source of pleasure — it will consider itself good, clean, beautiful and friendly. The difficulty is to avoid compulsive attitudes which so many progressives adopt in these matters when they want to do the right thing by their child while at the same time suffering agonies of guilt and insecurity.

Let us reiterate that self-experience of pleasure is the correct foundation for the communication of pleasure. The important thing is that with the sensation of pleasure in the natural functions these would cease to be considered as dirty, nasty and forbidden and the child would cease to regard its own impulses and therefore itself, as nasty and dirty and would not feel guilty about its bodily urges.

It is natural to love one's child but it is very difficult indeed to do so if you cannot love yourself. It is also very difficult to tell a parent to have pleasure in the natural functions of the child if the parent has unconscious fears and inhibitions about his own natural functions. While the intellect is a poor and limited instrument to break through the deep-seated taboos and compulsions it nevertheless can help transform innate predispositions by first making them conscious and by encouraging new attitudes. A start has to be made.

The satisfaction of the erotogenic zones in children depends to a large extent upon the sexual genital satisfactions of the parents, for should they suffer from sexual frustrations and inhibitions, then their attitudes to the child's pre-genital sexuality would be disturbed. So if parents want their children to be healthy and happy they must endeavour to have a happy sex life. No child can be happy or fulfilled if the parents are sexually unhappy. Sexual happiness is thus a duty to the child. (I am extremely conscious of the wry smiles this imperative will evoke in many people but I am in a hurry, we are all in a hurry, so let us just tell the truth. It might help.)

Besides the gratification of the child's erotogenic zones and the respect for infantile sexual needs there is the major problem of the genital sexuality of children. It is here that patriarchal

Sexual revolution and cultural transformation

attitudes have their major impact upon the psychic structure. We have seen that there are a number of genital primacies in children during which they experience genital sexual needs at the age of 2, 5 and 13, roughly speaking. The question arises — how are parents to deal with them? As I intend here merely to provide some pointers towards a new attitude let us take just a few aspects of the problem.

Freud has drawn our attention to the importance of the 'primal scene', i.e. the child's observation of parental intercourse and the emotional upheaval this creates in the child. From about the age of two years the child is extremely curious about sex and conscious of its parents' sexual activities. (This usually arouses disbelief in many people, even during psychoanalysis, but there are almost always memories, usually repressed, about the child's impression of parental sexuality.) What attitude can parents take towards the child witnessing their sexual relations? First of all the father must accept that the boy wants his wife sexually and the mother must accept that her daughter wants her husband sexually. Of course it would be impossible for a child of two or five years to have intercourse with the parent of the opposite sex but there are compensations — nature has seen to that. For instance if the boy knows that his father has intercourse with mother and if he further knows that father does not mind the boy's excitement and arousal on observing it, then the boy can identify with his father and take a vicarious pleasure in the act. Above all he can masturbate without guilt or anxiety, and in this way participate in his father's pleasure. This presupposes that the father is not afraid either of his own sexuality or of the sexual arousal of his son, that he does not fear his son as a rival.

There is no need for any ostentatious display of freedom or for anxious avoidance of traumatising the child. If the child is in the same room with his parents in a cot then some sign of acknowledgment of the child, some sign of open enjoyment and of acceptance of the child's libido (while he is listening wide awake with his eyes closed or half-closed) suffices to allay any anxiety or guilt in the child. People would be surprised to know how sensitive a child is about the parents' attitude towards it in matters of sex and what impact subtle and unspoken expressions of attitudes can have upon it. The father could acknowledge the boy's sexuality, not be embarrassed, the mother not be too coy to caress the child.

On the other hand over-stimulation of the child is also not desirable. For instance the mother should not play with his genitals but should accept and acknowledge his genital arousal with good humour. The acceptance of his sexuality is all-important to the little boy. Masturbation should of course be accepted and respected.

With girls the matter is not very different. Most little girls are left ignorant of the existence of their vagina, the mother never, *but never*, talks about it. That does not mean that girls do not feel sensations in their vagina; on the contrary, there is every evidence that they experience as much stimulation in their genitals as boys do. They often experience the equivalent of a boy's erection in vaginal spasms but these are invariably referred to as tummy pains or cramps and never for what they really are. There is much mystification of the tummy as some secret area where unmentionable things happen besides the ordinary digestive processes and the child quickly realises that vaginal sensations are not to be mentioned or acknowledged, in fact, are not supposed to be there. So while the girl is not supposed to have an internal genital she cannot help having genital sensations. No wonder that the child soon feels guilty and embarrassed by sensations that are not acknowledged as belonging to an internal organ. She learns to hide her sexuality, she becomes nonplussed and confused about it and she gets the impression that her femininity is unacceptable. No wonder then that she becomes envious of the penis. She feels that a boy's sexuality is accepted while hers is not.

The whole syndrome of feminine shyness, secretiveness, guilt and sense of inadequacy, the whole picture of some mysterious sinfulness about femininity is here engendered to become a cultural characteristic of the woman. Of course as with the boy there can be compensatory processes if a girl is shown love and affection. Not all girls grow up stunted and blocked as persons and it is indeed one of the miracles of human adaptability that despite the enormous psycho-sexual handicap imposed upon girls in our culture many develop into healthy, beautiful and intelligent beings. But the hardship of the non-recognition of the girl's sexuality as a child is responsible for a large number of neuroses and illnesses in women. Not realising that there is an organ behind her little opening many girls grow up with fears of the penis, with notions of violence and injury in sex, or with masochistic fantasies of having to be injured in order to experience sexual pleasures. The rape fantasies so prevalent in women are not merely an expression of sexual needs for which they do not wish to be held responsible but they are very often associated with pain and violence and the masochistic component creates considerable guilt and anxiety. Another aspect of this lack of acknowledgment of her own vagina is the assumption of passivity in the woman, her sense of dependency upon the male's sexual activity and the resulting envy and resentment against him on the one hand, and submissiveness on the other. In fact the vagina is every bit as active sexually as the penis but its activity is not as obvious as that of a penis and if it is repressed from consciousness can only show itself in a whole host of neurotic and somatic disturbances, hysterias and a high incidence of hypochondria in women. It is astonishing how many grown-up women remain ignorant of their vagina, are, as it were, unfamiliar with it, and how often they consider it as unacceptable, unattractive and something to be denied.

It is of the utmost importance that parents realise that a girl has a great need for genital acknowledgment. They should refer to her vagina, should signal to her verbally and pre-verbally that she has an important sexual organ behind her opening, they should look at it on those many occasions when the girl opens her legs and invites attention. The exhibitionistic urges of girls are more highly developed than those of the boy for the simple reason that she needs more reassurance that the hidden vagina is noticed, accepted and loved. Parents who do not acknowledge the little girl's sexuality, castrate her and make her feel inadequate for life.

Nakedness in families and in groups of children should be accepted as a matter of course in situations where nakedness is *functional* and *natural*. The curiosity aroused by natural nakedness should be fully respected and explanations of the differences between the sexes given at the earliest possible time. Sexual exploration between children should be fully accepted and even encouraged as a form of learning and discovery and the beauty of the genitals, male and female, conveyed to them. If people only knew what a traumatic experience it is for the boy to discover an opening between the girl's legs when he expects a penis there, having no idea that she has a genital of her own inside! Freud has observed that the absence of a penis in a girl arouses the boy's castration anxieties, he imagines her to be a castrated boy. Moreover, as he does not know that a woman has a receptive organ, his urge to penetrate her will arouse sadistic fantasies of cutting her open, forcing himself into her and injuring her. At the same time he will feel guilty about the aggressive aspect of his sexuality. He will project some of his aggression upon the woman who will then be seen by him not only as a victim but also as a threat. In his fantasies he will imagine her genital as a crab, as pincers or scissors which are likely to injure his penis. (Some men never get over this impression, remain terrified of women sexually and become homosexuals.)

When the vagina is acknowledged as an organ that receives without hurt or pain and its own desires are recognised, then the boy's penis is not a threatening and threatened object but an organ that gives pleasure to the girl and receives pleasure from her; then both vagina and penis are good objects embracing and intermingling with each other. There is no possible reason, apart from irrational anxiety, why sexual play between children from four or five onwards should be inhibited. Let parents be assured that if sexual curiosity and sexual play is accepted as natural and beautiful there would be no compulsion about it amongst children, unlike the hidden compulsions of sexual fantasies and symptoms so prevalent in our time.

If the girl's vaginal sexuality gains full recognition then the periods of vaginal repression and clitoral primacy would be reduced, and there would be far less conflict between the two sexualities of women. There would be much less penis envy among girls and castration anxiety among boys. The vagina is not merely a passive-submissive but an active-receptive organ with an embracing and incorporative sexuality as distinct from the pushing, penetrative sexuality of the boy. As an embracing receptive being, the woman has many psychological characteristics which are different from those of the male, but these differences are complementary to each other, and are not competitive.

Another aspect to be noticed here is that when the woman's vagina is given conscious attention in the formative years, then female cultural symbols will emerge: a female dimension will develop in our culture to complement the male cultural symbols which have, up till now, been dominant. Women would again develop their divinities, their principles and ideas in a recognisable manner as distinct cultural entities, and it is high time that this should happen if we are to be saved from the aggressive mania of the male Gods.

There have been great advances in the liberation of sexual relationships between young people. However, the important thing to remember is that up till now young people have had to fight for their sexual rights against parents and authorities: they feel a kind of persecution mania, are convinced that they engage in sexuality against parental authority, and often will do so in a spirit of defiance to affirm their independence and identity. Now, parental approval of a child's sexuality is important not only in infancy and childhood but particularly during the sexual puberty of adolescents. It is only when parents can feel pleasure in their children's sexual pleasure and can communicate it to them that young people will feel free to enjoy their sexuality rather than use sexuality as a kind of rebellion against their parents. If sexuality is used by adolescents as a weapon with which to fight authority then their sexuality acquires an aggressive quality and will lose much of its spontaneity. If parents communicate sexual acceptance and instil sexual confidence in their children then there is little fear that their sexuality will become compulsive. Nature has provided the rhythms of excitement and relaxation and intellectual and cultural activities would not suffer from free sexuality in adolescence. It may be that a different kind of culture will emerge — new symbols taking the place of the old. One must have a measure of trust in the future and in any case there is an urgent need for new cultural symbols and ideas.

How does an affirmative attitude by parents to their own and to the child's libido affect the oedipus complex? If the father does not play the role of sexual repressor then the boy will, to a large extent, cease to be afraid of his own sexual impulses and pleasure sensations. He will become less angry and aggressive, he will project less anger and aggression upon the father, father will not symbolise a forbidding and punishing object that, in turn, arouses the child's fear and anger. The child will not see father as a punishing castrating figure and he will not want to kill him. The boy will not stand in awe and trembling before father, he will not have to propitiate him and restitute him in worship, he will not have to glorify him into an omnipotent Godhead, and he will not be impelled to project his own aggressive urges upon the members of other tribes and nations and he will not have to fight them in order to defend father. He will cease to be paranoid, constantly seeing his God and his State threatened by the 'others'; he will not feel the need to wave a flag carrying father's image aloft and fight for it in the rituals of war and self-sacrifice.

Patriarchal totem worship of state and authority would become meaningless. When people feel acknowledged and accepted as persons then they will accept and acknowledge others as persons and not merely as members of other tribes or nations. When people are not made to feel guilty for their human needs then they can recognise the humanity of others.

The attitude to women would change. They would not have to be conquered. As sexuality would be an overtly accepted part of the life of an individual, so women would be individuals to whom one would relate according to one's own and her wishes without sin or compulsive ceremonials imposed from above. People would do their own choosing in sexual matters without the need for moral justification. This in turn would make the religious or State sanction for marriage unnecessary, and true marriage, the marriage based on love and the will of two people, could take place. People would either love each other or they would not and they would live together or they would not, according to their own feelings and their own choice. Indeed there would be no compulsion to imagine eternal love in a sexual attraction, no need to guarantee life-long fidelity. While sexuality would not be desirable without affection there would be no need to swear immortal love. Love goes beyond sexual attraction but of course includes it. It relates to the mind, the body, the thoughts and the personality of the other person and pulls people inexorably to each other and makes them want to be together. This is marriage — to share in each other's experiences, to discover the other and oneself in the other every day and to need this mutual discovery and sharing of experience. For this no contracts and no state sanctions are required.

But what about the family? If sex is not a sin or a source of anxiety, if love is not destroyed when sexual attraction towards another person occurs occasionally, then the coercive bonds of religion or state are not necessary. There would be no need for protective walls around the family. On the other hand the family would have to continue to exist just as long as the world outside is strange and hostile. The abolition of the family, in our sense, demands the creation of a society of non-alienated people; a society where people relate to each other without fear and mistrust, where sexuality, affections, pleasure and work and a sense of responsibility draw people together in comradeship, where every man is a creator and a source of pleasure to himself and to others.

When the patriarchal compulsions of mistrust and fear are overcome people can see themselves creatively engaged in the co-operative enterprise of making a human environment and of living in it; in other words where groups of free people can share in their work activities with no owners and slaves, no kings and authorities to exploit them and repress them. Then families can disappear because children can be members of a large group without being tied to their parents but related to them by natural needs and inclinations, while other members of the community or group would in some measure share in the parents' affection for the children. I do not think that parenthood and parental love for the children would disappear but I do think that children would have a wider circle of friends, uncles and aunts, brothers and sisters, to whom they could relate. The sharing in the care of children would be natural in such a society and would facilitate the sharing of the means of production.

The elimination of the oedipus complex would do away with the authoritarian and hierarchic compulsions and pave the way for a society of communalism of which, up till now, we have only the vaguest notions and which we all too often declare to be impossible in reality, relating it to the dream world of a heavenly existence. Who in the massed, mingled, apprehensive collective existence that is modern society still perceives what community is? As Martin Buber has written: 'Community is the being no longer side by side but *with* one another of a multitude of persons. And this multitude experiences everywhere a turning to, a dynamic facing of, the others, a flowing from I to Thou'.* Only when there is an *I-Thou* relationship between persons can we speak of *we*.

The ego, the self that can relate itself to other selves directly, as it were, could dispense with the old superego. The superego would be replaced by an ego-ideal that affirms the autonomy of men's humanity without the need for an internal and superhuman watchman to guard us against the libido. Just as the old superego has found its embodiment in authoritarian society, so the new human ego ideal would find its embodiment in a society which affirms man's pleasure in himself and in others, which would actualise man's freedom towards himself in the freedom of men to each other. The construction of such a society is necessary if we are to overcome the compulsions towards destruction which our civilisation produces. It is also possible, however strange this may seem to armoured and repressed people. Modern technology with its advances in automation and miniaturisation will make the hierarchical mass societies unnecessary and facilitate productive processes which are suited for a communalistic social structure. Furthermore, the liberation of the libido from its age-old negations would eliminate the compulsive need for substitute gratifications that has to be satisfied by a proliferation of commodities. The consumer psychology which was inevitable to alienated and repressed individuals will be seen as a pathological manifestation of a culture that has denied man his primary gratifications, that has

---

*Martin Buber: *Between Man and Man*.

estranged him from the sources of pleasure and joy that are innate to him.

While a detailed analysis of the politics of a non-patriarchal society does not fall within the scope of this book, it is imperative to realise that the social revolution is a dimension of the sexual revolution — that the two are interwoven and the one is not possible without the other.

There is a self-destructive drive in mankind which invades all institutions and ideologies. This is a fact which both the trauma of living in this century as well as the investigations of Freud have made abundantly clear. But this drive does not need to be seen as a divine force — Thanatos. It is a consequence of the thwarting of instincts, a secondary and not a primary drive however deep-seated and central it is to the human condition. It has to be taken very seriously. It is almost all-powerful. But it can be conquered and only Eros can conquer it. If we cannot love we are condemned to hate, and if we can love we have no disposition to hate — it is as simple as that.

Life and Religion

by Ola Raknes, Ph.D.

Formerly Vegetotherapist, Oslo
Fellow of the American College of Orgonomy, New York

Paper first presented at the Fourth Scandinavian Psychological Conference, in Copenhagen, 1956. Translated from the Norwegian by David Boadella.

Dr. Ola Raknes trained as a psychoanalyst at the Berlin Psychoanalytic Institute (1927-1929) and subsequently became one of the earliest analysts to study under Wilhelm Reich after he had developed the techniques of vegetotherapy (later, orgone therapy). Dr. Raknes has practised these techniques in Norway during the past thirty years. He has kept himself informed of Reich's later work after he had left Europe, by frequent visits to America, where he repeated many of Reich's experiments in basic energy research. He is the author of Motet Med Heilage *(Meeting the Holy: an investigation into the Psychological Foundations of Religion) (1927);* Fri Vokster *(Free Growth) (1949); and* Wilhelm Reich and Orgonomy *(1970). Dr. Raknes died in January 1975.*

After I had planned this paper, and sent in my resumé to the editor, one of my female patients related an episode from her life which seemed to me such a good example of what I intended to describe, that I will present the episode first.

 The young woman was then in her late twenties. She worked in a modest position, but was well thought of by her employer, and by her colleagues, and she felt happy to a reasonable extent. But it so happened that she had a disappointment in love, and was then for a long time very unhappy and depressed. Then one day, quite unexpectedly and suddenly, and without her being able to understand it, she felt that she was transformed. Her depression went, she felt a new liveliness and strength in her, a new life flowed through the whole of her body from head to foot. It was as if a new force had entered her from outside. She had grown up in a strict narrow-minded and moralistic environment, but had lived all the time with an inner protest against her environment and the whole religious life-view which she had been governed by. As soon as she felt herself strong enough she had left home and taken the training which she needed for her present occupation. Now that she felt this new vitality streaming through her she could find no other explanation for it, in her experience, but that her religion must have been right, and that God really could give people a new strength and happiness. She felt as though she was in a state of grace, and lived for some months almost intoxicated with happiness. At the same time she became discontented with her work, and took pains to train herself for something which seemed to her better and finer — a training which she carried through to completion. But she had not begun this for long before she noticed that her sense of new life left her, that she dried up more and more and froze up, without being able to understand why.

This short account is only an example of something we meet in all religions from the simplest and most primitive, to those which are thought of as the highest and most advanced and complicated — namely that the adherents of the religion believe that they have a share in a new, richer, and higher life than that which is available in the world outside. This other life has many different names in different religions, but they all have in common that the new life becomes looked at as something essentially different from ordinary life. It is sacred, in contrast to the profane everyday life. Those who participate in this new life also participate in the sacred, which it is religion's function to establish connection with.

In my doctorate thesis, *Meeting the Holy: an investigation into the psychological foundations of religion* (Oslo, 1927), I tried to show that all the specific religious feeling in a religion, in other words the sense of the sacred, can be explained by and leads us to certain psychic experiences which I called by the common name of 'ecstasy' and which other investigators, among them William

James, have called 'mystical states of consciousness'. I still thought nearly thirty years ago, that this explanation was successful, and that the so-called mystical states of consciousness gave a complete account of everything that was specifically religious in religions.

When it comes to explaining these same mystical states, or ecstasies, I have come to different conclusions today, conclusions which I believe give a deeper and better understanding of religion and its influence on human development.

At that time I believed that ecstasy arose in the same way that feelings and thoughts which had previously been repressed and unconscious may suddenly break through to consciousness; but in such an unclear or mystical form, that it was not recognised as such, but was taken as a completely new entity which took possession of one from outside. I still thought that there could be something correct in that. But what I believe now is that what breaks through to consciousness, in ecstasy, is essentially the very sensation of being alive, a feeling which is derived from the sense of vegetative liveliness. This sense is one which psychologists so far have not concerned themselves with, and the significance of which has been completely overlooked.

I shall now try to explain, briefly, what this vegetative liveliness is, how it manifests itself, how it can be suppressed, and how it can be made conscious again.

But first a few words on why, and by what right, we refer to this feeling as a sense of liveliness. First of all because all those who are aware of it experience it in this way, and speak of a vitality they did not know before, and feel themselves to be living in a new and enhanced way. Many say that before having this experience they did not really know what it felt like to be alive. But we also speak of this feeling in these terms, because it is derived from a central life-function, the biological pulsation, which I shall say more about in due course.

What then is life, and how is it experienced? It will not do at all, to quote different biological definitions of life, for none of those I have come across take the least account of how life can be experienced by the one who experiences it. The only definition which I know which takes account of subjective experience is

Life and religion

Wilhelm Reich's definition of life as a progressive process of rhythmic change from mechanical tension and bio-energetic charge to bio-energetic discharge and mechanical relaxation. I shall not describe here the origin of this definition, but only point out that the life-rhythms which are derived from it provide the possibility of direct experience of the vegetative processes, but only if the organism is free of tensions that would otherwise obstruct the free bodily rhythms, or would hinder those which did exist undisturbed from coming to awareness. Most people will need a certain amount of practice at taking note of their own bodily condition, before they begin to experience these life-rhythms. Those who do will sense them distinctly in two forms in particular: in the rhythmical streaming which goes through the whole body when the respiration is followed through freely; and particularly intensely during the sexual orgasm.

In the therapy of the neuroses that Wilhelm Reich developed, it is the goal of treatment to bring back to life and to consciousness the immediate experience of these living rhythms. He found that in all neurotic people the capacity for immediate experience of this kind was more or less destroyed or disturbed. He pointed out, moreover, that many patients recognised the experience as one that they had known before, but had forgotten, until the memory came back with the sensations. Usually these feelings are remembered from early childhood, but occasionally also from adolescence. Where patients had earlier experienced a religious conversion or awakening, they have spontaneously related that the life-feeling which was revived in them by the treatment was indistinguishable from what they had felt in a state of religious upliftedness. There are two comments frequently made by patients who experience these vegetative sensations consciously for the first time: that what they feel is on the one hand something new, remarkable, incomprehensible and marvellous; and on the other hand is yet felt as the most natural of natural events.

One of the earliest consequences of a person coming into touch with his own vegetative life, is that he develops greater capacity for contact with other people. This term, capacity for contact, may perhaps sound rather mystical or vague. Philosophical and psychological dictionaries do not define 'psychic contact', nor have I found it referred to in the usual text-books. I will therefore try to define the term myself, and will say that psychic contact is an immediate involvement in other people's thoughts and feelings. How this sense of empathy develops is a question I will not pursue further here, but will content myself with saying that for people who at first lacked and then later gained psychic contact, such contact is a clear fact of experience, just as the lack of such contact is an equally clear fact for others.

Everyone who is in touch in this way is agreed that children are alive in a way that one seldom finds in adults. The special quality of this aliveness is seen in many ways: there is a natural grace, in all movements, a fresh impulsivity with heart-felt actions in both affection and anger, a whole-hearted concentration on whatever task is undertaken, a free experience of bodily (sexual) pleasure, and finally a unique capacity for contact with other people and a sense of what is healthy and what is sick. For the majority of children, those who have undergone the usual type of upbringing, these expressions of natural vitality will be found until about the age of 3 or 4, sometimes a little longer, sometimes not so long.

In Christianity it has always been well-known that the religious mind has much in common with the child's mind. I have only to quote a few sayings of Jesus: 'Unless ye become as little children ye cannot enter the kingdom of God'; 'Suffer little children ... for of such is the Kingdom of Heaven'; 'the kingdom of God is within you'.

When one adds to this the comments from patients in therapy who have earlier had religious experiences, or who remember from childhood the same feelings of vitality which in therapy at first felt strange and alien, there is no doubt that this sense of vitality is the centre of that which a religious psychologist such as William James called 'mystical states of consciousness', and which I myself describe as ecstasy. The word 'ecstasy' originally meant to be beyond onself or taken out of oneself. Both these terms seem to indicate a condition that is more or less mystical, that is mysterious and enigmatic, and one might expect that such states must be vague and indistinct, but according to people who have experienced them that is rarely or never the case. Most of them and particularly those who had strong and intense experiences, are agreed that they are the clearest and most distinct forms of awareness that they know of. But it is a clarity of a unique kind, a clarity which affects every insight. Unclear states of mind on the other hand are not usually counted as mystical, either because they are weak and indistinct, or because they are strong but confused, as for instance in a state of conflicting emotion. How can it be that that which produces such an intense, clear, uplifting and pleasurable state of mind, can be so enigmatic and mystical?

If one calls any other condition mystical, it is easy to think that those who talk of mysticism have concealed part of the experience, with the result that it seems mystifying. Could it also be the case that in ecstatic states those who experience them have consciously or unconsciously concealed part of the experience, the part that has moved them towards mysticism? That is just what I think is so, and that I wish to discuss, moving from the hidden side of the experience towards the ecstatic state itself; in other words I intend to reveal the hidden basis of religious mysticism. Whether religion will be able to maintain itself when one removes the mystique about its origin, will be dealt with later. What can be predicted with certainty is that most religious people, and many others also, will protect themselves by all means from seeing the natural foundation of mysticism and with that of religion.

The natural basis of religion is nothing other than the sense of vegetative liveliness I tried to describe in the first place. St. Paul said, correctly enough, that the natural man could not understand the things which belonged to the kingdom of God, but by 'natural man' he meant the average man, and that meant in his day, as in our own, that most people lack this feeling, or the consciousness of it. When people in therapy first experience these feelings it is something so new that they feel themselves living in an entirely different way.

A patient who experiences himself in this way has no new name for the life-sensations. Most of them say that something streams, or moves like a wave, or is alive in a strange way here or there in the body. Usually it feels good, though some anxiety for the unknown is usually present. Some unacademic patients who have been familiar with traditional religious practice from childhood, but have never had any religious experiences of their own, say that they felt as if a stream of bliss flowed through their body, and understood for the first time what the mystics mean when they say that they experience bliss here already on earth.

I do not know how far it is recognised in medicine and in psychology, that a fully free respiration involves the entire organism. Those who are used to taking note of their own bodily sensations will certainly be able to sense the streamings which go through the whole body with a full and deep breathing. These wave-like movements give a feeling of being alive through and through. Those who have relaxed bodies and unclouded minds have these sensations as the regular and permanent background to all that they experience, and it is this which gives colour, taste, and freshness to their whole life.

In special circumstances, such as when one is seized with a novel insight, or engrossed in a major creative task, or in a state of full sexual surrender, these feelings increase so much in strength that one feels a stream of intensified life. But normally these life-feelings are in the background of awareness, and can then become so taken for granted, that one hardly notices them except at certain times when something or other draws attention to them. If something happens for a long time to inhibit one, or if one suddenly suppresses a natural impulse, then it gradually begins to feel as if one is not living properly, or as if life had lost its taste and colour, or no longer held anything. If the situation changes, and the tensions that had taken hold of the body are given up, then the vegetative streamings are felt again with renewed strength, and it may be in such circumstances that they first come into full awareness, whereas before they were so taken for granted as the background to all experience, that one hardly realised that they were there.

In therapy it sometimes happens, usually with patients who are not used to noticing their bodily feelings, that these sensations come to awareness without the patient being clear that they are his own feelings and are localised in the body. As long as they are not felt as arising from the body, these patients experience them as just as mysterious and bizarre as the religious mystic does, even if he recognises them in an inexplicable way, or as being a natural process. But once each patient has experienced his own organism as the source and ground for the sense of vitality, mysticism disappears and it becomes quite natural.

The vegetative sensations are fundamental to all pleasure feelings, whatever these may be induced by. Usually feelings of pleasure are associated with external things, which may be small or great, it may be a flower, the rays of the sun, or the creation of a masterpiece. Often people feel that the external events are the causes of what they feel and that these things alone give rise to the pleasure feelings. But it also happens that pleasure feelings can arise without there being any known cause. At the same time one often hears from people that the things which they expect ought to make them happy, leave them unmoved, or with at best a sense of cold satisfaction. This shows that the outer event which one expects should bring happiness is only the trigger for an inner process which only occurs under certain circumstances, the most important of which is that one has the capacity to experience the vegetative sensation.

What people seek in religion is just this sense of life and happiness; and the most important reason that people cling on to religion, perhaps with a sense of terror for what might happen if they gave it up, is that they expect to find life and happiness in it. Do people really find what they seek in religion, then, or is it only imaginary? Can one say that what religion gives is only a substitute for life and happiness? Before I try to answer this question, I shall digress to another issue, namely the matter of the truth of religion.

The essence of each religion is that all its adherents take something or other as sacred, and experience it as sacred. In *Meeting the Holy* I showed how sacred characteristics are determined by ecstatic experiences. Both the ecstatic experience and the sense of sacredness are psychological facts which in themselves are just as much facts as a stone, a river or the wind are facts. And just as we never think to ask if a stone or a stream or the wind are true, so there should be no reason to ask if the ecstatic experience or sense of sacredness is true.

But in all religions the ecstatic states and feeling of holiness are associated with different material or immaterial things. They can for example be linked to certain stones, trees, fields, houses (such as a church), or celestial phenomena; to certain ceremonies, customs, or individuals, and finally to certain theories or doctrines. And here we have the main area where it has some meaning to raise the question of truthfulness, in the following way: is there any truth in the different religious theories and teachings that are held to be sacred and which inspire a sense of holiness in believers? To that question all cultural history and all scientific research on religion gives an unequivocable answer: in all cultures and in all religions the characteristics of sacredness have been laid down with the same certainty as erroneous theories. The certainty is just as strong in the case of theories which are later shown to be false, as it is for those which may be confirmed by research. Sacredness in itself has never provided any guarantee for the truth of statements, and to ask if a religion such as christianity, is true, is only meaningless, and gives evidence simply of unclear thought processes.

I return now to the first question: is it true that people find life and happiness in religion or is this illusory, and can religion only offer substitutes? Following what has already been said about the vegetative feelings as the basis of the sense of vitality and pleasure, the question is whether religion can evoke these feelings or not.

To that question I can give an answer from my experience which may sound paradoxical until I have said more about what happens to the vegetative sensations during life. My answer is that religion may be able to arouse, at least in many people, the feeling for life which an authoritative religious upbringing has suppressed or paralysed. It seems that a religious awakening may be for some people the only accessible way of re-arousing the suppressed life-sensations. On the other hand religion may still prove for most of these people, to be a restriction, so that the sense of aliveness is incomplete, and not as all-inclusive as it could otherwise have been. For most people, in all cultures, who cannot accept the truth in religious teaching, religion becomes an effective barrier which prevents them recovering the lost sense of life, because what they were taught to look on as the only way to life is closed to them. Such people usually end up, like Freud, in his *Unbehagen in der Kultur*, by denying the factual core of truth in religion.

I hope that my answer will seem clearer when I have said more about what usually happens to the sense of vegetative life as a child grows up. No-one who has had anything to do with small children, and who is in touch with his own feelings, can doubt that a new-born baby has this vegetative liveliness. I have already mentioned the signs of this in children. Until recently there was no means of scientifically recording the difference between vegetatively free and vegetatively disturbed children, but it now seems that the diagnostic muscle-tests which Dr. Nic Waal and her associates have developed, can be used for this purpose. That such differences are there, many children know well, and can sometimes find words for them.

A patient, who behaved at times just like a child, complained that when he was out among people and 'loosened himself to be alive' (his own phrase), he became scared of all the dead people around him. An 8 to 9 year old boy, who until then had been unusually fresh and lively, was sent to me because he sometimes had such unruly outbursts of anger that the adults could not cope with them. When he trusted me not to scold him or lecture to him like other adults, he told me that he could control his anger; 'but then I became dead', he added. It was clear that he did not mean that he would die literally, but that his feelings of being alive would disappear.

I have already indicated that this child's life-feeling is closely related or identical with the religious sense of life. How it can disappear is well illustrated in the example above. How it can be that a child's sense of vitality is actually lacking in most cases is something we know much about from our therapeutic treatment of adults, supplemented with and strengthened by our experience of children at all ages. Unfortunately little of this material has been published, chiefly because for many reasons it is rather difficult to publish it. What I have to say here is therefore principally what I have learned from my own therapeutic work during more than 25 years.

As long as the child has his full vegetative liveliness, each impulse to activity will be followed through directly, provided that the impulse does not meet insuperable obstacles, and that the child does not tire of the effort to satisfy his needs, or forget one impulse and replace it with another. Even if he meets severe opposition, or he is tired out by useless struggle, or in disappointment and anger, he will still preserve his vitality and his impulsivity unharmed as long as he is allowed to assert his strength and his power, without punishment or reproach, for as long as he needs.

But once the child becomes punished for following his impulses, or learns that it is wrong to do so, then he begins to be careful, to hold his breath, and to make himself stiff in various parts of his body. In this way he suppresses the anxiety following the impulse, and with that the impulse itself. Little by little either the punished impulses or other things which remind him of them, become taboo, and the child becomes less and less alive, and more and more impulse-deprived. In the end he feels more or less dead and life-less, and has lost his original natural sense of vitality. Before that happens most children have tried different ways of obtaining some of the satisfactions they expected from their impulses. Active, vital children hang on to their anger, and can in this way for a long time retain their immediate feeling of life; but if anger is too firmly punished, or beaten down until it turns to anxiety, then these children will seek refuge in the same ways that weaker and less vital children do: they will comfort themselves with passive withdrawal, or sulking, with clinging and self-pity; or with compulsive masturbation, or finger-sucking, bed-wetting, or other masturbation substitutes. When in the end even these means of coping with the child's vital pleasure needs have been prevented, it is all up with the child's natural life-feeling, and the certain ground is laid for a variety of inhibitions which later on can lead on to a break-through of neurotic symptoms, or in softer form, to a religious break-through. Only in exceptional cases can this be overcome in a happy love-life, or in a creative work achievement.

I will say a few words here about what kind of obstacles lead to the loss of life-feeling, and in so doing lay the basis for inhibitions and neuroses and form the prerequisites for personal religion. According to earlier research, especially from the Freudian school, it was only sexual prohibitions which were the starting-points for neurosis. The basis of this theory was the fact that sexual inhibitions are found in every neurosis and that every history of a neurosis reveals sexual taboos, and a sex-negative environment. Professor Schjelderup advanced the theory, some years ago, that the basis for neurosis was not to be found in sexual taboos, but in inhibitions of activity. However, the contrast between inhibition of activity and sexual inhibition is an artificial one: each natural impulse that is prevented from getting proper gratification leads to a general life-inhibition, and with that also to a disturbance in sexual pleasure, which in turn is the basis for a neurosis.

I turn back now to the child who, due to inhibitions and taboos, has lost his natural vitality. Often it is only when this loss first takes place that the child feels unhappy or suffers consciously on this account. Later he feels a sense of emptiness, an unclear longing, which some children fill out with day-dreams and fantasies, while others seek to deny it by withdrawing and sulking, which turns them into over-dependent and discontented children. Perhaps the commonest response is to seek to drive the sense of loss away with noise and bluster and hooliganism, while others, finally, may seek to make up for it by being clever, and earning the esteem of adults in this way.

These different substitutes for the lost feeling of life, have the effect of making life tolerably bearable for most. Life may even seem merry and amusing, at least until the onset of adolescence. Until that time the suppressed pleasure feelings, including sexual feelings, are not so urgent for most that they lead into 'secret sins' which worry the conscience somewhat, but not so much as to stop them. But the intensification of instinctual impulses which sexual maturation leads to, means that the struggle against his own drives, and the anxiety on account of them, result in life becoming painful, or, if the inhibitions are strong enough, it becomes unbearably empty.

It is in this situation in puberty that religion has its first great chance to become a personal and living concern for the individual. Until now the children have accepted their religious teaching on adult authority, often with the result that God has become, for the young, one who forbids and punishes sexuality (so a priest told me after a discussion with Oslo youth). So far the religious teaching of a new and richer life in God has been empty words for them. But in the crisis of emptiness and psychic misery which most enter into at pubety, there are many who feel that life should be something different, something much richer, than what they have experienced so far, in as much as all have lost the time in childhood when life really felt alive and good. The religious preaching offers them a new life and a new happiness which passes beyond understanding, so that they will surrender themselves to it, indeed, and believe in their own salvation.

In surrendering in this way and getting the experience that they are saved, they can confirm that they really do gain a new life on conversion; and the same thing naturally holds if the conversion takes place in later life.

From my experience in treating religious people, and from the reports of converts, and from other religious-psychological writings, I am in no doubt that this new 'Godly' life, which the converted experience, is identical with a part of the natural vegetative life-sensation. But it is, in all cases normally, only a part of it, and sometimes only a small part. The strength and intensity of these feelings, in other words, provide no sure criterion for saying how inclusive they are, or whether they involve the whole psycho-physical organism, or only parts of it. What determines the intensity of these feelings is how strongly they have been suppressed, and how violently they break through into awareness. In a therapy where the experience of vegetative feelings is prepared systematically, with a gradual elimination of the muscular and characterological obstacles, one rarely sees the violent ecstasy that is met with in most religious awakenings.

A complete life-feeling, in which the whole of the psycho-physical organism is involved, will also result in sexual freedom — not to be confused with sexual licence, but I shall not develop this aspect here. The life-feeling which religion provides will not normally be free and all-inclusive, because the life-impulses which conflict with traditional religious morality are usually suppressed. This reduction or restriction of natural liveliness is the price that the religious must pay for their new life. But since the sense of vitality was even more reduced before, or even entirely suppressed as a result of a life-inimical upbringing, the converted will still feel that their new life offers infinite riches. But the life of most religious people is nevertheless narrowed down by these restrictions.

The new life, and the sense of being alive, which religion provides or arouses, will always be mystical or enigmatic within the context of religion because the bodily foundations for it are denied, or regarded in a different light. In doing so it is not realised fully that God's life has a bodily side, even though the bodily feelings may be interpreted as God's grace streaming through body and soul. As examples of religious interpretations of bodily sensations, I mention that when St. Theresa of Avila felt moved in her womb during religious ecstasy, she thought it was Jesus who touched her with an arrow; and when St. John of the Cross ejaculated under his ecstasy, it was simply that his body in this way participated in his heavenly joy.

In contrast to the religious life-feeling is the experience undergone under vegetotherapeutic treatment, which is not a bit mystical, except perhaps at first before the patient has become familiar with it, and sensed it as a distinct organic feeling.

I will now conclude by saying a few words about what is responsible for the life-feelings. All who have experienced them have felt that there is something which streams or ripples or pulsates through them, and most speak of it as like a force or energy. Since this feeling, and as a result, the energy, is not subject to conscious control, we may suppose that it is connected with and affected through the autonomic or vegetative nervous system in the body. This shows also that the experience depends on the vegetative body functions being at least partly in order. Many associate the streaming that they feel through their organism with an electric current, but on closer reflection they always admit that whilst an electric current always feels disagreeable, this streaming feels pleasant, in spite of the anxiety for the unknown which often accompanies it at first. Dr. Wilhelm Reich, who developed the techniques of character-analysis and vegetotherapy, and who first observed the signs of what he called 'vegetative streamings', thought at first that the underlying energy was a special form of electricity, bio-electricity. Later research led him to conclude that one is here dealing with a special hitherto undiscovered energy-form which he called 'orgone' because it was connected with the organism, and because he discovered it during studies of the orgasm function. Later he found that this energy-form was found not only in living organisms but everywhere, and was possibly identical with what physicists call cosmic radiation. Reich spent the last fifteen years of his life studying this energy, its laws, and its possible applications, particularly in therapy and weather-control. Here is not the place to say any more about this energy-form, but I will mention only that it is in constant movement, and that this movement, like all vegetative movement, is pulsating and rhythmical. I will also mention that what has been so far discovered of the laws of this energy-form provides the best explanation I have so far found for the life-feelings, whether they are experienced with a religious or other interpretation, or without such interpretation. The orgone hypothesis gives a natural explanation for the fact that the more comprehensive a person's life-feeling is, the greater his capacity for contact particularly with life-less nature. It lends probability to the claim that all mystics have advanced, that they feel themselves to be in connection with, or joined to, or at one with the whole universe, and that time as an independent reality does not exist. I maintain that it is possible, or even probable that wider study and application of the energy that we immediately experience in our life-feeling, can contribute to strengthening this feeling, and with that to increase the capacity for contact and understanding between people.

The Primary Personality and its Relationship to the Streamings

by Gerda Boyesen

Vegetotherapist, London

Gerda Boyesen has a degree in psychology from the University of Oslo, and a diploma in physiotherapy from the Oslo Orthopaedic Institute. She took a private training analysis with Ola Raknes, one of Norway's leading psychologists and Reich's principal co-worker in Europe. She took additional training at the University Mental Hospital and at the Bulow-Hansens Institute. She was Clinical Psychologist at Dikemark Mental Hospital, and a psychological consultant at Lorisenberg Hospital, Lier Mental Hospital, and the Vinderen Psychiatric Clinic, where she later worked as a full-time clinical psychologist.

She left Norway in 1968 and moved to London. Here she set up the Centre for Bio-energy where she trains therapists, sees private patients, and holds seminars in her methods of dynamic relaxation and vegetotherapy. From this base she also travels extensively to Holland, Germany, Switzerland, and France to hold further training programmes.

Wilhelm Reich discovered that after having removed a certain amount of muscle armour, the patient would report streamings. At first he called these vegetative currents, but later related them to the cosmic energy called orgone. This was, in my view, the most basic and essential discovery in connection with mental and physical health and well-being. His cosmic theory has been passionately disputed and discarded, and yet it is supported by the now increasingly influential Chinese medicine with its Ki energy, which is the same as Wilhelm Reich's orgone energy. Its existence is also supported by the Yoga concept of Prana, but the strongest support has come from America where, without knowing it, Professor Charles Bachman at Syracuse has reported the measurement — using his newly invented, ultra-fine measuring instruments — of electrical currents down the spine which can have no other origin than what Reich called the 'great cosmic sea'. Here I will begin with what in psychology is called the oceanic wave. Among psychologists, this oceanic wave, which is a theoretical concept, is supposed to be present in the child from birth, giving it an inner well-being, feelings of pleasure and security. The psychologists say it is later replaced by the secure emotional relationship with the mother. If we relate this oceanic wave to the Reichian theory, it has a literal and concrete existence as cosmic energy ('heavenly energy' in acupuncture) emanating from the cosmic sea (see Reich's *Cosmic Superimposition*), penetrating each pore of the body like a wave passing through it.

My own experience with patients shows that the oceanic wave is not naturally replaced by the mother. Only when it is lost, which is usually the case in our neurotic culture, is this necessary. But through the treatment of adults with vegetotherapy, people start to report what they often call 'rocking' movements, until finally they reach the 'genital' personality and regain the oceanic wave which gives them a natural well-being and security. Thus we see that the oceanic wave is the same as Reich's 'streamings' which flow through the body when there are no obstacles or armouring. We will now see how the loss of the streamings can give rise to a split and schizoid personality.

Psycho-sexual Development

If all is well, the streamings or energy potential in the body should give natural growth and self-realization both psychologically and physically. Such energy should be available as a sort of reservoir to be drawn upon in emotional or emergency situations and also in ecstasy and delight. If a critical situation arises, the organism has to draw from the reservoir the amount of energy needed to cope with the situation; but after this has been abreacted and the danger is over, the energy should be free to flow back to the reservoir and to circulate round the body giving the natural feeling of aliveness and well-being.

But if emotional expression is inhibited or stuck and the person is in a permanent situation of emotional provocation, the amount of energy in the reservoir is less because it is being used in the frustrated emotional block. This causes the organism to be exhausted or irritable and the natural feeling of euphoria disappears. But if the body is able to work out nervous energy, biochemical stress products are also released into the bloodstream and the organism can return to a free energy flow.

Each time the organism is not able to get rid of emotional stress products (adrenalin, lactic acid, etc.), there will be a build-up, an obstacle, for moving energy; and for each layer of restored neurotic defence or armouring there will be a fresh layer hampering the full streaming energy from coming through. Finally, if we think of it as chicken mesh with dirt in the holes, layers and layers of chicken mesh, we can see that the streamings cannot come through at all, any more than sunbeams can filter through solid material.

Self-actualization

Kurt Goldstein* has presented the view that neurosis has only one cause: the hindrance of self-realization. If we look at the bio-energy or life force as the basic stimulus for self-realization we see that if the streamings cannot penetrate the organism, the individual's awareness of his potentialities is lost. We can see this when a person is bent into a secondary shadow-personality, not knowing what he wants or what he is. Through vegetotherapy, we witness that as the person comes back into touch with his streamings and can feel his body, he always knows what he is and what he wants and he very often realizes that the work he does is not for him, and that the person he has grown into is nothing like his real self.

---

*in his book *The Organism*, Macmillan, New York, 1939.

Let us take a look at psycho-sexual development and character type, and their relationship to energy flow or fixation. It seems that the erogenous zones are highly related to orgone energy accumulation, for example a child's skin is very aware and ticklish, particularly on the stomach. You cannot even touch it without the child jumping and laughing. When a person is armoured, particularly a schizoid person, this ticklishness disappears and can only be regained when he becomes more alive and filled with healthy energy. People can be too ticklish, and this can be reduced to a normal level by massage. It seems that the accumulation or storage of energy in an alive skin makes for a high degree of ticklishness.

With a child in the oral phase, the energy accumulation is centred around the mouth so that this area has the highest level of permanent energy; when this energy reaches a certain level, the child will begin to suck.

When I talk about energy here, it is to be understood that the flow of energy is closely related to the nervous system and the autonomic blood circulation and distribution.

Strong and Mild Waves

We see in a child in the oral phase that there are two sorts of sucking — one greedy, aimed at taking in food, the other milder sucking movements destined for comfort and self-enjoyment. This distinction is very important. The strong sucking is connected with a high accumulation of energy which makes the muscles contract strongly. The other has a milder level of energy with gentler contractions, giving a lazy feeling of well-being, the energy going through the skin and downwards with a feeling of sweetness, quietness, and peace. Let me give an example: a woman in therapy where the therapy had reached the uncovering of the oral phase, relaxed and felt the energy flow up to the mouth. She felt a flood of sweetness with the mouth as the centre and a high level of pleasure. She felt no need for sucking movements but sensed the energy moving through the skin of the mouth and down around the outside of the mouth, giving a melting feeling and a bodily sweetness. When this stopped, she felt a pressure which she gave into to make sounds. This is a very important indication of how the baby's sounds develop through an accumulation of tension or energy which if responded to will result in sounds and mouth and tongue movements which are pleasurable. Thus the first sounds develop through the pattern: tension — charge — discharge — release.

When this adult woman allowed the pressure to guide her, she made babyish sounds which developed into 'mama', a 'mama' which did not come from her but from the movement of her tongue. The child, automatically receiving the reward of pleasure will thus develop the natural pattern of sounds, and this is most likely true also for birds and animals, following the pattern: tension — displeasure — release — pleasure. When this woman relaxed still more, suddenly the ocean of sweetness stopped and there came a strong ring of tension around the mouth bringing a feeling of unpleasure and anger and she felt that she was hanging onto a nipple. Later she went to her mother and asked her if she had ever hung by a nipple. And her mother told her that when she was a baby, she used to tease her by withdrawing her nipple, enjoying the sight of the little one's desperate attempt to hang on and its subsequent anger. When the mother was asked how often she did it, she said she had started almost from the baby's birth, doing it 3 or 4 times a day. The feeling of insecurity about the breast and the anticipation of withdrawal of the nipple, plus the anger connected with it, made my patient into a schizoid personality, orally fixated because the baby never had a chance to let the natural libidinous circulation of streaming in her body come through. Fighting back a scream while the experience was occurring, she built up a residue of anger in her body which became a barrier to her natural psycho-sexual development, to the development of the primary personality. Through losing the streamings in her body, she also lost the stimulus for self-fulfilment and self-realization and grew into a girl without any aliveness, but instead was compliant, dutiful, and 'good', all the characteristics of the pre-schizophrenic person.

Energy Circulation

Even in the oral phase, the energy should flow through the body stimulating also the anal and genital development through bringing pleasure to these areas. The energy flow should not be regarded as one channel, but as a lot of different channels. There are degrees of ability to experience pleasure ranging from the optimal level to complete lack of it. When the child is in the oral phase, it is predominantly the mouth and the arms that experience pleasure. Pleasure generates movement. In the anal phase, it is the lower part of the body which contains the pleasurable sensations, though in a healthy individual, the mouth will still retain its excitability, though the focus will be on the anal area. The anal stage is related to defaecation and the pleasure felt when the membranes are stimulated; but it is also connected to self-assertiveness, for example, temper tantrums, when the child kicks and presses backwards saying 'No, I won't'. Thus the anal phase has not only to do with the process of giving in to defaecation or holding it back, but is also to do with the development of an independent personality which can say 'no, I won't', or 'I want'. It seems that the child exercises this function during this period where it is stubborn or says 'no' or 'I want' even if it has no purpose and seems ridiculous to an adult. For instance, a girl of three, when her parents gave her milk, yelled for Coca Cola and for a whole hour she had temper tantrums until her exhausted parents gave in and said, alright, whereupon the girl started yelling for milk. This is a very important period for the development of the primary personality because the pleasure of kicking and the pleasure of self-assertiveness is strongly connected with the feeling of body streamings reaching the gluteal muscles, which are the point of 'standing on one's own feet'; they erect the body and make it independent and they also erect the neck. This gives a feeling of self, of being independent, and of self-worth, of value as a separate being. This process also makes the breathing freer and the posture erect and proud and with a natural dignity which is typical of the bearing of an independent human being with a primary personality. The opposite is when a child has guilt feelings about self-expression and asserting his will and his needs. Then he is bent both psychologically and bodily, his pattern is one of contraction; he will have a secondary personality and will be dependent on others for his well-being, with leanings towards the oral dependent character, questioning his right to exist. The important point here is that the streamings are blocked so that they cannot give more drive to the development of the primary personality and the individual's realization of his potentialities. Such people seem 'lost' and are dependent upon their environment to mould them, they have no real inner drive. When we see the attitude of most people towards bringing up children: 'Your will is in your father's pocket', with punishment for any expression of the child's feelings, with the emphasis on being a 'good boy' or 'good girl', we can see how the lack of outlet and the suppression of, for example, temper tantrums, become the crucial point at which the child's personality is bent, as is its posture, and only a secondary personality develops in order to adjust to the demands of the environment. There is a feeling of catastrophe in the child if it lets go. We can see why the Lowen kicking exercises are so important to procure a release of temper tantrums. But whatever method is used, these temper tantrums must be provoked because they bring expansion and independence to the individual and activate the frustrated stagnant streamings, causing them to move further down to the anal region and thence to the genital area in order to bring about a genital personality.

During this period of treatment, the person is often rebellious, wanting to change his job, and find another meaning in life because he realizes that the old pattern is not him, and he is right. He can see the stars far away and gains an inkling of his real self. In this period, homosexual tendencies often come up in men; in women there is a feeling of wanting anal coitus. This feeling in women is not catastrophic, but men are often very frightened because they become anxious about being homosexual. These feelings are quite natural because the energy has reached the anal membranes and tissue, making the whole area pleasurable and wanting touch. Preliminary to the feelings of pleasure is an itching in the anal region which indicates that the energy is trying to break through against biochemical resistances.

It would seem right to think — and case histories support it — that it is the orgone energy making both the tensions and pressure to use different parts of the body, which once again gives a libidinous feeling. For instance, the child has a period where it must move its fingers and touch everything, a touching which generates an almost libidinous feeling; if the sensation is not responded to, there is a feeling of tension and unpleasure. This happens with the hands, anus and mouth, as it does later with the feet and the need to walk. When the child first starts walking, this is a libidinous feeling.

The Genital Phase — period of transition

Wilhelm Reich describes the energy flow from the sacrum up the back, down the front of the face, down the stomach to the genitals where it finds release in orgasm; but in his description, there is one point lacking: the area between the anus and the sexual organs, the perineum. It seems that from the anal fixation, the energy moves during treatment towards the genitals causing excitability in the perineum where before there was almost no feeling; then it reaches the genitals.

The expression 'genital personality' might seem a very physical one, but it has tremendous implications for our whole civilization and for human happiness. It is not only the ability to experience orgasm and sexual fulfilment but has to do with the capacity for being a totally alive being. When we consider what our whole upbringing both within the family and at school is aimed at: forcing the individual to become a 'dutiful', 'kind' person, an industrious, laborious, almost machine-like worker who can fit into the various categories of society, someone with no will of their own, we can see that the production of a bent, anally-fixated, secondary personality is the best way of enabling society to exploit the individual and to form an obedient, robot-like community.

We live in the machine age where we have lost the exciting aliveness of being human and the natural well-being of body and mind. There is an increasing feeling of emptiness and purposelessness and the loss of what we had as children when we experienced everything as alive and pleasurable and exciting. The world has lost its shiny quality and we suffer from depression and anxiety, restlessness and loneliness; there is a feeling that we have to fill in something but we don't know what or why; there is a feeling of alienation from ourselves and others, a feeling that something is wrong and that the world is going in the wrong direction. It seems to me that the fixation of the compulsive being, stuck at the anal stage, where development cannot move on towards the genital personality, is the real reason for everything seeming so wrong, because as we are only secondary personalities, we build a secondary, twisted world. It may seem far-fetched to draw such sociological conclusions from physiological factors, but after all, without our psychology, we could not make a physical world.

Physiological Repulsion Against Cruelty

Here we have the real split and distinction between the alive being and the mechanical man. To illustrate it, I will take the example of the Nazis: we have been puzzled as to how humans could torture other human beings without experiencing a physiological revulsion against it. An alive being has a natural repulsion against planned cruelty which is not used in self-defence for survival. If an alive being were forced to perform torture, he would experience nausea, would get diarrhoea and be sick so that he could not go on with it. Under certain circumstances, he would be able to withdraw feeling so that his body could act as an efficient machine in an emergency. An example of this: one day when I was driving my car, a little girl suddenly ran across the road right in front of me. I was amazed how efficiently I reacted. There was no feeling in me interfering with the efficiency of avoiding the accident. This is a very important mechanism for survival, but after the emergency one should be able to regain the capacity to feel and should also be able to abreact the accumulated anxiety which has built up during the stress situation. This feeling of withdrawal, usually flexible, can under conditions of shock or following a prolonged period of trauma build up to such a degree that the flexibility does not return and one is stuck in a state of chronic and permanent withdrawal. This withdrawal of feeling is closely related to the withdrawal of streamings which give the feeling of being alive.

We will now take a look at how a mechanical, anal person with a secondary character structure, when he develops into a genital personality, turns into a live being. I call this 'people in transition' because it seems that they almost change into a different stuff. The transition from the anal to the genital phase is a crucial turning-point where the withdrawn energy flow and lack of feeling or aliveness are reversed and the energy stored in the sacrum travels down the spine. When there is a withdrawal of energy, this is connected to intellectualisation, compulsiveness in order to avoid real feeling, compulsive talking, obsessive thoughts, all related to the defence of not allowing the energy to move, because when the energy starts to travel and the person undergoes the transition from mechanical man to an alive being, he becomes so vulnerable and open that survival seems in jeopardy. Thus, and this is a very interesting point, as the energy is trying to come through from the sacrum to the genitals (the first crucial point), it always tries to come from the area of self-assertion between the shoulder blades and through the chest to the heart and out through the breasts: this may seem a strange combination, but if we consider how the breasts are organs for sexual energy parallel to the genitals, we see how natural it is that the energy should press from the sacrum towards the genitals and from the point of self-assertiveness in the back towards the breasts. On its way towards the breasts, it has to pass the heart. There are natural expressions in every language connected with the heart: 'I feel as though my heart would break', 'My heart is lonely', 'My heart is suffering', 'My heart is filled with joy' etc. A mechanical being (anal-fixated) uses the words but can never feel the reality of them. People in transition (anal-genital) literally experience what this is. In therapy, we can see these contradictions between patient and therapist: a nervous or mentally ill person has lost his defences and is literally on the way towards being more alive, but with all the anxieties and symptoms he is often more alive than the therapist who can still be of a mechanical-intellectual constitution where everything can be dealt with in a rational way and he can manage whatever he wants and can pull himself together because there is no live force pressing for expression and mercilessly refusing all compromise. When the streamings are released, there is no compromise solution, they have to be given in to, you have to go with the dynamic in your body and what it wants in order to gain release. The fewer psychological and muscular defences, the more one is a victim of the pressure to become an alive being and a primary personality. A return to a mechanical character structure can be achieved only through medications because they destroy the streamings. There is no natural pull from the unalive force and what there is can be dealt with on a shadow-mechanical, intellectual level which makes it easier to adjust to the expectations of the surroundings. But in doing this, one takes a step backwards from one's primary personality and the organism's unconditional demand for purification on the way to being a real alive being with its optimal possibilities for release. In our world with its mechanical standards and values, such a person is often regarded as 'going mad' or getting ill when he leaves his job and does not adjust to the ordinary standards of behaviour. This seems to be happening with the youth of our day, with the 'turned-on' people, whose aim is away from materialistic values, ambition, status and wealth, substitute values important only to mechanical man.

One of my patients said: 'My husband is not interested in people's feelings, he is only interested in psychology.' This is typical of mechanical man's need to control by knowledge what is going on, because when the streamings begin to move from their anal fixation on their way towards the heart, the person becomes interested primarily in people's feelings and does not want to hurt their alive being; new values develop which have to do with the soul; the person can feel himself and can be hurt and is therefore capable of an empathetic relationship with others.

In the period of transition, the patient often becomes physically low in health and exhausted. This is because when the energy is trying to move and to penetrate the body on its way outwards through the genitals and breasts, there will be an accumulation of energy and we have the situation of solidification of frozen energy (cf. Reich in *Cosmic Superimposition*). This frozen energy can be experienced as coldness, stasis in the pelvic region and in the region of the breast segment corresponding to the heart. Some patients with sufficient awareness report vibrations in the heart and are afraid of having a heart disease: they can feel a coldness around and in the heart, and in sorrow or emotional distress feel that the heart is full and swollen and on the point of breaking. At this point, there also develops an awareness of the suffering and distress of the world, its twistedness and the mechanical direction it has taken. The person becomes more sensitively aware of what is genuine and can relate only to real things; there is a revulsion against the plastic world, against the products of the mechanical world such as cars, asphalt, concrete. He feels a new aliveness and an awareness of how the body has not previously felt alive; he responds to other alive beings and feels their sensitivity and shining quality, their alive, sensitive faces and features. This is what is happening in the world where the youth is in transition, forming their own tribes, dressing differently both because they like the softness and aliveness of flowing clothes and hate the standardisation of the clothing of the mechanical world, and also to mark that they belong to the new generation, to a new world opposing the old one, one which stresses spiritual values instead of materialistic and mechanical ones.

So the process of becoming an alive being is closely related to the movement of energy on its way from the point of self-assertiveness in the back towards the breasts and genitals so that the ability for total sexual orgasm will develop. But the accumulated energy, because of former frustration may cause constant pressure with symptoms of stasis in the heart. This period can take a long time and the energy trying to get through draws so much from the reservoir of energy in the body that the patient may be very weak both because of neutral and free energy and through the stasis condition in the heart. Where this condition has existed for a long period, it takes time to penetrate the chest, and I have found it necessary to send patients to acupuncture where they treat the heart meridian. The patient now rediscovers the confusion and distress of his personality being violated and forced into a secondary personality, and he becomes painfully aware that the same process is happening to other individuals and to the world today. He feels a distress which has to do not only with his personal grief but also with a sense of Weltschmerz of a spiritual kind.

We are now coming to a very important point related to the sexual split between tenderness, the ability to love, and sex. In history, we have seen man's relationship to woman ruled by the split: that the one you feel tenderness and love towards, you do not feel sexual about, and vice versa — the split between the nun and the whore, the virgin and the gypsy. This period can be traced to the child's relationship to his mother: in the son, the Oedipal phase; in the girl, the period which as far as I know has not been pointed out: the period preceding the girls' Oedipal phase and which has to do with a fascination and love for the mother. A little girl will normally have a period of delight and really libidinous feelings for her mother around the age of 3. In this pre-Oedipal phase, she shows tenderness, the need to touch and kiss; and for both sexes, if they have to repress either their tenderness towards the mother because she is too possessive, or the sexuality they feel for her because of guilt feelings, then there is a split between heart and sex. As a solution of the conflict, there is a regression to the pre-genital and anal-fixated psycho-sexual stage. It seems then that there is an insoluable conflict. If there is a feeling of love in your heart of a streaming quality, then sexual feelings naturally result. If at this stage of treatment the patient dares to solve the conflict of love and sex, the Oedipal situation, then he can move on to the further process of becoming an alive being, but as long as this resolution is resisted, the energy pressing towards the heart and towards the genitals will accumulate without any release. When the energy is finally allowed to flow, the individual not only becomes a genital and alive being, but seems to move towards a spiritual personality. What makes this article so difficult to write is that it covers the whole range from physics and biochemistry to mysticism and spiritual development. This should not be so strange, but in our mechanical society, we have been accustomed to categories; and it will revolt the anal-fixated compulsive being to have this principle violated. It is acceptable to talk separately of psycho-analysis, physics, biochemistry, physiology, religion, mysticism, Buddhism, Yoga, and as long as they are kept apart, no animosity is aroused. And yet it follows almost like a law founded on case histories and empirical findings that these things become interrelated when the energy of sex and the heart are united and the person becomes naturally ethical, with a spiritual openness and understanding. Wilhelm Reich pointed out the tendency towards mysticism as being the cause of the split, because people could not experience sexual satisfaction and the energy went to the head instead and expressed itself in an inclination towards mysticism. This is true, but this is schizoid mysticism, that is alienated from the world and with hostility towards sexuality, as emphasised in most religions, with their consequent intolerance and superego doctrines and hatred of spontaneity and aliveness. This is often combined with ascetisicm and hostility towards worldly pleasures, which is a manifestation of the split. The unified, alive being, the being without a split, develops a spirituality where sexuality, heart, feelings and the third eye (intuition), together with parapsychological phenomena such as telepathy, are combined. People at this stage of the transition often get a feeling of being an instrument for higher forces, which in the view of the split and schizoid personality has schizophrenic implications. People in transition may even get a feeling of previous incarnations. There is a deep sensation of being embedded in the cosmic universe which may express itself as a feeling of being in touch with God,* a phenomenon which also often happens in LSD experiences — 'the good trip'. The patient becomes more psychic and has a radiance about him and is able to pass this radiance on to others. It seems that he is like an electro-magnetic field of cosmic emergy, where the aura lies outside and has not shrunken into the body, and through his aliveness, he is able to initiate both a process of aliveness in others, and also a process of hatred in mechanical beings not

---

*See the paper by Ola Raknes on 'Life and religion' in *Energy and Character*, Vol. I, No. 3, 1970, and on p.66 of this book.

ready for it, who cannot cope with the feelings he generates. Wilhelm Reich has described this phenomenon so well in his concept of the Emotional Plague, and in his books *Listen, Little Man* and *The Murder of Christ*. In our days of television and radio, which are based on the sending and receiving of messages through electro-magnetic waves, it is not so strange to think, if we dare, of a cosmic truth trying to influence our souls, in the form of a universal conscience ('primary conscience, ethical conscience' as opposed to the imposed superego) — our inner voice, which mystics call the voice of the Holy Ghost. People in prayer and those who meditate are trying to get in touch with this voice. There is also a natural honesty in all individuals: I have always been impressed by this in therapy. The individual has an unconditional honesty to himself that seems without exception to be related to the streamings which know no compromise; this is a deep dynamic in each person, driving us nearer to our higher selves and to self-fulfilment. The streamings always tell the truth and when we allow them to come through, we will always be honest to ourselves (Jung, Freud, Buddhism, Christianity).

Formerly, in my own mechanical period, I thought the prophets were schizophrenic and hallucinated. This was because the schizophrenic symptoms are similar. In the schizophrenic, the pre-morbid is a typical secondary personality (described above) with defences and blockages, both in the unconscious (hatred, repressed feelings) and the super-conscious (higher self). Ronnie Laing says in his book *The Divided Self* that it may be that the psychotic and the schizophrenic sees a higher truth that 'normal' people don't see. My own experience with the up-going and down-going energies show me that we are repressed in both. Under LSD, people speak about the good and the bad trip: these are connected with the up-going energy related to repressed hatred, anxiety, fear, etc., and the down-going energies related to love, tenderness, delight, personality traits such as honesty, compassion, humour, etc. ('the personality characteristic from the cosmic sea'). Tenderness is connected with down-going, melting feelings, non-sexual, and in tenderness, forgiveness and politeness; the hatred and impatience and hardness are melted and disappear.

Psychic people in the spiritualist movement develop the ability to get messages by a method where you open your shackles and your third eye. This ability is not psychopathic and one is not a slave to it and it does not interfere with thought; you can open to it or close to it whenever you like and it is very like the messages that the prophets and Jesus got.

Youngsters today are people in transition, moving into the genital spiritual personality, a phenomena we can relate to the fact that the younger generation did not have such a sex-hostile upbringing as earlier generations, so they are more open to the energies going through their bodies and are less mechanical. Independently of each other they have developed feelings of kindness and gentleness and have come together and speak about recognising each other as if they had met in an earlier life and had come back to earth as co-workers in a plan for a happier world — a phenomenon which among mechanical people would be considered schizophrenic. But more and more people who dare not speak about it officially, when you talk to them privately, express the same feeling.

People in transition are leaving their jobs, their secure positions, their countries, they seem to follow each other and it seems that not only people are in transition, but that the whole world is entering a more spiritual period, coming into what they call the age of 'Aquarius' when we will dare to speak about these things.

On the one hand, we have the mechanical world's increasing acceptance of sexuality in a pornographic, split way, and the acceptance of religion in a non-feeling, mechanical way. There was a TV programme in America where a young man moving more and more towards spiritual development told the story of how his parents could accept him being a drug addict or even going to prison, but what they could not accept and were shocked about was their children becoming religious in a devoted and genuine way. This is typical of the split and the need for control: our society is getting more and more 'permissive' so that one can do almost anything as long as one does it intellectually and rationally and can give reasons for it, if one is distant and has no alive feelings for it; but to be an alive being is associated with shamefulness. The world is trying desperately to get sexual pleasure in a split way, but without travelling the long path towards becoming an alive, genital being, which includes allowing oneself to become intuitive.

I want to add an example of the transition from the anal to the genital personality. A typical compulsive, pedantic, obsessive person on her way to the loosening up of her character-fixation reported during treatment that she felt as if there were a line from her back to her chest, as if energy were trying to flow there, and at the same time, she felt energy passing from her sacrum through the pelvis and causing a spasm in the lower abdomen because there was a spasm in the deep abdomen caused by a blockage to energy flow and the resulting increase in contractions and stasis when the energy tries to get through. When I asked her to try and get rid of the tensions in her upper back, she started to shake her shoulders like a belly dancer and when I asked her to try to get rid of the tensions in the pelvis, she also made movements like a belly dancer. This patient, who had lacked soft femininity, suddenly became very feminine and her rigid body loosened up and her face became alive. When she began to massage the deep tensions in her stomach and at the same time moved her pelvis in a pulsationary, snake-like motion, she felt beautiful streamings down her legs which spread to her whole body, showing that now the whole erotic personality was on the way to becoming alive. (Yoga considers the erotic personality to be the full personality.) She felt a warmth in her genitals and legs and felt as if she were pushing something out of her stomach: what she really meant was out of her vagina, but as she had no feeling in her vagina, she did not recognise the feeling. What she had to push out was something like a bad child. She had felt at other times during treatment that a bad naughty child was coming up from her throat. This pushing of the vagina, even if it occurs with no feeling of pleasure, seems to be the first indication of a beginning aliveness of the vagina. It begins as a tendency to contraction before the capacity for pleasurable sensations in the walls of the vagina is regained.

So this talkative, insensitive personality seems now on the way to the transition into a softer, more feeling, more sensitive person. It is as if a melting process has begun in her rigid way of being.

Part Two

Birth, Infancy and Childhood

BIRTH, INFANCY, AND CHILDHOOD : INTRODUCTION

Reich's interest in children arose from his concern to explore ways of preventing neurosis. If neurotic problems were the product of various forms of stress in infancy, then the most radical way of eradicating neurosis would be to revolutionise the ways that we bring up children. Freud fought shy of such a conclusion for he believed that some degree of repression was the inevitable price of culture. Reich was so scandalised at the many ways in which we brutalise the newborn that he considered most of the means we use to 'civilise' children as fundamentally uncivilised.

Reich watched the newborn baby breathing without inhibition, he watched the natural movements, the grace, and the expressivity of the young infant animal. He compared it with the stiff, unco-ordinated, over-controlled behaviour of the grown-up children who came to therapy. He came to see the baby as a marvellous example of unspoiled protoplasm that had far more to teach us about living functioning, than we had to teach it.

The work of Frederick LeBoyer today, on the simple needs of the newborn from the moment of birth, reflects the same straightforwardly simple concern for obvious realities that most people miss. Reich tried to tell us that in many ways we crucify our children on the cross of our cultural convictions. We mould them, and condition them, and bend them to fit our requirements, and to conform to our expectations and ideals. Reich held out a totally different concept of upbringing — the concept of self-regulation. Self-regulation, in the form of the biological idea of homoestasis, is now much better known. Organisms are equipped with the means to satisfy their needs. There is a lawfulness and a functional directness and economy in the movements and expressions of unspoiled children which provide the basis for growth and for natural socialisation. The focus of all Reich's work in this area is to deepen our respect for the capacity of children to indicate and fulfil their own needs, and to have equal rights to their 'elders and betters'.

Whatever it is that led to the historical aberrations of man — the big and little killings, the wars, and the regimentations, the neuroses and all the rest, Reich maintained that we repeated the process of damaging unspoiled life in each generation. And similarly, each generation provided a fresh chance to establish a more creative and pleasurable life-style. He had much faith in those he called 'the children of the future' — the generations of those unborn at the time of his death, who might challenge the life-negating patterns of an increasingly technocratic and mechanistic society, and help bring about a more worthwhile existence.

The Self-Regulated Child

by A.S. Neill

A.S. Neill was the headmaster of Summerhill School, England, for fifty years. His many books describing what is probably the most famous progressive school in the world have made him an international figure. 'For many years to come', said an article in The Times Educational Supplement *of 13th April 1962, 'teachers will need to sit at the feet of this great educator'.*

Neill was a close personal friend of Reich; he had therapy from him in Norway, and visited him several times in the United States. Reich recognised that many of his own views on child education had been put into practice by Neill for years.

The extracts that follow are taken from one chapter of his book The Free Child *(Jenkins, London, 1953) and are reprinted here by permission of Barrie and Jenkins Ltd, and of the Estate of A.S. Neill and Hart Publishers Inc.*

I never heard the term self-regulation until my friend Wilhelm Reich used it, and if he did not invent it, he, more than any other man, has understood and used the method. Homer Lane had spoken of self-determination and others had described self-government; these were not the same as self-regulation, for they referred more to children governing themselves communally than to self-determination of the individual baby.

There are so few self-regulated babies in the world that any attempt to describe them must be tentative and conjectural. The observed results so far suggest the beginnings of a new civilisation, more profound than any new society that is promised by any kind of political party.

Self-regulation implies a belief in human nature, a belief that there is not, and never was, original sin. This belief is not new; many have held it and tried to practise it, in, for example, the kind of education called Naturalism and associated with the name of Rousseau, but it was applied only to the child's psyche, not to his soul and body together. Self-regulation means the right of a baby to live freely without outside authority in things psychic and somatic. It means that the baby feeds when it is hungry, that it becomes clean in habits only when it wants to, that it is never stormed at nor spanked, that it shall always be loved and protected. It all sounds easy and natural and fine, yet it is astounding how many young parents, keen on the idea, manage to misunderstand it. Tommy, aged four, bangs the notes of a neighbour's piano with a wooden mallet, while his fond parents look on with a triumphant smile which means: 'Isn't self-regulation wonderful?' Another pair think that they ought never to put their baby of eighteen months to bed, because that would be interfering with nature; no, baby must be allowed to stay up when he is tired out, and then mother will carry him to his cot. What actually happens is that baby gets increasingly crossly tired. He cannot say that he wants to go bye-bye because he cannot speak. Usually the weary and disappointed mother lifts him and carries him screaming to bed. Another young couple come to me rather apologetically and ask if it would be wrong for them to put up a fireguard in baby's nursery. All of which illustrations show that any idea, old or new, is dangerous if not combined with commonsense.

Self-regulation should begin with birth. Every baby has the birthright of feeding when it wants to feed. This is an easy way to begin if the mother has the baby at home, but so many maternity homes are so far behind the times that many a baby cannot start self-regulation for a few weeks, and then no one knows what damage has been done already. If a maternity home takes the baby away at birth and does not allow the mother to feed it for the first twenty-four hours, who can say what permanent damage is done to that baby? In some homes a mother can discuss the situation before the child is born, and sometimes the home will agree to the mother's wishes, but usually to enter a maternity home means that one must accept the system as it is, and therefore, any mother who means to use self-regulation should be aware of going into a home that does not approve of self-regulation. The moral being: have your baby at home if you can.

Timetable feeding, so long the system of doctors and nurses, has been attacked so effectively that many old-fashioned practitioners have given it up. It was obviously wrong and dangerous; if a child was crying of hunger at four o'clock, he was being subjected to a stupid, cruel anti-life discipline of infinite danger to his bodily and spiritual growth. Hence baby must feed when he wants to feed, and in the beginning his wants will be frequent, for he cannot absorb large quantities at a time. The practice of giving a bottle of water at night is a bad one; the baby should be fed if hungry during the night. After two to three months the baby will regulate itself to larger quantities of food, and there will be longer interludes between each feed. At the age of about three or four months the baby will want to be fed — say — between ten and eleven p.m. and then in the morning between five and six, but of course there is no hard and fast rule about this. Remember that with timetable training the mother is always a few steps ahead of the baby, knowing what to do next and capable of rearing a mechanical baby that will give the minimum of trouble to adults, whereas with self-regulation every day, nay, every minute is a discovery, for then mother is always a step behind the baby and learning by observation all the time. Thus if a baby half-an-hour after a good feed is crying, I have no idea what the timetable merchants say about it, but I do know that the young mother will have to think it out for herself ... is he uncomfortable? Is it wind? Does he want attention from his mother because he feels lonely? The mother should react to all or any of these reasons with her spontaneous love, not with any wretched book rule. One fundamental rule should be writ large in every nursery ... *baby must not be allowed to cry itself out.*

It must be emphasised that self-regulation demands more giving out than a set system does; the parents will have to sacrifice more of their time and self-interest for at least two years. One dangerous custom is to park a baby in a pram in the garden, maybe for hours at a time. No one can know what agonising feelings of fear and loneliness a baby can experience on waking up suddenly to find itself alone in a strange place. Those of us who have heard such a baby's screams have some idea of the iniquity of the stupid custom. Self-regulation implies much selflessness in the parents; they must not play for the baby's love or gratitude; they must not look on baby as a show piece to perform smiles and tricks when relatives come visiting. I give this aspect prominence because I have seen young couples who thought that they were using self-regulation when they were making the baby adapt itself to their own convenience, e.g. trying to make the child have a sleeping time that will fit in with their desire to go to the cinema of an evening, or later on, giving the child soft, noiseless toys so that Daddy won't be disturbed during his after-lunch forty winks. 'But, hoy,' cried the parent, 'you can't do that to us; we have our own rights in life.' I say No; not during the first two years ... or maybe four years of a child's life. The first years must be years of the most careful watchfulness, because the whole of the surroundings are against self-regulation, and one is forced to fight for a child with a conscious intensity.

From the very beginning the recreational needs of a baby should be studied. Too many babies are shut in by the walls of a pram or a small room or a play pen; it seems reasonable to guess that the wider a baby's horizon is, the fuller will be its growth in all ways. Too many babies are sacrificed to furniture and adult precosities in rooms, and the withering: Don't Touch That, Baby! comes into force. In a small home of moderate or poor income one cannot make an ideal environment for the crawling baby, who will shove his hands into all sorts of pots and pans and knock over breakable dishes. Here there is a real problem for the most enthusiastic self-regulation mother, and one that demands much patience and invention. If a mother must take away something from a crawling baby, or a baby at any stage, the irate howls of protest should be placated in some way, preferably by substitution of a harmless for a harmful or fragile plaything. We found with our Zoë that she would not be placated with any Ersatz object, but our environment, a school, had so many opportunities for touching things, that our problem was much easier than that of the mother in a flat, with possibly neighbours downstairs who signal with a broom handle when baby is too

The self-regulated child

enthusiastically busy. There is no reason why a baby should not be allowed to play with kitchen material when it is not in use — noisy pot-lids, wooden spoons he can use as drumsticks; he is likely to prefer these to the usual toys sold in toy shops, most of which have not any element of creation or even construction in them. Indeed the average toy can be soporific, lulling baby into a dull somnolence, one similar to the dummy teat which gives a substitute pleasure for a creative joy.

All parents have a tendency to over-buy in the matter of toys; baby in the shop eagerly holds out its hands towards some gadget ... a tractor, a giraffe that nods ... and parents buy it on the spot; thus most nurseries are full of toys and books that the child never shows any interest in. Of all her toys the only one that Zoë retained a liking for was her Betsy Wetsy, a self-wetting doll I brought her from America when she was eighteeen months. The wetting arrangement did not interest her one bit, maybe for the reason that it was a puritanical fake, for the wee-wee hole was in the small of the back. Only at four and a half did she say one morning: 'I'm tired of Betsy Wetsy and want to give her away.' One should never show a child how a toy works, indeed one should never help a child in any way until or unless he is not capable of solving a problem for himself. The self-regulated children observed so far seem content to amuse themselves for long periods with their toys and games; they do not smash them about as moulded children so often do. Reich's little son, Peter, was making soap bubbles and delighting in their colours, but his moulded playmate kept smashing each one. 'Leave them,' cried Peter passionately, 'don't break them, they are so beautiful.' Yes, young parents, if your baby wants to destroy you have killed something vital in him that life will find hard to replace; you have converted his natural love of life into a hate of life. And all the Borstals and prisons and gallows and electric chairs exist because training has been making loving children anti-life for generations.

Mothers too often do not play enough with their babies. They seem to think that baby in a pram with a soft Teddy Bear solves things for an hour or two. Babies want to be tickled and hugged and larked with. One should ignore those life-shy psychologists who tell you never to have the baby in bed with you, never to tickle it, the idea being that any bodily contact might raise sexual emotions in the baby, thus giving it a fixed mother or father complex. There might be a danger, but only if the parent were so neurotic as to find self-centred pleasure for herself in so doing, but I am writing for more or less normal people, not parents who are still infants themselves.

When baby gets to the length of including his or her genitals in the play scheme, the parents meet the great test in their job. It may be that when a baby's life is full, the genital toys will come later as interests; so far I have not enough evidence to know. All I know is that, late or early, genital play must be accepted as good and normal and healthy, and any attempt to suppress it will be dangerous, and I include the underhand, dishonest attempt at drawing the child's attention to something else. A self-regulated girl was sent to a nice nursery school daily. She seemed unhappy. Her genital play she had christened 'snuggling in,' and when her mother asked her why she did not like school, she said: 'When I try to snuggle in they don't tell me not to, but they say: Look at this or Come and do this, so I can't ever snuggle in there.'

This infantile masturbation (genital play is a better term) is a most complicated problem because nearly all parents were conditioned in an anti-sex way in their cradles, and cannot overcome a sense of shame and sin and disgust deep down in their own personalities. It is possible to have a strong intellectual opinion that genital play is good and healthy, and at the same time, by tone of voice or by look of the eyes, convey to the child that emotionally you have not accepted the child's right to its own genital satisfaction. A parent may seem to approve wholly when baby touches its genitals, but when stiff-stomached Aunt Mary comes to call, the parent may have anxiety lest baby performs in front of the life-disapprover. It is easy to say to such a parent: 'Aunt Mary represents the anti-sex element in your repressed self,' but saying this does not help parent or child, and we do not know enough to say definitely what is due to repression and what is not. A familiar question asked by critics of child freedom is: 'Why don't you let a small child see sexual intercourse?' The answer, that it would give the baby a trauma, a severe nervous shock, is shown to be false among the Trobriands where, according to Malinovski, children see not only parental sexual intercourse, but birth and death as matters of course. I do not think that seeing sexual intercourse would have any bad emotional effect on a self-regulated child. The only honest answer to the question is to say that love isn't a public matter anyway, not in our civilisation.

The parental fear that infantile genital play will lead to sexual precocity is a fairly wide-spread one. It is a rationalisation of course; genital play does not lead to precocity, and if it does, what about it? The best way to make a child take an abnormal interest in sex at adolescence is to prohibit his or her genital play in the cradle.

So far I have no personal knowledge of how one self-regulated child reacts to another such in genital play. Boys who have been taught that sex is wrong generally link up genital play with sadism, and girls who have had a similar anti-sex training seem to accept the sadistic genital play as the norm. I can only guess, not via wishful thinking but because of the absence of aggressive hate in the self-regulated child, that genital play between two free children would be gentle and loving.

Yes, yes, I hear young mother say impatiently, get back to practical things. Tell me in detail what I ought to do about my baby and its sex, and not only its sex, but such things as thumb-sucking, head-rolling, bed-wetting. Tell me what I should do when baby gets into tantrums and tries to match its sense of power against mine. But how can I tell? I can only say: interfere with your baby's natural growth and certain results will appear, unpleasant results, but which ones they will be I do not know. I know that thumb-sucking does not appear in a self-regulated child, at least not in any I have seen, but I do not know enough to say exactly why. I could make the guess that in timetable feeding thumb-sucking might arise because nature was quicker than the clock; I could suggest that bottle feeding, by depriving the baby of the warmth and orgastic emotion of the breast, could lead to habitual thumb-sucking. Such guesses do not help; I have seen self-regulated children brought up almost all the way on the bottle, and they did not suck their thumbs. I fancy that too much is made of the bottle feeding breast deprivation; if the baby is loved warmly, bottle feeding does not appear to make any difference. We cannot of course tell, but we can observe that bottle feeding does not automatically lead to symptoms that are negative and soul destroying. Such symptoms are more likely to arise after training in cleanliness and habit formation. The habit formation fetish is one that ought to be fought against; there is no merit in a habit in itself, and nearly all habit formations have the aim of making the baby as little of a nuisance as possible to the parents.

I have sometimes thought that, if human excrement were as easy to touch as that of sheep or rabbits or horses, children would stand a better chance of growing up with emotional freedom. The disgust that adults have for human faeces must play a great part in forming the negative, hate-forming part of the child psyche. A mother may have no feeling of disgust when washing out the nappies, but three years later may show considerable emotion when she has to wipe up a small pile from the carpet. No emotional anger is ever lost on a baby; it sinks in and stays and is registered in the character. Hence the young mother must be very careful in dealing with the excrement situation. The child, owing to the geography of the lower body is bound to associate sex with excrement, and parent disapproval of the latter will almost certainly associate with the child's disapproval of the former. In practice then, never attach any importance to excrement ... unless the child is proud of its production in which case you have to show your admiration. If the child has an 'accident' treat it as something normal and unemotional.

I have had no experience of the self-regulated child's reaction to the arrival of a new baby. Whether jealousy is an everlasting trait in human nature I do not know, but the absence of any visible sexual jealousy among the Trobrianders suggests that it may be a by-product of our more complicated civilisation. Jealousy arises from the combination of love with possessiveness about the loved object, and it has yet to be known whether the self-regulated child has a strong possessive attitude to its parents. The Trobrianders are under a matriarchal rule, and if the absence of jealousy has any connection with this fact, it may be that the self-regulated child will be less jealous than the trained one, for in a self-regulation home I take it that the patriarchal and the matriarchal are blended, so that there is no 'authority' either dual or single. In jealousy is always a definite fear of loss, and not only in sexual jealousy; the easy illustration is that of the opera singer who hates the other prima donna, dreading that her applause will suffer in volume and intensity, indeed it is possible that fear of loss of appreciation and esteem accounts for more jealousy that all the love rivals in the world. Much depends, therefore, on the elder self-regulated child's feeling of being appreciated. If self-regulation has given him so much independence that he does not need to ask for his parents' approval and appreciation all the time, then his jealousy of a newcomer will be less than it would be in the case of a moulded child, that is, one tied for ever to mother's apron strings, and therefore never independent and outgoing.

This does not mean that the parents should stand aside and merely observe how the elder takes to the younger. From the start any actions that might aggravate jealousy should be avoided, such as a too obvious showing the baby off to visitors. Children of all ages have a keen sense of justice, or rather of injustice, and wise parents will see to it that the younger child is not in any way favoured, given preference over the elder, although this is almost impossible to avoid to some extent. That baby has mother's breast may seem an injustice to his older brother, but it may not if the older one feels that he lived out naturally his breast-feeding stage. Here we need much evidence before we can be dogmatic.

So far as I have observed the self-regulated child does not need any punishment. Punishment forms a vicious circle. A child is spanked; spanking is hatred and each spanking makes his hate more and more; so his behaviour gets worse and more spanking is applied. The result is a bad-mannered, sulky, destructive little hater, so inured to punishment that without it he would feel lonely, and thus he 'sins' in order to get some sort of emotion from his parents (a hate one will do when there is no love one); he is beaten, he repents ... and begins again next morning. But the self-regulated child does not go through this hate cycle. He does not need to behave badly; he has no use for lying and breaking;

his body has never been called filthy or wicked; he has not had occasion to rebel against authority or to fear his parents. Tantrums he will have but they will be short-lived and not tending to neurosis. My knowledge of anthropology is almost nil, but I am told that roughly there are two schools of thought about primitive man; one, that he was a savage, a killer, a wife-snatcher, a brute: the other, that he was peaceful, social, kindly. The adjectives used suggest the differences between the disciplined and the self-regulated child. Children when allowed to be themselves are peaceful and social and kindly. The view held by so many psychologists, especially the Freudians, that the inner man has to be restrained, disciplined, sublimated, has no meaning to those who have seen free children. The fundamental difference between the Freudian school and Reich is simply the one I am examining now; Reich believes that life isn't evil, that the Unconscious isn't a devil, that all individual and social evils are man-made, made by interference with the life process; I do, however, know that, since some educators and parents do not interfere with the life process, adult interference is not a fixed and final attribute of human nature.

Self-Regulation in Birth

by Paul Ritter, M.C.D., B.Arch.
and Jean Ritter, B.Sc., Dip.Ed.

Directors, the Planned Environment and
Educreation Research Institute, Perth, Western Australia

Paul Ritter has an international reputation as an architect, city planner, and in sociology and education. His books show his original contributions in these fields. He acknowledges his debt to Reich, and regards all his work as developments in the theory and practice of orgonomic functionalism. Jean Ritter, wife and close co-worker for thirty years, is a biologist and an educator who has been particularly active in the natural childbirth movement and as a member of the Council of the Kindergarten Association of Western Australia. They edited Orgonomic Functionalism *from 1954 to 1964, and the* Wilhelm Reich Memorial Volume *in 1958.*

What follows is taken from their book The Free Family, *Gollancz, London, 1959, describing the creative experiment of bringing up their family. 1972 editions of the book in Germany include extensive contributions by their six children (aged 10 to 22), which answer some of the sceptical reviews of the first edition which appeared when the eldest child was ten years old. Copyright: Ritter Press 1954.*

Pleasure and Pain in Birth

There are new and unusual elements in our positive attitude to birth. Dr. Dick Read and others have for some thirty or forty years tried hard to convince society that birth need not be the ordeal that has commonly been assumed. Dr. Read found that fear of the birth is the fact which is largely responsible for pain. To lose the fear and to learn to relax is such a help to many people that they manage to have their babies with joyous effort.

If there is pain it is incidental, like cutting your hand in a tug of war.

But even the admirable propagandists for natural childbirth look upon the whole process of birth as something only the mother experiences. The baby is not considered. We, on the other hand, look upon birth as an experience which involves mother and child in a relationship. We recognize the baby's 'I-want-to-get-out' as a factor as real as the mother's equally involuntary 'I-want-to-push-you-out'. Both can be pleasurable and indeed both baby and mother move. But, usually, the wriggles of the baby to get out are ignored as unimportant.

In this we differ again from the psychoanalysts, who, with Rank assume the bad effects of birth in birth traumas only, but leave out of account that, as a creative process, birth may not result in trauma at all but be a pleasurable experience. Observation confirms this.

Although Dr. Read limits his estimate of the influence of the birth process on the child to saying that the mothers who have had their babies while conscious and relaxed have a better breast-feeding relationship, it is in very far-reaching ways the effect on the baby, every bit as much as that on the mother, which justifies the quest for the natural birth.

Once again, if we look to the emotional limp of society, the situation becomes clear and the understanding helpful. It is just because deep emotions are involved in birth that fear envelops the subject and taboos keep it secretive. Blocked against the strong feelings involved, women and men consider unconsciousness at the time the best way out.

This is typical of society. In fact, so strongly anchored (even in the musculature, as Reich has shown) are the fears of emotion which are awakened by birth, that many attempts to learn to relax fail. Dr. Read does not make allowance for the emotional fears that are not rational and whose origin lies in childhood. In fact, as with upbringing, so with birth. As our society is sick it must from the beginning be regarded as a therapeutic process to train for childbirth. And training for what is a dramatically important phase of life for mother and child and their relationship is obviously worthwhile, once our view has been accepted.

Only with that concept of energetic flow which springs from

Self-regulation in birth

Reich can we understand why consciousness at birth is so important to the emotional relationship between mother and child. That it is so cannot be doubted any more. Ironically enough, one of the clearest bits of evidence is the experiment of a religious helot to prove that pain at birth is ordained as necessary by God, to expiate the sin of intercourse, no doubt. Wrongly assuming that conscious birth is painful, even to the antelope, with crass naîvety this person gave anaesthetic to one antelope in a herd. This antelope alone, in contrast with the demonstrative motherliness of the others, did not acknowledge her offspring. If we understand that birth is to the antelope a deeply satisfying emotion and not excruciating pain, then we realize that the emotions felt during birth, and missed where there is fear, are a very important tie between mother and offspring, and obviously the only healthy start to the infant's life, and to self-regulation. If they are missed, by accident or design, the relationship must at once be regarded as an unhealthy one, and it will take much effort to put things right and to make self-regulation fully applicable.

So rarely is the right and sensitive attitude found in those professionals who help in birth that the husband's presence can be a very valuable safeguard to his wife and newborn child. The very deep emotional involvement of the wife makes her almost as vulnerable to the bossing of the attendants about her bed as the new-born. It is therefore only proper for the father to read up the facts and arguments regarding natural birth and to make sure that he is a real deterrent to the unconscious and casual cruelty and harm which are part of the routine behaviour of the medical and nursing professions. This professional detachment is not surprising. University courses in medicine and nursing brutalize notoriously. The husband needs a proper emotional capacity to grasp and be unafraid of the event. He should certainly not feel guilty that he has in some way caused pain, and, if he does, or is panicky for some other reason which he cannot overcome, then some close friend can often take his place by the bedside of the wife. The criterion is her choice. The mere presence of someone emotionally close is of great help during much of the time of the birth.

The taboo on full knowledge of birth is continued, perhaps unconsciously, even by Dr. Read. In his latest book on ante-natal training and exercises, the class photographed, all quite fully dressed, is treated with that standard, depersonalizing white strip that renders faces in medical textbooks anonymous. Once again the traditional assumption that birth is not quite nice, and has to do with hospitals, is backed from a most unexpected quarter. Even now, when films and records of births have emerged, there are no pictures showing the emotions in healthy birth. Yet this might reassure many frightened women most convincingly. It is because of this that the photograph in this book, of the beautifully relaxed face, even at the crowning of the head, the climax or crisis of any birth, is of inestimable value. It should have a great and direct effect in dissolving fears and mystery. This photograph, together with another showing the ecstatic and transfigured face of the mother immediately after the birth, are reassuring evidence that the emotional aspects of birth are delicate, precious and important.

What all this means in terms of everyday happenings in this country will emerge clearly from the accounts of the births of our daughters. These, because of their circumstances, illustrate remarkably well a wide range of what is typical. Even before the first pregnancy we had been convinced that birth could be a great experience. From the first we knew also that this was not generally appreciated or understood in our culture, by our doctors, hospitals and even midwives. And so we tried hard in all cases to choose a place and personnel which would be, in our belief, conducive to a good birth. That means cheerful attendants who agree that birth is a strenuous but great occasion, who understand the healthy physiology and psychology of it — people who do not fuss and who allow and encourage relaxation when it is required, who are aware of the sensitivity of the baby and the mother, and the delicate intimacy of their emotional relationship.

In describing those instances in which, despite our efforts, things went wrong, we hope we will not make others afraid. We merely wish to show distinctly how important it is to make sure, in very many ways, that atmosphere and personnel will be right. We

Self-regulation in birth

want to reduce fear of the unknown, to counter the gory stories whispered so often in puberty, confided anxiously to those in the teens, and told with pathological relish in the waiting-room of clinics.

The general ignorance of the physiological happenings in labour is also due to the emotional limp. It is a source of guilt to many men, and of fear to women. To counter the ignorance resulting from this we give a short summary of the biological process. Without this it might be difficult to follow the accounts.

There are three recognized stages of labour, known respectively as the first, second and third stages.

First Stage, Stage of Dilation — From the commencement of labour until complete dilation of the cervical canal. As a rule, the membranes rupture at the end of this stage, but not always, for at times the membranes are not ruptured till late in the second stage, or, rarely, the child may be born without their being ruptured; while in other cases, and these the more common, the membranes may rupture long before the external os is fully dilated. In the case of a mother having her first baby, this stage lasts about sixteen hours, in subsequent births, about eleven.

Second Stage, Stage of Expulsion — From the complete dilation of the cervical canal till the birth of the child. This stage usually lasts, for a first baby, between two and three hours, and in subsequent births, one.

Third Stage, Placental Stage — From the birth of the child till the placenta and membranes have been expelled.

The average duration of labour is: in a primigravida, or mother pregnant for the first time, eighteen hours; in a multipara, twelve hours.

The durations given above are those found in textbooks. In physically and emotionally healthy birth they tend to be shorter.

Birth as it Should Be, and Recommendations

Joy Nicola was born at 11.35 p.m. on January 2nd, 1956. There had been a false alarm on the Friday. The doctor listened in accidentally to a 'practice contraction' and sent the midwives along. They got the room ready. The pubic hair was shaved off, but an enema, which was to be given as a matter of course, I flatly refused. I was convinced that labour had not started, and, in any case, by eating a healthy diet I do not suffer in the slightest degree from constipation. There was some argument, and the midwife insisted that when labour did start I should have to have one. When Paul arrived home I was shaking and depressed from the effort of resisting their authority, so I decided that, as the midwives lived very near, I would not call them until the first stage of labour was almost complete and should thus avoid further dispute, the disturbing enema or further examation (also largely unnecessary).

The first stage did in fact begin at 6 a.m. on Monday, three days later, and fourteen days after the nominated date. Contractions came more or less regularly at ten-minute intervals. I felt that, as in previous pregnancies, it would be a slow process. I got up and carried on normally, cooking lunch, doing housework and playing with the children, relaxing only at the height of each contraction. The waters broke at about 9 a.m., and when the doctor looked in a little later she cautiously stated that she thought the baby would be born that day.

After lunch I decided a rest would be a good idea, in case the night was badly disturbed. I lay down fully dressed, but about 4 p.m. I realized that the first stage was really well established and so undressed and went to bed. I managed to relax comfortably, and was able as usual to read a story each to Leonora, Erica and Penny, stopping only when contractions were at their climax, to be able to relax toward them. The children followed the whys and wherefores of this easily. At 9 p.m. the contractions came closer together and stronger, and from then on I was extremely glad of Paul's company. We talked of a great variety of things, and the longer and stronger the contractions the more I found talk, on subjects such as holidays we had enjoyed in the past, helped. Dr. Dick Read says just this, and we thought of that too.

When the contractions were at their fiercest and I felt the end of the first stage could not, nay must not, be far off, I found tremendous comfort in the green fields and illimitable blue of a Van Gogh reproduction and the smug dog face of a cheap Czech china money box. (In the official hand-out on 'Preparation for

Home Confinement' the first paragraph says: ' ... All ornaments, mats and other small articles should be put away, leaving only a minimum of furniture in the room ... ' — an example of the fetish for cleanliness leading to complete disregard of the emotional factors.)

Dr. Grantly Dick Read speaks of this period as the true pain period of labour. I felt the muscles of the cervix stretched to their extreme by the baby's head. With the few final contractions, my capacity to relax was now fully extended also. Keeping my breathing going evenly and deeply during the contraction, I managed to keep off the excruciating pain which results when the baby's head is forcing tense muscles of the cervix apart. I tried and used many more different positions than during this period in other pregnancies, and was helped by the wonderful peace and absence of all fuss and attendants.

Suddenly, about 11 p.m., I found the contractions ceased. No longer did I feel the need for companionship, I wanted to be quiet, by myself. Paul retired across the room to type a letter (the study had been converted into a temporary nursing home, a very unhygienic one!).

I made myself comfortable on my left side with the right knee well drawn up and my right hand hooked under the knee. I practised deep breathing and relaxed. The outer world receded. I was utterly at peace and withdrawn.

Then came the first contraction of the second stage, the process of the actual expulsion, and I used it to the full, my deep satisfaction expressed by the tremendous grunt, and my right hand gripping my right knee and the left pulling its hardest on the pillow slip.

I vaguely remember the typewriter stopping, Paul crossing the room and asking, 'Jean, has the second stage started?' I felt furious at this meaningless disturbance and ignored the question. He left me alone again. More typing. I was glad he left me alone. Again, a few minutes later, an even more tremendous expulsive push, set off by the convulsion from within, and an even louder throatier grunt. Again Paul spoke to me. This time I came a little way out of my natural amnesia, said 'Phone midwives', and said that I was ill at ease because excreta had been pushed out by the baby, and I knew the midwives' view.

Having rung the midwives, Paul returned to clean me up before they arrived, but he was met by my curses at the disturbance mixed with the most sustained and powerful of the tremendous grunts which brought the head through the perineum into his hands.

It was all too good to be true. I enquired anxiously why my baby wasn't making a grunt or cry, 'It's you who are keeping its mouth shut, as yet,' said Paul, and then the midwives were in. I found that the panting required to slow down the expulsion, to avoid stretching and tears, came spontaneously, even before it was ordered by the midwives. One more push brought the baby's body. The satisfaction was the deepest of my life. They told me it was a girl. I wished they'd have let me ask.

The doctor arrived too. There was no tear, no particular discomfort and, awaiting the afterbirth, I felt quite different from last time, when it had refused to budge. The midwives left me utterly alone, the baby was handed to me in a towel, and within ten minutes of the birth two gentle contractions brought the afterbirth away complete and without loss of blood.

The atmosphere became highly elated and light-hearted, it was just like a party, Paul taking photographs. I was not even very tired.

I was made comfortable, the baby was gently bathed and weighed (6½ lb.); it cried, and had the healthiest, lovely colour when the brown meconium mess had been gently removed from its body and face.

At 1.30 a.m. Nicola lay in her cot and cooed. Paul and I lay side by side. All of us slept well till the morning. Nicola slept most of the next twenty-four hours. I was able to walk across the room within twelve hours, and had no need of a bedpan at all. On the eleventh day I went out for a walk. The birth was really the most satisfying and invigorating experience of my life, like any physical work well done, and it had a very profound and relaxing effect on my whole being and character.

To summarize: capacity for relaxation and emotion, for deep pleasure and orgasm — in short, health — is necessary for good birth, and it is desirable to take pains to get as near to this condition as possible. Indeed capacity for relaxation is more fundamentally needed than exercises. At home the atmosphere and the carefully selected personnel are likely to increase the limited capacity of a woman to enjoy birth, whereas in hosptial a woman and her offspring with full capacity may well be robbed of their invaluable relationship by unfavourable conditions and inexperienced, ignorant or over-worked attendants.

Summary of Points for Thorough Agreement Between Doctor and/or Midwife and Parents

1 The shaving of the pubic hair to take place days before the birth if the mother feels apprehensive, and therefore tense, about it.
2 No artificial inducement of labour if there is no danger in waiting.
3 No injections or drugs of any sort without a clear explanation of why they should be administered.
4 Enemas only when constipation makes them essential; then only as much as is needed.
5 Comfortable position for second stage, which means *not* the traditional 'leg over midwife's shoulder' position.
6 The baby in the second stage may slip back somewhat between contractions, so there is no question of 'holding it' tensely where it is. Relaxation is the aim until the next involuntary contraction makes itself felt, and then the tremendous push, holding one's breath, is the voluntary reinforcement of what is an involuntary reflex.
7 No routine cutting of the perineum to 'facilitate' birth, as advocated by 'cut-happy' people like the otherwise progressive Prof. Nixon in his book.
8 If the baby breathes, it does not need slapping to make it cry on being born.
9 Immediately on birth the baby is to be handed to the mother.
10 The baby is not to be bathed, but only wiped gently.
11 There must be a waiting period of fifteen minutes minimum for the afterbirth (unless there is considerable loss of blood). A squatting position should be tried to let uterus expel placenta naturally. No pummelling of the placenta in the tummy!

12 The foreskin of any male child is to be left strictly alone.

13 If the baby cries, or the mother wishes it, the baby is to be given the breast immediately after birth and before the afterbirth has been expelled.

14 The blood group of the mother should be known in case of emergency, also the telephone number of the Flying Squad.

15 The parents are prepared to go to another doctor/midwife if agreement is not maintained.

16 It is essential to arrive at a supple body, which in most women means adoption of the exercises as given by Randall or others.

17 The husband to be present at the birth.

The Use of Vegeto-Therapy in Childbirth

by Peter Jones

Peter Jones studied vegeto-therapy with Ola Raknes in Oslo between 1969 and 1971. When his account was published in Energy and Character *in May 1973, it aroused considerable interest in natural childbirth circles.*

I first became interested in the application of vegeto-therapy in childbirth when my wife became pregnant in 1968. (The pregnancy ended in a miscarriage.) We bought several books giving basic information on pregnancy and the various methods of preparation for 'natural childbirth'. I knew very little about the physiology of labour, but an important observation made by Wilhelm Reich and which is an essential part of the theory of vegeto-therapy had always remained in my mind, even before I had had any therapeutic training myself. This observation (1) was that the innervation of the autonomic nervous system is not random, but that the organs function antithetically in two 'directions' and that the parasympathetic innervations correspond to an outward-going, relaxing movement, 'away from the self, out towards the world', as Reich put it, and the sympathetic innervations to a holding in, retaining movement, 'towards the self, away from the world', and that in a state of anxiety or tension one withdraws 'inwards' physiologically. Some examples of parasympathetic functions are intestinal peristalsis, micturition and defecation. Examples of the sympathetic are constriction of the peripheral blood vessels and spasms of the bladder and anal sphincters. He did not mention the innervations that take place during childbirth, but before I actually knew about it, it occurred to me that the muscular contractions that expel the foetus, if Reich's observation was correct, would be parasympathetically innervated and that the cervical sphincter, which holds the womb closed would be sympathetically innervated. Taking this further, a painful or difficult birth or even uterine inertia were caused because the woman was functioning 'sympathetically' when she should be functioning 'parasympathetically'. When I went into this later, I did in fact find out that the contractions of the longitudinal muscles of the uterus are parasympathetically innervated.

A trained vegeto-therapist knows that his patient is always neatly locked in an inappropriate sympathetic condition. As Reich pointed out, a healthy person's organism can alternate between the sympathetic and parasympathetic in accordance with their physiological needs. One of the aims of vegeto-therapy is to help the patient regain this capacity for free alternation. Although this is far too complex to describe in detail here, in the therapy we usually do this by helping the patient to breathe completely, concentrating on establishing smooth, unified expiration (another parasympathetic function). The therapist is trained to recognise things the patient habitually does that prevent natural breathing, and can help him to give these up. In this way an expansion and relaxation of the organism is brought about which has its functional parallel in the way the patient feels and thinks. For instance, a patient might arrive for a session constipated or anxious and irritable. If these withdrawals were reversed therapeutically he would be able to do an easy bowel movement or feel alive and able to go out towards life again.

To those who are completely unfamiliar with vegeto-therapy and the theory behind it I must emphasize here how very far-reaching the positive effects of this therapy can be. In this lies its efficacy in childbirth. People who prepare women for childbirth in relaxation or psycho-prophylaxis classes say, 'Oh yes, we do that. We get our women to breathe properly'. But they have no idea of the deep disturbances present in most people's breathing caused by chronic muscular tensions which have existed since childhood, nor how badly these tensions affect physiological processes. Nor are they trained to recognise the many 'tricks' people use to hold their breathing and control their feelings or to help the patient abandon these practices and breathe naturally.

Vegeto-therapy is of course mainly a form of long term psycho-therapy, but it is also a very effective form of first aid in acute depressions and other situations where stress is likely to make us tighten up unnecessarily and where this tightening up will interfere with a physiological functioning organism. Childbirth is an example of such a function and one, too, where the results of vegeto-therapeutic first aid, if my expectations are borne out, are most positive and worthwhile. In many ways the use of vegeto-therapy as first aid is simpler than its use as a long term, deep psycho-therapy. It may take months, even years in some cases, of hard therapeutic work to loosen a patient's shoulders permanently, but this can be done temporarily, and if necessary, repeatedly during labour.

Readers may be interested to know of some connections and contradictions between the theory outlined here and the theory behind the most popular method of preparation for 'natural childbirth' — psycho-prophylaxis. This is not in fact natural childbirth at all, except that if successful it helps a woman to give birth to her child without analgesics or medical intervention. But it does not enable a woman to give birth in the way nature intended, that is, with her expulsive processes working harmoniously and effectively without any interference from permanent muscular tensions.

Psycho-prophylaxis is a set of highly artificial breathing exercises which help the woman in childbirth to control her response to her contractions, so that she does not contract unnecessarily in the rest of her body, so causing herself pain and tension and also wasting energy holding unused muscles in a state of tension. It is based on Pavlovian conditioned reflex theory which sees all human and animal activity as a pattern of stimulus and response, ignoring the fact that a human being, or any other animal, is an energy system with spontaneous impulses from within.

Psycho-prophylaxis explains the difficulties that many women have in labour by the concept of 'neuro-muscular mechanisms' (2). When a uterine contraction occurs, this is the 'stimulus'. The woman feels that it is such an enormously strong 'stimulus' that she has got to react to it in some way, and because of her many neuro-muscular mechanisms she reacts by tightening various muscles throughout her body. Why one has to react negatively to a stimulus is not explained except by an *a priori* assumption. This reacting will be familiar to vegeto-therapists. Often when a patient starts to have a feeling in his body he immediately looks disconcerted, even if the feeling is a pleasant one. On enquiry he will reply, 'Well, I don't know what to do with it'. If you suggest to him that he simply let it grow and be felt he is amazed at the idea that one does not necessarily have to react to something but can just let it happen. A woman who is functioning harmoniously in her labour would be able to let her contractions happen without feeling a need to fight them or 'disassociate' herself from them.

However, the concept of neuro-muscular mechanisms does not explain why some women have easy deliveries and some very difficult ones (even women of the same culture, who presumably have similar patterns of 'neuro-muscular mechanisms'). Nor does it explain why animals, who, too, must have their neuro-muscular mechanisms, if the Pavlovian theory is correct, can all give birth to their young without difficulty. These neuro-muscular 'mechanisms' are what Reich called character armouring and it is this that interferes with the natural functions of the birth process. This character armouring will also affect the maternal organism during pregnancy and thus the vitality of the foetus. I think it would be possible for an experienced obstetrician or midwife with vegeto-therapeutic training to assess expectant women and their armouring and pick out in advance those who were going to have difficulties in labour.

Psycho-prophylaxis overcomes the woman's 'response' of contracting her body when she has a uterine contraction by reconditioning her with the technique of 'muscular disassociation'. As the contraction starts she breathes more shallowly than usual, thus disassociating what is going on in her uterus and abdomen from the rest of her body. The stronger the contraction the shallower the breathing becomes until it has become a shallow panting during the fiercest part of the strongest contractions. This disassociation from what is going on in the abdomen and pelvis by shallow breathing will be familiar to students of vegeto-therapy.

I must point out that psycho-prophylaxis does work with the right type of woman, but seems to be more effective with articulate, educated women than with less educated ones (as one would expect) (3). This is a drawback that I think would be overcome with a vegeto-therapeutic method and its more direct approach to the body. Also, even if a woman has had psycho-prophylactic preparation, she may still run out of psychological resources, lose her nerve, and get into a chaotic predicament from which the only escape is more or less severe medical intervention. In this situation an assistant trained in vegeto-therapy would be able to help a woman out of her predicament and re-establish harmonious physiological functioning again, so that she could give birth to her baby spontaneously and without danger to it or herself.

Another obvious drawback to psycho-prophylaxis is that if a woman pants shallowly for a period of 30 to 60 seconds when the enormous physiological effort of a contraction is going on, she is cutting down the oxygenation and detoxification of the blood, which goes on automatically as long as one is breathing enough. Grantley Dick Read (4) points out the bad effects of a poor supply of oxygenated blood to the uterus and says that waste matter in the muscular tissue as a result of physical effort may cause pain.

This reduction of the breathing must also mean that the oxygen supply to the foetus is also cut down, and any successful method of delivery (if one can use such a word of natural function) should have as one of its main aims the maintenance of a good supply of oxygen to the foetus. Natural breathing brought about by vegeto-therapeutic assistance assures this.

No childbirth can really be called natural until women's bodies function as nature intended them to, that is, without disturbances brought about by chronic muscular spasms. And this can only come about if children are allowed to grow up with unimpaired biological vitality and with their reproductive functions unaffected by these spasms. It may even be that this armouring, as Reich called it, thwarts the natural growth pattern of the pelvis, thus constricting the space through which the foetus has to pass at birth and so necessitating a Caesarian section in some cases (9).

Even advocates of psycho-prophylaxis or adaptations of it pour scorn on the idea of 'natural childbirth' as some cranky back to nature figment of the imagination (5). Of course truly natural childbirth has nothing necessarily to do with 'squatting down amongst the leaves with the squirrels and little wild creatures'. What it does mean is an unarmoured woman giving birth to a biologically vital baby that has grown in an alive uterus. Under such circumstances birth can be truly natural whether it takes place in a field or an urban block of flats.

My wife, J., (at 33 an 'elderly primagravida'!), went into labour after a very difficult end of pregnancy with a severe rise in blood pressure and a certain diagnosis of pre-eclampsia by the clinic doctor who examined her on referral by her own doctor. (She had been hoping to have her baby at home.) Fortunately this diagnosis proved wrong and her blood pressure fell considerably after rest in hospital. On admission it was 170/120, at the beginning of labour about 140/90. She had been to psycho-prophylaxis classes at the National Childbirth Trust and was expecting to use her training during labour. She used this training for the first few hours and it worked fairly well with the mild contractions. But as they got stronger she became more and more breathless with each contraction. This tired her quickly and her morale began to droop after about 4 hours' labour. I had gone into the labour room with her with my therapeutic training in reserve, but did not for a moment think we would use it together. My ideas were just a hunch, I had no obstetric knowledge or training, and I thought that psycho-prophylaxis, in spite of its shortcomings, would prove far better than an untried technique in the hands of a beginner helping his wife in her first labour.

As her contractions became stronger she found psycho-prophylaxis less and less satisfactory and was rapidly becoming very exhausted and demoralised. I was putting a brave face on it, but was really wondering how I was going to keep up her morale for possibly another 10 hours. Then she suddenly said in utter frustration, 'I can't go on with this any more, I simply must breathe ... Help me Dr. Raknes!' (with whom I studied vegeto-therapy and with whom she, too, had had some therapy). To which I replied, 'Well, he can help you even though he's not here. You can apply what you learnt from him about breathing naturally'.

Without further ado she abandoned psycho-prophylactic breathing (using shallower breathing the stronger the contractions were), and changed to the natural deep breathing that she had become able to do as a result of her vegeto-therapy, and which the therapist aims to establish in every patient. The sudden change in the character of her labour was amazing. Before it had been hectic and hurried. Now an atmosphere of peace and harmony filled the room and I could see from the expression on her face that she was now feeling her body and foetus as one. Her first comment was, 'Oh! The baby feels much nicer this way!' She started to have streamings in her legs, even during contractions. (This is something that all patients in vegeto-therapy feel when their breathing is loosened up sufficiently.) She said she felt like a tube with a baby in it and that the baby was gradually moving downwards. Before, while she had been doing psycho-prophylactic breathing, she had looked to me like a box cut in half by a rigid heavy partition. In therapy one often has such impressions of patients. These impressions usually correspond to the physical reality of their particular type of armouring and the way their tight muscles break up their body into disharmonious compartments. This change affected me too. From feeling discouraged and exhausted I suddenly felt peaceful and energetic and capable of helping her for another 24 hours if necessary. This transformation in her labour was a deeply moving experience.

She was now in the middle of the first stage and everything progressed smoothly for 4 to 5 more hours. Between contractions she lay back peaceful and joyful now that an ordeal had come to an end and her labour was going happily. About every hour I went over her therapeutically, loosening up by direct manipulation any parts that seemed to be tensing up, in her case the jaw and the adductors of the thighs. J. said she felt the contractions more breathing naturally but that she did not feel she was fighting them any more. Significantly, after her delivery she told me that while doing psycho-prophylactic breathing she had had images of people shouting at her all the time, while when she changed to natural breathing she saw beautiful waving trees. Until the change in her labour she had been looking greyer and greyer and more and more weary. Now her colour returned, her eyes became bright and alive, and she looked as if she could deal with anything. Her energy level rose and she lost her feeling of exhaustion. This of course must have been reflected in the oxygen supply to the foetus. Throughout her labour her blood pressure remained steady and the foetal heart rate strong and even. (All this was in spite of the fact that she had had hardly any sleep the previous two nights because of two false starts that had come to nothing during the day.)

She now continued happily until the transition stage. Here the contractions became very fierce and confusing, and she started to lose her grip a little, arching her back and saying, 'I can't, I can't'. I pulled her shoulders forwards, pushed her chest down helping her to exhale deeply and the panic passed. With this assistance she took these very powerful contractions well. It was at this point that my therapeutic assistance was most useful, I think. Now her tendency to tense her jaw and thighs was very strong and I had to work hard to help her keep them loose.

There was then a pause in the contractions and a feeling of respite and recovery. Throughout this successful first stage we had been in very close contact and I had been quite aware of her needs and wishes. This is yet another positive aspect of vegeto-therapy. As a trained therapist one is in unspoken contact with the patient. In childbirth this is of great value as it makes a lot of fussing and questioning unnecessary. This respite was then interrupted by a very powerful contraction and the membranes broke.

When eventually one of the nursing staff turned up, J. was examined, her cervix was found to be fully dilated, and she was transferred to the delivery room. Until now we had been completely unattended apart from occasional visits by nursing staff to take her blood pressure and check the foetal heart rate. But now she was under continuous medical supervision and, of course, the doctor delivering her knew nothing of the therapeutic assistance I had been giving her. By now she was very tired. This was her third night without any real sleep, and by the time of her delivery (10.13 a.m.) she was rather weak. Things were not improved by the doctor's superficial bantering and the complete lack of contact between him and J. He just wanted her to push like mad whenever a contraction came without any feeling for the right rhythm. Nor did he seem to know how to help her to push so that her own effort harmonised with that of her contractions. Consequently she wasted the first few contractions pushing furiously but applying very little effort in the right place. The interruption to her efforts and the quietly progressing hard work of the first stage upset her very much and she was on the verge of giving up. She was really very, very exhausted now and I was beginning to think it would have to be a forceps delivery. (The registrar who had been watching from outside the delivery room through a see-through mirror had thought the same too, as we found out afterwards.) The atmosphere of haste and pressure in the delivery room, even though J. had only been fully dilated for half an hour and the foetal heart rate was still steady, did not help either.

However, between contractions I was again able to help her to relax and exhale properly by pressing her chest down. Her breathing rhythm became more harmonious again, she rested peacefully between contractions and regained some strength. The doctor was prepared to do an episiotomy, but by now J. had got the feel of pushing in time with her contractions and while he was anaesthetising the perineum the head started to descend and we saw the surface of the baby's skull appearing. Now that I was able to tell her that we could see the head she was much encouraged and was pushing very effectively. The head crowned easily within 3 to 4 contractions of coming into sight and she expelled the baby with no trouble. Unfortunately she suffered some laceration, but I felt this could have been avoided if there had been a less hectic ambience about her and she had been allowed to expel her baby at her own rate.

The baby when born was in excellent condition. She had started breathing as soon as her head crowned and she was a good pink colour when her body appeared. (She had a beautiful expression of peace, and her face and head were undistorted by pressure which makes so many newly born babies look ugly.) She did not scream at all but lay breathing easily and steadily. (This silence was not one of exhaustion or weakness, as she lay 'looking around' and gently moving her limbs and cooing softly.) During the first few weeks of her life until she learned to make more articulate sounds this was one of her characteristic pleasure noises.

I would sum up the advantages of this therapy when applied in labour as follows:

1   It establishes a harmonious functioning of the body's natural processes and helps to mobilise the natural capacity to give birth to her child spontaneously, which must exist biologically in every woman.
2   It can be used to re-establish this harmony and capacity if a woman in labour is getting into difficulties. It could obviate the need for forceps deliveries in some cases, and possibly even save some mothers from the need for a Caesarian section (where this is brought about by a woman's inability to go through with her labour, and not, of course, when indicated because of obstruction).
3   It ensures a good supply of energy and can even raise a woman's energy level during labour.
4   It means that full respiration takes place, so that the blood is fully oxygenated and the foetus is kept well supplied. (I think this is why our daughter was in such good condition at birth.)
5   A doctor or midwife trained in this technique would really be able to help their patient to use her energy most effectively and harmoniously. They would have a lot of contact with and control over the birth process from outside, and if things got difficult, be able to intervene to re-establish the expulsive process safely without resort to mechanical or analgesic means, which must to some extent carry some risk to mother and/or baby. As a method of rendering help to a parturient woman it is completely safe and always on the positive side, encouraging rhythmical breathing, smooth contractions, and a good supply of oxygen to the foetus.

In the present state of obstetric knowledge it seems that if things do go wrong there is very little a doctor or midwife can do

The use of vegeto-therapy in childbirth

to re-establish the natural expulsive processes of birth. So they have to resort to mechanical intervention or surgery with inevitable disappointment to the mother and possible risk to the baby.

6 I think it would be possible to work out a method of preparation for pregnant women in small groups which would enable them to breathe naturally and, particularly, to give in to the complete reflex when exhaling, and which could help to make them aware of things they do that stop them breathing completely. Such preparation, if it proved possible, would go much further than 'relaxation classes' or psycho-prophylaxis. It would take into account the fact that most women (and men of course) have been suffering from chronic muscular spasms since childhood, and it is that that interferes with the physiological activity of labour. It would take research and practical experiment to devise such preparation though.

Footnote on the Origins of Muscular Tensions and their Effects

The chronic muscular spasms which interfere with the natural process of childbirth (and many other physiological functions) usually originate in childhood when babies and infants suppress their awareness of basic needs that have not been satisfied, or when they have to suppress negative feelings towards their parents or teachers that result from their not having these basic needs satisfied. These tensions restrict the child's capabilities and damage his vitality, often causing illness or a predisposition to illness.

This tightening up, to which Reich gave the name armouring (as it protects the individual from unpleasant experience both from the outside world and from within himself) is not a simple tensing of the muscles. It is a biological withdrawal from the world, of which the muscular spasms are the most obvious feature. This withdrawal is a sympatheticotonia and the organs affected depend on the particular type of armouring that a child forms. This in turn depends on what difficult situations he has to deal with. The various patterns of local chronic sympathetic actions and the part these play in different diseases have not yet been investigated in detail. For available work see reference (6). The far-reaching effects on the organism can be readily understood if one remembers how many organs and functions are governed by the autonomic nervous system. Some commonly found sympathetic actions are: spasms of the cervix, anus, bladder, pylorus, constriction of the peripheral blood vessels, tachycardia, inhibition of the salivary glands, digestive secretions, excessive secretion of adrenalin.

In vegeto-therapy one aims to restore to the patient his capacity to alternate healthily between sympathetic and parasympathetic functioning. As these functions are autonomous and not easily subject to conscious control the breathing is used as a gateway into the autonomic nervous system. This is why one can help a woman's birth processes by helping her to breathe naturally. The therapy is a long process with adults who have had their tensions for years, but it can be used to dissolve muscular spasms in children much more quickly and easily. Usually simple manipulation is enough to loosen them (7). (Of course, if the spasms are not to form again the parents would have to be consulted, and, if possible, helped to find out what they are doing or not doing that has made the child withdraw by armouring himself. Thus parents would have to discuss their problems and receive positive advice on how they could best satisfy their child's needs. At present community welfare services only give very limited advice on medical and feeding problems. There is no one to turn to for help with complex emotional problems that may well originate in the first months or even weeks of life.)

Thus this therapeutic technique in midwifery and child care would lend itself very well to a community health project. A group of mothers who were all interested in taking part could all give birth to their babies with the help of vegeto-therapy, and the therapeutic knowledge could be used to advise them during their pregnancies. With counselling and, where necessary, therapy for their infants where difficulties had arisen and they had formed some armouring (this is almost inevitable where the parents themselves are armoured as this restricts their natural contact with their children and their ability to satisfy their needs), a close check could be kept on these infants and detailed records kept, so that at the ages of, say, five and ten one could sum up the experiment and see how children's vitality and emotional stability could be safeguarded, and if possible, see in some detail what situations cause children to armour. Obvious negligence and brutality cause armouring (psychological damage as most people would call it), but there are many subtly damaging things that can cause a child to armour, and often the armouring forms before one is aware that a child is even under stress (8).

The question of how parents would bring up their children so that their vitality is not impaired and they can regulate their energies themselves, is a complex one that is outside the scope of this paper.

AFTERWORD

I wrote the above article, a rather prosaic account of a very moving experience, in the hope that I might be able to interest some medical people in the use of orgone therapy in childbirth. For this reason I explained it in orthodox physiological terms and omitted any reference to the 'energetics' of labour. Any connection between physiological functions and the emotions seems incomprehensible to most doctors, so I thought even bringing in this aspect would be a novel enough approach without introducing energy discharge functions, etc. However, the little research I have been able to do and the experience of helping my wife have convinced me that the capacity to tolerate the enormous rise in energy level is the key to a healthy birth. At the most harmonious stage in my wife's labour, before she got tired, I was aware of a prodigiously expanded energy field round her and felt complete unspoken orgonotic contact with her, as one does occasionally in therapy when a patient's energy field expands greatly.

I have explained this therapeutic method to two advisers of the National Childbirth Trust, who run preparation classes for expectant mothers, but they showed no interest. However, Dr. Raphael's successful intervention, when he was able to restart a woman's birth process after she had been in labour for 40 hours and was in a state of uterine inertia, proves that my wife's healthy delivery was no accident. A woman who had a few sessions with me before her delivery would have as many as 8 or 9 Braxton-Hicks contractions in an hour, whereas she would normally have 2 or 3 in a day.

It is certainly possible to prepare a woman for delivery in private sessions, but I hope to devise a method based on vegeto-therapeutic techniques which could be used in groups. My research so far suggests that this will be possible. Of course the effectiveness of such preparation depends on who assists at the birth. A midwife/doctor with therapeutic training would be able to help a mother use her preparation more effectively during birth. During the next 2 to 3 years I hope to set up a pioneer group to prepare expectant mothers and would be pleased to hear from anyone who would like to collaborate.

Helping a mother to give birth in joy and dignity, so that her child feels glad to be born is the very core of preventive therapy, and is the child's first step along the road to health and happiness.

REFERENCES

1. Wilhelm Reich, *The Function of the Orgasm*, p. 257-263
2. Ema Wright, *The New Childbirth*, p. 80-85
3. Sheila Kitzinger, *The Experience of Childbirth*, p. 12
4. Grantley Dick Read, *Childbirth without Fear*, p. 36-37
5. Sheila Kitzinger, *The Experience of Childbirth*, p. 17
6a. Wilhelm Reich, *The Cancer Biopathy*, ch. 5 The Carcinomatous Shrinking Biopathy, ch. 8 Results of Experimental Orgone Therapy in Humans
  b. Robert Dew, The Biopathic Diathesis, *The Journal of Orgonomy*, Vol. 3, Nos. 1-2, Vol. 4, Nos. 1-2
  c. Elsworth Baker, *Man in the Trap* (Chapter on Psycho-Somatic Disease)
  d. Wilhelm Reich, *The Function of the Orgasm*, p. 255-265, The Basic Antithesis of Vegetative Life
7. Elsworth Baker, *Man in the Trap* (Chapter on Paediatrics)
8. Wilhelm Reich, *The Cancer Biopathy*, ch. 9 Falling Anxiety in an Infant of Three Weeks
9. Frederick Sypher, Psychorthopaedics, *Energy and Character*, Vol. 2, No. 3, Sept. 1971

For further discussion on this subject see:

10 Elsworth Baker, *Man in the Trap* (Chapters on Obstetrics and Paediatrics)
11 Chester Raphael, Orgone Treatment during Labour, *Orgone Energy Bulletin*, Vol. 3, No. 2, 1951
12 Michael Silvert, Orgonomic Practice in Obstetrics, *Orgonomic Medicine*, Vol. 1, No. 1, 1955
13 Paul and Jean Ritter, An Orgonomic Theory of Birth, *Orgonomic Functionalism*, Vol. I, No. 2, 1954

Some Thoughts About Breast-Feeding and Health: The Role of Information and Support

by Alice K. Ladas, Ed.D.

Psychotherapist and Marriage Counsellor, New York

Alice Ladas is a licensed psychologist, a certified social worker and a member of the American Association of Marriage Counsellors. She studied at the Smith School of Social Work, the Washington School of Psychiatry, the Teacher's Center at Columbia University, the Orgonomic Infant Research Center, and the Institute of Bio-energetics of which she is a founder member. She has trained with Dr. Ola Raknes, and with Dr. Nathan Ackerman. She ran the Department of Child Guidance in the public schools of Caldwell, New Jersey, and was on the staff of the Payne Whitney Clinic of New York Hospital. Currently she is on the faculty of the Ballard School of the YWCA. Her article "How to help mothers breast-feed" appeared in the December 1970 issue of Clinical Pediatrics, *but the paper below was written specifically for* Energy and Character *(Vol. 2, No. 3, September 1971).*

In the course of my professional activities, two things stand out: one is that a great many of the people with whom I have worked had problems which could be traced or related to difficulties occurring very early in life; the other is the manner in which parents seemed to want to fight the natural pace of development of their offspring. With remarkable frequency, mothers complained that their small children were not growing up quickly enough and that their teenagers were growing up too quickly. These observations led me to wonder how mothers could become more in tune with their children. It was thus that my attention became focused on the crucial early days and years of life and on how we can help mothers during that time. It seems to me that in matters of prevention, mothers are our largest and most promising group of potential allies. My interest turned first to educated childbirth and then to breast-feeding.

Although currently in popular disfavor and in rapid decline as a method of infant feeding throughout the world (1), breast-feeding has, it seems to me, the potential of helping infants off to a healthy start. By itself, breast-feeding is no guarantee of good mothering. But it is a natural function of substantial value to the nursing couple, if successfully carried out over a period of some months or more. Yet our society discourages women who wish to breast-feed which makes it difficult for those stalwart souls who insist on trying it anyway, to succeed. Why? Are modern women less able than their forebears? Do the conditions of contemporary life make breast-feeding too difficult? Or bottle feeding too easy?

My view, based on experience with my own children, observation of friends and of many other women, was that modern women are just as capable of breast-feeding as their forebears. What they lack is the information and support which was once available to them through other women (2). Giving birth in hospitals is a recent social invention and so is the almost exclusive reliance upon men (who have little or no education on the subject and no personal experience with it — as adults at any rate) for help with breast-feeding. Centralized nurseries, which interfere with the contact between mothers and infants, are also a recent innovation and the manner in which they are customarily administered, facilitates bottle rather than breast-feeding.

To find out whether my view had merit, I decided to study the relationship between information, support and outcome of breast-feeding.

Fortunately an organization of mothers, the La Leche League (LLL) which has more than 1000 groups throughout the world, agreed to help. The LLL was started by chance when three nursing mothers took three would-be breast-feeding friends on a picnic in Franklin Park, Illinois, in 1956. Their person-to-person method of helping on that picnic proved so effective that they held a small meeting for a few other interested women the following month. Today the LLL is helping women all over the world. Not only do they offer information about breast-feeding and support to those who seek it (by mail, phone, in person, through their book *The Womanly Art of Breastfeeding*, and through a series of four meetings) but they also offer help with the art of mothering.

Background Information

Contrary to popular belief, breast-feeding in humans is not a purely instinctive activity and probably never has been. It is a womanly art passed down from generation to generation in almost every culture but our own. The image of so-called natural nursing in primitive societies is a fallacious one and 'fails to allow for the high degree of stylization' which accompanies these acts (3).

As recently as 1920, medical authorities warned that, 'bottle feeding is a difficult matter and not without risks.' (4) Yet today breast-feeding is the lesser-valued method of infant feeding and in rapid decline throughout the world (5). This decline has serious enough consequences in countries like the United States where most mothers are able to obtain adequate protein substitutes and have sufficient education to feed their infants artificially with proper sanitary precautions. In developing nations (where the United States is often copied especially in the realm of technological innovation) bottle feeding is often a disaster. Many of the women in lower socio-economic groups, who believe that bottle feeding is the status thing, have neither the education to bottle feed under proper hygienic conditions nor can they obtain the needed protein substitutes. The result is marasmus, infantile diarrhoea and kwashiorkor, which often leads to permanent brain damage (6).

Breast-feeding is not a universal panacea. Some women

cannot breast-feed because of illness, death and other factors while other women do not choose to breast-feed. According to the mothers in the study, the reasons for this have to do with distaste, stemming from our puritanical heritage and the notion that breast-feeding is 'animalistic', 'dirty', 'associated only with the lower class'; and inconvenience, 'because our culture promotes detached, free mothers.' Lack of education and ignorance of the medical profession were among other reasons they suggested why mothers do not choose to breast-feed: nevertheless, a far larger number of women might breast-feed than one would assume by looking at the available statistics on its decline, if they were given proper information upon which to base an intelligent choice.

Advantages of Breast-Feeding

On a physiological level, human breast milk is by far the best food for human babies. Among other things, it is more easily assimilated and digested, it conveys immunities, reduces the incidence of allergies, promotes proper formation of the oral cavity, and comes in warm containers which babies find most agreeable and well suited to their needs (8). Breast-feeding is also beneficial for the mother. It helps her uterus return to normal, aids in the prevention of postpartum hemmorhage when initiated at once, and produces a hormone, prolactin, which makes one feel motherly (when injected into male animals, prolactin makes them act motherly too) (9). It also provides her with a close continuing contact with the life that has so recently dwelt within her and reduces her chance of contracting breast cancer (10). Breast-feeding is also good for the father. It is more economical, his baby smells sweeter, he doesn't have to get up and help with a night bottle, and his wife is likely, in the long run, to be more loving and warm towards him.

Behavioral scientist, Niles Newton, suggested recently that being a mother without breast-feeding and the pleasure which normally attends it, is like being a wife without the pleasure of sex (11). While there have been no conclusive studies about the emotional value of breast-feeding due to the difficulty of controlling multiple factors, a number of clinicians have made relevant observations on the subject.

Said orgonomist, Elsworth Baker:

> Contact with the mother is particularly important in the infant. For nine months it has been part of the mother and even after birth is greatly dependent on her. The two organisms mutually excite each other providing that sparkle and intensity of living so necessary for development and growth. This excitement reaches its peak during nursing if the mother's nipple is warm, erective and alive and frequently produces an oral orgastic convulsion in the infant. Food from a bottle can be made as nourishing from a nutritional standpoint, but it does not provide contact and excitation (12).

Writing in *Love and Orgasm*, Alexander Lowen said:

> Infantile oral needs include the needs for bodily contact, food, affection, and care. The first two of these needs are ideally fulfilled in the natural function of breastfeeding. The relation of the mouth to nipples is the prototype of the later genital relation of penis to vagina (13).

A non-clinician mother and writer, Karen Pryor puts it this way:

> The oneness of the nursing mother and baby has always fascinated mankind. Like lovers, they are united both physically and spiritually ... For one mother, nursing the baby may be an intense, joyful experience, while for another mother it is as casually routine as pouring a cup of coffee. But all successful nursing mothers unite in regarding the bottle-feeding mother with pity — the same pity a happily married woman feels for a frigid wife. She just doesn't know what she's missing (14).

Wilhelm Reich expressed it in more objective terms:

> The pre-eminent place of contact of the infant's body is the bio-energetically highly charged mouth and throat. This organ immediately reaches out for gratification. If, now, the mother's nipple reacts to the sucking movements in the proper biophysical manner with pleasure sensations, it becomes vigorously erect ... Every healthy mother experiences the sucking pleasurably and gives herself over to the experience (5).

One might deduce from the latter that only 'healthy' mothers can successfully breast-feed. It is interesting to find, however, that many mothers whom Reich would probably not have judged to be healthy by his standards, are able, with the aid of correct information, and a bit of support, to succeed with breast-feeding and to enjoy it. In the study, which will be described below, pleasure in breast-feeding was found to correlate highly significantly with information ($p < .005$), significantly with individual support ($p < .01$) and highly significantly with group support of the type offered by LLL ($p < .0005$). What better way to work at prevention than through pleasure?

Summary of Research Procedures

A judgement sample of 74 LLL groups throughout the United States took part in the study. Under the supervision of LLL group leaders, a questionnaire was filled out by 1124 women who attended a regular LLL meeting. One hundred percent of the groups returned the questionnaires. Some of the women had been members of the LLL at the time of the birth of their first child while others joined later. Only breast-feeding experience with the first child was studied. 756 women who breast-fed their first child, and had finished breast-feeding that child, were selected to test the hypothesis of the study. These were:

1 Women with information of the type given by the LLL have a better outcome to their breast-feeding endeavors than women who lack such information.
2 Women who have support have a better outcome to their

breast-feeding endeavors than women who lack support.
3 Women who have both information of the type given by LLL and support have a better outcome to their breast-feeding endeavors than women who have only information or only support.

The independent variable, *information* was studied through questions about breast-feeding which the respondents rated 'true', 'false', or 'don't know' according to their views at the time of birth of their first child. Questions were limited to those about which there is agreement among persons interested in breast-feeding e.g. how often to nurse, whether to nurse from both breasts, when and how frequently to introduce the bottle, when to introduce solids, whether to nurse lying down, etc. The independent variable, *support*, was studied in two ways: *individual* support based on the attitudes about breast-feeding of persons (mother, father, husband, sister, friend, physician) towards whom the woman felt close at the time of birth of her first child; and *group* support, whether there was any, when it occurred, and from which group(s) it came.

The dependent variable, *outcome of breast-feeding*, was studied in three ways: a Guttman-type scale based on whether a woman who wanted to breast-feed actually tried to, whether she breast-fed for as long as she wanted to, and whether she enjoyed breast-feeding; duration of breast-feeding; and speed of weaning.

Choice of an ex-post-facto design was made with full awareness of the limitations of such an approach but in the belief that a more controlled type of experiment, if at all feasible, would have been unethical. The opportunity to study a social experiment in progress (the effect of the work of LLL) seemed to more than compensate for the problems involved, particularly since results might be of immediate practical importance to persons involved with pregnant women and newborns.

Findings of the Study

All hypothesis of the study were confirmed (see Table 1).

Information related to outcome of breast-feeding to a high degree (p < .0005). Individual support by itself related to outcome of breast-feeding to a high degree (p < .005). Group support alone related to outcome of breast-feeding to a high degree (p < .0005). Information and suport combined related more highly to outcome than either information or support alone. The findings indicate that mothers who wish to breast-feed should be offered information and support. The fact that individual support by itself relates less highly to outcome is probably due to the association of group support with information.

TABLE 1. *Correlations of Outcome Scores with Information and Support Scores of Noncurrent Breast-feeders*

Information and Support Scores	Scaled Outcome	Duration of Breast-feeding	Speed of Weaning
Information	0.3839	0.4432	0.3757
Individual support	0.2977	0.2568	0.2349
Group support	0.3741*	0.4488*	0.4021*
Individual and group support	0.4046	0.4591	0.4243
Information and individual support	0.4398	0.4707	0.4053
Information and group support	0.4229	0.5119	0.4537
Information and both types of support	0.4665	0.5287	0.4708

*Correlation ratios rather than Pearson's r.

Although amount of individual support is significantly related to all three outcomes, the amount of conflict in individual support is not. This confirms the findings of social psychologist, Solomon Asch, that as long as some support is present, the existence of persons who disagree does not significantly affect behavior (16). The same holds true for group support. As long as a woman belongs to a group which favors breast-feeding, her behavior is not significantly affected if she also belongs to one opposing breast-feeding. The practical implications are that if other mothers, friends, physicians, offer a woman information and support, she can breast-feed successfully even if some persons in her immediate environment disapprove of what she is doing.

This finding appears again in another form when one considers why women who wanted to breast-feed, stopped before they intended to (see Table 2). Those lacking in proper information were much more likely to have 'mother difficulties' (e.g. not enough milk, cracked or sore nipples, breast abcesses). They were more likely to be stopped by doctor of hospital intervention (e.g. mother given medication to stop milk, hospital gave baby bottles and infant lost interest in breast, baby not allowed to nurse frequently enough, physician told mother to stop breast-feeding.) Baby difficulties (i.e. baby could not suck or rejected breast, baby had jaundice or diarrhoea, didn't gain or lost interest in the breast) were also significantly related to lack of information as was the effect of social pressure (e.g. baby's father disapproved, someone else or many persons disapproved). Lack of information was significantly related to all the reasons why mothers stopped breast-feeding before they wanted to.

TABLE 2. *Relationship between Information and Reasons for Stopping Breast-feeding before Mother Wanted or Intended to by T-tests (n = 754)* (t754, .0006 - 3.30)

	Information Scores of Those Who Did Have Difficulty	t-Tests	Information Scores of Those Who Did Not Have Difficulty
Mother difficulties	$\bar{x} = 2.496$	10.577*	$\bar{x} = 9.142$
Baby difficulties	$\bar{x} = 3.569$	5.042*	$\bar{x} = 7.767$
Doctor/hospital intervention	$\bar{x} = 1.000$	9.687*	$\bar{x} = 8.593$
Social pressure	$\bar{x} = 0.212$	7.063*	$\bar{x} = 7.762$
Personal inconvenience	$\bar{x} = 3.462$	0.501	$\bar{x} = 4.390$

*Significant $(p < .0005)$

Effects of Membership in LLL on Other Mothering Customs

In addition to helping mothers who want to breast-feed, membership in LLL had an effect on other mothering customs.

Some thoughts about breast-feeding and health

Members tended to breast-feed their children longer and wean them more gradually, allowing the children to participate in the weaning process rather than imposing it on them. If members used a bottle at all, it was introduced later and mostly to replace a feeding (when they were away from the baby) rather than to supplement the breast. Into the bottle they put water or breast milk rather than formula. Solids were introduced later by members than non-members.

LLL members allowed a great variety of persons to be present while they breast-fed and did many more things while nursing (including housework and even horseback riding). Quite significantly, they allowed more body contact between mother and child than did non-members. This included carrying their babies around more between feeding, allowing their children to rest or sleep in bed with them more often (and with fewer clothes on both mother and baby) and using carrying devices where the babies' bodies were in contact with the mothers' bodies rather than the plastic devices which do not permit this kind of body contact. Members of LLL also took their children to more places with them at an early age and left them less frequently with baby-sitters other than the father in the first months of life.

LLL members were more likely to seek and to obtain educated childbirth, to use little or no anaesthetic, to have their husbands present during labor and delivery, and to want and get rooming-in. Members were also better prepared for the difficulties they might encounter with breast-feeding in the hospital.

It is my impression, from the data gathered and from observation of hundreds of LLL mothers that a large percentage of the group provide the close contact and consistent mothering which many believe important to the well-being of the human infant and to the development of his capacity to love (17).

Another interesting finding of the study, which must be viewed with caution since it is based on self-reports of women about a highly-charged subject, is that those who were successful with breast-feeding were also likely to be more successful in other aspects of their sexual responses. 30% of the respondents reported improved sexual relationships after weaning the first successfully breast-fed child. Only 2.5% reported that it had worsened. 22% reported improved sexual relationships after contact with the LLL, while 0% reported that their sexual adjustment became worse. Most of the women who reported an improvement in sexual functioning were women who felt their sex life to be excellent in the first place while all the women in the 2.5% who felt it became worse were women who reported that they had a poor sexual adjustment to begin with. Nursing and contact with LLL merely made them more aware of the lacks that existed in their relationships with their husbands. Concerning the connection between breast-feeding and sexual adjustment, a number of women made specific comments.

Question: Did you notice any changes in yourself after breast-feeding?

Answer: Tremendous changes. I became a much better mother. And I have a feeling that comes from within that makes me closer to my children. My husband and I are much closer for some reason ... I feel that there is something very earthy about nursing a child and this can pleasantly affect the husband-wife relationship. All aspects of your life are more pleasurable. And I feel also that a good breast-feeding experience makes you more open and womanly. In my case, I had a sexual problem and the breast-feeding made me want to find out what was wrong, so I went for help ... Because of nursing and realizing I had such a closeness with the baby, and yet I loved my husband and still didn't have such a closeness with him. So I knew there was something wrong ...

Another woman commented:

Because of nursing, I felt there ought to be a better feeling between husband and wife ... and with a bit of help, it didn't take long. I was able to have orgasm which I had never had before.

Some thoughts about breast-feeding and health

Asked if nursing had affected her relationship with her husband, a nurse replied:

> Well, I've always been pretty successful at that. But I think probably that if you were inclined to be a little cool, it would warm you up. Not in the sense necessarily of feeling sexual, but more tender feelings, more loving feelings.

A high-school graduate from Wisconsin wrote:

> I was very shy about the whole thing ... but secretly I totally enjoyed it ... The psychological closeness that breast-feeding affords, and the pleasure, to me has to be a necessary part of the continuing maturation process of a healthy female. Anyway, my husband thinks I'm more fun.

From San Diego, a woman wrote:

> Without the association afforded me by the LLL, the sexual side of my marriage might have deteriorated. Intelligent and frank discussions and reading materials suggested by and sometimes available through LLL will continue to broaden my attitudes and help me to give more of myself in this area.

Some Conclusions About Breast-feeding

If one accepts the premise that breast-feeding has enough advantages so that women who want to breast-feed should be encouraged and even helped to do so, then some rethinking about the training of personnel who come into contact with pregnant and parturient women is in order. Institutions that train physicians and nurses should include information about breast-feeding in the curriculum. Only a few of them do so now. Since physicians and nurses are subject to the same cultural pressures as the rest of us, they can hardly be expected to become knowledgeable and supportive on the subject of breast-feeding without special training. Nor is it likely that hospital administrators, without some education on the subject, will understand the consequences of their policies for running central nurseries. Such common routines as a four-hour feeding schedule, offering supplementary bottle feedings and withholding the infant from the mother for up to 24 hours after birth, are not conducive to success with breast-feeding (18).

One might go a step further and argue that it is advisable, without pressuring women who do not wish to breast-feed, to tell expectant mothers about the advantages of breast-feeding so they are in a better position to opt for it. It is simply not true that bottle feeding is equally advantageous, even in the United States, although bottle feeding is a perfectly acceptable safe method of infant feeding where breast-feeding is not possible.

When a woman is making the decision of whether or not to breast-feed, she is entitled not only to the clinical facts, but she should also be made aware of certain other viewpoints, typical of the successfully breast-feeding mother. For example:

> What a beautiful experience ... I simply cannot describe what breast-feeding did for our family. I became a truly happy person for the first time in my life, my marriage is close and I can *love* my husband and children as I never knew how before.

> With my first child, I knew nothing about breast-feeding and I have learned, learned, learned. I am thankful beyond words and I feel I owe it to other mothers to tell them. They can make a choice once they know the facts. Just because your husband or some other person says he was breast-fed isn't enough help.

Whether or not breast-feeding once again becomes a popular and widespread method of infant feeding has relevance to some other problems which face mankind today. Breast-feeding is not *the* answer to the problem of food shortages, but it is one part of it. For infants, human milk is an excellent, readily available, sterile and high quality protein. Breast-feeding is also one SMALL part of

Some thoughts about breast-feeding and health

the answer to the population problem. Breast-feeding *without food supplements* is associated with a decrease in fertility. This decrease is not absolute. Lactating mothers do conceive but not as soon as non-lactating mothers (19). In areas where birth control is not available or not acceptable, *unsupplemented* breast-feeding acts as a deterrent to ovulation. (Where women have access to oral contraceptives there is a conflict, since breast-feeding is contra-indicated for mothers using this form of birth control) (20).

Some General Conclusions

Although the effect of support and information were studied, in this instance, only with respect to the culturally lesser valued activity of breast-feeding, it seems likely that information and support would be helpful to individuals undertaking a variety of other activities as well.

There are, it seems to me, implications in these findings about the value of information and support for parents and children, husbands and wives, supervisors and employees, therapists and patients, and people working together in any kind of joint enterprise whether generally sanctioned or not by the group in which the individuals are living. Although the findings of the study suggest that even the rugged individualist might be well advised to find at least one other person he respects who approves of what he is doing.

It is a widely accepted premise of education that the offering of correct information is importantly related to behavior. It is less widely accepted that support of students may be as important in its effect on behavior as is the offering of information. On the other hand, therapists often recognize the value of support but sometimes fail to supply needed information which might facilitate treatment.

In every person who has survived, there is an element of health, however small it may be. One of our jobs is to get at that push towards life, and to strengthen it through information and through support. As one woman from LLL wrote:

> It seems to me that unlike several people interested in

various types of psychiatric cures for neuroses, those of us whose interest lies in building happiness by prevention are in remarkable agreement about how to proceed. Helping mothers and babies off to a loving start with breast-feeding lots of skin contact, minimum separation, working with natural rhythms rather than trying to suppress them, all these really important things are not among us a subject of debate. This is surely a great source of strength and offers a ray of hope.

REFERENCES

1. Meyer, M.F.: *Breastfeeding in the United States.* Clin. Pediat. 7:708, 1968
  Newton, Niles and Newton, M.: *Psychologic Aspects of Lactation.* New Eng. J. Med. 277:1179, 1967
2. Rapael, Dana: *The Lactation Suckling Reflex within a Matrix of Supportive Behavior.* University Microfilms, Ann Arbor, Michigan, #69-15580
3. Mead, Margaret: *Changing Patterns of Parent-Child Relations in an Urban Culture.* Int. J. Psychoanal. 38:1. 1957
4. Wood, Alice: *History of Artificial Feeding.* J. Am. Dietetic Assoc. 31:5, 1955
5. Newton and Newton, *op. cit.*
  Meyer, *op. cit.*
6. Jelliffe, Derrick: *Breast Milk and the World Protein Gap.* Clinical Pediatrics, 7:2, 1968
7. Gunther, Mavis: Instinct in the Nursing Couple. *Lancet,* March 1955.
  Mead, Margaret: Changing Patterns of Parent-Child Relations in an Urban Culture. *International Journal of Psycho-analysis,* Vol. 38 Part VI, 1957
8. Kon, S.K. and Cowie, A.T. (eds.): Milk: *the Mammary Gland and its Secretion.* Vol. I and Vol. II. New York: Academic Press, 1961.
  Haire, Doris and Haire, John: The Medical Value of Breast Feeding, *Implementing Family Centered Maternity Care with a Central Nursery.* Hillside, New Jersey: Childbirth Educational Assoc., Ch. V, 1968
9. Newton, N: *Maternal Emotions.* New York: Paul B. Hoeber, Inc., 1955
10. Gerard, Alice: *Please Breast-Feed Your Baby.* New York: Hawthorn Books Inc., 1970. (Introduction by C.D. Haagensen, M.D.)
11. Newton, N: Speech, 3rd International Cong. Psychosom. Med. in Ob-Gyn., London, March 1971

12   Baker, Ellsworth: *Man in the Trap.* New York: Prentice-Hall, 1952.
13   Lowen, Alexander: *Love and Orgasm.* New York: the Macmillan Co., 1965
14   Pryor, Karen, *op. cit.*
15   Reich, Wilhelm: *The Cancer Biopathy.* New York: Orgone Institute Press, 1948
16   Asch, S.E.: *Studies of Independence and Conformity, a Minority of One against a Unanimous Majority.* Psychological Monographs, 70:9 1956.
17   Montague, Ashley: *Human Heredity.* Cleveland: World Publ. Co., 1959
18   Haire and Haire, *op. cit.*
19   Gioiosa, R.: *Incidence of Pregnancy during Lactation in 500 Cases.* Amer. J. Obstet. Gynec. 70:162, 1955
     Schaefer, O.: Letter to editor. Canad. Med. Assn. J. 99:915, 1968
20   *The Pill:* adapted from the FDA. Child and Family 7:1. 1968

The Needs of Children

by Herb Snitzer

Director of Lewis Wadhams, New York

Herb Snitzer is a founder of Lewis Wadhams School in upstate New York, which is based to a large extent on the principles of Summerhill School in Suffolk and the work of A.S. Neill. Snitzer had a close relationship with Neill until his death, and also co-operates closely with several of the bio-energetic therapists in exploring the possibilities for the use of therapy in the school situation.

A child is a fragile, defenseless and dependent human being whose early needs must be fulfilled in order for the child to begin his or her own growth process feeling secure. Children are born with a drive towards what is life-giving and life-fulfilling, namely that which is open, therefore vulnerable; peaceful, therefore compassionate and trusting; sensual, therefore intuitive and emotional.

This drive, call it life force, begins to diminish and in far too many children seemingly disappears altogether. Upon birth, a symbiotic relationship forms which in the first few days will determine just what the child will get or not get from the mother specifically, and from the parents generally. It is the mother who establishes and carries out the initial physical and emotional contacts and these ties will grow, develop, and deepen depending on what kind of a person the woman is and how emotionally secure she is in her own right.

In our society very few people are emotionally mature. Whatever deficiencies exist are at play and passed on with devastating results to children. For example, a woman has a child because her life is unfulfilled. She believes that having a child will make her life fuller. Her life will become active, complicated, and busy, but whether it will become fuller is another matter. It simply does not work. As one mother stated, 'I waited all these years to have a baby and when I did, she didn't do a thing for me.'

I am the father of five children ranging in age from sixteen down to five years of age. I speak with great sympathy and compassion for parents, even though I know that we as a group are doing a fairly lousy job of rearing children. Rearing children is perhaps the single most difficult job adults have. With each passing day, there are millions upon millions of children absorbing hurts which they will never get over. Perhaps one day they will know and recognize that early hurts need not be kept buried; that hatred and anger can be expressed in ways which will not be destructive and by so knowing begin to recover and express the early childlike beauty that they and we, at one time or another, felt and knew. I believe that behind all the torment, all the anger, all the rage, is the beauty and gentleness of the child wishing to be expressed.

So, what are these important and necessary needs of children? Early on I mentioned unquestioning acceptance as a fragile, totally defenseless human being.

A child has a need for closeness and warmth, to be held, cuddled, caressed. Obviously the man or woman who had difficulty in touching, in accepting warmth or love, is going to have a terrible time of it. A newborn baby is operating on a rhythm of instinct and will respond to a cold touch, a rigid holding, a conditional relationship.

The Freudians used to take the position, I don't know if they still do, that very young children should never see their parents naked, should never be in the bathroom at the same time as their parents, should never have physical contact unless there is clothing worn by either the child or the adult. I'm not quite sure why Freud's teachings hit so big in this country, but I have a suspicion that his Victorian attitudes towards sexuality fitted in very well with the puritan concepts that continue to dominate this country.

Children growing up in a house with an absence of physical contact slowly begin to feel something must be wrong with touching another or themselves. Locked bathrooms will be taken as meaning something secret is going on. A psychiatrist once 'jokingly' told me that he is doing his work because he never knew what was happening behind his parents' closed bedroom doors.

And so children grow and develop, absorbing their immediate surroundings, evaluating, questioning. They are wide-eyed with wonder, interested in all kinds of things, excited about themselves and the lives of others. Yet, I also know that many children, by the time they are four and five, are already partially destroyed, already locked up with fears.

And so we then come to the socialization of the young in group play and group functioning. And from this point on, the life of a child is filled with the most subtle, insidious conditioning and indoctrination man has yet devised. They are placed in environments which will, by the time the child is seventeen, attempt to mold, condition and break their spirits. A system whose basic function is to prepare young people to eventually take their place in and perpetuate the existing society. This may be the need of society. It is the furthest need a child has. Paraphrasing Dr. Kenneth Clark, we read the same old reports, we talk the same old words, we hold the same old meetings, and we have the same old inaction. Today, schools mean factories thorugh which children are production-lined — at the end of which they are 'educated'. They are not educated, they are trained, and we are all the less for it.

Today we have the opportunity to make dramatic changes, important changes in education, and I suggest we begin to do so by listening to and feeling young people — not the angry college students however valid their complaints may be — but the words and feelings of ten-year-olds who would rather play, jump and run, with an inexhaustable supply of energy. A young body just cannot sit quiet and still for long hours unless the body is dulled, the energy bottled up and held in check. And we all know these energies are held in check by a system of rewards and punishments — a vile system perpetuated by people who admire control and power.

Is it really so complicated to know why children become socially deviant, unresponsive, inattentive to the wishes and demands of teachers?

All the protestations of children, especially young adults on the college and high school level, can be viewed as their need to be seen and heard as people; for others to accept them as people. They want to be listened to and accepted for who they are, to associate with whomever they please, to grow at their own pace, to fight their own battles. They have a need not to be brutalized by parents or teachers. It is a terrible thing to know that with each passing day, two children die at the hands of their parents through beatings; that over 2.5 million children are hit and hurt each year in the United States alone. Children need to grow in safety, secure in their own person. Any adult who beats a child for any reason should be tried and convicted of brutality, yet I know this condoned violence is just another weapon sanctioned by the adult world.

How different it could be if we were to say to each other and to children, 'we want to grow in harmony with you. What can we do?' And at that point, the adult world, either as individuals or groups, must just sit back and listen and feel, quietly, openly, compassionately. The needs of children are no different than the needs of adults. At given times, certain needs are paramount and must be fulfilled for any semblance of emotional health, but we never really outgrow those early basic needs. We all look for love, warmth, security and stability, and the searching for what is personally meaningful and enriching. Perhaps one day we can put away the slogans, the revolutionary rhetoric, and get down to the business at hand — to live life fully and to rear children in a stable and secure atmosphere. Perhaps then will we see the changes in the world we all hope for.

Youth and the Meaning of Growth

by Ronald Rybacki

Educator

Ronald Rybacki trained as an educator and has a particular interest in creativity. He is the author of a book of poems called The Earth, the Sky, and the Body, *and is currently living in New York.*

Most schools, unfortunately, are only a continuation of that civilizing process begun in most homes, the final result of which is a severe split in the personality. Very few people emerge as healthy adults because the civilizing process, even today, works with a deep-seated bias against the body. The civilized person loses touch with his body and does not sense his ties with nature. Because the body is used as an instrument of the will, most of the tender feelings in the body are lost, and the person loses his natural sensitivity towards other living things. A result of this is that in this century we have before us the grim spectacle of a dying natural environment.

Most people do not realize that culture and nature are intimately related. This is due to our civilization's attempt to raise man above the animal level.

This is a short paper, and the complexity of the problem does not allow for briefness. However, I may be able to say a few things which would dispel some of the confusion which I know students have in regard to their homes, their schools, and the society into which they are expecting to emerge.

Youth and the meaning of growth

Youth was meant to be a period of great excitement and responsiveness and perceptivity. Life, to the young person, is new and fascinating — and to life each young person brings a fresh vision of reality. This is why so many philosophers and poets have eulogized youth.

In primitive cultures, such as the Eskimo or Indian, the child's nature was deeply appreciated. Breast-feeding was the natural close tie that a baby had with its mother, and this was not severed early; a baby, also, had continual close contact with its mother's body apart from nursing, by being carried most of the time.

Children in our society are deprived emotionally. If you have ever seen a baby breast-feeding, you probably did sense the pleasure the baby felt in receiving food, warmth, erotic contact, and maternal love. In humans, nursing is a face to face relationship. Great awareness of the other person is possible, and through the eyes child and mother are aware that each is giving pleasure to the other. The baby needs this oral pleasure. Through nursing, the baby comes to know the bodily truth of joy and love. The contentment on a baby's face who has fallen asleep at the breast is unmistakable. One is aware of a sweetness and openness, like that of a flower.

Because the baby sucks energetically on the breast, the way is laid for a natural development of the child's breathing capacity. The child who has been deprived of the breast is a poor breather, at the same time revealing the other problems which result in most homes where the importance of breast-feeding is not recognized.

That breathing is important, most people will not deny. However, to say that breathing is 'the breath of life' will appear to some just a misuse of metaphor. But I am not speaking metaphorically. Try breathing very deeply for a moment, and see how it makes you feel.

It will make you dizzy. Now if you breathe deeply and also move briskly, for instance in running, your body will become enlivened. For some people, walking, running, and generally moving about during the course of the day is a pleasure. This is so because they do not work compulsively, they do not move at the mercy of the will — rather, they are in touch with the pleasure of the activity. A disturbance in breathing disqualifies a person from pleasure in work.

Pleasure in one's movements, and pleasure in meeting the basic needs of the body provide the basis for emotional response. The person who has no pleasure in his own body, independent from others, cannot love — or at least suffers in his capacity to love. And the adult who has little pleasure, and who does not have an adequate sense of self through the body, was deprived as a child.

Parents on the one hand mean well, and on the other enforce upon the child codes of behavior which split the integrity of the personality. A little child who is crying is asked to stop, and the method used is often shame or fear. Parents often say: 'STOP CRYING!' 'Big boys and girls don't cry.' Or they may shout: 'Stop that this minute, or else!' Or they may leave the child to cry himself out. In the case of being shamed or scared, the child will automatically catch his breath, and this will stop his crying. If these experiences continue, chronic tensions in the diaphragm, chest, and throat will develop which destroy the natural breathing pattern. Since crying is the child's way of calling for help, and is a direct expression through the voice of disharmony in the body, the child becomes bewildered when his need for comfort is met with hostility. I have seen people squirm when a child cries and this is due to the sadness they have had to repress in themselves in the face of a hostile reaction from their own parents.

Children have a natural desire and need to follow their parents' suggestions, and they have the need as they grow a little older to identify with the parent of their own sex. But if the parents' behavior and guidance go against the needs of the body, the child will become confused. A split will develop between thinking and feeling, between the mind and the body, and between the child and the world. The child will fall prey to words. He will go to school and join others in our society who pursue the 'reasons' for life and work; but the meaning of life will escape him.

It becomes a vicious circle. The child who loses his pleasure and his feelings, or the child who simply never experiences the growth of his identity because of the lack of pleasure — will ask the painful question, 'Why?'

Children eventually turn against their own bodies because of the extreme pain its unmet needs give them; the pain itself is shut off by chronic muscular tensions which stop all movement and feeling. The body loses its emotional aliveness. Painful memories, which would awaken early conflicts, are barred from consciousness. Emotionally, the child does not know who he is.'

At the high-school level, problems seem to multiply. These are not carefree years for the student. More and more of the *world's* knowledge and problems are put upon the shoulders of the student, and this comes right at the time when the emergence of sexual feeling and desire is met by the student's own doubts. Added to this is the guilt and shame which is attached, by our society, to adolescent sexuality.

Often, the high-school experience 'makes' or 'breaks' a student. In my opinion, neither outcome is good. At a time when students most want to understand themselves, the school curriculum becomes more abstract and more difficult. The more problems, questions and puzzles we push at the student, the more distraught and painful school becomes.

The real questions go unanswered.

Schools are only beginning to recognize that a problem exists. By an obsessive emphasis on thinking processes, they have in fact furthered the split between the mind and the body which, for the student, began in the home. As schools gained in prestige and national importance, especially at the time when scientific exploration was incited by the power struggle between countries, the acquisition of factual knowledge and the ability to discern cause and effect relationships became idolized. These specialized and limited ways of thinking give man control over organic and inorganic processes in nature. This control yields manpower.

Everything is focused upon power these days. Faster cars, more money, recognition, success, and fame. The illusion is that power will bring pleasure and fulfilment, and so people become engaged in the struggle for power. Unfortunately, power cannot bring love. Love arises between two people whose hearts are filled with the gladness of just being alive. The person who enjoys being alive lives in the present, and is in touch with what is going on in his body. The person who craves power hangs on the future, and is unaware of the state of his body.

When the body is in a state of pleasure, it vibrates smoothly. It 'hums'. With each intake of breath, streaming sensations are felt down the front of the body. One feels light-hearted. Such a person is said to have a 'vibrant' personality.

I have known a few people like this. One is aware of a beautiful resonance in their voices, of a warmth and depth of personality in their eyes, and of a grace and harmony in their physical movements. They are individuals who know the real meaning of joy and love.

Man is a cultured animal. Animals are graceful and spontaneous, and we all love to hear their voices in the woods. The singing of birds, the wonderful sheen of a fox's fur, the elegant leap of a deer — these are all direct expressions of the vitality, beauty and joy that belong to living organisms.

I am sure that people, despite the forces which go against feeling in our society, still have some natural insight. Many people express a love for nature, and we have even come to call this earth of ours 'Mother Earth'. At the same time, we all like to walk in the sunshine on a fine summer day. The sun in the sky is a very pleasing sight. It means growth, fertility and fruitfulness.

The earth and the sky work together. You can't think of one without the other. We would all be very disappointed if the sun were not there tomorrow. We are not very happy when we think of this earth becoming spoiled by pollution. These things we all talk about.

How is it that we can think of a child, and not realize how intimately related a child is to its mother?

The answer, of course, is that the civilizing process has made us live more in our thoughts and less in our feelings. If one does not *feel* the relatedness of all life, one tends to think about life in an abstract way. If one can feel, one can think creatively.

School would be more exciting. A violin, for instance, would be thought of as an instrument that was designed somewhat after the human body. It has been called the instrument that most closely resembles the human voice. The violin has a 'neck' to which are attached strings (we have vocal strings), and these strings when touched set up vibrations which are amplified in the 'body', the wood of the violin.

Naturally, people love harmony. Harmony is pleasant to us.

Harmony is the union of rhythm and melody. However, the music is not in the music, but in our bodies. Music is created by a person who can express harmony.

You might say modern man is out of harmony with his body. He does not know his body, he does not feel it. Sure, you can feel your body somewhat when you walk across a room. But more and more, we are losing the capacity to be 'moved' from within. Children are easily moved, and the staidness of adulthood is a sign that the child was slowly immobilized.

Students want help and need it. They are willing to explore the things which disturb them because they are very apprehensive about their futures. The way to meet this need is to encourage emotional expression in school, and to set up programs for therapy. Bio-energetic therapy is the only way I know of to help a person gain a better sense of self, and schools here in Newfoundland will sooner or later be faced with the problem.

By an acceptance of feeling and the major role of the body as the basis for identity, the school could become a center for re-integrating society — rather than remaining an institution which is only arming young people to compete in a power struggle.

Should anyone think that an exploration of feeling would lessen teachers' and students' interest in knowledge, I can offer some reassurance. The person who is in touch with himself and who knows that the wisdom of the body is inspired, ultimately, by a spiritual source — has an appetite for life and learning.

On the Creation of a Masochist

by Eric Edwards, M.R.C.S., L.R.C.P., D.P.M.

Eric Edwards was a Consultant Psychiatrist at the Portman Clinic, London. He trained in character-analysis with John Kelnar, and worked as a consultant at the Lincoln Memorial Clinic for Psychotherapy. When Alexander Lowen introduced the bio-energetic approach into England in 1968, Eric Edwards was among the first to welcome these new ideas. His contribution here is taken from a talk on 'Masochism and Violence' given to the Howard League for Penal Reform in October 1969, and published in Energy and Character, *Vol.1, No.2, May 1970.*

Each new generation is exposed in childhood to the social pathology embodied in the parents. This 'behavioural infection' (1) is transmitted by the mechanism of projective identification (forcing into others conflictual behavioural patterns) to produce a conformity to the parents' pathology. This mode of infection is complemented by the reciprocity of introjective identification — an accommodation response out of fear. ('If you can't beat them join them.') The resulting 'superego' (Freud) may be considered as a pathological formation for transmitting cultural pathology through the generations.

There is no such thing as a biological wish to suffer, children being initially innocent victims of this process which produces in them reactive violence which can then be used to justify further repressive measures. The *distortion of any individual life produces hate* which renders the false logic of repression unassailable, since there is always a fund of hostility awaiting expression and which is readily tapped. When hate turns back on the self and in the self, sadism becomes masochism as the impulse is re-directed along internal lines. Hate does not magically turn back on the self: it is bent back by further outside force. In desperation the child takes its own ego as hostage in severe interpersonal strife with parents and educators. Suicide and murder are closely linked in this way.

A 'battle of wills' is found in the history of every masochist and although the forces used to subdue a child may not be crudely physical, they often are, in which case the struggle is hopelessly unequal, creating profound feelings of impotent injustice. Too often, alas, the doctrine that 'might is right' prevails and when the child is too old to be beaten or otherwise forced, moral aggression takes over and, by steady indoctrination of anxious guilt, mental murder is produced, even though the parents may be quite oblivious of the harm they are causing. The right to complain and answer back is denied, so dialogue and communication essential to human intercourse is blocked.

What happens when a child is beaten?

1 It is hurt, frightened and shocked. Bodily feeling is withdrawn from the area under attack, usually the pelvis. In boys fear for the penis is experienced. The muscles of the whole body stiffen to take the blows and to deal with the fear. Petrification may ensue.

2 Anger and hatred are mobilised and combine with the impotence to create a deep resentment which smoulders and is withheld, biding its time for re-expression as revenge and a desire to get even. Contempt and scorn for the bully co-exist.

3 Being forced into submission is deeply humiliating and if the punishment takes place in front of others the hurt to pride is so much greater. There is no respect for feelings.

4 The loss of love implied by punishment creates fear of disapproval, and tender feelings are held in abeyance.

5 There is conflict about weeping owing to competition with the anger. 'I won't give them the satisfaction of seeing I am deeply hurt in my pride.'

6 A profound distrust of others is engendered.

7 Because the attack is not understood by the child and if it is shifted from another quarrel (redirection from parental strife), the sense of confusion, injustice and insecurity

increases.

8   Finally, the exhortation to 'take your punishment like a man' reflects the tendency of the human race to regard the infliction of pain as 'man-making'.

What happens if a child is given an enema or otherwise forced in this natural function? Again, a deeply humiliating experience is created where bodily privacy and right is invaded with the same disrespect for natural feelings. Strict and punitive toilet training has already produced resentment, disturbance of biological rhythm and a resulting constipation. This leads to the enema assault of breaking and entering. This trauma is usually to be found in every severe neurosis, in my experience. Threats of illness force the child to force itself to do the impossible, which renders the function physiologically impossible in any case. The enema produces fear of incontinence (already a punishable offence), and, together with the engendered fear of continence, a deadly oscillating anxiety is created, often manifested in later life in women who move about the world from one lavatory to the other in perpetual uncertainty.

In addition, the feeling of being used by the parent for covert sexual interest adds a dimension of rape to the situation. An extremely conflictual situation is now produced between rage, fear, humiliation and pleasure. One patient told me she hated herself for feeling pleasure as well as hating her mother for being forced into shameful submission. It is dangerous to give in and dangerous to give out without disastrous effects on later genital functioning.

The child is learning that it cannot function unless forced, and belief in natural ease of bodily processes is lost. There is chronic muscular spasm of the pelvic floor, which interferes with the orgasm reflex and which Reich considered as specific for this character disorder.

It will be apparent that feelings in general will be withdrawn and jammed up and, since the attack is on one of the major expressive outlets of the body, a blockage takes place.

Moving from the tail end to the head end of the organism we encounter the same blocking. The head end is for assimilation of food and oxygen (for charging up energy), and this area is also for the active deployment of intelligence, man's greatest asset which he never seems to utilise.

Intelligence functions with the aid of the special senses: vision, touch, hearing, etc. Apart from direct blows on the head the following lesser assaults occur.

Vision: 'You must not look' but 'Look at me when I talk to you'. The Russells explain how important the looking function is in primates, in relation to anxiety.

Eating: An over-anxious mother can produce a fair bit of damage to this function, e.g. 'You will eat what is put in front of you and not leave the table until I say so'. Or in a recent example, 'Mummy, can I have some more chicken?' 'No, you don't need more chicken, you eat more greens, they are good for you.' The child happens not to like greens *so the right to have likes and dislikes is undermined*. What you want you cannot have and what you don't want you have to swallow. Children can suffer greatly though having to swallow food they loathe, e.g. fat meat. The whole process can be seasoned with a sprinkling of guilt. 'Some poor children would be glad of that, you and your fads.' This means that you are guilty if you do not swallow what you do not want and guilty if you swallow what you do want.

If the reader begins to feel slightly confused at this point, it will illustrate the effect of the trauma of confusing and contradictory signals with which the brain has to deal.

The 'You will be glad of that one day' theme evokes fears of future starvation and the total process is the training ground for indoctrination and the prototype of brain-washing. If the 'grown-ups' go to a restaurant, they order what they like, sometimes vehemently. The 'You don't know what is good for you' gambit contributes to a gradual undermining of the child's belief in its own judgment.

Can anyone say how one can cry and eat and be angry all at the same time and express it all through a narrow channel with some impulses going in one direction and some in another as they compete for the nervous pathways? Finally, the 'You don't want that surely' or 'You don't really feel like that' approach cements in the idea that the child has barely the sense to be alive and functioning at all.

Breathing: Easy relaxed breathing only occurs in the absence of stress. Children hold their breath if frightened and this helps to withhold feelings from expression. I have witnessed patients who are too frightened to move or breathe.

Gradually in this way *authority for functioning comes to lie outside the child and natural self-regulation is lost sight of altogether*. A further variant is to play off one function against the other, one end of the body against the other. 'You can have some sweets if you go to the lavatory.' Thus a bargain arrangement prevails between one end of the gut and the other. It is hardly surprising that masochistic characters are always 'bellyaching'.

How can the brain and mind codify and classify such a welter of contradictory stimuli without seizing up? It resembles watching TV and trying to conduct a conversation at the same time.

We are considering in some detail a variety of pathogenic influences acting on natural functions to produce conflictual emotional situations of confusing complexity.

Let us continue. Children are often told to 'shut up'. They retire hurt and sulk maybe. They are then told off for sulking. 'Haven't you got a tongue in your head then?' 'If you don't stop crying I will give you something to cry about.' This piece of illogicality implies that the child is crying for nothing (usually basically true in view of the oral deprivation). Or what about the mother who screams at her children to convey the message 'stop shouting', as I encountered recently.

Such illogicalities have been studied in detail by Bateson et al (2) in their theory of the Double Bind mechanism and its disastrous effect on mental functioning. The child being always in a vitally important relationship, however unsatisfactory it may be, cannot afford to ignore such a battery of alternating and contradictory signals and thus endeavours to gear himself up to a neurotic or psychotic parent. The Double Bind is a mental strait-jacket par excellence, and will eventually produce mental fragmentation, a docile zombie-like conformist or extreme violence.

Let us be clear about such processes. If I stamp on your feet and you are hurt and angry and protest furiously, I then turn round and imply that you ought to feel guilty for having such bad feelings. In addition, I deny that I have injured you. How often do we hear parents admit they are in the wrong or explain a course of action which vitally influences the child's life? The overall effect is to 'put on the spot'. 'You can't win 'em all' is the popular saying today. For the child in this position you cannot win any (or anyhow), and in addition there is no way of being right or comfortable. Speaking of existential anxiety, during the war (a debilitating sado-masochistic experience in any case) I had the misfortune to be pinned down by a sniper as I sheltered behind an overturned vehicle. I deemed it wise to 'dig in' until a soldier from an adjoining trench shouted that I was digging in a mine field. I was caught in a situation where neither action nor reaction was possible and the effect is rigidity and a dissociated zombie-like condition ensues. The Russells remind us that when Trotsky created the Red Army he said the soldier must have the 'choice' of advancing against probable death or retreating against certain death. It is regrettable that this social prescription of impossible dilemma is in a lesser degree inflicted on many children.

Many of these difficulties arise through a fundamental belief in 'original sin', in which case the child has to be trained to be good. It is a question of being guilty until by some perfect performance one can prove oneself innocent and acceptable — a treadmill of performance position.

The essential injury we are considering is one of suppression directed to both body and mind so that the natural outlets of the person are blocked. The masochist is imprisoned in himself, and spontaneous functioning is quite out of the question. Often he has been the whipping boy (or girl) in the family: the scapegoat attracting all the hostility available for redirection. To appreciate this mechanism (akin to the analysts' 'displacement') I must refer the reader to the Russells' book.

The feeling life of the masochist has suffered a severe set-back. He cannot experience bodily feelings naturally; *their normal perception is damaged* and in serious cases there is a schizoid contactlessness. A gradual transition of severity may be seen from the child who 'plays up' to gain attention, gets slapped and bursts into tears, which relieve, to the more serious cases. The individual is not seeking punishment, he is seeking relief from intolerable inner tension and the deeper pain of blocked lovelessness. He is saying in effect, 'Force me to feel something' in accordance with his learning pattern. Harold Searles, in his book on schizophrenia (3) makes the same point when he describes the apparent physical violence of some patients as a desperate attempt to get in touch and out of isolation.

However, the mechanism of salvation through suffering should not be elevated into a doctrine and we should not lend support to the fiction of 'learning to take your punishment like a man'. To summarise:

> The beating is for feeling-enforcement.
> The passivity is for appeasement.
> Identification with the active rôle is for revenge.

The hatred in the masochistic character is shared out in a three-way split. The ego is resentfully obedient and/or rebellious towards a crushing superego (internal sado-masochism), and the remainder is redirected outside in provocative and spiteful relationships. This may be verbalised as 'I hate myself and I hate others'. This pathological splitting is forced into new relationships, including those with the new generation. The child is constantly learning how the 'grown-ups' solve problems by not solving them. The basis of the process is that 'might is right', backed by physical force or mental coercion (psychological warfare). Circumcision should be mentioned as an initial provider of a fund of anxious guilt to be drawn on. We must now consider items of parental behaviour, which in any other context would be regarded as criminal, such as blackmail, extortion and false pretence. These are found in varying mixtures as part of the daily fare of upbringing. 'If you are not a good boy Mummy will run away — or fetch a policeman — or a doctor.' 'What would the neighbours say if they saw you doing that — nobody will love you if you carry on like that.' Or the threat of being sent away is frequent. In very serious cases mothers may threaten suicide as the ultimate form of blackmail, but usually the lesser forms of martyrdom are effective weapons of control. Fears of the unknown are conjured up by 'all right you go off and do that and see what happens to you'. Mothers who lay claim to a hot line to God present an unassailable blocking combination for the expanding child, and the introduction of the supernatural dimension as a weapon of control opens up the path to psychotic breakdown, in my experience.

False pretences may be seen most obviously in the sphere of sexuality. Apart from the downright lie — storks and all that — the lesser lie persists in the denial of the pleasure aspects of the sexual act. Another area of false pretence occurs when the parents pretend to a happy relationship (pseudo-mutuality) despite the evidence of the child's senses, who perceives a cold war as the true state of affairs. Nevertheless he has to gear up to the falsity.

Love is used quite blatantly as a means of control, and this accounts for its persecutory nature for some people. Paralysis is produced when a parent says, 'If you love me you wouldn't do that' or the variant, 'How could you let me down'. This manipulation of the tender feelings and appeals to the 'better nature' are difficult to resist, since the child needs vital supplies of love and approval, and so far as he is concerned the parents have cornered the market. Any mother has a monopoly of such supplies and is thus situationally omnipotent. There are no alternatives. Many a child would run away if there was somewhere to run to. Neither of the biological reactions of fight or flight are of the slightest use in such a pathological set-up. You can't win, you cannot escape and you cannot comment on the situation. In addition, you are expected to feel grateful.

The masochist has a deep distrust set in a profound matrix of injustice and resentment with potential reactive violence. In therapy, which is always difficult, he shows the typical negative therapeutic reaction, which is another way of stating that he is out to murder the therapy, if not the therapist. His good will has been destroyed and he will, out of revenge, destroy the good will of others. He invariably proceeds by putting the therapist in the wrong, which is simple revenge for having been placed in a similar situation, and everything which unfolds in the therapy is a question of doing unto others what has been done to him. If the therapist can withstand being forced into submission by extreme provocation and insult, and can tolerate the projected guilt and impotence, there is a chance that the deep suffering of blocked lovelessness will emerge which is the ultimate pain of the masochistic illness.

If a child is faced with the impossible situational dilemma of abandonment versus submission, the latter will be the 'choice'. This enforced submission will inevitably produce further resentment, and sooner or later the whole abortive rebellion is forced underground in the-process of internalisation. What can be done at five cannot be done at seventeen, in exactly the same way that the abortive 1905 revolt in Russia was savagely put down only to erupt again in 1917.

Each new human child is learning how problems are solved by 'the authorities', and these early imprints are not easily rubbed out, as every psychotherapist knows. There is no question of any polemics against parents, since they are equally victims of the general 'behavioural transmission' (Russells). Did not the biblical writer say, 'the fathers have eaten sour grapes and the childrens teeth are set on edge', a view which Reich strongly endorsed. It is to be hoped that ethological study will underwrite the study of the social process to complement the study of the individual and thus enable social criticism and sociological science to advance on a firm foundation, rather than by the hopelessly confused activity we call polictics.

The Clinical Problem

The majority of cases do not show overt beating behaviour in their sexual life, and in fact the whole character-structure may be masked. Beating phantasies are more usual, with the idea of

On the creation of a masochist

being physically bound or tied up as a condition for sexual release. Overt beating behaviour requires beating with studded belts to achieve orgasm — often indeed until the blood flows. The overall impression is that of a caricature of sexual functioning, and the thinly disguised spite and resentment may be discerned together with a profound contactlessness. Such a person cannot feel normally towards others, and more and more punitive stimulation has been required to bring about orgasm. They have, as it were, to be forced more and more as they feel less and less pleasure. They live out forced functioning in obedience to their training in early childhood, which means they have to find a partner who will supply this enforced activity which their characteristic way of being demands. It is a question of doing things the hard way, there is no spontaneous ease of functioning — it is not within their experience. There is an all-pervading 'bloody-mindedness' in their behavioural dealings with others, and the sadistic partner is required to take responsibility for the whole episode in the sense that the masochist has a great fear of assertiveness (active role) in any form.

The inner split of force versus force is reflected in the lack of will-power — the will is divided and the self is a battle ground between ego and superego (the concern of psychopathology). This conflictual state is re-projected into the social environment *from whence it came in the first place*, and where it readily finds resonance and validation, with others who are behaving likewise.

Reich laid down the essential features of the masochistic character as follows: 'Subjectively a chronic sense of suffering which appears objectively as a tendency to complain; chronic tendencies to self-damage and self-deprecation (moral masochism) and a compulsion to torture others which makes the subject suffer no less than the object. All masochistic characters show a specifically awkward atactic behaviour in their manner often so marked as to give the impression of mental deficiency.' (4).

The latter, as previously mentioned, is due to insults to the exploratory drive of intelligence, such as punishment for curiosity, e.g. 'don't ask questions', 'curiosity killed the cat', 'mind your own business', 'don't show off your knowledge here' —

the list is endless, plus the contradictory opposite injunctions: 'Why didn't you ask?', 'You never think,' 'You have always got your head in a book,' 'Why don't you use your initiative and common sense?' The process is continued at school, where lack of knowledge is a punishable offence and liable to lead to ridicule, which is greatly dreaded by sensitive children. It is only possible to have a viable teaching situation if one party wants to learn and the other teach, and yet learning is compulsory.

There is no doubt that A.S. Neill (5) has the right approach to education. Examinations are a special variety of forced functioning where the person has to sit down and make a concentrated effort against the clock — an echo of having been forced to sit on a pot as a child and produce 'results' regardless of biological time. In this connection we must not forget that suicide rates and breakdown are high among students.

The whole process of functioning against obstructions takes place in a learning context with the effect that the world is experienced in unvarying patterns of domination and submission — a pattern which achieves a stereotypic and automatic quality more reminiscent of the instinctual functioning of lower forms of life as illustrated by the Russells in their 'Human Behaviour'. Intelligent life could take a very different course were it not for the kind of mental castration described. Once a character pattern, i.e. an organised defence system, has been set up it is virtually impossible for people to act 'out of character'. The same old patterns are repeated again and again despite repeated failures and this is seen with particular monotony in the field of delinquency.

There are many masochistic characters in delinquency who live out their lives in running battles with 'the authorities'. The character who kicks a policeman where it hurts most, thereby provoking equal and opposite retaliation with interest, and then announces that this proves the police to be sadistic brutes, is a masochistic character. Violence begets violence, besides being unintelligent.

This brings us to the important matter of the individual and society between which there appears to be a logical discontinuity. In 1964 in a survey of delinquent adolescents, sixty-six in all, I found that there was an average of four gross traumata in the early life of each individual (6). They had been subject to severe stress — a kind of emotional car crash with multiple and sometimes irreversible injuries to emotional development in early life. The admixture of deprivation and the kind of suppressive injuries discussed in this paper make an especially bad combination in which the quantity of suppressed injustice demanding revenge is truly enormous.

If strong punitive authority is brought to bear on an individual, clinical experience indicates that the following reactions may occur:

1 The strong will defy.
2 The less strong will revert to indirect forms of expression.
3 The weak will break down.

Mixed reactions occur, and there is always the important mechanism of 'identification with the aggresssor'. The ultimate evil of this process is the Nazi concentration camp officer who is merely 'acting on orders'. Moral courage is the courage to question 'authority'. It is imperative for 'society' to be aware of the fact that by punitive measures it continues to manufacture the very problems it aims at solving.

It is the widening gap between the needs of the individual and the insane social process producing a complete logical discontinuity in the emotional field which causes so many difficulties. Man is a social, intelligent animal living in a social framework originally designed to deal with primordial fears. This is why he clings to it so tenaciously and I have tried to show that this social arrangement of dominance hierarchy cannot be the right medium for translating the biological process of living life, since it compresses too much energy, with the inevitable tendency toward internal violence, i.e. revolution; or by mass redirection of violence to foreign fields, international war — a phenomenon only possible to regimentable herds.

REFERENCES

1. W.M.S. and Claire Russell, *Human Behaviour: a New Approach.* Andre Deutsch, London, 1961
2. Gregory Bateson, et al., Towards a Theory of Schizophrenia. *Behavioural Science*, Vol. 1, No. 4, Oct. 1956
3. Harold Searles, *Collected Papers on Schizophrenia.* Hogarth Press, London, 1956
4. Wilhelm Reich, *Character Analysis.* Vision Press, London, 1950
5. A.S. Neill, *Summerhill.* Gollancz, London, 1962
6. F.H. Edwards, Aetiological Patterns in Delinquent Adolescents. *Psychotherapy and Psychosomatics,* 1965

Part Three

Emotional Expression and Therapeutic Contact

EMOTIONAL EXPRESSION AND
THERAPEUTIC CONTACT : INTRODUCTION

Reich was the first psychotherapist who moved beyond talking to the heads of his patients, and learned to read the language of their bodies. His work is the foundation for the many therapies which have sprung up in the last decade or so, in which analytic work and the acquiring of insight is complemented by work on breathing, muscular tension, and posture.

But Reich was no physiotherapist, or yoga teacher. His work on the body was rooted in his deep understanding of the flow of life through the organism, and the ways in which people's energies became bound up in their character-structures, the set patternings of mental attitudes and physical tensions by which they were often trapped and inhibited. Work in dissolving fixed character attitudes, led naturally to the release of more energy and to an enhanced sense of aliveness. Because he was dealing with nervous energy, often expressed through the vegetative nervous system, which governs the involuntary reactions — trembling, blushing, blood pressure and so on — Reich called his technique 'vegetotherapy'. When his work moved from Scandinavia to America some of the later therapists he trained moved into more direct body-work, involving heavy massage of tense muscles, and the focus on character became less important.

'Bio-energetics' has both restored and deepened the original focus on character in which it had begun, and extended and enriched the repertoire of ways of activating the energy by physical means. However, there are many strands of thought and styles of therapy that have developed on the basis of Reich's original insights, and the dialogue between these various schools is a healthy one that reflects a vigorous and rapidly developing therapeutic commitment.

No therapist working in the tradition of Reich works with the body alone. The language of the body and the language of words reinforce and nourish each other. Deep insight affects the flow of blood and the tonus of the tissues. Deep physical release of tension liberates repressed memories and generates new insight. The Reichian therapist works with the basic expressive language of the living organism. His basic tools are empathetic touch, the capacity for emotional contact, the ability to understand the subtle nuances of tension and relaxation, and the underlying rhythm of tissues. He seeks to create out of the bound energies of neurosis, a pulse of life which can help to form and sustain a whole person.

Bio-energetic Analysis: A Development of Reichian Therapy

by Alexander Lowen, M.D.

Director of the Institute of Bio-energetic Analysis, New York

Bio-energetic analysis is an extension and systematization of the body-mind concepts developed by Wilhelm Reich. The fundamental thesis underlying Reichian therapy is the functional identity of muscular armoring and character armoring or of an individual's bodily attitude and his ego structure. This concept of physical and psychological unity allows a therapist to diagnose personality disturbance from the expression and motility of the body. One can for example recognize an up-tight person from his bodily posture. This approach to the personality through the body is not new. Every person sees another as a body, that is, he has a picture of the other in which bodily form, movement and gesture convey significant information about the other. Reich, however, was the first to integrate this information into the analytic procedure.

A second basic Reichian concept relates the inhibition of emotional responsiveness to the restriction of respiration. As early as 1935 Reich had observed that resistance to the analytic process was manifested physically by an unconscious holding of the breath. When the patient was encouraged to breathe deeply, his resistance fell apart, resulting in a flood of repressed material together with its accompanying effect or feeling. This observation led Reich to the realization that emotional responsiveness is dependent on the respiratory function. By limiting his oxygen intake a person reduced the metabolic process of his body and effectively depresses his energy level. Banking the metabolic fires cools the passions of the body. Children seem to know that holding the breath cuts off painful feelings and suppresses threatening impulses.

Apart from its effect upon metabolism, limiting respiration also restricts the natural motility of the body. The respiratory movements flow like a wave over the body, moving upward in inspiration and downward in expiration. These movements which constitute the matrix for emotional expression are blocked by chronic muscular tensions mainly in the throat, chest, diaphragm and abdomen. The throat tension results from the inhibition of vocal expression. It constitutes an unconscious repression of impulses to cry, scream and shout. Chronic tensions in the chest wall are closely associated with muscular spasticities in the shoulder girdle which hold back the reaching out with the arms. Thoracic rigidity suppresses the feelings of longing for love which would seek expression in crying and and reaching out. These feelings are suppressed because repeated disappointments in childhood have made them too painful. Muscular tension or spasticity in any part of the body affects one's breathing, because breathing is a total body activity. A set jaw or a tight ass reduce the respiratory movements and restrict the respiratory intake.

Broadly speaking, it can be said that if these tensions are predominently in the superficial muscles of the body, the result is an overall rigidity that is both physical and psychological. When the main muscular tensions involve the deep and small muscles that surround the joints, the result is a flaccidity and fragmentation. These produce a loss of integrity on both the physical and psychological levels. Bio-energetic therapy aims to release the chronic muscular spasticities of the body and to restore, thereby, the natural motility and expressiveness of the organism.

The third basic tenet of Reichian therapy deals with the role of sexual fulfilment in regulating the energy economy of the body. Reich postulated that full orgastic gratification discharged all the excess energy of the organism and so left no energy available to support neurotic patterns of behavior. He recognized that this discharge fails to occur when energy is bound in chronic muscular tensions and that these must be eliminated if full orgasm is to be achieved. It was his belief that if an individual developed the capacity to discharge all his excess energy through orgasm, that is, if he became orgastically potent, this would guarantee his emotional health since there would be no energy available for neurotic attitudes. Orgastic potency thus became the goal of Reichian therapy and the criterion of emotional well-being.

These three concepts constitute the framework of Reich's character-analytic vegeto-therapy and they have become the foundation, with some important modifications, of bio-energetic analysis.

Reich however moved further afield in his pursuance of his interest in the energetic processes of life. He developed the concept of orgone energy which he called the special life energy. He did some work in cancer research where I believe he made important contributions. He investigated many physical phenomena in terms of his orgone energy theories. This development led him to change the name of his therapeutic approach to orgone therapy. Bio-energetic analysis proceeded in a different direction. It focused all its attention upon the bodily functions with the aim to integrate bodily processes and psychic phenomena in a more comprehensive way than Reich had done. The result is a deeper understanding of personality disturbances and the development of more effective techniques for treating these disturbances.

A good illustration of the effectiveness of bio-energetic techniques is the treatment of depression. Cinematic studies have shown that motility is markedly reduced in the depressed individual. Our observations clearly indicate that respiration is also severely limited in this disturbance. The effect of this reduction in the basic biological processes of the body is a decrease in emotional responsiveness. Ignoring for a moment whatever psychological factors are operative in this condition, the fact remains that any procedure that stimulates breathing and augments the body's motility must lift the person out of his depressed state. Using the special techniques of bio-energetic analysis it is often possible to produce a fairly quick temporary improvement in these basic functions. The result is often astonishing to the patient who had no idea that what he viewed as a mental disturbance was intimately and directly connected with the body's activities.

This immediate release from depression is only temporary since the dynamic factors that create a depressive tendency in the patient are still untouched. It can be anticipated, therefore, that depression will recur. Consequently I advise these patients that recurrence is probable. But having experienced the release they also know that continued work to improve the breathing and motility of the body will overcome the tendency to depression.

What is this tendency? I may surprise you when I say that depression occurs when an illusion that the patient entertained collapses. These illusions, which are just under the surface of consciousness, have the function of sustaining the spirit against an underlying feeling of despair. A child's mind cannot accept parental rejection and disapproval. It conceives the idea that the love which is not forthcoming could be earned by good behavior, success, achievements, intelligence, cuteness, etc. This leads to the illusion that if one could be different, everything might work out. The child rejects its own nature, its feelings and its way of being to fulfill an ego image which was imposed by the demands of its parents.

The tendency to depression is based on the rejection and denial of the self and the attempt to gain approval by being what someone else wants. No matter how much acclaim one gets for success or achievement, it is not an adequate substitute for love. Love accepts the other wholeheartedly without conditions or demands. The primary illusion is that one can earn this love. The illusion collapses when one senses that the goal is meaningless and the struggle was futile. Even without fully understanding what is happening, the individual gives up all effort and becomes depressed. Every depression indicates that a person has reached a position of 'what's the use.' It signifies a return to the original despair reinforced now by the failure of the conscious endeavor.

The sequence of despair, effort, failure and depression must be worked through psychologically so that a patient can gain an understanding of the vicious circle in which he is trapped. But I have found that this understanding is generally incapable of overcoming the depressive tendency without a reversal of the self-rejection and self-denial that powers this tendency. To achieve this reversal, one must remove a secondary illusion to the effect that one's attitudes are subject to ego control. Another aspect of this illusion equates the self with the mind and the ego image and ignores the body as the basis of one's being in the world. As we get older we realize that the ego is not master of the body. In our youth it had driven the body relentlessly in pursuit of its goals and now the tired body cannot go on. We are beset with illness and we have a premonition of death. We feel somehow that we missed the boat. The pleasure and joy of living escaped us. We feel helpless and, again, a feeling of 'what's the use' overwhelms us. We become depressed.

The person who lives in terms of his body does not get depressed. He knows that pleasure and joy depend on good body feelings and he is sufficiently in touch with his body to sense their absence and to take appropriate measures to restore them. He is aware of his bodily tensions and he knows that as long as they persist, they condition and determine his emotional responsiveness. Being in touch with the body means being in touch with reality, the basic reality of one's mode of existence. He has no illusions about himself or about life. He accepts his feelings as an expression of his personality and he has no difficulty in voicing them. When a person can return to this way of being, the depressive tendency is eliminated. He may be disappointed and feel sad about events of his life but he will not collaspe into depression.

Being in touch with one's body is the guiding principle of bio-energetic analysis. The more emotionally disturbed a person is the more out of touch is he with his body. Bio-energetic analysis attempts to bring a patient into contact with the fundamental relationships of his existence, his relationship to the gaseous environment in which he functions. The quality of contact between the feet and the ground determines how well grounded an individual is, whether his feet are firmly planted or whether he is 'up in the air', whether he stands on his own feet or is a dependent person needing the support of others. Most patients soon become aware that they do not feel that their feet are fully in contact with the ground. Some even say that they are standing on their knees. But not to know how one stands is equivalent to not knowing where one stands or to have no standing as a person.

Poor contact with the ground is caused by chronic muscular tensions in the feet, in the legs, in the pelvic girdle and throughout the rest of the body. High arches and narrow feet indicate a pulling away from the ground. Flat feet and collapsed arches signify an inability to move over the ground, or away from the ground. In addition to these tension areas one often finds chronic spasticities in the muscles of the legs and thighs, the calves, the hamstrings, adductors and others. Each of these chronic tensions reflects a limitation of movement and, by extension, represents a limitation of expression and of the self. Each has a history which must be elucidated psychologically if the tension is to be released.

The ground is always interpreted as a symbol for the mother. Ground equals earth equals mother is a basic concept of bio-energetic analysis. The way a person stands tells us much about his early relationship to his mother. The insecurity of that relationship becomes transferred to an insecurity in standing and becomes the basic insecurity of life.

The other major relationship is to the air and the quality of that relationship is reflected in one's breathing. The air or breath is equivalent to the spirit, it is the pneuma of ancient religions, a symbol of the divine power residing in God, the father figure. Breathing is an aggressive act in that inspiration is an active process. The body sucks in the air. The way one breathes manifests one's feeling about his right to get what he wants from life. In breathing we are identified with the male principle, the active or aggressive principle of life. This concept shows the broad base upon which bio-energetic analysis rests. With this concept it is possible in many cases to analyze a person's relationship to his own father.

There are several kinds of respiratory disturbance that relate to personality function. Two are important enough to describe in this presentation. In the schizoid and schizophrenic patient, for example, one quickly finds that the chest is depressed in the expiratory position. Breathing in is severely constricted as if the muscles of the chest walls, the diaphragm and the throat were partially paralyzed. Actually in these patients there is a partial paralysis of all automatic and involuntary functions of the body. This partial paralysis is related to a state of terror which is mainly unconscious in the schizoid patient but rises to consciousness in the schizophrenic. I have described these aspects of schizoid functioning in my book *The Betrayal of the Body*. In the neurotic, on the other hand, one finds that the chest is held in the inspiratory position. It is generally over-inflated and the patient has difficulty in breathing out fully. He holds on to the air as a security measure. Breathing out deeply often provokes a feeling of panic as if he would not be able to get more air. He holds in whereas the schizoid individual just holds on. In both cases working with the patient's breathing soon uncovers his basic anxieties and furthers the psychological working through of these anxieties.

This distinction between schizoid and neurotic breathing is not absolute. It is, in fact, no more absolute than the distinction between schizoid and neurotic behavior. What one can say is that a restricted inspiration denotes a schizoid tendency in the personality whereas restricted expiration denotes a neurotic tendency. And even this distinction is less important than the fact that the patient is not breathing freely and fully.

It is beyond the scope of this presentation to describe the bio-energetic techniques used to free the respiratory function from the chronic muscular tensions that restrict it. One of these techniques, however, merits some attention. It involves the use of the voice. The range and quality of sound production is a measure of personality. The word personality is derived from the expression per sona which means 'by sound'. By his sound you can recognize a person, and by the sounds he utters, you can know what a person is feeling. Persons who are inhibited in crying, shouting and screaming are restricted in their breathing by the tensions that block these expressions. Getting a patient to cry or to scream is one of the most effective ways of releasing the blocked emotion and freeing the respiratory function. Screaming can often be provoked by selective pressure on the anterior scalene muscles while the patient is making a sustained sound. The involuntary scream sends a flow of feeling through the body from the top of the head to the bottom of the feet and produces a total and unified body awareness.

Whatever the personality problem, it is reflected in a disturbance of the flow of feeling in the body. This flow of feeling is the basis of all emotional responses. If it is suppressed, the person's emotional responsiveness is flat. If it is fragmented, the emotional responses are conflicted and ambivalent. Only in the emotionally healthy person is the flow full, free, and rhythmical. Such a person is capable of expressing his feelings of love, anger, fear and sadness easily and with complete ego control. He has self-possession.

When the flow of feeling is blocked by chronic muscular tensions, self-possession is limited. It becomes important, then, to remove these tensions. To accomplish this three steps are involved. First the patient must become aware of the tension, that is, he must feel the tension and sense the impulse that is blocked from expression. For example, he must sense that his tight jaw holds back biting impulses, his tight shoulders hold back hitting and reaching impulses, etc. Every chronic muscular tension represents an inhibition from expressing certain feelings. The tension is the physical counterpart of the psychological inhibition. But tensions are not isolated phenomena. They are interrelated and all together they determine the characterological attitude of the individual. The patient must become aware of this attitude and understand its role in determining his behavior. This is what Reich called character-analysis.

Second, the patient must discover the origin and elucidate the history of the inhibition or tension. This is the analytic aspect of bio-energetic therapy. If this aspect is ignored, the patient remains unconnected with his past and the underlying conflict that produced the tension is never fully resolved. In this step, too, the focus is never limited to the individual tension. The 'why' of a particular tension is extended to include the 'why' of the whole character structure. The patient must see himself as a product of a unique historical development. When he gets the full picture into focus, the jigsaw puzzle of his life makes sense. These concepts are developed in my book, *The Physical Dynamics of Character Structure*.

Third, the blocked impulses must be released in appropriate

movements. Unless this occurs, the analysis remains sterile and no significant changes occur in the total personality. The term appropriate movements means also appropriate circumstances. Acting out the blocked impulses in social relationships is a destructive form of behavior. Whether one feels guilty about such behavior or not it negates the dignity and integrity of the self and the other. Bio-energetic therapy provides the means whereby these impulses can be expressed in the controlled setting of the therapeutic situation. Blocked anger can be released, for example, by pounding or kicking the bed. In this procedure there is no danger that the patient or anyone else will get hurt. In all the years of my practice I have never been hurt by a patient. The full range of emotion from the deepest longing to the most violent rage can be expressed in this way.

One advantage of working with these techniques is that the patient can do much to help himself. Gaining contact with the body is not a one-hour-a-week activity. Every waking moment and every movement provides the patient with an opportunity to increase his body awareness. The patient develops a feeling awareness of himself instead of the intellectual awareness that resulted from analyzing one's thoughts. In addition my patients do many of the therapeutic exercises at home thereby furthering their physical health at the same time that they promote their emotional well-being.

Among the many modifications which bio-energetic analysis made in Reichian therapy is the shift from orgastic potency to pleasure as the therapeutic goal. By pleasure I do not mean any momentary self-indulgence but the enjoyment of living. The aim of therapy is to help a patient gain the capacity for pleasure and joy. This is a broader aim than Reich formulated for it includes sexual pleasure and orgastic satisfaction. While the analysis of sexual conflicts is still a focal point of the therapeutic endeavors in bio-energetic analysis, this therapy avoids the preoccupation with sex that characterized the Reichian approach.

At the beginning of this presentation I mentioned the growing interest in the body and in immediate experience as the main features of the new psychotherapeutic approaches. The value of this focus is illustrated in the following short case-history of one session. The patient, a young woman of twenty-five, consultd me because of a severe depressive reaction that culminated in an attempt at suicide. She was released from a hospital for the consultation. After discussing her situation, I put her through some of the bio-energetic procedures designed to increase her breathing and motility and to promote the expression of feeling. At the end of the session her color was better, her eyes were more alive, and her body had more feeling. As she left she said to me, 'Dr Lowen, I came in feeling hopeless but I am leaving with a feeling of hope.'

In psychotherapy the approach to personality through the body also provides a new hope for the understanding and amelioration of problems that verbal techniques leave untouched. These are the character disorders such as the schizoid personality, the oral dependent personality, the masochistic personality, and the rigid, compulsive personality. Verbal techniques are relatively impotent to affect these personality problems because they are structured in the body. The schizoid personality, for example, is determined by the dissociation of the conscious mind from the body and based on a reduction of feeling in the body. Increasing bodily sensation and mobilizing body awareness are the immediate procedures which can overcome this mind-body dissociation. The oral dependent personality is determined by feelings of insecurity stemming from inadequate contact between the feet and the ground. Getting feelings into the legs and the feet overcomes the feeling of insecurity and reduces the dependency needs of this personality. Broadly speaking, the masochistic personality is determined by chronic muscular tensions that constrict the neck and pelvic outlets. The masochist can be considered a bottled-up individual one of whose main complaints is the fear of bursting. When these tensions are released the masochistic tendency to whine, complain and suffer diminishes. Rigid, compulsive types are characterized by rigid, tight bodies and the psychological rigidity is only softened when the body rigidity is relaxed. The interested reader is referred to Reich's and my books for a fuller analysis of these personality structures.

Being in touch with the body offers a new hope to individuals for meaningful existence in these confused times. Every value but one can be questioned today. The one value that is beyond question is bodily health. The person who is in touch with his body is aware of its tensions. He senses when his breathing is disturbed and he can do what is necessary to restore his bodily function to its optimum state. Thus he can take the responsibility for his emotional and physical well-being. The person who is out of touch with his body projects his problems onto others and seeks a solution to his personal difficulties in radical social change. The illusion that society can change without a prior change in the character-structure of its members was exposed by W. Reich in *The Mass Psychology of Fascism*. The inevitable collapse of this illusion will plunge the social radical into depression sooner or later.

Bio-energetic Concepts of Grounding

by Stanley Keleman, D.Ch.

Bio-energetic Therapist, Berkeley, California, Director of the Center for Energetic Studies, Berkeley, California

Stanley Keleman is a practitioner of the bio-energetic approach developed by Alexander Lowen. He has studied with Nina Bull, at the Neurological Institute, Columbia; at the Institute for Integration of Religion and Science, New York; at the Alfred Adler Institute for Individual Psychotherapy, New York; at the Dasein Analytical School of Psychotherapy in Zurich; with Karlfred Durckheim, at the Centre for Religious Studies in Germany, and with Dr. Ola Raknes, in Oslo. He has lectured and given courses on his work at hospitals, psychological associations, and growth centres in different parts of America, Canada, Mexico and Europe. He is the author of The Human Ground, Sexuality, Self and Survival, Living your Dying *and* Your Body Speaks Its Mind. *This paper first appeared in* Energy and Character, *Vol.1, No.3, September 1970.*

The primary ailment I am confronted with as a bio-energetic teacher is the split in my students' human processes. Almost universally, we have made a separation between what we call our selves and our bodily processes and feelings. We are like trees uprooted from the earth; we have lost our nourishment, support, and ability to grow. In my language, we are not grounded.

To me, grounding means being anchored in our physical-psychic growth processes; expanding, contracting (contact, withdrawal), charging, discharging. Grounding means being rooted in and partaking of the essence of the human animal function.

First I say that man is totally animal in his foundation, that we

have to learn to surrender to and accept that animal state. We
share our basic modes of life with the other animals and respond
in the same way that they do in our involuntary muscular and
nervous systems. Too often we try to deny our animal, the result
being grave psychological and physical disturbances in our
Being.

At the same time Man has the possibility of making a widening
choice in the life he leads; we háve a voluntary system that allows
us to take charge of our experiences and to create value
consciously. The premature birth and extended childhood of the
human infant create new dimensions of freedom and
experimentation in the human being. All of these attributes
combined produce the deepest difference between man and his
fellow animals: his possibility for a dynamic deepening feeling,
expression, movement and love, a capacity that allows us to
understand and experience in an ever deepening way the
meaning and joy of biological life.

The opposite of grounding is flight, or interference with our
human essence; its products (our common ailments) are fear,
rage, frustration and dissatisfaction. Separation from the
biological ground results in anguish and despair instead of the
great potential for vitality, love, contact and growth with which
we have been endowed.

In this paper I will relate some models of grounding and
interference that I have developed in the course of my work, in
the hope that by working together on these problems we can
increase the possibility for pleasure and growth in ourselves and
in future generations.

I

I have come to see the human animal as an energy system. In
bio-physical terms we are each like a huge energy chamber that
receives, transforms and discharges (externalizes or redistributes)
energy which we metabolize and convert into feelings, expression
and movement, in three ways. First there is an energy flow that is
always moving toward the earth and away from the head and
world. (The movement of energy toward the head has been
over-emphasized in our world.) Interference with this flow

produces anxiety and unsureness. Second, there is throughout the organism the build-up and discharge of tension, which can also be seen as expansion and contraction. Frustration, anger and despair are characteristics of interference with this function. Finally there is what I call the containing or revealing function, the phenomenon of growth in the lower center of the body. This is the sexual function, the way in which we develop another pole of our existence. Maturation by containment also occurs in the other poles (the chest and head), developing possibilities for feeling, and Being, revealed to us through time.

Grounding in terms of this bio-physical model means functioning on each of these primary levels; it means allowing energy to flow through the body in each of the three ways I have outlined. There is a relationship between the flow of energy and the physical structure of the body. We disturb the energy flow by creating muscular spasms, deep contractions that inhibit the normal flow of energy through the organism. Deep contractions of this kind disturb the whole (proprioceptive system) relationship to space and gravity; the ability to hold, transform and discharge vital substances from the environment is interfered with. And the person who is thus distorted naturally begins to have feelings of anger, despair, and frustration. Even the form of the organism determines flow direction.

When we examine the causes of these inhibiting contractions and their emotional results we reach the place where the psychological and energetic approaches to man come together. We can begin to see some of the causes and effects of separation from the biological ground.

II

For example, closely looking at some people you will notice that the head seems mature but the body seems immature, squashed together as if it has never unrolled, the legs tight and contracted. What does this mean and how did it happen? We know that the natural development of the child takes him from the flexing position to extension, a natural unrolling, which is a very deep and dynamic learning process. To be able to create extension in relationship to gravity becomes one of the most dramatic adventures of the growing child and provides him with a great enjoyment and pleasure. This takes place against an emotional background, the relationship to the parents; while tied emotionally to the parents, he learns to lower his center of gravity, gain his independence and his self-esteem.

But when I ask a student who has not unrolled properly to take a physical posture that represents 'standing on his own feet', that produces a temporary unrolling which usually evokes fear, anger, and insecurity. Like many of us, he will be strongly resisting that. Sooner or later the person reveals specific emotional conflicts in his early years. There may be an overly anxious mother who forces the child to stand on his own feet too early in his dynamic relationship to gravity; or conversely, perhaps a mother who is overly protective and instills fear in the child. Not only is a structural immaturity produced, but also a whole emotional tone of anxiety and unsureness that remains structured in the individual in later years. When you have the student loosen the contractions, you find the whole mother complex coming to the front.

On another much broader level you have the relationship of the person to the Great Mother principle, which is the connection to the background environment represented individually by every mother. Relationship to the ground has an unsteady background; relationship to our own instinctual alignment (which is the unconscious) will have a certain shakiness. We are never in a firm relationship to the mystery of life. All of this is structured physically; this is an interference with the energetic and emotional potential of the individual.

It becomes apparent that the Oedipal complex is an expression of a development actually physically structured in the body in the form of deep muscular spasms that interfere with the natural development of energetic flow.

III

When I speak of muscular contraction limiting the flow of energy, I am speaking of a deep, pervasive process. That is, I see every part of the body, including the organ systems, as functioning on the same principle of impulse formation, containment, transformation and expression of substances. Strong muscular contractions distort the bone structure development, tissue development, and even the chemical functioning of the body.

There are different chemical substances that are released according to the body's internal clock that enable us to develop structural configurations at the proper time. Inhibition of this timing produces an observable infantilism.

So I look for places in the structure with infantile traits meaning that the growth potential has been disturbed, indications of the separation from the developing ground and diminution of motility. The prevalence of infantilism in our culture is manifest; in the emotional realm it exists as the inability to maintain, develop and express appropriate feelings. The ability to respond emotionally, to develop deeper and deeper feelings and gain satisfaction, depends upon the state of tissue receptiveness and motility; muscular contractions may arrest and impede the maturation of our tissues.

Maturity, as seen in biological terms, is the ability of the tissue, the ability of the total organism, to be motile, take in, contain, transform and discharge energy and substance in an ever deepening manner. Biological maturity to me is defined in terms of how the tissue, how my body, how my being is able to maintain, express, and develop feeling. We have emphasized in the Western world a maturity of thinking and reasoning, a maturity of one end of the structure, while we allow the infantilization of our feeling side, a lopsidedness of too much knowledge with too little feeling.

Maturity from the perspective of stimulus-response is the ability to respond directly to the incoming impulse, to allow it to change us, to act without a distorted conditioned response that bears no relationship to the impulse. When somebody approaches me and I don't know what I am feeling, I must hold to see, follow stereotypes, etc. Maturity means being able to take him in and go out to him without a pre-conditioned response; I have an open receptive feeling in my responses. To be able to do this, again, depends upon a state of tissue development and motility. As a model we can look to the difference between a young tree and an old tree, a puppy and an older dog. There is a qualitative difference in the state of tissue as the tissue matures that needs to be deeply understood. In sexuality, it is the difference between frustration, anxiety, and inhibition on the one hand and deepening pleasure, satisfaction and growth on the other. You can have neither a deepening flow of the river nor direct response to stimuli unless you have the tissue to support them. Allowing development of the tissue is part of the organism's naturalness; it is disturbed by the formation of muscular contractions.

IV

Another expression of the biological ground is expansion and contraction, basically the way we get the sustenance of our biological existence. By this process we take in oxygen and expel carbon dioxide; we consume food and water and eliminate waste materials; the heart beats its two-fold rhythm of systole-diastole. Bio-physically, the human being builds up energy to a certain point and then expresses it; there is compression and tension. The orgastic release operates similarly, a building of energy followed by a focused release.

The muscular contractions and their attendant psychic content disturb the expansion and contraction function, lower the capacity for taking in and discharging substances. Many people, for example, inhibit the breathing apparatus. They may have puffed-out chests or hunched shoulders; or they impede the function of the diaphragm and restrict their ability to inhale and exhale. Some people have contraction in the digestive and elimination systems, and almost universally in our culture there is an inability to allow the build-up and energetic outpouring of body/love/sexual feelings.

Along with the physical diminishing of possibilities and actual distress that accompany inhibition of the expansion-contraction function are invariably, again, both a psychic discomfort and a psychic cause. Helping to open up the chest and tight diaphragm of a young man I worked with prompted expression of a deep and murderous rage; he had been unable to express his anger as a child and now could express neither anger nor tenderness directly. Even experiencing his own tender feelings was too much for him to bear and he attempted to dispel them with an outpouring of rage. He had kept all this locked in by inhibiting his chest, by actually diminishing the breath and depth of his Being.

A young woman I worked with had separated herself from her body ground by inspiring her chest and contracting the abdomen, buttocks and urethra. She experienced feelings of being withdrawn, out of contact. In the course of the work she revealed an inability to cry, to melt, to experience any deep satisfaction. Much of this was directly related to the prohibitions against strong emotional expression that had been placed upon her by her father: Daddy's good girl does not cry, or in any way indicate that she is unhappy, because Daddy does not have the emotional strength to deal with it directly and honestly. To stay in his favor she learns to physically suppress any strongly felt physical or emotional sensation.

As can be seen from just these two examples, interference with the contraction-expansion function produces a rigidity and diminishing of the individual that manifests itself in both physical structure and emotional expression.

V

Perhaps the most relevant and deeply felt dissatisfaction in our culture is the sexual, and also it is the most misunderstood. We are conditioned to put violence and sexuality together or we are conditioned to split sexuality and love or passivity and sex. Most of my students have arrested in one way or another the development of their sexual expression, are unable to understand or express their sexuality, and are confused and bewildered by questions of perversion, orgasm, or meaning in sexuality.

I have called this sexual expression the containing or revelation function. Containing, as I will explain in greater detail later, is the development of the ability to hold, allow, and be transformed by feelings. By living with and from our feelings, by allowing them to change us and growing with them, greater possibilities for love and expression are progressively revealed to us. I see the sexuality as an ongoing deepening process that dynamically increases our possibilities throughout an entire lifetime when allowed to. What I see happening in nature is that the whole phenomenon is linked to man's having greater sexual availability than there is possibility for having children. In contrast to the kind of licentiousness that only assumes a shallow 'fun' in this extra sexual availability, I see it linked to the human possibilities for greater integration, movement, feeling and love, which is contact.

We can see this in another perspective if we look at the biological development of the individual. After birth we begin to get movement downward; as the oral dependent needs are being taken care of, the arms become free and begin to explore the world; the legs kick and develop strength. As the child gets older there is a repolarization that takes place anatomically with an enriching of the blood supply in the lower part of the body that was not so rich at birth. He begins to have feelings from and control over areas of the body that were beyond him previously, such as the bladder and the anal sphincter. At first the lower abdominal structures, the genital structures, and the lower digestive structures do not have the rich blood supply; the first commitment of the organism is to the head, the mouth. Gradually the movement descends and is committed to the legs, genitals and bowels. Another pole is developing in the organism. Finally specific sexual functioning begins and continues to develop throughout the person's life.

The process continues to develop during sexual experience. The movement going downward and having expression (orgasm) in the pelvic world tells me that the energy moving down is helping to bring alive the layers, the segments of feeling that the person is actually building, a series of tubes from the inside out. As the energy is moving down, it is moving out, bringing more aliveness, more integration, more possibilities. It brings the head down, discharging the head and allowing the head to open for new possibilities to come in. There is movement toward more and more meaningful expression, taking in more oxygen, putting more roots, developing more and more feeling and more and more movement and independence.

It is important to emphasize that this development of an energy reservoir in the genitals and the intestines, an analogue to the energy of the head, is the natural development of sexuality that most of us are not used to and are afraid of. We have developed mental images of sexuality while denying the lower pole of our existence, and so have become afraid of and intimidated by our own feelings. We contain our energy in the head and are afraid to release it into our lower structures and in a very real way rigidify our being into mistaken ideas of what we are or should be. This becomes very clear in the case of students who, when the energy is pulled out of the head, when the energy flow is zooming down and is discharging the head, get pale and light in the face and experience dizziness or fear. For them it is concomitant to loss, the loss of some long-held, idealized image reinforced by repression of their lower pole.

As is the case with the other basic modes of expression, we inhibit the development of the sexual pole through muscular contractions that are linked to emotional contexts. For example, children are taught to function in the lower pole by contraction rather than by containment, to avoid rather than allow feelings and growth to take place. We teach them that anal and genital functions are 'dirty', pleasurable sensations 'evil'. Our toilet training and sexual preparation are commandments to withhold energy and feeling from anal and genital areas and children are taught not to trust their energetic feelings by forming contractions that prevent them.

Or we teach people how not to move with and express their feelings. There are people who have come to me who are able to develop beautiful feelings, but are unable to let the feelings flow to expression. They create a split between inside and outside and have settled for an incomplete, arrested existence. You will see many people who have an inability to express their good feelings, who have a rigid musculature, who cannot melt. There is an inability to discharge and consequently an inability to grow. One woman that I worked with recently, for example, reported that she cried silently and not very often. She had the appearance of a certain hardness and felt that when she allowed herself expression she was at the mercy of something else. She was afraid to allow herself to soften, to actively melt. She could not mobilize the legs and diaphragm or the pelvis to move with what she was feeling and was unable to experience, as a result, orgastic expression. She had been taught from early childhood how not to cry, how not to trust the expression of her most basic feelings.

As we grow older we are taught further distortions of the life process. We are taught to live in a sexual world of high level stimulation but no orgastic expression. Women are taught to tease, to stay in what I would call a clitoral state, and men are taught to live from what I would describe as an 'end of the penis' attitude. Both of these assume stimulation without growth, and external rather than internal feelings. They are characterized sexually by a splashing, sparkling tingling that is electrifying but does not involve the deepest structures of the person. Stimulations come from the outside in contrast to the deeper orgastic states in which there are feelings, movements and pulsations coming from the inside out. In a workshop I conducted recently there was a girl who came to the point where she was experiencing the pleasure inside her and this made her anxious. It was perfectly all right for her to have feelings from the outside, feelings that she was not a part of, but it was not all right to have feelings and pulsations and movements from the inside that she was responsible for. She had been conditioned to deal with outside events, but not her own. She had been taught to be anxious and ashamed of her own feelings, and this distrust caused a holding back, an inability to experience satisfying expression, a feeling of being gypped in life, and an underlying attitude of desperation.

On another level we have developed images and other advertisements of what to expect from sexuality, and these, combined with our frustration and longing, cause us to impose hard, wilful moving that screws everything up. It is another expression of our locked and contracted lower pole. You can't achieve the expression that is satisfying with wilfully shaking, violent, banging, pushing movements. There are in reality a statement of panic and conflict, an expression of 'I can't get through'. The result is incomplete experience, a feeling of lack of meaning, and dissatisfaction.

In the natural state the personality is involved. The movement is gentle and small in the beginning, the two pelvises moving and reacting. And then it becomes very intense and strong; there is a lot of movement finding its way to expression. It is not a hysterical thrashing thing but rather a simple soft penetrating. Bigger and deeper pulsations and penetrations develop until there is a peaking release. Expressing oneself is the key to allowing something new, for allowing old forms to dissipate and the emergence of deeper potentialities. The releasing mechanism is the key that allows you to experience the world in continually new ways. Satisfaction is not in a job well done; it is in experiencing something newly, deeply.

For the woman this releasing expression takes place in the uterus itself. In both the woman and the man, the movement has grown spontaneously and developed on its own. The body has in one sense directed itself, needing no direction from the head; they have both become involved in and moved with the flow of energy through their bodies. Afterwards, and the orgastic state can be best qualified by what happens after the event, the natural deep expression that I have described leaves a person with a deep feeling of satisfaction, pleasure and gratefulness. This is in strong contrast to the partial release of the thrashing, hysterical, or non-moving contracted experiences which promote the dissatisfaction that I have previously described.

It is this place where we have all the confusion about positions, roles and perversions. The natural development of sexuality allows, when the ego is open to what is happening, a fluctuation of roles and experiences. The one primary condition is to allow yourself to go to the final place, to allow yourself full involvement with your entire structure. You can begin to see the consequences of not involving the lower structures, of, in effect, making love with your head alone acting out some learned role. Men for example are taught to be strong heroes in the world, to hold back emotion, to change things rather than be changed by them. Generally they come to resent this, and experience the conflict of wanting to be loved on the one hand but being unable physically and emotionally, to be receptive or passive. Or many women are taught to be aggressive in the world and passive in bed, a conflict that is difficult to endure. They often end up in a castrating position or at war with the men they have chosen, or in some cases they revert their sexual energy to an adolescent role. The development of the lower pole, the ability to experience and discharge feelings and energy, allows the fulfilment of the various role needs between man and woman without rigidity and with growing depth and understanding. In a very real sense the function of sexuality is the creating of more possibilities, the ongoing development of feelings, expression, movement and Being.

What I am getting to is that sexuality does not simply mean genital interplay, it means the development and expression of the whole person in terms of his building ever deeper feelings and contact with his universe. A person moves through life doing whatever work he is doing — walking, washing dishes — and there is movement, creative fields backed by sexual feelings, internal feelings spreading outward. And you live from these feelings and express them with the person you are with. This is biologically how it works; that is the meaning of mature sexual feelings: that you have this back and forth relationship with your environment that builds, and makes more feelings from which you create the world; and you go out into it and express these feelings and begin to create anew. And out of this creating and discharging, involving the whole of your self, a deeper and fuller self continues to evolve greater and deeper possibilities of Being, loving and acting. This kind of life-style, this deepest biological truth of what we are, is never revealed. Rather we are taught to live in fear of our feelings and our expression of them; we are taught to cut off and to try to control the essence of what we are.

VI

In the previous sections of this paper I have tried, in describing each of the three modes of existence, to contrast unity and fragmentation, misery and pleasure, inhibition and expression as they are manifested in the body states and attitudes of my students. When the basic functions begin to be refounded, when movement through the system and pulsations begin to come, people experience a change in both their perceptions and their values. They report an increasing pleasure, satisfaction and meaning in life; they develop an ability to sustain that kind of excitement, an ability to allow it to happen, to allow it to develop a quality of aliveness that changes them and their relationship with the world. They begin to know love and Eros, the deep contact and outpouring experience of the Self and other that deepens the self, bringing it to an ever greater knowing and expressing of itself. This dynamic aliveness becomes the central value and mode of Being in the world for them; the central question in their lives becomes how do I develop and transmit this aliveness; this humanity, this love.

All of this comes in contrast to their former muscular rigidity that carried with it values such as: how can I be secure, or superior, or rule the world. Biological grounding in the ways I have talked about allows the development of a person who is an energetically alive, pleasurable, and loving body, and I think that it would be impossible for such a person to go to war, to make or create war, unless he was really threatened. It is impossible to think of this kind of person as killing or repressing others, not because he is spiritually developed in the traditional sense, but because he is humanly and tenderly alive.

The contrast of grounding and interference, as it has been developed here, implies to me choice in the ways we look at the world, live our lives and raise our children. At present we teach our children how to hold back and contract rather than to contain and hold. We teach by discipline, punishment and creating spasms rather than holding and containing and growing with. One model of education is the creating of spasms, which I hope one day you will all outgrow, and the other is real growth phenomena based on the growth potential and the ability to expand.

In our lives, the question is not for me whether I'm over my Oedipal situation, but whether or not it is working for me or against me. As my childhood attachments and inhibitions become more and more conscious, they release more and more feeling for me; as I take from the past and give to my present situation I become more and more free. And all the feeling that's been locked in or not allowed to develop, trapped inside because of contractions and distortions, is a reservoir of energy which when released gives me greater and greater possibilities for feeling and loving (contact).

For me, the dynamic deepening of love, the potential for deepening of affection, tenderness and Being is the principal difference between Man and the other animals. I share with the French Jesuit Teilhard de Chardin the belief that this deepening and developing of love is man's uniqueness and responsibility in the Universe. I hope that all of us can begin to work together toward our ground and reap the rewards promised to us by virtue of our living.

Notes on Gounding

The essence of our work is to remove the blocks to our split-off parts and help us to deepen our contact with ourselves and the world, and to learn how to live with our heightened aliveness.

The function of the blocks is to decrease our energetic availability, and expression and to force it into 'socially acceptable' pathways of these times, e.g. cerebral aliveness over bodily aliveness; love as a doing, concerning concept, rather than a sexual bodily contact. The function of the blocks on this level is to be constricting to the available energy.

Strange as it may seem, the most serious problem does not turn out to be to bring more aliveness to people, but to educate them to deal with the aliveness they have. It makes no sense to increase aliveness if it cannot be tolerated or lived with.

A person has three levels: (1) peripheral, (2) middle layer, (3) core; a block can exist on these levels.

The outer layer is the social layer: the roles and the attitudes we adopt, the limitations or scope of movements we allow ourselves, the feelings we permit ourselves, and the ideas we have. This level is in conflict with what we are actually doing with our bodies, and our thoughts.

For example, if you tell a person who has grandiose ideas about himself that his chest is inflated, he does not feel it, especially since he cannot deflate it or let it relax.

So this first layer is really a layer of pseudo-contact, or really contactless-ness; it prevents contact with the inner and outer worlds.

This layer involves the muscular system (the organ systems and brain), inhibits the breathing (all blocks must affect the breathing) and is an intimate part of the role-playing system.

The second layer contains all the so-called and real anti-social impulses: the blocked anger, rage, fear, sadness, crying, sexual, sucking, touching, looking impulses (defiance, stubbornness, etc.) and the inhibited impulses of who we are. The second layer contains the converted primal energetic impulses like touching, loving, sucking, and the rage component. This is the area most folks are afraid of, they think. Actually it is the core one is afraid of. This second layer will involve deep muscular patterns and vegetative organs and nerves. It is a distortion of the innate capacity of the organism to hold, or rather contain impulses and feelings for proper discharge; or better still expression. We must use all kinds of tricks to learn to hold, hold back; the whole organism participates, muscles as well as brains, guts, etc. We hold with contraction and fear, instead of containing the expansion and pleasure. This containing function, instead of being used for proper assimilation in expression, is used in the service of repression.

(I may add here a note that discharge is not the goal, expression is; consciousness is not the goal, expression is; to know is not the goal, to be is.)

Expression has as its opposite not repression but impression, to prevent the natural inner flow, or impression to find expression.

The third layer is the core, that dynamic pattern of life forces, with its constancy and change that is reflected in deep feelings of aliveness, or peace, or at-homeness, or a knowing, without overstressed cognition, of a contact we call love, a force that moves us and gives us a feeling of connection with the cosmic world, social world, and natural world. This layer that most of us yearn for frightens us until we learn to bear pleasure and recapture our true identities, not our false ones, where we can allow ourselves this flow and expression which at one and the same time allows contact and individuality.

One of the truly remarkable things about us humans is our gift of ever-increasing range of movements, both gross and minute, which allows us novelty of expression. We have this over all

Bio-energetic concepts of grounding

animals, and we have three organ-systems to live this: the core; the container; the muscular system.

The body can be symbolically as well as expressively divided to look at these areas:

Head and pelvis:	organs of reality, containment and expression
Torso (core):	organs of core and containment
Arms, legs (which are connected to the head, pelvis and trunk):	organs of expression and contact, grounding.

In these areas we can look for the expressive quality of aliveness. For example, legs that withdraw instead of support; arms that clutch instead of reach and explore; a flat belly, tight and hard, instead of soft, containing, vulnerable, impressionable. In short, these characteristics of weakness, or overdeveloped strength (weak muscles, over-rigid muscles, weak eyes, an over-determined jaw). When we look at the breathing, we may see it is only in the lower half of the body, or restricted in the chest. This may indicate either an overcharged sex life or feeling life, and a weak social function; or in the reverse situation, breathing may be overdeveloped in the chest, and we may have an overdeveloped social function and underdeveloped instinct. Both these disturbances talk about difficulty in loving and having pleasure.

We can in psychological language look at it so:

Schizoid	*Compulsive*	*Phallic*
Fragmented and over-stiff	Over-riding, over-stiff, not fragmented	Over-hard, over-rigid, no softness, energetic
Oral	*Masochistic*	*Hysteric*
Weak, under-developed	Muscle-bound, oppressed, constricted	Over-hard, rigid, little softness, too much or too little form

Breathing is the same way:

Diminished breathing, repressed breathing equals a low energy level, deep holding, little expression and aliveness.

Over-excited breathing equals no containment and shows one to be over-reactive and impulsive.

The freeing of breathing is not understood by most people, for it means full uninhibited breathing, which is concomitant to full emotional expression. If the diaphragm is prevented from fully crying, or anger expression, etc., there will be a blockade to the full movement. The swinging of the diaphragm builds sensations and feeling; if these cannot be tolerated there will also be a block.

A block can be seen in another way:

Too much form (expressive muscular rigidity) corresponds to a personality that is over-rigid, compulsive, egoistic, with no ability to let down, that must leave no empty spaces or empty feelings, and is governed by a power drive, with too little feelings, and little pleasures. Too little form (underdeveloped muscular expression) equals a weak, fragile ego that cannot contain but collapses, is impulsive and overwhelmed by feeling, that can swim in the global feeling of pleasure, but with no experience of individuality.

A well-balanced person has form that he or she can surrender and is always swinging between form and formless-ness; or better still, between creating form and giving form up. That is: always growing, finding new ways to express oneself.

In this work we seek to establish contact with the core, and between the core and the whole self; a flow of expansion-containment, expression-contact-withdrawal. (To do this we use an active technique* that mobilizes the breathing and the expressive organs of the body.)

This is seen most clearly in the flow of the breathing: to take in, to assimilate or pause, to exhale, to express. The flow of life is not to discharge, it is to express and impress you on the world (you reaching out), as much as to let the world express itself and impress us. In this dynamic process we are and become ourselves. We are grounded in ourselves, in our bodies. We are grounded as bodies in our parent body, the earth. We are our bodies; to the degree we are, we are grounded.

---

*See Alexander Lowen, *Betrayal of the Body*.

BIBLIOGRAPHY

Wilhelm Reich, M.D., *Character-Analysis*, 3rd edition.
Alexander Lowen, M.D., *Betrayal of the Body.*
Caron Kent, Ph.D., *Man's Hidden Potential.*
Karlfried Durkheim, *des Durchbruch zu Wesen.*

A Developmental View of Bioenergetic Therapy

by Robert A. Lewis, M.D.

Robert Lewis is a practising child and adult psychiatrist in New York. His personal background and training over the past ten years has been simultaneous exposure to bioenergetics and analytically-oriented, developmental psychiatry. This paper is, therefore, the first part of a statement of his personal attempt to integrate ego psychological developmental thinking and bioenergetics. It appeared in Energy and Character, *Vol.5, No.3, September 1974.*

I   Theoretical

Bioenergetic Analysis has always been an inherently developmental way of understanding life: the more literal and explicit this can be made, the deeper the understanding and sharper our clinical focus will be.

Reich's insights have had a profound influence on the principles which underlie Bioenergetic Analysis (1). Two examples of such Reichian concepts are (a) the unity and antithesis of all living processes, and (b) unity is an organismic phenomenon, i.e. no matter how complicated any living organism is, it functions on the organismic level as a single cell.

Until recently, perhaps partly in reaction to the unbalanced, dissociated preoccupation of ego psychology on psychic reality, many of us working in the Reichian tradition have seen the principle of self-regulation as referring to the core of the organism, its deepest pulsations, instincts, feelings (figure 1).

From this view, the tendency is to see ego functions (motility, motor co-ordination, perception, self-expression) negatively, i.e. in terms of their defensive, adaptive function: the word adaptive is seen as implying an adjustment to reality which diminishes the

A developmental view of bioenergetic therapy

Figure 1

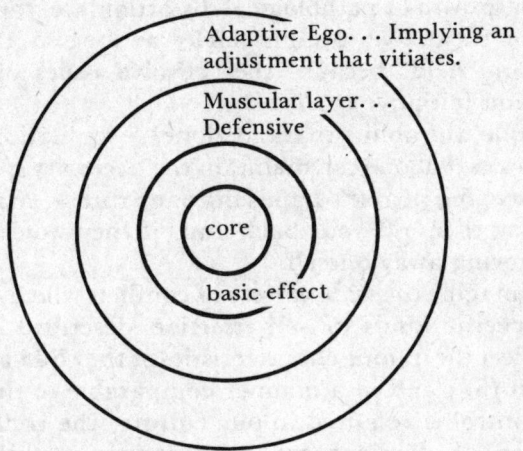

vitality of the organism.

It is true that the principle of polarity (2,3) transcends this conflict of antithetical functions such as body and ego, feeling and thought, etc. *But somehow, in practice*, until recently, we have not explored adequately the ego functions which enable the originally helpless infant to assume a vertical position, and become a self-supporting organism whose core impulses surface with definition and clarity. This more recent emphasis on being able to interact effectively with the environment in accord with the reality principle is stated clearly by Dr. Lowen, 'a strong ego depends on the ability to see clearly (perceive, imagine and conceptualize) and to express oneself adequately and appropriately in verbal and motor activity'(4).

So we are referring not to psychosexual development, but to ego functions such as motor co-ordination; functions which ego psychologists call autonomous (5). Emerging motor co-ordination enables a child to begin to control its movements, to execute its desire to reach for something, or move with enough predictability, that it can experience itself as an effective self with continuity in time and space. The child reaches, grasps, stands, walks; like sucking and anal sphincter control, these areas of development are subject to their own stresses, vicissitudes, nuclear conflicts, and potential for growth or pathological distortion, i.e. they don't just take care of themselves automatically as long as the child is nourished and held, because they involve issues of emerging autonomy and initiative (6, 7).

For example, the ability to stand alone — in relation to others, already assumes that one can maintain the necessary space around oneself by keeping people's hands off one's throat, making elbow room, getting them off your back and, if they won't keep their distance, moving away oneself.

One can imagine the wide variety of conflicts which often result from the specific kinds of self-assertion described above; the conflicts reflect the unique characteristics of the child and its early environment (6) ; and in a manner comparable to the way anal sphincter control is acquired in our culture, the conflicts range along a line of development of autonomy, which can be accelerated, delayed, or otherwise interfered with. The conflicts leave a story structured into holding patterns in the neck and shoulder girdle, and in degrees of falling anxiety; they result in *people who show degrees of being able to stand alone*. A simple clinical example is a thirty-year-old patient, loathe to feel her legs, which she sprawled akimbo, whenever deep infantile sobbing occurred. Told to stay on her flexed legs while sobbing, she suddenly looked stunned, and sensed her terror and anger 'about taking a step forward ... I'd be separated from mother ... I won't ... she would only accept me as a helpless baby.'

There is, in other words, a biological urge to stand and walk, just as there is to suck. It may be developed prematurely to compensate for oral deprivation; it may be delayed and denied in the face of threatened rejection (i.e. the above patient); it may be partially immobilized by its use as a chronic survival mechanism, i.e. legs held in reserve for escape from threatened oedipal seduction. As the child follows its innate motor urge to stand and move away, it may experience *degrees* of rejection, denial of warmth and support from parents, in relation to a function that is at first tenuous and takes *years* to fully develop. It is, therefore, clearly unrealistic to expect some patients to relate to, and integrate the feeling of standing on their feet: they have lost too much ground in the process of growing up, and should be able (figure 2) to rock back and forth on the ball of the foot (almost all the weight on the forward leg and foot) until they can feel their ankles and feet ... and *begin to find their footing*: the hands touch lightly to lend the balance that people don't have enough of in the lower extremities.

Figure 2

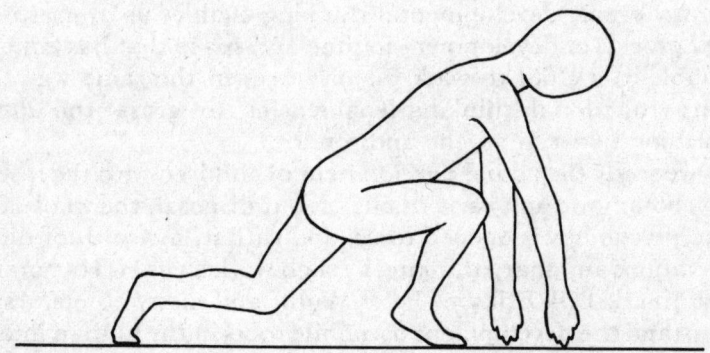

In this position, one can feel the ground as the source from which one springs. It can be followed by the rising movement which Dr. Lowen describes (8), but it is the developmental understanding that is more important than any specific technique.

To digress briefly, and yet illustrate my emphasis on epigenetic, autonomous development with biological and phylogenetic analogies:

(a) For the growth of a tree, the initial nourishment and matrix in the ground is necessary, but not sufficient: the tree needs space and light in which to flourish; similarly, the child's initial nourishment and matrix in the mother's body is also necessary, but not sufficient: it needs space — to move away — elbow room — ultimately to go its own way. (b) In primates, upper extremities, lower extremities, and tail *are each used* to grasp, to support, and for locomotion. Human infants initially grasp with their mouths, then wrap their legs around you (hugging) while being carried on the hip. Later, while crawing and standing up, they use their arms for locomotion and support. While the functions and their organs of execution have become highly specialized in the adult human, *the older, fused function is still an underlying reality*, i.e. the quality of one's footing is related to the ability to hold or grasp the ground with one's foot, *almost as if it were a hand*. Conversely, one has no footing if one can't hold the ground, and without solid footing, one can neither support nor move one's self.

In any event, developmental thinking enables us to grasp the *literal* process of development in time and space that has gone on to enable to a child to walk for instance, in the same way that Reich's functional thinking enabled us to grasp the *literal* connection between psyche and soma.

As we study the actual development of children with the insight of psychosomatic unity and duality at our disposal, the whole area of ego psychology is opened to us; and with it, a wealth of direct observations and sharp thinking by such workers as H. Hartmann, Anna Freud, Erik Erikson, Peter Wolff, and many others. As we understand the development of mobile roots in the human infant, the functions of the lower extremities become *finding* one's footing rising from one's roots, getting on one's feet, standing alone, walking away.

II Clinical

Spiral of Growth

The organism pulses from its core — out into the world — moment by moment. This movement also occurs as a process (spiral, schematically) of growth in time (figure 3) — over months and years — during which there is a change in the organism's basic orientation in space, in relation to the earth: from totally dependent to relatively independent.

Figure 3

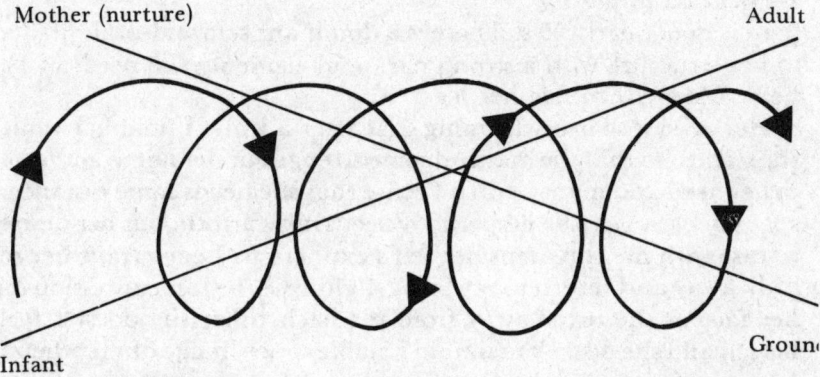

In both ontogeny and philogeny there is a long evolutionary process from floating in a liquid-filled womb, to being held and warmed at the mother's breast and body, to crawling the earth as a quadruped, and, finally, to standing erect as homo sapiens: the dependent infant and the erect adult are extreme points on a continuum that has a whole range of *normal* intermediate stages: during the first two years of its life every infant struggles to sit up, crawls on all fours, pulls itself upright with its arms, walks with help, and finally begins to take tentative steps on its own as balance, co-ordination and strength evolve. A profound change occurs in its experience of itself as upright in space vis-à-vis gravity.

We will broaden our diagnostic and therapeutic effectiveness if we understand this process as we help a patient to literally regain the feeling that he can walk on the earth, that the ground is under him. It is normal in the child's development to use its upper extremities as supplemental support until its legs offer secure enough support. In this process, the infant constantly falls and rises a little higher each time.

It has been my experience that as I work back and forth with a patient from bed to the standing positions, sensations, needs, experiences, and expressive movements *spontaneously* arise which seem to relate to these early stages of development.

Clinical Example 1
Joan is in her early 20's. There is a dominant schizoid-oral quality to her structure with a strong paranoid element. She needs to be held, warmed, to feel her legs.

Her need is so overwhelming that after a while I hold her while she stands (so that she may feel some strength under her in addition to her need and my support): I sense that she needs some distance, space between us; she desperately needs my warmth, but her desire to fuse with me threatens her self's extinction. I encourage her to walk away and return to my arms: I glimpse the lost expression on her face as she turns away from me each time; she doesn't feel herself and she doesn't maintain a stable inner image of me when I am out of sight — the first fifteen and last ten minutes of our sessions (return and separation) are traumatic for Joan: one can feel her charge contract into the inner core.

Joan has a deep disturbance; but some of her vulnerability has been highlighted in a process which *we all go through normally*, and which she must be helped to re-experience, perhaps step-by-step, constructively this time: the process, extensively described by M. Mahler (9) and others in the analytic literature, occurs (concomittantly with the motor development I've described in the first two years of life) intensively for the first three years of life and, derivatively, for more than any of us would care to admit: it begins as a state ('symbiosis') in which the infant's gradually emerging sense of self is first fused with the nurturing figure, and continues ('separation-individuation') as the infant slowly begins to experience itself as a separate self. The infant, for instance, will crawl farther and farther from the mother, tolerating the physical separation, but turning its head and taking mother in visually, and then will crawl into another room, out of sight, but within earshot of mother's voice, now holding onto mother and taking her in only via the distance receptor — hearing.

It is true that Joan experienced profound deprivation of her oral-erotic needs, and may have been so stunned or shocked that she has very little sense of self: to the extent that she regains contact and trust in her body and life, she will, in some way, go through a process of climbing onto her feet and practicing the distancing and rapprochement with her therapist (taking in his energy and faith) until she feels enough self to be alone. A valuable dimension is gained if such a patient feels her legs (some strength) under her at the same time that she practices separating and rapproching, just as the infant practices separating on the way towards its individuation.

This is particularly true of a patient whose underlying sense of identity is weak enough that too much regression fostered by the helpless position on the bed may be too threatening to their tentative sense of separateness: the loss of ego boundaries and fusion with the mothering figure needs to be balanced with later positions in development if the patient is to leave the session having had a constructive experience.

Clinical Example 2
Mike — in his early 20's — borderline schizophrenic — comes into therapy in a state of collapse — work, pleasure function, relationships are practically non-existent.

Mike will not stand on his legs to do bioenergetic work for the first few months; rather, as I gently encourage his right to be, he spontaneously twists into bizarre infantile positions on the bed, spits, emits infantile sounds. Then, tentatively, he stands on his legs — grounding begins — he extends his arms and asks me to hold his hands — I find that he has given me a good portion of his weight and is half hanging on me: his communication comes through vividly: 'I'll try to stand — give me two helping hands — I never had two parental supports under me'.

Mike's movements and positions on the bed and floor serve several functions: in part, they release blocked, spastic muscles, in part, they are mouthing, rocking and the exploring of extremities seen in infants in the first six months of life as the early body coalesces. This patient may never learn to just be, to come into the world, if his getting to know his body is not understood and accepted.

Clinical Example 3
Jane, a less disturbed patient, around thirty years old, standing on her legs, reached out and took my hand: she felt and said the following, 'I've never felt that in my hands before; I felt my legs and backbone for the first time — so I felt I really took your hand actively in mine': the arms have the natural functions of reaching, taking, giving: you cannot reach, take, or give if you do not have (feel) the ground under you — you can only clutch, grab or shove. This patient immediately sensed and integrated the fact that when she reached out with feeling legs and backbone under her, it was a responsible act; she also sensed her usual state of reaching out (clutching) from an unfeeling base and falling on her face.

In other words, in a standing adult position the *interrelationship* of functions (i.e. dependence, independence) becomes apparent *as they occur in life*, in *interpersonal situations*, and heightens the dynamic understanding of and working with bioenergetic concepts.

A person stands before you as a developmental unity: how much did he ripen on the vine? How strong are his roots now? In one moment in time, he can actively experience what was a *real developmental sequence* in his past, taking many years.

This last patient re-emphasizes an important point that was stated earlier: it is not only people with weak egos and low energy levels that have given up ground in the process of becoming civilized. There are a variety of issues in a child's development during the resolution of which a parent may damage a child's initiative, other than when it first reaches out for pleasure: it may be when he first starts to move away, wants elbow room, wants them off his back, i.e. whatever action a child takes that no longer permits the mother to relate to the child as a continuation of her own narcissistic self.

To mention a few of the endless ramifications: a) correlations regarding a person's sense of balance, alternatives, ability to step aside or to make a stand when appropriate. b) The fact, for instance, that if a person's shoulder girdle is partially immobilized in the unnatural service of support and locomotion, they can't *really reach with joy* when leaping, because the lift is coming from the shoulders instead of the spring in the legs. c) Dr. Lowen has extended this approach by having the patient reach out to him and then pulling away so that the patient falls flat on his face (the mattress): the whole past experience around being held, abandoned, has been given current expression.

An important note of caution! These are not maneuvers; *they are a developmental focus on a process of growth within a character-analytic framework*. It takes sensitivity on the part of the therapist to see that these are experiences *felt in the body* — not pieces of behavior dominated by imagery; it is not so much that you do something as a therapist, but that your feeling understanding (in your own tissues) of your legs under you and the longing and reaching in your chest and arms, will create the conditions under which the patient can have the experience and integrate it; your appreciation as a therapist, of whether a conscious voluntary movement in a part of the body is based on that part feeling warm, streaming, vibrant, or is merely that conscious movement in a cold, unfeeling limb, will prevent acting out behavior.

III Discussion and Summary

When we read theoretical, clinical and research work in ego psychology, we are left unsatisfied by its inability to reach the level of unity in the mind-body duality, to have the working ability to look from two points of view all the time. While it is intelligent, its view from the top causes it to miss the heart of the matter, and to become technical, mechanistic, and even shallow.

In spite of this, however, there is in ego psychology a great deal of research, clinical observation and careful thinking done by gifted people over decades, that we can use to enrich our understanding.

There is a long evolution between the infant's first reaching out to the world with its mouth, held in its mother's arms, and the adult capable of maintaining, even under the best of conditions, a grounded pulsating state of function anchored at genital and ego levels. It takes a long time before we can stand alone. Erikson feels that standing up, per se, leaves a child, and later an adult, under stress, vulnerable to feelings of smallness and shame: smallness, because it takes measure of itself in the vertical dimension; shame, because it now has a front and a back — especially a behind which 'cannot be seen by the child and yet can be dominated by the will of others'(7).

Whether this last point is cultural artifact or not, it stems from the kind of developmental thinking that raises good questions.

It is a well-established principle in biology that later, more complex forms and functions are more vulnerable than their earlier, simpler counterparts: the later, more highly evolved function is lost first under stress. Standing erect is a function acquired relatively late in the development both of the species and of an individual possessing consciousness ... doesn't that very consciousness threaten us with the possible loss of the standing, an *inherently* vulnerable function, no matter how perfect the child-rearing, and how vital the organism that comes out of the womb? In Western culture today, when the child stands vertically, doesn't the inherently comparative, and therefore, on some level, competetive nature of the parent-child relationship, become a visibly apparent theme? Even if more questions are raised than answered by such considerations, they may leave us with a healthy degree of uncertainty in working with people's problems.

We sometimes overemphasize the pathologic aspect of *positions that fall inbetween* the dependent infant and the more independent adult, because in our patients they are neurotic fixations or arrests in a line of development, now inappropriately structured into an adult. This does not mean, however, that these early maturational stages weren't as necessary in the normal development of the child as its oral-anal-genital evolution. The organism's grasp and exploration of the world begins with the mouth at the breast; the eyes and hands become extensions of the mouth as they grasp and explore the breast (world). Later, now grasping and exploring with its feet, the individual walks the earth.

REFERENCES

1. Lowen, Alexander: What is Bioenergetic Analysis? *Energy and Character*, Vol. 2, No. 3
2. Lowen, Alexander: *Pleasure*. New York, Coward-McCann and Geoghegan Inc., 1970
3. Lowen, Alexander: *Depression and the Body*. New York, Coward-McCann and Geoghegan Inc., 1972
4. *Training Manual in Bioenergetic Analysis*. New York, the Institute for Bioenergetic Analysis, 1973
5. Hartmann, Heinz: The Mutual Influences in the Development of Ego and Id, *Psychoanalytic Study of the Child*, Vol. VII, 1952
6. Sander, Louis: Issues in Early Mother-Child Interactions, *Journal of the American Academy of Child Psychiatry*, January, 1962
7. Erikson, Erik: *Childhood and Society*. New York, W.W. Norton and Company, 1950
8. Mahler, Margaret: *On Human Symbiosis and the Vicissitudes of Individuation*. New York, Int. Universities Press Inc., 1968

The Role of Affect Expression and Defense in the Character

by Carl Kirsch, M.D.

Carl Kirsch is a leading training analyst at the Institute of Bio-energetic Analysis, in New York, where he also has a private practice as a bio-energetic therapist. He has led numerous professional training workshops, and is Director of the Energy Research Group in New York. This paper first appeared in Vol.4, No.1, of *Energy and Character*, in January 1973.

This paper represents a preliminary theoretical approach to the problems of the personality considered from the point of view of affect expression and defense. It attempts to integrate this approach into the basic characterology utilized in bio-energetics. Following the introduction, the general concepts of character will be reviewed. Then the problem of affect in terms of expression, defense and placement in the personality will be discussed. The specific character types will then be integrated into this schema and a therapeutic approach utilizing affects considered. A future paper will present case studies from this point of view. Finally, I would like to thank Dr. Alexander Lowen for generously providing inspirational and critical help in developing these ideas.

Introduction

In bio-energetic therapy the concept of the character structure of the patient is continually emphasized. There are many reasons for this. Reich (1) showed that character was synonymous with the resistance and that without understanding the character, one would be unable to meet the resistances that occurred in treatment. Thus in order to modify the personality, the character, which is egosyntonic, must be analyzed so that it can become egodystonic. Treatment of symptoms also requires an understanding of character. If one works simply on the symptom level without understanding the basic character of the patient, and how the symptoms are generated by this character to maintain homeostatis, the treatment plan will be inadequate. The diagnosis and dynamics of specific character types has been discussed in detail by Reich (1) and Lowen (2). Few people are pure types, however, and it is the unique combination of these types that makes the character structure or personality of the individual.

Bio-energetically, we can look at the therapeutic problem the individual presents in at least four ways:

1 Physical Aspects of Character-Structure
   The form and motility of the body tell the therapist what problems are present in terms of drive and discharge, energy flow, and the stages of psychosexual development.

2 Interpersonal Relations and Adaptive Functioning
   The presenting complaints, the history, the present-day situation and the transference, further delineate the character structure and the ego's defensive solutions to the basic conflicts.

3 Specific Problems Within the Character-Structure
   In addition to the character-structure which is made up of various combinations of character types, the individual can have specific problems that are central to his personality. Some of these that have been written about by Lowen (3) are the clown, the doll, the demon and the monster. There are others including the problem of horror and the fear of death or insanity. These areas need further exploration.

4 Affect Expression and Defense
   Each personality struggles with five basic affects which press for expression and are defended against by the ego and the body. This struggle in turn modifies the individual's relationship to the environment. This will be further explored in this paper.

Characterology

Analytically, character can be defined as (4) 'that aspect of personality (the image of the person and his ways of reacting perceived by others) which reflect the individual's habitual modes of bringing into harmony his own inner needs and the demands of the external world. It is a constellation of relatively stable and constant ways of reconciling conflicts between the various parts of the psychic apparatus to achieve adjustment in relation to the environment. Character therefore has a permanent quality that affects the degree and manner of drive discharge, defenses, affects, specific object relationships, and adaptive functioning in general'. Ego psychology considers both neurotic symptoms and character traits as compromises between instinctual impulses seeking discharge and the defensive system. The major difference is that symptoms are egodystonic whereas the character traits are egosyntonic. Freud (5) stated that 'The permanent character traits are either interchanging perpetuations of original impulses, sublimations of them, or reaction formations against them'. This statement shows that character attitudes or traits are never free of conflicts and even though some attitudes or traits may not be defensive, they represent ways of compromise within the psychic and somatic defensive structure of the individual.

Is there a healthy character-structure and are there healthy character traits? Fenichel (6) stated that some character traits are of the sublimation type and represent successful solutions of the instinctual conflict. The genital character who could bind anxiety by genital orgastic gratification and sublimation was considered healthy by Reich (1). Lowen (2) believes that health would be an absence of character structure (and thus character traits), that is, an individual who functions freely and spontaneously from his instinctual feelings or core. Yet we know that the basic character-structure of an individual remains the same even after treatment. Thus, from a pragmatic point of view, we could say that (4) 'Whether character traits are healthy or pathological is not dependent upon instinctual gratification permitted or on the defenses against such gratification, but on the ego's capacity to achieve a degree of flexibility, mobility, and even reversibility within a framework of constancy, which will lead to optimal mental functioning'.

Since flexibility is also essential from a bio-energetic point of view, the important point therapeutically will be the restoration of this flexibility. The more the individual perceives his own feelings and can choose the mode and manner of expression, the healthier he is. The more he functions on a self-regulating energy economy in contact with his body, the healthier he is. There it is the less flexible elements in the character-structure that will be focused on therapeutically.

Therapeutically, character-analysis has as Lowen (2) stated 'one basic objective to make the patient feel his character is a neurotic formation which limits and interferes with vital ego functions'. Since as Reich (1) pointed out 'economically the character in ordinary life and the character resistance in the analysis serve the same function, that of avoiding unpleasure, of establishing and maintaining the psychic equilibrium — neurotic though it may be — and finally that of absorbing repressed energy', this task becomes all the more difficult. The difficulty of the task is even further increased by the fact that the analytic situation reproduces to a great degree the same type of infantile experiences through the transference that led to the character formation. Reich (2) has discussed this in great detail. The only solution to this problem is to make as many character traits ego alien as possible while at the same time helping the individual identify with the more positive aspects of his character and ego. Only in that way will the flexibility of the person be increased. In order to do this, one must determine what the character-structure is and what are its characteristic defenses and modalities of expression.

Affect Expression and Defense
The accompanying diagram represents the person in terms of affects and defenses in four layers. This diagram considers the basic affect states and the defensive structures used to modify them. It does not consider the personality from the standpoint of drives and at a future date, this may be worked into this schema. This diagram is an expansion of one presented by Lowen (7) and

can also be used to understand some of the energy dynamics of character-structure. We will first consider each of the layers separately. (See diagram.)

Core

The core is the center of the individual. It functions both as an energy center and as the center for the deepest positive feelings. The core contains cosmic feelings (feelings of harmony with the universe and with the self) and the undifferentiated feeling of love. The core represents the feelings that each individual wishes to have as much as possible. Many religious sects are based on the individual's striving for these core experiences. The ability to have core feelings depends on how well the other layers are worked through. If a lot of holding remains in the structure layer, any cosmic experiences that occur cannot be fully integrated into the personality. The core can also be viewed as the area from which impulses originate (id area).

Central Affect Layer

This layer contains the five major feelings that play a role in determining character-structure. It is how these feelings are handled (expressed and defended against) and which ones predominate that determine both character types and the unique character-structure of the individual. This will be illustrated for the specific character types later in this article.

a) Pain

Pain is the reaction to the suppression of the growing organism's basic rights. It is the unexpressed hurt that reflects questions like 'Why wasn't I loved?', 'Why didn't they accept my sexuality?', 'Why did they frighten me?', 'Why did they hit me?', etc. Pain is present in every character-structure as a reaction to the betrayals suffered by that person. Sometimes in therapy the person will feel the pain and a concomitant sense of confusion with a lack of recall for specific events. This reflects the childhood experience when the events occurred. The confusion will disappear when recall and working through occur.

Role of affect expression and defense

b) Anger
   This includes not only anger but also the murder and rage present in the person. This occurs both as a reaction to similar feelings from the parents and to the suppression of the individual's spontaneous movements, expressions and growth.

c) Longing
   Longing is the need to be held; the longing for the parent, the closeness, the touch, the nourishment. Sadness occurs as a later development related to the unfulfilled longing.

d) Terror
   Terror is the fear of annihilation by the parent's rage and hatred. It is related to feelings of incipient death or insanity but in many people represents the reaction to severe threat in in the first six months of life.

e) Erotic
   Erotic feelings begin with the infant's early quest for pleasure (infantile sexuality) and centers orally. Other erogenous zones also give the child pleasure. Erotic feeling is finally centered primarily on the genitals during the Oedipal phase. Adult sexuality can be considered the fusing of core love with feelings and erotic genital feelings.

The Structure Layer
The structure layer represents the layer of muscular defense. It is the body layer. Here the character-structure of the individual is evident in form and motility. The primary defensive function of this layer is suppression, the holding in or back of affect. This expresses the negativity, i.e. the no, the distrust, the hostility in the person. The muscular system is utilized in one of three ways to accomplish this:

a) Holding
   Using tight, spastic muscles and either the voluntary or involuntary musculature, conscious and unconscious affects are suppressed by the individual. By blocking different areas, the connection and integration of affects into the personality is kept from occurring. This type of defense is predominant in

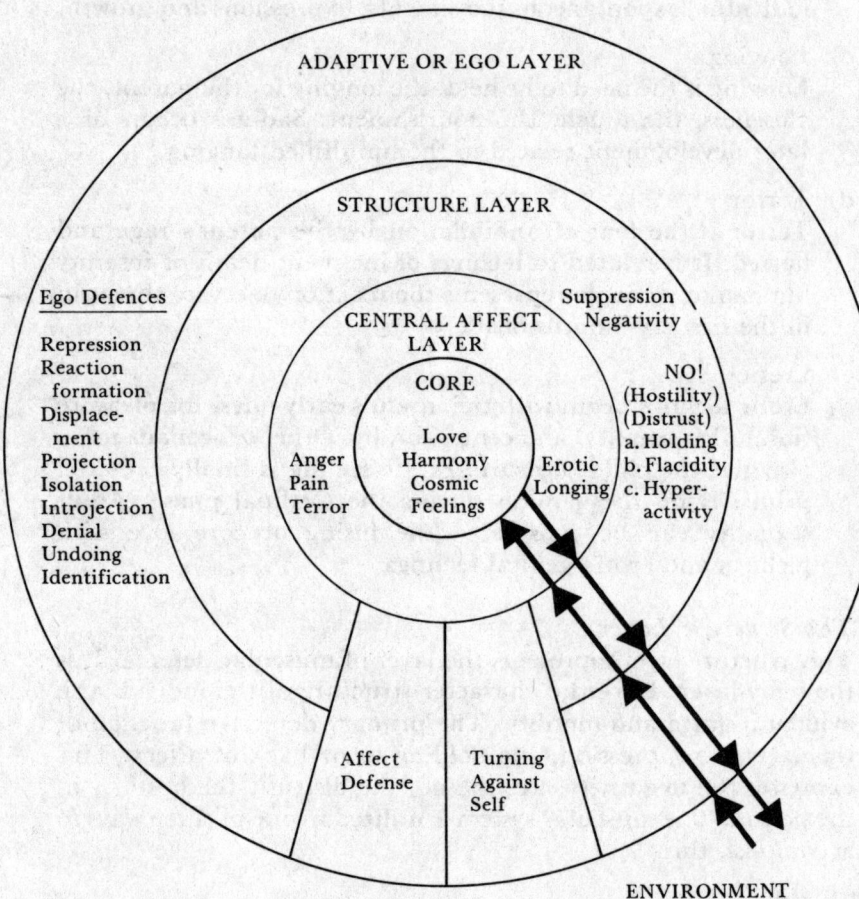

more organized character types and expresses its negativity by binding the affect.

b) Flaccidity
Flaccid, hypomotile muscles can be used to block affect. This type of individual's body is unusually flexible, with joints that hyperextend. In their aggressive movements it will seem that they have no muscular strength. Terror tends to be high and the personality is often not well organized. The negativity is expressed by paralysis as a response to affect.

c) Hyperactivity
The muscular system is hypermotile with a lability of affect expression. There is a diminished ability to maintain and increase affect. The personality may or may not be well organized. In those that are more organized, this takes on the quality of 'meshlike armor' (2).
The negativity is expressed by the discharge of unfocused affect.

The Adaptive, or Ego, Layer
This is the layer that deals with the outside world and is the final modifying layer of the impulses that come from the core and the central affect layer. Psychological symptom formation occurs in this layer. Psychosomatic symptoms involve the structure layer as well. The ego defenses (some of which are listed in the diagram) are the main determinants here. For consistency, repression will be confined to mental ideation and suppression to affect.

Cross Layer Defenses
There are two defenses that cross both the structure and the adaptive layer. The first one is the affect defense. This defense utilizes denial and displacement as well as muscular discharge, in an attempt to defend against a specific affect. For example, in schizoid individuals the central affect problem is terror. Some of them can express murder, rage or longing without great difficulty either initially or after some therapy. However, when terror is felt in life or approached in therapy, the individual will avoid it by expressing either longing or anger. Similarly, in other character

types, one will often see individuals use one affect (with good discharge and a relatively complete expression) as a defense against the central affect problem of their personality.

The second defense that crosses both layers is called turning against the self. Here the anger or rage, which is pressing for discharge, is stopped by redirecting it back to the self. Since a person will not usually assault themselves physically, flaccidity develops and the individual expresses a negative self-image. When the person is asked to hit the couch, for example, he will do it weakly if at all. If you try to get him to hit harder, he will not want to do it. When asked why, he will answer that the only one he is angry at or hates is himself.

Many aspects of this schema are artificial. Defenses usually function in multiples, and behavioral determinants can rarely be separated out layer by layer. It is useful, however, to try and understand the character structure in terms of this diagram and to see which defenses are being used against which affects.

Using these ideas, character can be defined as the characteristic way the outer two layers modify the individual's expression of the inner two layers and his response to the environment. As the arrows indicate, impulses from the central layers of the person must pass through the outer layers before being expressed, to the environment. Similarly, environmental stimuli must pass through the outer layers of the person before they can reach the core. Thus it is the dynamic equilibrium between each of the layers that maintains the homeostatis and determines the personality.

The energy of the individual lies in the inner two layers. Any therapeutic work that taps those layers will liberate energy which is necessary for the dissolution of the pathological elements in the personality. There is no energy in the outer two layers, although they function to contain affect and thus energy. Initially, when the muscles act to defend, they use and contain energy. When the defense becomes chronic however, the muscles no longer contain energy. When any block other than the respiratory block opens, the individual does not have more energy, only a better energy flow and more contact with himself, and thus, more energy available for use. It is the increase in respiration that increases the energy level. A further discussion of the energy dynamics of respiration and respiratory blocks requires a separate article.

Character Types

By using the concepts considered above, each of the character types can be understood in terms of the affect and defenses that are central to the problem. This is a simplification since few are pure character types and other feelings in the central affect and core layer are present, and important dynamically in even pure character types. Yet, there is always a main central affect problem for each type, and unless this problem is reached, therapy will not be successful.

Oral Character

The affect that must be reached is the longing, since deprivation in childhood is the central issue in the oral character. At the ego layer, he defends against this by denying the loss and by displacing his needs for mothering and support onto others. He feels that it should be done for him. On the structure level, he defends with flaccidity and will not reach out. His arms hang limp, he will not reach with his lips or eyes. His negativity is clearly shown by his inability to ask the therapist for help and yet he expects the therapist will help him. In the depressions that usually accompany this type, the anger associated with the pain of the unfulfilled longing is handled by turning it against the self.

Masochism

The central issue of the masochistic character is anger. There can be no therapeutic success until anger and a concomitant sense of assertion is openly expressed. On the ego level, some of the defensive maneuvers include turning against the self, projection ('You've done it to me'), isolation of affect (contemptuous and whining) and reaction formation. On the structure level, the body is heavy and holds in but also collapses. The negativity is expressed by spite especially at the cardiac and anal sphincters.

Rigid Character
For the rigid character the central issue is the frustration of his genital erotic needs and the pain of this betrayal. These affects must be reached and the individual realize that he can open up and not be betrayed and function even if defeated. At the ego level, all the defenses are utilized with the main ones being reaction formation, isolation and displacement. Much of the aggressiveness evident serves a defensive function. Structurally, the individual either holds back or utilizes hyperactivity (flexible or inflexible armoring). Anger is often used as an affect defense against the pain. The negativity is expressed by indirectness and holding back.

Schizoid Character
The basic problem in the schizoid character is terror. This must be resolved if therapy is to be successful. The main ego defense used by the schizoid is denial. He denies the threat of annihilation and his rage and longing. Structurally, he will either hold (holding together) or use flaccidity in order to suppress the terror. His negativity is expressed in paranoid ideation and his lack of response. Affect defenses are quite commonly used: for example, sex to fulfill longing or to ward off terror and anger or longing to avoid terror.

Psychopathic Personality
The central issues in the psychopath are longing (especially for the father) and erotic (sexual) feelings. The main ego defenses are denial, projection, displacement and reaction formation. These maintain his sense of superiority. Structurally, he holds up (upward displacement) and also uses hyperactivity (acting out). His negativity is expressed in superiority and contempt.

Therapeutic Techniques

Therapeutic work with the character-structure can be carried out on different levels. The problem can be approached from the ego layer working towards the center. This involves interpretive work related to life functioning, interpersonal relations, transference, etc. The character is delineated and exposed before any interpretations are made on an infantile level (1,2). At the structure level, the individual needs to become aware of his blocks, understand their meaning and feel them as dystonic. Finally, the individual is helped to experience and express the central affect and core layers.

Attacking the character from the structure layer working outwards towards the ego and inwards towards the affects, is central to bio-energetics. The person primarily needs to identify with his character on the body level. He has to understand where he is blocked, what those blocks mean and how they interfere with full pleasurable functioning. As this understanding develops, he then becomes motivated to get rid of these blocks (they become egodystonic). How this is done is one of the key issues of therapy.

First, respiration and contact with the body must be increased. This will increase the person's energy and make interruptions in flow (blocks) more noticeable and uncomfortable. In addition, this will provide more energy for affect release.

Secondly, maneuvers encouraging affect release are used so the person will see the difficulty he has in expressing anger, pain, longing, sexuality, etc., and how that interferes with full emotional functioning. The blocking of affects is a major part of the character (resistance) and must be interpreted. This can be done by pointed out that the individual had no choice but to erect these defenses since this was the only possible solution to the childhood stresses. Today, however, their maintenance represents an inappropriate solution (2). Later in therapy, the active role the individual played as a child in determining his defenses, can be explored.

Thirdly, the issue of negativity must be handled. The individual can verbalize these feelings, associate to them and act them out in a therapeutic setting. In addition as the individual identifies more and more with his blocks and feels the character to be egodystonic, the dynamics of why he continues to suppress his own natural functioning must be worked through.

In working with affects, an alternation technique we can call 'ping-ponging' is often used. This technique is done by alternating affects in order to deepen them and make their dynamic interrelationship in the personality clear. An example of this is the issue of terror in the schizoid character. Since terror is the central affect problem in the schizoid, it needs to be expressed. On the other hand, the individual has to be able to tolerate it and realize that he will not be annihilated now. One way of doing this (in addition to increasing grounding and contact) is to alternate terror with anger thus increasing the expression of each. By doing this, the individual's ability to sustain the depths of the terror is increased. The relationship of terror and rage is also clarified, as well as increasing aggressive expression. Similarly, in the schizoid, the terror and longing can be alternated to show and work through the problem of reaching out. In the rigid character, one can alternate between fear and longing. This will deepen both of those feelings and bring the central problems of fear of betrayal and defeat clearly into focus.

These simplified examples show how the alternation of affects can deepen their expression and aid the working through of the dynamic conflicts. With erotic affects, for example, the alternation may need to be between anger and terror or anger and pain, depending upon the current personality problem. Clinically, we sometimes see that when a person is working over the stool and rapid pelvic movements are instituted panic or terror may develop. This should be alternated and the individual's memories and perceptions explored so that this can be worked through in terms of the underlying incestuous drives and fear of surrender. Anger or rage may occur when pelvic movements are initiated. This expression should be deepened and alternated and the sense of violation, betrayal and revenge worked through.

It is interesting to note that the alternation of affects follows the energetic principles of pulsation. Just as increasing the pulsation rate yields greater lumination so alternating between different affects yields greater intensity and expression of each.

Finally, we can say that in the same way that affects are used defensively, they can also be used offensively in therapy to undermine resistance and to focus on the central problems of the character structure.

Summary

This formulation gives the therapist an additional way to understand the character structure and dynamics of the individual and to formulate his therapeutic approach and treatment goals. A detailed discussion of the treatment approach to the different character types is covered elsewhere (1,2,3,8). Here the central issues and the defenses for each type have been discussed. Only a limited aspect of bio-energetic therapy has been presented. Work with increasing respiration, contact with the body, grounding, etc., are the basic foundations of therapy upon which the restructuring of the individual is built. Work with the affects of course, is integral to grounding since the individual will become more in contact with his body, the psychic determinants of his personality, his sexuality, and his standing as a person. However, releasing affects alone will not accomplish grounding. The ability to experience and express affects will give the individual the energy and positive feelings which will be the impetus for further changes in the personality.

REFERENCES

1. Reich, W., *Character Analysis*. 3rd Ed., New York, Orgone Institute Press, 1949
2. Lowen, A., *Physical Dynamics of Character Structure*. New York, Grune and Stratton, 1958
3. Lowen, A., *The Betrayal of the Body*. New York, the Macmillan Co., 1967
4. Moore, B., and Fine, B., *A Glossary of Psychoanalytic Terms and Concepts*. 2nd Ed., New York, The American Psychoanalytic Association, 1968
5. Freud, S., *Character and Anal Erotism*, in "Collected Papers", Vol. 2, New York, Basic Books, 1959
6. Fenichel, O., *The Psychoanalytic Theory of Neurosis*. New York, W.W. Norton and Co. Inc., 1945
7. Lowen, A., Talk on April 25, 1972, to a Bio-energetic Trainers Seminar, New York
8. *Training Manual in Bio-energetic Analysis*. New York, The Institute for Bio-Energetic Analysis, 1972

Why Touch?

by Jerome Liss, M.D.

Jerome Liss received his B.A. from Bard College, and his M.D. from the Albert Einstein College of Medicine. He did his internship at the Jewish Hospital of Brooklyn and trained in psychiatry at the Massachusetts Mental Health Center in Boston, and in London with the Philadelphia Association. He practised as a psychotherapist and family therapist in England between 1967 and 1973, and was one of the first doctors in Britain to help introduce encounter groups into this country. He is the author of Family Talk *(1972) and* Free to Feel *(1974). 'Why Touch?' was first published in* Energy and Character *Vol.4, No.1, January 1973. Dr. Liss is currently living and working in France.*

Freudian theory states that oral feeding is the infant's most crucial relationship to its mother. That is why the first period of life is called 'the oral period'. Freud did not study infants directly, but based his findings on his work with adult patients. From a common sense point of view though, wouldn't you say Freud was right? After all, it does mean that the most obvious characteristic of the small invant is that it will howl when hungry and show great satisfaction when fed.

However, if we examine the experimental work of Harlow as presented in John Bowlby's excellent and comprehensive book *Attachment and Loss*, Volume 1*, we see that Freud was definitely wrong. The infant's emotional life is not as affected by periodic feeding as it is by the availability of touch. Harlow's experimental work is carried out with infant monkeys (thank God!) but there is nothing to suggest his results would be reversed for human infants.

---

*Bowlby, John, *Attachment and Loss*, Volume 1, the Hogarth Press, 1969.

Touch Reduces Fear, Feeding Doesn't

Harlow's general procedure is to provide infant monkeys with either a cloth model of an adult monkey or a wire model of an adult monkey. Each adult model has a baby bottle attached to it from which the infant monkey can feed. The obvious difference between the cloth and wire models is that the cloth model feels good to touch while the wire model does not. Bowlby describes one experiment where eight infant monkeys were raised with both the cloth and wire model monkeys present. Four infant monkeys were fed on demand on the cloth model and the other four were fed by the wire model. Harlow measured the time the infants spent on each model and the results were striking. No matter which model provided the feeding, the infant monkeys spent most of their time on the cloth model. More specifically, the infants of both groups spent an average of fifteen hours a day clinging to the cloth model while none of the infant monkeys spent more than an hour or two a day with the wire model. In fact, 'Some infants, whose food came from the wire model, managed to lean over and suck the teat whilst still maintaining a grip on the cloth model.'*

These experiments show that infant monkeys will spend most of their time on a cloth model mother whether or not that model feeds them. However, one may ask how do we know whether the infant's 'emotional life' is more affected by a touchable cloth model or a feeding wire mother? Two further experiments deal with this question and again the results are clear-cut. In one experiment the infant monkey is brought up in the presence of a cloth mother which gives no feeding. When the infant is made frightened and alarmed, it at once seeks out and clings to the cloth mother. This behaviour is analagous to monkeys in a natural setting who will run and cling to the mother whenever alarmed. Furthermore, after the infant has held on to the cloth mother, it apparently becomes less afraid and may even begin to explore the object which was previously frightening. In marked contrast, the infant brought up with a wire mother which has

---

*Ibid., p.214

provided feedings will *not* seek out this mother when alarmed, but will instead remain frightened and immobile. Thus the feeding mother which gives no physical touch comfort will not be sought out for reassurance when the infant is frightened. The cloth mother, however, is not only sought out but actually gives enough contact to subdue the fright and allow the infant to once more explore its environment, a natural transformation of emotions.

The same type of results were obtained when the infant monkeys were placed in a strange test room with unfamiliar toys present. The results:

> 'So long as its cloth model (for touch) is present, the young monkey explores the toys, using the model as a base to which to return from time to time. In the absence of the model, however, (which means "no touch") the infants would rush across the test room and throw themselves, face downward, clutching their heads and bodies and screaming their distress ... The presence of the wire mothers (also "no touch") provided no more reassurance than no mother at all. Control tests on monkeys that from birth had known only a wire nursing mother revealed that even these infants showed no affection for her and obtained no comfort from her presence.'*

I can envisage someone saying, 'That may be true for infant monkeys but how can we be sure it holds true for human infants?' My response to this is to ask investigators who study infants in their natural setting what they have observed.

Can an Infant Reach Out for What It Needs?

Let us for the moment approach the problem from another angle. Let us assume that infants are, from their very beginning, dependent upon direct physical contact for comfort. We might ask, then, how come we have not known this before but only see it so clearly when infant monkeys are investigated. The reason,

---

*Ibid., p.214

Why touch?

which I shall elaborate upon in a moment, is that infant monkeys from right after birth have the ability to reach out and therefore show what they need. In contrast, human infants are less developed at birth in accordance with the general principle that the more mature the organism becomes, the more time it takes to ultimately reach that higher level of maturity. Therefore, the less mature human infant, in contrast to the infant monkey, does not have the *capacity* to reach out for the comfort it needs. The less mature infant is more dependent upon its higher developed human mother than the more mature monkey infant is upon its less highly developed monkey mother to know what it needs. From an evolutionary standpoint, this makes a lot of sense, but in terms of where our complex civilisation has brought us to, it hasn't worked out so well, since infants are not held enough. Let us look at further data presented by Bowlby.

Touch Deprivation can be Transmitted from Generation to Generation

Bowlby presents in orderly sequence data which describes the amount of direct, physical contact ('ventro-ventral contact') between mothers and infants of different primates. The principle which emerges is that in the more developed species, there is greater duration of continuous physical contact between mother and infant than in less developed species. Starting with the lowest developed primate, the rhesus monkey, Bowlby writes:

> 'During the first week or two of its life the infant is in continuous ventro-ventral contact with its mother with hands, teeth and mouth, and at nighttime being held by her. Thereafter, the infant begins to make short daytime excursions from mother and she from it.'*

The more highly developed baboon 'spends almost the whole of the first month of life clinging to its mother in a ventro-ventral position, exactly like the rhesus monkey.'** The still more highly

---

*Ibid., p.186
**Ibid., p.188

developed chimpanzee spends its first four months clinging to its mother in the ventral position with only brief periods of sitting beside her. The gorilla (man's nearest relative) matures at about the same rate as the chimpanzee and is in continuous body contact with its mother for about the same period of time, the first four months of life. Thus, the rhesus monkey, the baboon, the chimpanzee and the gorilla each need more and more sustained mother-infant body contact as one goes up the ladder of species development. The more developed species start out more vulnerable at birth and require more nurturing before the members reach independence.

In terms of evolutionary development, how much continuous mother-child contact would be expected of human beings in a natural setting? Six months? Even more?

Bowlby points out, 'Only in more economically developed human societies and especially in western ones, are infants commonly out of contact with mother and often during the night as well.'* One possibility is that this is as it should be. Perhaps the principle that the more developed the primate, the longer duration of mother-infant body contact, does not apply when we make the jump to the human being. Certainly it does not seem to apply to practice.

There is another possibility: that human mothers have lost their natural and intuitive relation to their own body experience and that of their infant children, and so have failed to recognise that need for continuous body contact which is so important for the infant's development.

Can this be possible? Let us look at one more item of information offered by Bowlby.

> 'During the first two or three months of life the young gorilla (closest to man) lacks the strength to clasp its mother's hair securely and *receives support from its mother's arms*. By the age of three months, however, it can cling efficiently and may begin to ride on its mother's back.'**

---

*Ibid., p.199
**Ibid., p.191

The infant gorilla, like the human infant, does not have the capacity to clasp and so is instead supported by its mother. How does a mother gorilla know to clasp its infant? Obviously, animal knowledge. Another way to put it is that the mother gorilla *needs* to hold her infant for her own bodily satisfaction. But if the human mother has been cut off from her own 'animal awareness', from her own knowledge that she needs to be held, because she was not sufficiently held as an infant and because of the other bodily deprivations of civilised life, then her own body no longer tells her that her infant needs continuous holding, she does not respond fully to her child's need to be held, and she unwittingly perpetuates the process which entrapped her. And this can continue for generations.

The need for changes in child-rearing, such as to respond more fully to the infant's needs to be held, is just one implication of Bowlby's data. The very fact that our civilisation has missed awareness of this need for more body contact, and has missed seeing how we suffer from its lack, is to my way of thinking a sign of how civilised awareness with all its institutions to promote that awareness, has been off the bat. We have to reconsider our civilised ways of life from the word go. For example, might there not be deep interconnecting links among the following characteristics of today's civilisation: lack of body contact in the home, authoritarian censuring of 'selfish' pleasure, condemnation of 'them', that is, those who are not like 'us', fear of failure, shame of being 'weak', competition in the schoolroom and the fear and hatred it produces, societal control of intimate relationships through marriage laws and norms — a control which solves that most anguishing problem of sexual jealousy by taking the matter out of an individual's hands, and thereby abrogating a freedom in sexual choice which people may not anyway be prepared for because of their authoritarian family life; and then there is overpopulation, the destruction of trees with spreading urbanisation, the four-cornered, flat-walled rooms and buildings causing angular movements, the oppression of 'underdogs' (children, women, blacks, the insane, and the poor) by 'top dogs' without compassion so that paranoid fear is justified for all concerned including those top dogs who, out of fear, act oppressively; and this connected to large institutions which lack small group intimacy and decentralised decision-making for the functions of work, education and politics; and this connected to dulled senses, mass media living and war with cellophane violence because from behind a trigger, rocket or bomb, you don't see who's killed and actually how it happens, so you don't need to feel much about it; and more. It's all too complicated to tease apart and, besides, who will set it right? Therefore, let us return to touch therapy and our needs for body touch.

Body Touch Arouses and Releases Feelings

Touch affects the body's vital forces. Touch brings energy into the body and also allows for its discharge. Some people who lack sufficient body contact or, more importantly, that body contact which is just right for oneself, are in direct contact with their anguish. 'I need to be helped', 'I need somebody to hold on to' or 'I need you to hold me'. But, as Kierkegaard said, 'There is despair over not being in despair', and so there is a different body anguish in not feeling the need for body contact, even though there is insufficient bodily gratification: 'I don't need anybody to hold me,' or 'I don't need to be touched, not by anyone'. Body tension turns into numbness, coldness, emptiness, frozenness and the feeling of being dead. The body ache and yearning turns into neutrality and from there into 'Stay off!' The thought of being touched by anyone one knows becomes repulsive.

The touch therapies are meant to help people open up their bodily needs and at the same time find daily life relationships that will give complete bodily satisfaction. That is their overall purpose. Alexander Lowen and Arthur Janov use assertive methods, while body touch therapists use direct body touch to aid a person's emotional arousal, awareness and relief. The touch therapies may be divided into two groups: the soft touch school of Gerda Boyesen and the hard touch school of Ida Rolfe.

Soft Touch Therapy

The soft touch method of touch therapy has been developed by Gerda Boyesen. Mrs Boyesen is originally from Oslo, Norway, and has been practising her form of body-oriented psychotherapy, which she terms 'dynamic relaxation therapy' in London, England, during the past four years. She describes her special form of massage therapy as 'furthering abdominal respiratory relief, and, in this way, giving a relaxation so deep that underlying repressed emotional patterns are awakened and especially those containing autonomic responses.'*

The massage technique is to give gentle, circular strokes to areas of muscle tension. The timing of the stroke is important. They are brief in duration and there is a brief pause after each stroke in order that the body has time to fully react. This is based on massage methods developed by Aadel Bulow-Hansen, who was Chief Physiotherapist at the Ulleval Psychiatric Department for Women in Oslo.

Soft Strokes Relax Muscles, Deepen Respiration and Arouse Buried Feelings

The purpose of these regular strokes, which Mrs Boyesen calls 'shock impulses', is to provoke abdominal respiration, meaning a deeper respiratory response which originates from the diaphragm at the base of the lungs. Abdominal respiration helps emotions well up and find release, in contrast to 'chest cage breathing' which is more restrictive and limits emotional experience.

Mrs Boyesen states that the abdominal respiration was originally lost when processes of emotional repression resulted in muscle tension throughout the body. She compares the process of emotional repression to be like a person's reaction to a pistol shot. 'The body stiffens by contraction and the flexors of the body over-rule the extensors, at the same time as the breathing is held in in an inspiratory pattern.' She says the body stiffens as a reaction

---

*Boyesen, G. Experiences with Dynamic Relaxation, *Energy and Character*, Abbotsbury Publications, Abbotsbury, Dorset, England, Vol.1, No.1, January 1970, p.32.

to 'traumatic psychic situations ranging from simple daily stress reactions to the more dramatic ones reported during times of war.' In other words, the muscles tense and feelings are cut off.

She continues, 'Residual startle patterns can build up upon one another with attendant respiratory inhibition patterns and corresponding non-abreacted vegetative reactions. Unabreacted emotional tensions are then built into the organism's defence system and locked there in an encapsulated form.'* Therefore, the 'startle' response to emotional situations results in shortened, tense muscles and lack of feeling. 'Non-abreacted vegetative reactions' refers to reactions of the autonomic (vegetative) nervous system which are blocked ('non-abreacted').

To recap: the startle reaction of emotional repression involves contraction of the muscles, inhibition of breathing and cut off feeling. The gentle strokes of 'dynamic relaxation therapy' (and undoubtedly of other soft-touch methods) relaxes the muscles, promotes deeper respiration and allows feelings to come to awareness and find relief. The feelings that are thus aroused will bring with them their associated memories of origin and the 'working out' proper involves discharge of the feelings, remembering their origin and assimilation of the experience through talking it out.

The Arousal of Warm, Buzzing, Electrical, Vegetative Streamings of Pleasure

Mrs Boyesen makes one more important observation which she quotes from the work of Dr. Ola Raknes concerning the arousal of 'vegetative streamings'.

> 'By means of this loosening of the cramps and tensions, one could bring into consciousness emotions and memories which had hitherto been completely repressed, even supposing the therapist had managed to guess what they were from the patient's dreams and associations.
>
> 'Not only repressed emotions and memories came to light, but also things that nobody had thought of before or paid

---

*Ibid., p.35.

attention to, things that should prove to be of the utmost importance both to psychotherapy as it exists and for further discoveries. These new and unexpected experiences were feelings of streamings in the patient's body — streamings which to most of the patients were formerly unknown, and which, to most of those who knew them, had been of little or no significance. Such streamings were of a pleasurable nature, mostly soft and rather weak but also, occasionally, so strong that the person felt they would overflow him. In these latter cases, sometimes even if they were of moderate strength, they represented a new and unknown danger to the patients and made them afraid.

'These streamings seemed to stem from the vegetative or autonomic nervous system, and Reich therefore called them vegetative streamings. It soon became evident that they only appeared when a considerable loosening of spasms and tensions had taken place, enabling the patient to relax, and breathe fairly freely; they always inaugurated a more general feeling of well-being. They duly became signs of therapeutic progress and, as such, assumed an even greater importance for the valuation of what had been attained.'*

'Vegetative streamings' are experienced as warm, buzzing or electrical sensations which run up and down through the body and through the limbs. As Dr. Raknes points out, they are pleasurable. They are promoted by soft massage or any method which aids emotional arousal. Not only do they feel good and afford a sense of well-being, but they seem to come up when the vital functioning of the body is improved. Body therapists for decades have speculated that they are signs of autonomic nervous system functioning. More specifically, however, they are most likely a 'parasympathetic reaction', the parasympathetic being one component of the autonomic nervous system.

Mrs Boyesen described the 'dynamic relaxation' treatment of a young married actress. The patient had a severe anxiety attack at

---

*Ibid., p.33

the premier of a new play. She had to be carried from the stage and following this became victim to strong, repeated attacks of anxiety so that she was unable to leave her home. The initial treatment started with the patient lying on her front and Mrs Boyesen giving the gentle stroke 'shock impulses' to the muscles of her back. At first there was no reaction, but when the strokes came to the right upper trapezius muscle of the patient's shoulder, the muscle, formerly tense, suddenly became soft as butter. At the same time, the patient's face turned pale green and she began to shiver violently. The patient then lay quietly and for the next ten days experienced almost constant nausea, vomiting and diarrhea. No further treatments were given until this 'autonomic reaction' subsided.

Two weeks later Mrs Boyesen found that the right upper trapezium was still soft but that the other muscles of her body were as tense as ever. An identical treatment was given to the left upper trapezius and there was the same reaction: softening of the muscle, violent shivering, face turning pale green, nausea, vomiting and diarrhea. The reaction again lasted for about ten days and then another treatment session was arranged.

Mrs Boyesen continued to work on different muscle groups in the same manner, each time obtaining the same reaction. After a period, however, the patient's reactions became milder and at the same time her anxiety lessened. Thus Mrs Boyesen was provoking the patient's warded-off anxiety reaction and permitting its discharge. The therapeutic response was positive. The young woman began to go out into the streets again with her husband and with friends. Mrs Boyesen also reports the following item:

> 'Finally, as the shivering reactions grew milder and milder she exclaimed one day: 'This is just like it was at the beginning. I would shiver a little, just like this. I used to be so nervous about going on to the stage but I managed to make myself do it and used to cut off the shivering'."*

Therefore, it appeared that the patient had somehow managed to cut off her anxious feelings each time she went on the stage,

---

*Ibid., p.42

but these feelings were nevertheless 'stored up' and eventuated in her severe anxiety attack. The soft strokes provoked and tapped the dammed up energy through the autonomic discharges of vomiting, nausea and diarrhea. And eventually the patient was clear. (Talking about 'energy' being 'dammed up', 'discharged', 'released' and 'cleared' is the language of body therapy.)

It is interesting how this correlates with ecological studies of 'instinct behaviour' in all animal species. If the instinct (e.g. sexual, flying, hunger, nest-building) cannot be expressed, its energy seems to build up and up, since the threshhold for its being triggered off is continuously lowered. Once the instinctual behaviour is carried out, the dammed up energy appears to be depleted, because for a period of time it is hard to provoke, and even if provoked, the intensity of the act is low. Mrs Boyesen's patient's anxiety worked somewhat like this and so do many people's anxieties. Somewhat anxious, one is more easily made anxious once again. If the anxiety is not discharged through full emotional expression then one is still more easily made anxious. The situations that arouse anxiety spread: talking to the boss, talking to some fellow employees, the building where one works, going shopping downtown, going shopping in the neighbourhood, stepping outside one's doorstep, seeing strangers, acquaintances, even friends. The area of safety diminishes. The continuous anxiety of undischarged feelings mount. Though 'insight' may help one work out the mapping, I think it is clear that discharge of the feelings at the deepest autonomic level are required for a 'clear' — clear thinking, clear planning, renewed functioning. I believe the symbolic reworking through the talking out process of verbal psychotherapy is extremely important once the clear has been achieved, in order to avoid re-entry into the traps of unwieldy anxiety. But for a therapist to carry on lengthy verbal discussions with a person screaming with inner pain doesn't make treatment sense to me. First, discharge the pain, then talk rationally. Mrs Boyesen reports that her patient, 'having rid herself of anxiety, attained health and maintained it for many years.'* As a footnote she adds that ten years later the

---

*Ibid., p.42

patient called her again, describing how well she had been doing, but added, 'But this autumn my mother died after long and exhausting circumstances. I feel the old anxiety returning but this time I want to start treatment before it really develops.' Treatment was resumed. This time reactions were very slight. Anxiety feelings disappeared after a month, and the patient's menstrual periods, which had disappeared six months before, resumed again.

Most of Mrs Boyesen's work, and that of other body therapists is not so severe. The massage goes on for a while before feelings are aroused. The first feelings are usually of fullness, such as in the throat or the belly. The therapist very gently touches the area that feels swollen (swollen with feeling, but undoubtedly reflecting tissue changes as well.) The swollenness or tension dissolves into trembling, vibrating or convulsive feeling — grief or panic. 'What comes to mind?' But the therapist need not even ask the question in intensive therapy because the patient knows this is at issue. 'It's my mother,' or 'It's my sister-in-law', or 'It was my best friend'. When? Where? What happened? Experience the details, though they need not be described, then, 'Tell them!' and the patient replies: 'I want you with me!' 'Please!' or 'Get away!' The words come from the feelings to provoke more feelings, more memories, more words, more feelings, more memories, more words, and so on. The cycle of working out problems is continuous. Although Janov claims his patients are 'defenceless' and 'cured of neurosis' in three weeks or six months of primal therapy, I think that position is ridiculous. We are too early in our ignorance to know the end point of the revitalising process.

Pulsation and Feeling

by Laura Dillon

Laura Dillon learned to understand and work with pulsation and counter-pulsation of the body energy in the training programme at the Radix Institute (formerly the Interscience Work Shop), and this treatment relies heavily on the concepts of Charles Kelley, Director of the Radix Institute, and of his teacher, Wilhelm Reich. However, the article expresses the way she has learned to observe and work with pulsation and counter-pulsation in her own practice as a teacher of neo-Reichian techniques.

For over two years I have been working with people in neo-Reichian body work. I use deep emotion release techniques to help my students contact deep levels of fear, anger and pain. Many people have held these feelings in their bodies in the form of muscular tensions since early childhood, and their bodies reflect it in the way they move and express themselves. I have become aware that the people I work with are able to feel and to allow the expression of their deep held feelings to the extent that they are able to allow a flowing, rhythmical, pulsating movement of their bodies. A major objective of my work is to help bring about spontaneous emotional discharge, and unless some degree of pulsation of the body is attainable, this will not occur.

What is Pulsation?

Pulsation may be understood as rhythmic contraction and expansion. In contraction there is a moving toward the centre, a pulling in; and in expansion, the movement is directed out from the centre. The jellyfish is a good example of a pulsating creature. Pulsation implies a flowing movement of whatever it is pulsating.

Pulsation occurs in both living and non-living nature, ranging from tiny microscopic forms to rays from the cosmos. Day and night create a pulsation which is responded to by seemingly every animal and plant on earth. For most creatures the day is the expansive, active time when energy is being discharged. At night the system contracts and recharges during sleep. The seasonal pulsation of nature, coinciding with our yearly trip around the sun, has its constant rhythm. In the expansive heat of the summer, plants 'discharge' their fruits and reproduce. The cold of winter is a time of contraction, dormancy, and recharging.

Dr. John Pierrakos of the Institute of Bioenergetic Analysis has explored the pulsation of the energy field in man and nature through his ability to see this field. The energy field associated with inner biological processes has been seen to pulsate at varying rhythms depending upon the emotional state of the organism and its degree of physical activity. Pierrakos reports that plants vary in their energy field pulsations according to whether they are flowering or dormant. The atmosphere over the ocean has a field pulsation, and all of us can observe the pulsation of ocean waves which varies according to the time of day, winds, and perhaps other, non-mechanical factors.

There are millions of natural pulsations occurring at all times all over the earth. Many of them affect us, if not consciously, then unconsciously, through our bodies. We respond to the emotional pulsations of other people and creatures too, and they respond to us. Cleve Backster of New York, with his lie detector experiments, has gathered evidence that plants respond to violence or threat of violence as well as positive emotions. While working with a patient bioenergetically and during deep emotional release, Pierrakos states that the energy field of a nearby plant was invaded by radial beams resembling porcupine quills, which shot from the patient's head. Plants exposed to deep emotional release work for several days withered and died, according to Pierrakos.

Energy

I understand the human energy field to express the biological, emotional, and mental energetic activities of the organism. The energy field is known to pulsate, that is to contract and expand, to charge or take in energy, and to discharge energy. When I speak of energy I am referring to the energy which Reich called 'Orgone'. Others have called it the life force, the radix (Kelley), Chi, and vitality. 'Orgone' energy fills all space and is present in varying concentrations in living systems.

This energy flows through the body in rhythmical, pulsatory waves causing movement of the liquid contents of the body. The movement of energy through the body plasma is experienced subjectively as feeling. Because animals have no control over their feelings as they interact with their environment, their bodies spontaneously express the emotions they feel. In other words, the pulsation of energy in the bodies of animals remains uninhibited and they experience their feelings fully. Humans, on the other hand, by virtue of our volitional capabilities that evolved along with the ability to reason, have learned to control feelings (Kelley, 1970). When the movement of the energy results in a feeling too painful to experience, we tighten our muscles against the flow of energy, thus cutting off the feeling.

If this cut-off of feelings occurs often enough the tension of the muscles, which holds back the feeling, will become chronic. This chronic tension is referred to by Reich as *muscular armouring*. In neo-Reichian body work, as these chronic tensions loosen, the energy held back by the tensions is released. The emotional discharge that results is due to the energy flow that was blocked previously by the muscular tension. After a full discharge the body is relaxed and often expansive in its movements. The pulsation of energy has been restored and so have the pulsatory movements of the body.

Charge

A discharge of body energy is possible only after a sufficient charge has built. This can be accomplished by increasing the breathing pulsation. Breathing is the most obvious and emotionally the most significant pulsation in the body. The belly and chest rise and expand as the air is drawn in and fall as it moves out again. Breathing can assume many different rhythms. When the body is at rest the breathing pulsation is relatively shallow and slow. During more strenuous physical and/or emotional activity the breathing becomes deeper and faster. Many feelings are blocked in the muscles which control breathing and simply by altering the 'chronic' breathing pattern of control a person may experience much more feeling.

Not only is breathing a primary pulsation of the body, but it also literally inhales and exhales free atmospheric 'orgone' energy. The body becomes charged with a surplus of energy. With more energy pulsating through the body, feelings become more intense. If the feelings are not very blocked they soon emerge in discharges of anger, fear, pain, or any number of mixtures. Feelings which are more heavily blocked will show themselves as muscular tensions which impede the natural expressive movements of the body. Sometimes direct manipulation of a muscle will give the student the awareness that he or she needs to let go of the tension and allow the expression of the feeling. Or I may ask a student who is blocking anger to pound the arms and kick the feet as in a child's temper tantrum. This breaks through the tension, using voluntary movements which gradually become spontaneous as the feeling behind the tension discharges.

The Sexual Pulsation

Reich's early work with body energy was concerned with the sexual pulsation and its characteristic four-beat rhythm: tension ⟶ charge ⟶ discharge ⟶ relaxation. Kelley prefers to see the pulsation as: charge first, then tension ⟶ discharge ⟶ relaxation, and I agree with him. The body builds up an excess charge of energy from day to day pulsatory activity which results in a tension. The feeling of tension may be experienced as desire. In love-making the charge is increased by deeper breathing and voluntary pulsatory movements of the body. At the height of the experience pulsation deepens into convulsion and the movements become involuntary as the energy is discharged in orgasm. When the orgasm has been complete, involving the whole body in involuntary convulsion, a deep relaxation follows in which the energy pulsates freely in the body.

The structure of the Radix Intensive (which is the way we work with a person individually) is patterned after Kelley's modification of Reich's orgasm formula. The *charge* is built through breathing and voluntary body movement, and the muscular *tensions* become exaggerated. As the pulsation deepens, the tensions loosen, the movements become involuntary and the feelings *discharge*. *Relaxation* of the body results in a restored pulsation of energy and movement.

Lower Life Forms

Reich studied pulsation in lower life forms (Reich, 1951). Every living organism, regardless of its complexity, is a concentration of 'orgone energy' separated from free atmospheric energy by a peripheral membrane. The energy circulates within the membranous boundary of the organism. The striving of the energy to extend beyond the boundary results in a characteristic shape which Reich called a basic form of Living. Seeds, plant bulbs, animal reproductive cells and embryos, organs of the body, single-celled animals, and animal plant bodies as total forms, all fit this model.

While observing a microscopic form one can see the movement of the plasma which describes the flow of energy. The plasma moves around and around, not continually but in rhythmic impulses — pulsations. The surging forward of the energy at the head produces movement and growth; and at the tail end, genitality.

Consider this basic pattern of energy movement in the human form. The energy moves up the back, over the top of the head and out the eyes, giving to and receiving from the environment. Then it moves down the front of body toward the genitals where the energy is discharged in orgasm. The flow of energy through

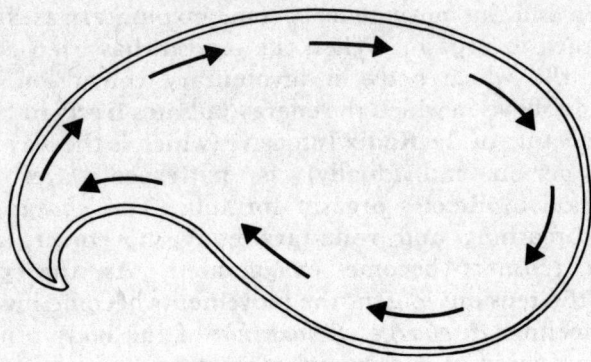

(For original, see Reich's *Cosmic Superimposition*, p.42)

Figure 1

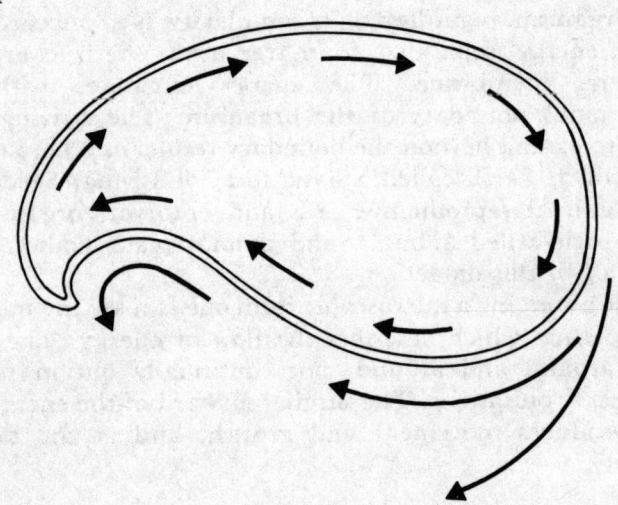

(For original, see Reich's *Cosmic Superimposition*, p.45)

Figure 2

Pulsation and feeling

Figure 3

the legs and feet into the ground gives us stability, contact with the earth, and together with the flow through the eyes, contact with reality. The flow through the shoulders, arms, and hands allows manipulation and energy exchange through physical contact with the living and non-living environment.

The Segments

Expressive movement in the human body is made up of many different pulsations, and the body is divided into pulsating units. Reich referred to this as the segmental arrangement of the body and likened it to the sphincter-like structure of worms and caterpillars. The peristaltic movements of the intestines and other organs of the body follow this pattern.

(For original, see Reich's *Cosmic Superimposition*, p. 33)

Figure 4

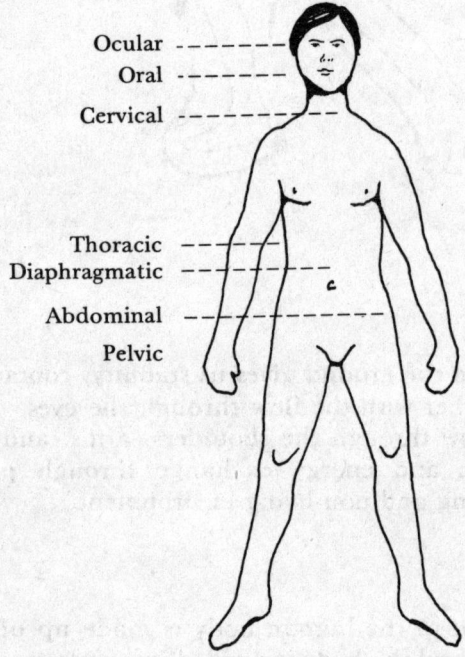

Figure 5

Pulsation and feeling

The segments are arranged in seven rings around the body beginning with the top of the head and the eyes and ending with the pelvis, legs, and feet.

Each segment contains muscle groups which, when relaxed, allow spontaneous pulsations of energy and movement through the plasma in the segment. When the muscles are tense pulsation and movement are inhibited and the feeling is dulled. Ideally, the energy flows freely up and down the body and each muscle segment is co-ordinated in its expression and movement with all the other segments. Thus, the overall pulsation of the body is made up of a group of smaller pulsations. If one or more of the units stops or reverses its pulsation ('counterpulses') the overall expression of the body is blocked and loses its integrated quality. The person feels scattered, diffuse, or out of touch with himself.

Counterpulsation

Muscular blocks are actually a case of energy turning back on itself, countering the normal flow in the body. Kelley calls these active blocks *counterpulsations*. The blocking process is not static, as Reich's term 'muscular armour' implies. Counterpulsation occurs when the flow of energy through the body plasma results in feelings that are judged (usually unconsciously) to be too painful or frightening to experience. Instead of being discharged, the energy and the feelings behind it are locked in the musculature of the segment. As the rest of the body expands, the blocked segment contracts. We attempt to get the segments pulsating, or contracting and expanding, together. When this happens, the whole body pulsates as a unit and the blocked feelings have a chance to emerge.

When a feeling begins to emerge as the student works, it is expressed through movement. The expression of the feeling, or feeling discharge, will be complete to the extent that the whole body participates in the movement. Energy blockages become apparent as we observe that certain body segments attempt to express the feeling by pulsating in unison and other segments are immobile or counterpulsating. It is my job as a teacher to indicate (mostly non-verbally) where the blocks are, and to teach the student how to let go of the tensions and allow the expression of the feeling in the total body.

Anger, Fear and Pain

The body moves in particular ways when expressing each of the three basic 'negative' emotions — anger, fear and pain. That is, each feeling has a characteristic pulsatory expression in the body which is inhibited when the feeling is blocked. Anger is an outward directed, expansive emotion and the emphasis in its expression is, on the expansive stroke of the pulsation. The direction of anger is from the centre to the periphery of the body, and from the self to the outside world. The body pulsation of the person blocking anger is 'stuck' on the outward direction. It is necessary to encourage outward directed expression in order to re-establish the full pulsation of the body.

In fear, the emphasis is on the inward stroke of the pulsation. Fear is a contraction into the core of the body and a drawing into the self from the outside world. The body pulsation of the person blocking fear is 'stuck' on the inward or contracted direction. As the fear is felt and expressed the inward stroke is completed and the body is again free to pulsate fully.

The expression of pain, or sobbing, differs from the expression of anger and fear. Pain is expressed through a convulsive movement, or successive contraction and expansion. When pain is blocked in the body the whole system contracts against awareness of feeling. As the muscles tighten to hold back crying, the overall body pulsation diminishes. Sobbing allows the pain to be felt, releases the muscular contraction, and restores pulsation to the body.

I use many different neo-Reichian techniques to release blocked feelings and energy, but the underlying theme of my work, whether with individuals or with groups, is pulsation. I emphasize contraction and expansion; coming in to the self and moving out toward others; charge and discharge; and always rhythm with movement. Breathing is the single most-used pulsation. I teach exercises which emphasize pulsatory movements of the body. The movements include the eyes, mouth, neck, shoulders and arms, the trunk of the body, and the pelvis and legs. Even the structure of the one-day, the weekend, or week-long workshop reflects a fundamental pulsatory design of charge and discharge.

The process of discovering my own body pulsations continues to be a source of joy for me. Learning about feeling pulsations entails learning about the blocks and experiencing the feelings connected with the blocks. Although the experience of the blocked feelings may be frightening or painful, there is also an element of pleasure that comes from surrendering psychologically and physiologically to the natural process of feeling. People vary in their ability to surrender to their own feeling pulsations, and it is this ability that I work toward developing in my students.

As the capacity to surrender to feelings of anger, fear and pain develops, one also becomes better able to experience more fully love, trust and joy. The 'negative' and 'positive' feelings are paired in such a way that if one is blocked, the other is blocked to some degree. For example, the person blocked in his capacity to experience fear is also unable to trust another person fully. The capacity to love develops out of the capacity to express angry feelings. Many couples find that making love is more pleasurable and expansive after a 'good fight'. As the negative feelings are released from the body they make room for the positive feelings and expressions.

Conclusion

Pulsation is a basic characteristic of living things and it is a natural biological movement. Whether we are aware of it or not, pulsation is a major energetic activity of our bodies. The awareness of body pulsations brings awareness to our connection with nature and the roots of our existence. This is important in a time when man's vital relationship with nature is often forgotten or ignored.

Experiencing neo-Reichian re-education is one way to become aware of pulsation in the body and how it relates to the expression of feeling. Tuning in to my body pulsations has helped me to perceive the energetic pulsations outside myself. Learning to live in ever finer harmony and resonance with living pulsations all around is a life-long process of growth which has no perceivable end-point. It just keeps getting better and better.

BIBLIOGRAPHY

Kelley, Charles R. Notes from The Radix Institute Teacher Training Program, 1972-1973
Kelley, Charles R. *Education in Feeling and Purpose.* Santa Monica, California, Radix Institute, 1970. Revised 1974
Pierrakos, John C. *The Energy Field in Man and Nature.* Monograph, New York, Institute of Bio-energetic Analysis, 1971
Reich, Wilhelm *Cosmic Superimposition.* Rangeley, Maine, Orgone Institute Press, 1951

The Kick of Life

by Nadine Scott

Bio-energetic Therapist, London

Nadine Scott moved to London from New York two years ago to run a private practice as a bio-energetic therapist. She has co-ordinated several intensive training courses for therapists in Europe. She is a Fellow of the American Psycho-analytic Society, a Member of the New York Gestalt Institute, and of the Institute of Bio-energetic Analysis.

D.H. Lawrence says the baby kicks his way to freedom, Alexander Lowen says kick your way back into your body, and the junkie on the streets talks about needing to kick his habit.

One might say that the meanings and dimensions of this word are enormous. And that is perhaps because the meanings and dimensions of this action are indeed enormous.

Anyone who has worked at all in the bio-energetic process soon begins to understand the meaning of his kicking, how one can tell a lot about what a person's way of being in the world is, just from his kicking.

In the early days of treatment with a patient, his kicking tells me a great deal about how much space he allows himself to move in, about how much effort or driving force he applies to life, about how firmly he can feel himself, or about how little he believes his own affirmation of life. It can even tell me how much he feels life from within, how much he respects life, or how much there are ingredients of his desire to die.

Three years, ago, when I first began working in New York, I had occasion to work with several young people who were using drugs as a habit. The drug use went from uppers to downers to some extreme cases of using speed, by shooting it directly into the vein. On one occasion I worked with a young man who was on heroin.

This was my first experience with a heroin user, and the following is his story. It is presented as an example of the beauty and power that the bio-energetic approach to life contains, not as a suggestion that this process could cure all drug users.

Joe came to me through his sister with whom I had been working for almost a year. He was hooked and he had been for a little over a year when I first met him. We made an agreement from the beginning that my participation in his life was to help him to feel his pain, not to cure him of something that I myself had had no experience with and could not begin to understand from his point of view. So, initially, it was stated that he was not coming to be cured. Secondly, since I could not work with a vegetable he had to agree to not 'shoot up' for at least twenty-four hours before his session. Finally, I wanted no part of any money he received from dealing in dope, so if he did not have the money for his session from earnings that he had saved or from some other positive place, he would be truthful about it and we would work from that place. And so we began ...

This was hardly a matter of gathering information from the past, or even from the here and now. The here and now for Joe was very far away, in a haze that made no connection with himself, that always stayed numb and protected him from any pain at all. I felt so little was happening in the early sessions that I often was surprised when he would appear for his appointment. He would take off his things and lie painlessly on the bed, hardly breathing. His body was contracted and the colour was a yellow brown. He looked to me like one big sore that, if agitated, would turn crimson with irritation and scream with pain.

Slowly the sessions began to go deeper, with the breathing and some body movements, and he gradually moved from clutching and doubling up the mid-section, to being able to let the breath flow more and to let the tears out. For some weeks following he would begin to breathe and grimace from the pain and, with encouragement, gradually let himself feel. And I would hold him in my arms and we would both weep, the words never being full flowing sentences but rather little sharp knives of hurt about his mother and father.

Joe's father had taken Joe away from his mother at an early age as he felt she was not able to care for him. Joe was caught somewhere in himself between rage and heartbreak, and also very strong positive feelings for his father who really wanted to take care of him. Joe's father had married again and he had one step-sister (my patient) and another sister.

During the time I worked with Joe I moved my work from New York City to Scarsdale, where I was living, and I wondered if Joe would make the trip. I felt he was really serious, even though he couldn't really show it, when he in fact did manage to travel from New York City to Scarsdale for his sessions.

Sometimes he would come on the day of the evening group. Several of the young people in this group, including his sister, would stay after their sessions for dinner and group therapy and, since they were all coming from Staten Island, they would stay the night. This not only allowed them, in a practical level, to travel only once a week on the train to Scarsdale, but it also gave them all a feeling of community and family that had the ingredients of people really having fun together, preparing meals and doing up dishes. There were a lot of good feelings at the table and discussions were open for free thought, with due respect for the questions and philosophies in their own young minds. They were all getting off dope now and they could give Joe a lot of support and love, without judgments and shoulds.

It was during this period that a series of things began to happen outside of Joe's sessions which were expressing his desire to really help himself. First, he got arrested and put in jail for dealing dope. I called the police station and asked to speak with him as I knew he could be in there for some time without getting his necessary shot.

The officer was kinder and more helpful than one might imagine and he allowed me to speak with him. Yes, he was frightened, and had good reason to be. I encouraged him to let himself feel his fear and panic and to breathe deeply and remember his pain, let himself have it, rather than to settle for trying to maintain an image of the street addict.

He did. And when he was released he very soon afterwards gave himself a case of hepatitis and was put in the hospital. After that time Joe went on the Methadone programme.

When he was able to he came back. With the care he got while sick, with his ability to pass a major crisis in jail, and with the Methadone, he was a stronger and 'more there' Joe. We then began working with the bio-energetic processes much more strongly and elaborately. He would kick and kick and I would say again and again, 'Kick, Kick, Kick', and he would say it too, never talking about the double meaning, just being, kicking.

Feeling began coming fast, more than pain and tears ... now anger, spite, fear. Gradually we began to work with Joe on his feet, and I began to provoke him, and taunt him to see if he would react. The beginnings of his spontaneous reactions began coming first in facial expression and in his eyes. Finally, one day I pushed Joe (I played the 'Pusher' all the time). Joe pushed back and I landed on the floor, Joe looking down at me, not with sympathy but with determination to make his 'NO' stick. And it did.

It was Spring then, late Spring, and I was planning a Marathon with some of my patients, in July in the country.

Joe came ...

We worked through the night and Joe managed to participate as little as possible. Throughout the next day he held out but, finally, he began to work. We moved the group around so that the women were on the outside of the circle and Joe at one point realized he was surrounded by men. He had to deal with them and they stayed with him every step of the way. One of the men was an ex-dealer and he knew all the clever manipulations of the dope world. He worked with Joe in a beautiful, creative way, and Joe gave in.

He destroyed his needles and poured out the last of the Methadone, a gesture that I feared was a bit too dramatic to be real. But later we all discovered that it was very real, as Joe then made his arrangements to stay with us in the country for a week after the Marathon was over, to try to make it on his own.

The following week was, for me, most anxiety producing. I had not really hoped for this, and yet some place inside myself I guess I had secretly hoped for it all along. And now it was here and I was caught between my own real feelings for Joe, my fear, and my ego that wanted to take all the credit. I worked with Joe a little each day. He wanted his girl to be there, so we sent for her, only to find that we were faced with the alcoholic-wife syndrome ... the lady who really doesn't want him to kick. Also there was dope in the community where we were and it seemed to me that, externally anyway, the odds were too great against it for it to work. Joe was extremely afraid of the pain of withdrawal, even though we were told that withdrawal from Methadone is supposed to be much easier than with other drugs.

As time passed symptoms began to appear that would frighten Joe ... a runny nose and weeping eyes ... some of the early stages of withdrawal. Mid-week in the evening Joe was sick and scared. Those who had stayed on after the Marathon gathered around Joe by the fire. He lay on a couch as if waiting. We did not speak or try to work with him in that way. Instead, someone kept the fire going while someone else played the music. Each person just gave their energy to Joe, silently and lovingly. I began to massage Joe and, as I did, I remember that I was really praying. I don't know how to describe that massage; I never gave one like it before. My hands fully moved themselves in a rolling, palming motion that seemed to be endless. And I was never tired. Eventually Joe fell asleep. The room seemed to be lit with the good feelings present. Then something very lovely happened. Robin, Joe's sister, began to weep, not from the surface, but from a place that went very deep. Her whole body cried as she gave in to her feelings completely and wept with everything in her.

The Psycho-Diagnosis of the Body

by Nic Waal, M.D., Anne Grieg, and Mogens Rasmussen

Dr. Nic Waal was one of the foremost psychiatrists in Norway. She trained with Reich at the Berlin Institute of Psychoanalysis in the early nineteen thirties, and was one of the few therapists at that time who were able to understand his development from character-analysis to vegetotherapy.

Dr. Waal was formerly the director of the Child Psychiatric Department of Oslo University, the Head of the Mental Hygiene Clinic in Oslo, and President of the Association of Child Psychiatry and Clinical Child Psychology, in Norway. She worked as a training therapist to physicians and psychologists at the Child Department of the State Hospital in Copenhagen, and at the Paediatric Department of the Copenhagen University, before becoming director of the Institute for Psychotherapy (later the Nic Waal Institute) in Oslo.

She lectured extensively on muscular tensions and respiration as treated in vegetotherapy, at International Congresses of Psychiatry in Zurich, Paris and Toronto, and gave courses on therapy and child development to psychiatrists, nurses and teachers, in many parts of Sweden and Germany as well as Denmark, Norway and Holland. From 1947 onwards she developed her own form of personality diagnosis — known at first as the Nic Waal muscle tests — which was later published as a monograph by the Nic Waal Institute in 1956. The material that follows is taken from that monograph, in English translation by David Boadella, and is reproduced by permission of the Nic Waal Institute.

Anne Grieg and Mogens Rasmussen were members of the Nic Waal Institute who collaborated with Nic Waal in describing the muscle tests.

Part I: The Development of the Research Method

Nic Waal's method for the psychodiagnosis of the body (hereafter called the Nic Waal method), is a somatic research method for psychiatric and psychological diagnosis. The method is based on the fact that there is always a correlation between muscular tension and the type of respiration on the one hand, and emotional conflicts and affective states on the other. Starting with this assumption it follows that it should be possible without speaking to a patient, without using psychological methods of research, but simply by noting the patient's expression, local muscle tensions, and breathing, to map out the patient's psycho-dynamic structure (1).

More precisely the fundamental assumption can be put in this way: an individual's total personality will express a synthesis of environmental processes and inherited biological potentials. Permanent psychic and somatic changes will take place if a child comes into continuous conflict with his surroundings, or is exposed to severe frustration (2). This viewpoint implies that both the somatic and psychic changes will be specific to the child's stage of maturity, and the patterns of functioning which characterise the phases of development. A detailed recording of special features of the body structure can therefore explain both a patient's actual psychological condition and indirectly the conditions which brought it about.

The Nic Waal method assumes that each person is a psycho-biological unity, but it has wider consequences than are found in modern psychosomatic medicine. This branch of medicine still often shows a dualistic viewpoint. With a background in conventional concepts of a parallelism between mind and body, it seems unthinkable that somatic research alone could provide the basis for a diagnosis of personality as adequate as personality tests on a purely psychological basis. Most psychologists will doubt the possibility of this kind of advance, and so will most physiologists. The Nic Waal method offers in many ways the first real bridge between the two research realms.

The Nic Waal method has its roots to a great extent in Freud's epoch-making work on the origin and treatment of neurotic illness. The development of psychoanalysis represents a milestone not only in the understanding of mental illness, but also of psycho-dynamic principles generally. In the course of twenty years Freud and his closest followers were concerned more and more with the phenomenon of 'resistance' in psychoanalytic treatment. Originally psychoanalytic technique consisted in bringing the patient's repressed experiences and conflicts to consciousness in the present day by means of free association and the interpretation of dreams. Used with hysterical patients and patients with easily provocable emotional reactions, these techniques were quite adequate. Many patients, however, brought up childhood memories without any feelings. Treatment gave these people significant intellectual insight, without being able to change their life situation to any important extent. Others could not associate freely, found they had blocks to their thinking, etc. These phenomena were called 'resistance', and occurred after each meaningful analytic observation. The phenomenon of resistance can also be seen even with people who seem specially suited to the technique. Resistance was explained by the view that there were drives in the personality — the so-called 'ego' drives — which were formed in the process of adjustment to the conflict experiences and repressions, and which later had the effect of hindering the present day awareness of these repressions. The study of these drives and psychic mechanisms resulted in psychoanalysis moving from a pure impulse psychology, to an *ego* psychology, whilst at the same time the technique developed a concentration on the repression mechanisms and resistance processes. Many psychoanalysts began, often unclearly and half-heartedly, to concern themselves with character formation.

The clearest theoretical and technical formulations were mady by Reich (3). The development of his character-analysis represents an important advance in methods of treatment. Character-analysis today is recognised to be the most essential concept of modern psychoanalytic technique. With Reich's work on studying his patient's manifest character, he was led steadily to pay close attention to the patient's muscular expressions. An arrogant man carries himself in a characteristic way, holds his back and neck arrogantly, has an arrogant facial expression, etc. A submissive personality stoops, holds his head and neck bowed and sunk into the shoulders, etc.

In his efforts to get a patient to experience his character, and his bodily posture, Reich discovered a whole range of new phenomena. Many patients lacked the experience of themselves, had no bodily awareness, and could not recognise the muscle tensions which formed a typical part of their bodily posture. Whilst Reich's technique at first was verbal-descriptive, these blocks led to an increasing use of 'somatic' technique. With contact and palpation, later with massage and pressure on local tense muscles, patients began not only to experience themselves more fully, but a series of new phenomena came to light. Pressure on muscles, for example, can often release spontaneous cries, biting, whimpering, etc. Touching can set the contracted muscle, even the whole muscle complex, into movement, and this can result in the release of infantile impulses and feelings. What is released is so full of memories of childhood situations and infantile conflicts that the material can be worked on consciously and verbally immediately afterwards.

Reich called his technique 'vegetotherapy' (4), a term which in some ways is a little obscure. At that time the technique provided no overall therapy or somatic understanding of the physiological background of the phenomena. Reich took the patient's unspoken affective and impulsive reactions to be primarily a result of his having stimulated his autonomic (vegetative) nervous system.

Reich's technique and empirical observations led to a great interest, among his students, in physiology, neuro-anatomy and reflexology, and in the theories of James Lange, Cannon and Pavlov, on the somatic basis of emotional and expressive behaviour.

From different medical schools, from dance, ballet, gymnastics and theatre, a steady flow of new insights developed, in the nineteen twenties and thirties on the influence of muscle tensions on human emotional life, on the physiological balance of the body, and as causes of different functional illnesses. These views are associated particularly in Berlin with Schultz, in Chicago with

Jacobson, in Copenhagen with Gerda Alexander, in Oslo with Seyffarth, and in England with many orthopaedic specialists.

The connection between vegetotherapy and the different relaxation techniques which were started in these thirty years has been recognised, but never examined in a thorough-going way (5). Relaxation techniques offer a completely educational treatment of the patient: the patient learns to relax, but his fantasies and feelings are still repressed. These techniques provide a purely symptomatic treatment, which often results, in fact, in an increased repression of the conflicts and of the irrational infantile feelings and impulses. The role of respiration and the special dysfunction of the hypotonic (over-relaxed) muscles is on the whole not understood by many of the teachers of relaxation.

In contrast to the usual relaxation teaching, the aim of vegetotherapy is to use the stimulation of muscle tension and blocked respiration to release and later to abreact the reaction patterns which are bound up with the early conflicts between the organism and its environment. The abreaction of the blocked feelings and impulses brings about a restoration of natural tension in the muscles, that is to say, the capacity for flexible use of the musculature which before treatment had a different function — the blocking of feeling. The difference between relaxation methods and vegetotherapy is quite essential in the matter of the contact between the therapist and the patient. A condition for successful results with vegetotherapy seems to be an earlier working through of the quality of the patient's contact, and his attitude to the treatment. In work with psychoses for example, the working through of the distancing and withdrawal processes takes on a central importance. This is in sharp contrast to the advice of some relaxation teachers to their patients, to let their eyes gaze into the distance (6).

In spite of lacking systematic work on the contact problems, many relaxation teachers have experience of strong outbreaks of feeling from their patients. This is because the muscular system not only has its purely physiological role as an effector, but also acts as a regulator of affective stimuli. In contrast to vegetotherapy, the relaxation teachers usually look on the release of feeling as a subsidiary phenomenon, and therefore fail to analyse its specific contents or dynamics.

Reich's later energetic work and cosmic theories have had the effect that his vegetotherapeutic theories have generally not been given the attention that they deserve.

The vegetotherapeutic technique as it was developed by Reich in the middle of the nineteen thirties, has since passed through many changes, some of them of a major kind (7). The significance of the quality of contact, mentioned above, is in many ways, for example, a new idea in vegetotherapy.

It is important to point out that vegetotherapeutic technique does not consist in a mechanical provocation of affect, but is a means of helping patients to accept themselves and to assimilate the walled off impulses into their personality. Vegetotherapy has as one of its principal aims a reorganisation of the whole personality.

It is this reformulated and extended vegetotherapy that has given the Nic Waal method its theoretical anchoring and the foundation for its special psycho-somatic hypotheses.

In the course of a continuous and longstanding experience with vegetotherapeutic technique at Gaustad and Ulleval hospitals, there were two observations which were very significant for the development of the method.

On waking up after cardiazol shock treatment, many patients (but not all) showed marked infantile behaviour patterns. Often impulsive childish sexual expressions came out, sucking, crying, masturbation, etc. Research with schizophrenic patients using X-ray photography, often showed a notably small outward movement of the diaphragm. In schizophrenic patients who improved after shock treatment, there was usually found an increased motility in the diaphragm, while patients who did not improve had an almost motionless diaphragm.

On the basis of the above observations at Gaustad hospital, Nic Waal concluded in an article in 1939:

> 'From a vegetotherapeutic point of view one might say that the shock treatment is a kind of mechanical gymnastics of the vegetative nervous system and the autonomic functions; thus it liberates vegetative energies. Where this liberation succeeds,

there is considerable improvement. But since the treatment is purely mechanical, since it does not take in the whole personality, it will never really change the personality.'(8)

The Nic Waal method first took on systematic form in 1947. The first scientific tests were planned in connection with Rappaport, who was then the Head of the Research Department at the Menninger clinic in Kansas. The aims of the research was to show how far psychiatric diagnosis and psychodynamic structure-interpretation, derived from the study of muscle tensions, showed agreement with psychological test results and clinical observations. The results of this research were very exciting and encouraging.

In all four investigations on these lines were carried out:

1 Out of 46 adult patients at the Menninger clinic, a diagnosis based on muscle tension showed complete agreement with the psychiatric staff diagnosis in 39 cases, and complete agreement with the psychological test diagnosis in 41 cases. Only in one case was there a decided lack of agreement between the results of the two methods.

2 In a sample of 33 child patients at Southard School at the Menninger clinic, there was full agreement between the Nic Waal method and the usual psychiatric diagnosis in 30 cases, and with the test diagnosis in 29 cases. In 3 cases there was no agreement between the diagnoses.

3 In a sample of 39 patients with psychosomatic symptoms at the Veterans Hospital, Kansas, the Nic Waal method showed full agreement with the usual clinical psychiatric diagnosis in 28 cases, partial agreement in 8 cases, and complete disagreement in 3 cases. Further, the psychosomatic symptoms were correctly predicted for 26 patients. For the remaining eleven, the predicted symptom was either not found or the patient's complaint was directed to different symptoms.

4 In a total sample of 48 asthmatic children at the Rikshospital Polyclinic for children with allergic illnesses, in Copenhagen, the Nic Waal method showed full agreement with the psychological tests and behavioural observations, in 45 cases. In no

case was there a direct mistake, but in the 3 remaining cases there was an important lack of agreement over detail.

As a supplement to the above research the Nic Waal method was combined with Rorschach investigations and clinical observations in a series of individual cases. In all, the method has been used so far (by 1957) with 1200 patients, including 60 children at Barnbyn Ska, outside Stockholm, 78 children at the Child Department of the State Hospital in Copenhagen, 78 school children in Aarhus, 162 children having psychiatric treatment in Oslo, and a number of children treated together with their parents, in all about 850, who had therapy since 1953 at Dr. Nic Waal's Institute, in Oslo.

The Nic Waal method of psycho-diagnosis uses chiefly the following methods of investigation: inspection, palpation, and passive movement. The method employs in all 114 individual features to be recorded, and all observations are recorded according to a special schema.

Part II: Muscular Tension and Muscular Activity

Findings with Passive Movements.

Passive movements are used to assess the motility of the jaw in relation to the rest of the head, the degree of movement between the head and neck, between the neck and body, and movement in different parts of the limbs.

For all passive movements it is important that the tester should carry out movements many times in succession. In this way the tester can change the rhythm of his movements and also change direction many times so that the full range of movement can be reached. The tester's movements must therefore not be jerky or abrupt, but easy, smooth and continuous. To achieve this the tester needs to make sure of breathing freely, and to be naturally relaxed in his arms.

With passive movements there are two phenomena we are concentrating on observing* namely, *tension*, and a greater or

---

*The word 'observing' includes everything we notice by whatever method, whether it is simple inspection, palpation, or findings from passive movements.

lesser degree of *activity* in movement.

To describe these phenomena more closely we will here give a concrete example. To observe the movement of the lower arm in relation to the upper arm, passive flexion and extension are used. The patient is instructed, before the test begins, to be as relaxed as possible and to let the tester carry out the movements. The tester grips round the patient's forearm with his own hand, and lays his other hand on the front of the upper arm over the thickest part of the biceps muscle. The tester bends the patient's lower arm at the elbow joint, straightens it out again, and does this several times in succession, while changing the rhythm of movement. With some patients one finds some degree of resistance to the passive movements. Such resistance we call *muscular hypertension*.

Resistances can be assessed as:

1 Isolated resistance against flexion. The patient has a tendency to keep his arm stretched; or

2 Isolated resistance against extension. The patient has a tendency to hold his arm bent; or

3 Resistance is found against both flexion and extension. Resistance may then be equally strong against both kinds of movement, or it may be stronger with one kind of movement than with the other.

The research method has quite a resemblance to that which is used in neurological investigations to demonstrate spasticity, but the resistance phenomena observed in these cases are often significantly greater than in such neurological findings.

With some patients one does not find resistance, but a characteristic looseness and slackness. It can vary between lazy, dull, 'dead' or can be recognised by a strange lightness. Such slackness we call *muscular hypotension*.

Often we find in combination with the tension or in place of it, an active movement on the patient's part. Patients are unable to carry out the instructions to let the tester make the movements and not help, but join in themselves with a greater or lesser degree of movement. This phenomenon we call *'activity'*. We distinguish between three different kinds of such movement:

Type 1: Obedient activity
Type 2: Self-assertive activity
Type 3: Impulsive activity.

Each of these three forms of activity has its own special characteristic feature.

Different Forms of Activity

a Obedient Activity (type 1)
It is characteristic of obedient activity that the movements the patient makes seek to follow the tester's movements so as to please him. Such movements can in some cases be felt immediately by the tester. If it is weak, the patient can however manage to conceal this type of movement quite well. The phenomenon is revealed by the tester changing the rhythm and direction of his passive movements. If activity is present, the patient will not manage at once to follow when the tester moves in a different direction, or will not be able to change his movement tempo to synchronise with the tester's change of tempo. The more sensitive the tester is, or the stronger the activity is, the less dependent the tester will be on using special tricks to reveal the activity.

Activity of type 1 is experienced by the tester as if the patient moves actively but in over-unanimity with what he understands as the tester's intention, and as if the patient through his movements is saying 'I ought to help you do it the way I believe you want it'. In contrast to a sensitive perception of the tester's intentions, there seems to be a moment of doubt or eagerness in the patient's reactions. The patient meets the stimuli of the passive movements with a fixed reaction-pattern.

b Self-assertive Activity (type 2)
It is characteristic for this form of activity that, to a much greater extent than in the previous group, the patient seizes the initiative himself. The tester feels that even if the patient apparently follows the passive movements, there are strong moments of self-assertive activity at certain points on the patient's part. This

activity has a wilful quality as if the patient himself will carry out the movement and determine the tempo, yet still keep control enough over his own movements to carry out the movement the tester indicates.

Compared with activity of type 1, there is less correspondence here between the tester's intentions and the patient's movements. The phenomenon is felt by the tester as if the patient was saying: 'All right, I shall try to do *what* you want, but I will decide myself *how*, for you can't tell me that.'

Activity of type 2 is much easier for the tester to recognise than activity of type 1, but the tester may also need in this type to make changes in movement direction and tempo.

A specially pronounced form of self-assertive activity we call *constant leading*, where the patient can hardly let the tester move him passively, but must make all the movements himself completely actively. The patient may also continue his movement after the tester has let go his hold, and the need to lead can most easily be made clear by pointing this out. Sometimes the leading is so marked, even when it is constant, that the tension level cannot be assessed.

c Impulsive Activity (type 3)
Here the patient's movements are jerky, uneven, and rough, with quite strong force. The movements change tempo on the patient's side independently of the tester's changes of tempo, and the movements have an uncontrolled and involuntary character. Impulsive activity prevents assessing the muscular tension at the same time.

Different Forms of Tension

a Muscular Hypertension
Muscular hypertension will show itself to the tester as a resistance on the patient's part to the passive movements. When the resistance is clear, but not specially pronounced, we record a tension of grade 2. If the resistance is not only clear, but particularly marked, it is recorded as grade 3. If the resistance is so strong that it is not possible to carry out the passive movements

because the part of the body concerned is held too stiffly, we record a tension of grade 4. With hypertension of grade 2 or 3, the resistance can be either stiff and stretched, or stubborn and tough. Grade 4 is always a stiff resistance in this definition.

b Muscular Hypotension

Muscular hypotension is indicated when the tester observes a very marked slackness and looseness during the passive movements. According to its intensity, hypotension is graded in two steps: grade 0 which is used when the slackness is present, but not to a marked degree, and grade 00 is used with severe slackness. Sometimes we can also distinguish between two qualitatively different forms of hypotension, namely *sluggish* and *light* hypotension. With sluggish hypotension the body part concerned feels inert, 'dead', slack and dull, and falls dully down when the tester takes his hand away.

Light hypotension gives the tester the feeling that the part of the body he is holding is lighter than its real weight.* It can be recognised also that the joints are specially loose and dangly.

The more marked the hypotension is (grade 00) the easier it is to distinguish between sluggish and light hypotension. Whichever form is present should be noted. If the form is unclear, it can be recorded as uncharacteristic, but one can still record the degree of hypotension.

c Natural Tension

Natural tension is characterised by the fact that the patient can let a particular body part follow the passive movements calmly, supply, and with a living response, without any slackness or sluggishness or any marked looseness, without resistance and

---

*We do not know the neuromuscular physiological background for the phenomenon of hypotension. We have changed the nomenclature from the usual term 'hypotonia' to the more neutral 'hypotension'. When the tester observes light hypotension, and feels that the weight of the body part is reduced, it may result from over co-operative movements of the patient. Often, but not always, such activity can be noticed at the same time as the light hypotension.

without active movements. Natural tension feels to the tester as if the patient has such a full and undisturbed capacity for bodily perception that he manages to carry out the tester's intentions completely. Even when the tester changes the tempo or the direction of the passive movements, the patient can still respond fully to them. The stimuli which the passive movements and the test situation give, result in a reaction in the patient which is in complete harmony with the instructions, without the patient either giving up all readiness to contract (as seems to happen with hypotension), or initiating contractions (as in hypertension and activity). The patient is in a condition all the time to change his reactions according to the stimuli, in a flexible and plastic manner. He shows no sign of fixed reactions patterns. Such a response we record as tension of grade 1, without activity.

d Simultaneous Occurrence of Tension and Activity

We find all grades of tension without simultaneous activity, and these are usually the simplest to observe. Often we also find a simultaneous activity. Individual combinations of these two factors occur relatively easily.

With continuous tension of grade 4, no movement takes place, and as a result we can find no activity in this case. With sluggish hypotension it is unlikely that activity can occur at the same time.

Conversely, no tension is recorded if the activity is of type 3. If the activity is of type 2 and especially the form known as 'constant leading', tension cannot always be recorded.

Sometimes activity of type 1 or 2 can be observed, without finding resistance (hypertension) or hypotension. In such cases we record tension of grade 1, *with* activity. Such a finding is essentially different from tension of grade 1 without activity.

The tension can sometimes change while the passive movements are being carried out. We distinguish between three different forms of such changes in the tension level, even if there are gradual transitions between them: even change of tension, single tension jerks, and irregular shifting tension.

e Even Change of Tension

With even change of tension, we see that the tension shows a continuous increase, or a continuous decrease, during the course of the investigation. It is characteristic of this phenomenon that the degree of tension found at first during the passive movements at the beginning seems to be constant. In the course of the test, however, while the passive movements are being carried out, one finds that the resistance increases or decreases to a higher or lower level which is maintained during the particular test. An initially high tension which decreases momentarily, when one begins the passive movements, should not be recorded as a reduction of tension. Signs both of tension-reduction and tension-increase are recorded as 'even change of tension'. Theoretically there are many combinations possible of reduction or increase between the different grades of tension, but only few seem to be found clinically. Tension-reduction together with obedient activity seems to be the most usual.

Tension-reduction and tension-increase can be recorded only if the transition from one tension level to another extends for more than one interval (difference in tension grade) unless there is a qualitative difference between the two tension grades. For example, we don't think it is possible to diagnose tension-reduction between grade 3 and grade 2. However, it is easily possible between grade 4 and grade 3, where we can distinguish between complete stiffness and marked resistance. Correspondingly we can register no tension-reduction or increase between grades 0 and 00.

f Single Tension Jerks
Sometimes we can see along with a particular degree of tension (with or without activity) that during the passive movements there occurs a *sudden momentary* increase of resistance. The higher tension disappears again at once, and the tension goes back to the initial level. These jerks or twitches of increased resistance usually occur during bending or stretching in the lower arm, but can also occur with other movements. When the jerks only appear in isolation and on single occasions, they are recorded with the sign 'R'. We don't try to indicate the tension level in the jerk, but to record the background tension level from which it arises.

Sometimes we often see repeated jerks which last during many movement tests with the same section of the body, and this indicates either a sign of impulsive activity, or of irregular shifting tension.

g Irregular Shifting Tension

An example of this form of tension is the following: the tester notices during the passive movements first a tension of grade 0, then a sudden shift to grade 00, then another sudden change to hypertension, eventually to grade 3, and then complete rigidity (grade 4). In one moment activity is going on, in the next there is no activity, and so on. The essential feature of this phenomenon is the irregular leaping changes between different levels of tension. There is no even reduction or increase.

The patient's reaction changes are here independent of the tester's changes of stimuli. The stimuli given by the test situation result in no consistent reaction patterns, but a range of different tension responses. Such irregularly shifting labile tension readily extends over large areas of the body, for instance during all arm tests.

With passive movements of the limbs, we find in most cases an agreement between the findings on both tension and activity, between the left and right limbs. All the tests are carried out bilaterally, and when this is done any asymmetry can be noted, and the differences between the two sides recorded separately.

NOTES AND REFERENCES

1   For an overview of the different dimensions which occur in psychodynamic structure, see Bjorn Christiansen, B. Killingmo and Nic Waal, *Personality Diagnosis in Relation to the Description of Structure*, Nic Waal Institute, Oslo, 1956 (in Norwegian)
2   This viewpoint has been strongly emphasised in Norwegian psychoanalytic thinking. See Trygve Braatøy, *The Nervous Mind: Medical Psychology and Psychiatry*, Oslo, Cappelen, 1947. Harald Schjelderup, Personality-changing Processes of Psycho-analytic Treatment, *Acta Psychologica*, 1956

3   Reich, Wilhelm: *Character Analysis*, Berlin, 1933
4   For the technical and theoretical basis of vegetotherapy, see:
a   Reich, Wilhelm: Psychic Contact and Vegetative Current, in *Character Analysis*, 3rd edition
b   Havrevold, Od: Vegetotherapy, *Tidsskrift for seksualokonomi*, Copenhagen, 1939; and *International Journal of Sex-economy and Orgone Research*, 1942
c   Reich, Wilhelm: *The Function of the Orgasm*, New York, 1942
d   Raknes, Ola: The Orgonomic View of Health and its Social Consequences, *Nordisk Psykologi*, 1953. Included in: *Wilhelm Reich and Orgonomy*, New York and Oslo, 1973
5   Waal, Nic: Muscle Tensions, Muscular Relaxation, and Psychotherapy, in *Ugeskrift for laeger*, 1951 (in Norwegian)
6   Jacobson, Edmund: *Progressive Relaxation*, Chicago, 1937
7a Waal, Nic: A Case of Anxiety Neuroses in a Small Child, *Bulletin of the Menninger Clinic*, 1948
b   Waal, Nic: Psychotherapeutic Goals: Health and Adjustment, *Nordisk Psykologi*, 1953
c   Waal, Nic: A Special Technique of Psychotherapy with an Autistic Child, in *Emotional Problems of Early Childhood* (ed. G. Caplan), New York, 1956. Reprinted in *Energy and Character*, Vol. 1, No. 3, 1970
d   Borgen, Carl Martin: *Combination Treatment of Schizophrenic Psychoses*. Lecture at the Psychiatric Association, 1954
8   Waal, Nic: Shock Treatment as a Subjective Experience, *Tidsskrift for seksualokonomi*, Copenhagen, 1939. Also in *International Journal of Sex-economy and Orgone Research*, Vol. I, 1942

Muscular Tonus and Integrated Respiration

by Lillemor Johnsen

Psychotherapist and Physiotherapist, Oslo

Lillemor Johnsen has worked both in private practice as a psychotherapist and physiotherapist, and at the Tonsberg Hospital, the Ulleval Hospital, the Oslo Psychiatric Univesity Clinic, and Dikemark Mental Hospital. She was strongly influenced by the methods that Trygve Braatøy learned from Reich in dealing with muscular tension, and by the work on somatic diagnosis of Dr. Nic Waal.

What follow are edited excerpts from her two booklets on *Psychic Aspects of Muscular Testing and Therapy* and *Integrated Respiration Therapy*, translated from the Norwegian by the author.

Introduction

Various forms of treatment of neurotic patients, based on physical aspects, have previously been described in literature, either as special forms of treatment or combined with more typical psychotherapy.

Professor J.H. Schultz has described his experience as to the release of affects in *Das autogene Training* and mentions that such affects are most often aroused as detached from their natural connection. His statement bears witness of disintegration of affects, especially in the cases of neuroses of the heart. He mentions that in about twenty cases sudden death has occurred, while such patients were undergoing treatment. Subsequent experience with this method also indicates that it is unsuitable for patients in a highly affected mood.

The Vienna analyst Wilhelm Reich gradually developed a method based on the physical conditions of the patient.

Such methods have since gained a footing in my country. In his later publications (1951-1954) Dr. Trygve Braatøy had in his mind treatment according to these methods when he centred his own method on the muscular tensions of the patient.

This treatise is based on the theories of tensions, and is founded on experiences gained from clinical studies of about 150 patients. Fundamentally it is motivated by the desire that in future, indications of muscular treatment may be founded on a more detailed examination of muscular qualities.

History

In the course of the years physiotherapy has become a part of a wide range of treatments, such as post-treatments for polio patients and in other neurological cases. It has also been applied in surgical post-treatment and in the treatment of medical cases with muscular troubles of various kinds.

Standard treatment mostly comprised massage, exercises, short-wave and other mechanical treatments. Various aids and special exercises were adopted varying with the facies morbi picture. The purpose of the therapy was to restore the patient as closely as possible to the functional state existing before the illness.

Gradually physiotherapy also came to embrace treatment of mental patients. At first it involved a treatment of symptoms, based on the local somatic troubles. Later on the treatment aimed at nervous mechanisms. The results, however, were not always up to expectations, the reason apparently being that the conditions of the tensions were considered a thing apart, and not connected with the patient's general mental state.

During the past fifty years psychiatry has seen in the literature various references to the use of physiotherapy for mental patients, as either the treatment of choice, or as an adjunct to the more typical type of psychotherapy. It was the Viennese psychoanalyst Wilhelm Reich who coined the term 'Character armour' and who eventually developed a method of treatment designed to focus on the muscular state of the patient. Braatøy in his book *Fundamentals of Psychoanalytic Technique* demonstrated the implication of body tension release in treatment of neurotic individuals.

Thus his interest was not only focused on the dynamic and deep-psychological aspects of mental disorders, but he also paid attention to the posture and the respiratory patterns of patients. He wanted to break the incessant wandering of the patients from one treatment to the other, as had previously all too often been their sad lot. He was also willing to try new methods and was not afraid of trying ways of treatment opposite to the traditional one. This was also his approach to the task in trying to solve problems as regards muscular tensions.

He considered muscular tensions as a physical aspect of the patient's defence against unrelieved impulses. His basic view was that massage applied to tense muscles would mobilize and realize impulses and affects, and that this would in turn modify the central nervous mechanism provided that it was properly followed up and assimilated to the patient's mental state.

His point of view was that muscular tensions were an important factor in the resistance to relieve repressed impulses and affects. This naturally brought him into communication with physiotherapists. The idea contained in his later publications were largely the result of this co-operation.

The collaboration brought about a change of muscular approach, which in many ways was the opposite of usual physiotherapeutic approach: correction of posture, mechanical massage, and muscular training carried out under the instruction of the therapist.

Treatment may confront the patient with his emotional deadness, and it was therefore of primary importance to further the patient's 'liberation' and 'spontaneous activity'.

He switched the emphasis from correction and training to the feeling of confidence and relaxation of tense postural musculature, maintaining that 'not orders, but security, relaxation and time release spontaneity'. In this connection Dr. Braatøy introduced the supine position in the treatment of neurotic patients, in order to bring about relaxation of posture, necessary for giving the treatment its effect with a view to furthering the patient's spontaneous activity. As an important means to give the necessary feeling of security to the patients, he proposed an 'actively sensing' attitude on the part of the physiotherapist, that he/she adapt and co-ordinate the approach to the musculature to the respiratory rhythm of the patient.

Treatment of muscles would cause the patient to release gradually his blocked impulses. This was the task of the physiotherapist. The psychological following-up of the impulses was the field of the psychotherapist. The psychotherapist should take over with special knowledge and technique, and further an intimate psychological analysis of the mobilized material. Physiotherapy and psychotherapy should work closely together. In other words, the aim was an integrated physio-psychotherapeutically combined treatment.

In my experience especially respiration is an important guide to sensing the patient's overall mental condition, and particularly to the sensing of his reaction to muscular approach.

The introduction into the treatment of the supine position made it possible to assess the patient's respiratory pattern, and furthermore to observe how the therapeutic grip on the patient's muscle affects his respiration.

This procedure enabled me to obtain a clearer diagnosis and to further the progress of treatment.

Appraisement of the Results of Treatment

Which therapeutic results have been obtained by this method of treatment? Judging from my own three years of experience with the method, from the past fifteen years of experience with patients having previously received such treatment, and also from experience acquired from the anamnesis of patients in institutions, results vary greatly.

There is no doubt that many have benefited by the treatment. There is likewise reason to believe that the greater number of them would not have benefited to any extent from traditional physiotherapy. However, what is important is that positive results should not be permitted to hide the fact that the method did not always yield encouraging results. There were cases where no improvement could be detected in either mind or muscle. In other cases again signs of more aggravated conditions appeared. My attention was particularly drawn to the patients whose conditions became worse. I have, however, often felt it difficult to find sympathy for my — at times critical — appraisals of this form of treatment, especially among the professionals who apply the method. In this treatise I will attempt to demonstrate the need for more closely examining the process and aims of treatment, and to try to find the reason, if any, why the treatment failed. I am not only thinking of the negative results themselves, but also of a number of discontinued treatments and deteriorated conditions. Some patients showed signs of an increased tendency to cleavage and were often brought into a chaotic state of mind. Other patients continued treatment for years and gave the impression of having resigned to a condition of emotional defence. These cases were found with comparatively well-integrated patients. In other patients progress was found to have stopped after a successful first phase, resulting in diminishing symptoms. Continued treatment did not have any decisive effect, but took the form of 'comfort and support'. The attitude of the patient was one of resignation and physically one of muscular defence. In reality there was no improvement in these patients, but rather an 'easing down'.

What was the reason for this? Was it just chance, or were any common factors present where the treatment failed? I will discuss and substantiate this in later pages, but it seems reasonable to assume that e.g. the following factors determined the results of treatment.

1. The muscular treatment was directed solely towards especially tense muscles on the assumption that these tensions in particular constituted the physical aspect of the neurotic defence. To recognize this defence would help the patient so that the underlying causes could be mobilized, realized and treated by psychotherapy.

2. The concentration on the tension, the defence, became too

predominant a part of what was intended to be combined physio/psychotherapeutic treatment, since the patient often received excessive muscular treatment. This precluded the possibility of muscular treatment being followed up by psychotherapy. In the end the patients mostly received only muscular treatment, which went on for several years, and could lead to hospitalization becoming necessary. According to the theory this treatment respresented a one-sided assault on the patient's defence mechanism, without being linked up with the rest of his personality. It was therefore neither possible nor natural for the patient to follow his impulses. The emotions had not been experienced by the patient and assimilated by him/her. They were not self-realized. Emotions were awakened without having any bearing on the patient's situation, and thus did not acquire meaning. Not seldom crying, anger and anxiety were the results of physiotherapy and completely forgotten by the patient after the treatment.

3 The tensions were treated isolatedly without taking the overall muscular pattern into consideration. The position of the muscles in the total dynamic pattern had not been weighted and studied. This could lead to the patient being deprived of his defence, which in turn resulted in disintegration and further suppression of spontaneous activity, the therapeutic process thus running contrary to its objective. In this way the psychotherapist in various cases was left without any possibility of profit by the previous physiotherapy. Even though the two kinds of treatment followed each other without interruption, they often looked like two forms of treatment completely separated from each other. Again the question arises: Could this have been avoided? Is there a possibility that a more detailed assessment of the muscular structure of the patient could have resulted not only in avoiding cases of doubtlessly erroneous therapy, but even possibly in a fully positive reaction. In my view there should be a fair chance for such results.

Summing up one may assume that it was — and is — not the case that the underlying repressed affects would automatically be released when tensions were removed. My own experience shows that spontaneous activity is not promoted by concentrating the treatment on tense muscles.

Failure to obtain a complete picture before planning the treatment and the one-sided form of treatment probably constitutes the main weakness also in these courses of treatment. On a sound empirical basis I have reached the conclusion that attention must be directed towards *the underdeveloped muscles*. Research into the material available concerning the functional part played by underdeveloped muscles in psychotherapy, is of the utmost importance at our present stage of development. Here, too, the aim must be to promote spontaneous activity.

The treatment, however, is rarely directed towards tense 'defence muscles', and far more often towards the underdeveloped muscles, which represent the repression — the affects which are held in check. My interest in underdeveloped muscles was aroused years ago, when a couple of cases were brought to my notice showing a clear discrepancy between the patient's facies morbi and the conditions of his muscular tensions. In 1954, keeping in mind the disintegration problem of the tension theories, and supported by the experience which gave grounds for assuming that there is a relationship between the patient's muscular and respiratory pattern and his psychic mood, I started scrupulously to chart and compile records of the patient's somatic symptoms, and details of the muscular consistency found were rendered in different shades on my charts. I was especially absorbed by what I at that time termed underdeveloped musculature, particularly with regard to the different qualities of consistency in this musculature and the disturbances in personality represented by these muscular qualities, in psychological sense, disturbances of stages of development of patients. My interest in this aspect of the problem was heightened when I later became acquainted with Dr. Nic Waal's method of somatic psychodiagnosis. She used the terms hypotonic and hypertonic in her somatic appraisals, although in relation to the patient's reaction to 'passive movements', and not in relation to the muscular consistency, the field which had aroused my interest.

The underdeveloped muscles are easily recognisable to those who have learned to look for them. It was the patient's respiratory reaction to the treatment, which proved that these muscles constituted an important part of the overall muscular structure. They definitely have a different consistency as compared with normally relaxed muscles. The slackness which characterizes the underdeveloped muscles is a weak consistency, which is characterized by inelasticity. They have various degrees of slackness which indicates shades of qualities.

Correlatives in the Total Muscular Structure

The hypotonic qualities are not isolated phenomena, but ought to be viewed in relation to the general patterns of tonus throughout the body. The hypertonic muscles have different qualities of resistance. The grip on hypertonic musculature reveals that the tense consistency gives way, tight consistency will also give way, although to a lesser degree. Nodose muscles will only give way slightly and unevenly, whilst a hard and bony consistency does not give way at all. These degrees of tenseness should be given values and appraised against the hypotonic qualities. Most important, however, is how the different muscular qualities are distributed throughout the body and the correlative of tonic qualities in the various segmentary sections. In the most favourable cases, the findings may reveal even patterns giving adequate forms of expression:

Certain tonic conditions in the neck will reveal correlated conditions in the nose, back, chest and leg, with secondary correlatives in other mimic face musculature and in the thigh, hips, crown and toes. The correlatives in the surface musculature have counterparts in deeper muscular layers. Further, special attention should be paid to the significant consistency symptoms to be found in the regression phase, the therapeutically favourable regression. A harmonious selection of the findings will be of great significance and it may be possible to establish fixed and well-founded variations with ample clinical material. Most important is, however, the consistency conditions in the surface musculature in relation to the deeper layers. All such symptoms must in turn be considered in relation to the posture of the body, as a whole, and to specific anomalies of the posture in the upper parts of the body. For example uneven hips, dislocation of the spine and their effect on posture.

Like tensions, anomalies in posture are a defence mechanism. In fact, segments of muscles directly related to the carriage anomaly will be an object of stimulation in the same way as other musculature. The actual alteration in posture will be brought about through knowledge of the connection with the patient's consistency and resources as a whole.

In appraising the degree of pathology, the ascertaining of hypotonic regions which represent the more infantile stages is very important. In other words, the overall structure can collectively provide the answer as to how far physical spontaneity can be expressed and how intact this tendency is. The hypotonic qualities are the key to whether primary activity is present. The reaction of a healthy child reveals no differentiation. Thought, movement, spontaneity, respiration and emotions function as one. The purpose of the new method of treatment is to promote a differentiation of these functions. The individual spontaneity factor varies, since rhythm, strength and manner of movement differs from person to person.

Negative forms of expressions, and their naturally ensuing forms of affirmative and intermediary expressions, having been repressed, will vary from person to person. With adequate stimulation they will manifest themselves in many different ways. It is this complete realization which it is so important to encourage in the patient.

Against the background of the total pattern of tonus, respiration and posture, it will be possible to mobilize the repressed expressions and thereby reintegrate the total muscular pattern, the respiratory and emotional components being released at the same time.

As a confirmation of this, we can take the example of the psychological/physical reaction pertaining to shyness. The closed mouth, the crooked smile, the shifting gaze and twisted body. Arms hanging loosely, slightly to the fore and the shambling gait. In this example, the hypotonic qualities are characterized to a large extent by a feeble consistency. The respiration will be even, halting in the expiratory phase, indicating that anxiety is held back during the missing stage of expiration. In other words, respiration in fact becomes the barometer showing the patient's degree of constraint. Individual frequency varies, but the general respiratory function in relation to musculature is the same for everyone. I do not believe that the different psychic ailments have each a special pattern of respiration. One finds all degrees of constrained respiration, which vary in breadth, depth, rhythm and form. When, however, respiration and hypotonic consistency are studied together, they reflect and complement each other and will reveal the situations and levels of spontaneity at which respiration assumes a defensive function, or at which it can become unconstrained.

The expressive motion, muscle consistency, posture and respiration will indicate the degree to which spontaneous activity is present, and in practice one will find that the lack of spontaneous activity reveals constrained respiration, overwrought egotism, exaggerated facial expressions and gestures. In other words, communication is inharmonious, the spontaneous forms of expression being locked within the personality structure, communication becoming inadequate, acting or dull, since there is no depth of feeling.

The well-known Norwegian author A.O. Vinje once said, in connection with emotion aroused by natural scenery: 'It impresses me so that I can hardly breathe'. The realization he speaks of is an unalarming general experience, where the breath helps to fill the body with the experience to retain the impression longer. His remark could also have served to describe an alarming experience which could have brought about a respiratory condition which would drain the total physical expression, and have a disintegrating effect on the personality.

A simple phrase such as 'turning weak at the knees' also implies a disintegrating experience. Here, instead of experiencing the situation, repression takes place, when at the same time defensive mechanisms are accentuated in the form of tense muscles around the neck, arms and shoulders. This is accompanied by resignation (weakness) represented by hypotonic musculature in the thigh and calf. The anxiety has settled in the mind, with constructed respiration, weakness and tensions as feeble and taut muscles in the body.

The author Sigurd Hoel says in his *Selected Essays* 1962, under the heading 'Depth-psychology and the Writer': 'The repression will be maintained as long as the body stays rigid.' This naturally falls in with the views on which the tension theory is based. We remove the stiffness of the body and the patient is relieved of his complaints. 'The repression will be maintained as long as the body stays rigid' may be an established fact, but is not a correct principle on which to base treatment. An essential link is missing in the total structural development, the surrender. Surrender, the hypotonic state, is the essential part of the picture and is of primary importance. As long as this is present, a defensive mechanism for what is repressed is equally present.

Sigurd Hoel goes on to say: 'Repression is fundamentally caused by anxiety. We know that we can become paralyzed, we can become stiff with anxiety.' Here he broaches upon what I have tried to demonstrate via the muscles. We become paralyzed (hypotonic) and stiff (hypertonic) with anxiety. This constellation is anxiety. The anxiety remains in the mind, the tensions and laxity remain in the body, as two aspects of the same phenomenon. (An adequate experience of a situation, which unexperienced may lead to the same constellation, would be fear.)

Sigurd Hoel has touched upon the problems connected with a newly-formed pattern of carriage. This evidence of physical reactions forming part of a complete realization, may be found in widely different connections in nervous patients.

On the basis of the foregoing, it is my hypothesis that:

Underdeveloped (hypotonic) musculature represents what is remote or latent; the tense (hypertonic) musculature represents the defence mechanisms in the total pattern of muscular tonus.

The inhibited, checked emotion finds expression in the body through constrained respiration and various degrees of resignation (hypotonic state) in the different parts of the body. Those bodily factors serve to keep spontaneity in check. For both diagnosis and treatment, the relation between respiration and muscle tonus indicates the degree to which spontaneous activity is checked.

From what has already been said, it will be realized why many patients worsened by a treatment based on a theory that the treatment of tensions should release the emotions. It is also understandable that in many cases the treatment did not bring the desired results. Muscular stimulation of barriers for unmanifested impulses did not necessarily lead to these impulses manifesting themselves during the subsequent psychotherapy. Feelings were awakened and could be realized, but not in relation to the patient's situation or in relation to definite experiences, so as to acquire a meaning. As a rule it was simply an emotion all by itself, without any special significance, quite often an expression of impatience because the treatment had not fulfilled the patient's expectations. The psychotherapist therefore had little opportunity of employing muscular therapy as a basis for psychotherapy, even though the latter could be given immediately after the muscular treatment. In many cases the two treatments might even have operated at cross purposes, since the therapeutical processes to the patient seemed to have different aims. Difficulties could particularly arise because the two methods of treatment affected different levels in the personality.

Treatment according to the tension theory could not but result in chaotic states in some patients. The tense muscles, which were the seat of the strongest defence, were subjected to treatment. The patient was then deprived of his defence mechanism against an unrealizable subconscious matter far beyond the level of conscious experience, without anything being given him in its place. No understanding of a possibility of integration is available. This is the main weakness of the tension theories. Treatment is carried out according to a theory based on only half of the causation. The emotions which were awakened were often diffuse forms of anxiety combined with restlessness, failing power of concentration and similar troubles which occurred simultaneously. Such a state could be quite foreign to the patient.

This conforms with the warning which exists in all 'surgical' methods of therapy for neuroses, namely failure to stimulate the least excitable defence mechanisms, the patient's most vulnerable point. The patient's response must then be to remove the emotive matter further from the conscious mind. In muscular treatment as in psychotherapy, this process will lead to further repression in persons with a strong ego, and to resignation in those with a weak ego. In patients approaching the psychotic mood, the effect of the treatment could be exceptionally unfavourable. In such cases, the emotions awakened may manifest themselves as completely isolated. When more serious degrees of tension are subjected to treatment, the consequence will be to remove the defence mechanism against impulses, which are too far removed from the patient's level of consciousness, thereby giving him/her no possibility of realization or of integration. When starting treatment, the patient may have been characterized as:

1 Well integrated (defensive) or
2 Poorly integrated

When the muscular barrier is subjected to treatment and partly disappears, the result in the well-integrated group will be that the degree of integration present will be weakened. The consequent anxieties and depressions are often such as cannot be remembered to have been experienced before. This condition may last for years. In the case of patients in the less well-integrated group, muscular treatment might have resulted in a condition which necessitated hospitalization. They had been robbed of the defence mechanism which had upheld them during their previous state of poor integration, and the psychotic level was just around the corner.

The treatment will take an altogether different course if one begins with the underdeveloped, hypotonic musculature and treats only the muscular consistencies belonging to this category. Treatment of the underdeveloped musculature makes realization and integration possible. The tensions (defence mechanisms) give way as the patient gets insight as a result of this process. The hypotonic musculature represents the content we wish to awaken in the patient. It is this lacking content which upholds the stagnation and disturbances in the development of the patient.

The treatment will also assume a different character when dealing with the prefunctional hypotonic qualities, the level which is on the borderline between activation and consciousness. The patients show by involuntary signs that the treatment is really reaching them. At first this is expressed by responses such as bodily movements and the uttering of single words. According to the individual structure, these forms of expression will also be manifested in other simple ways like yawns, sighs, etc.

By shifting the aim of treatment from hypertonic to hypotonic muscles, I experienced a noticeable change in the results obtained. The patient no longer showed signs of any excessive affects. By directing further treatment to functional hypotonic muscles, a more complete picture was obtained. The tensions subsided and disappeared when the experience was realized and assimilated. The activity of the patients was expressed both in verbal comment and in bodily activity. The treatment was felt by the patients as something familiar, which they could realize as their own emotional experience. The course of the treatment was guided by the aim of obtaining an active synthesis in the patient's personality, and so vivid that the patients themselves could continue to explore the connection with something they felt as personally relevant and sensed.

I shall later return to the subject of the further perspective connected with the spontaneous forms of expression in relation to the total pattern of resources.

Treatment given in this manner helps to bring resources to the fore, since its focus is on latent personality content. It is also performed in a different manner from the massage-like grips used on tense muscles. The muscular approach applied to underdeveloped muscles will be an appealing grip, adjusted to the patient's level of spontaneity. The approach on hypotonic musculature which is capable of being mobilized, will then be felt as something familiar which concerns the patient, making it possible for him to give spontaneous expression to the content of the impulses which are pushing forward. If and when the respiratory response indicates the presence of doubtful emotional tones, the grip may become lighter, although still firm. If the grip is too hard, the patient's respiration will become inhibited and the therapist will notice the absence of the expected, adequate muscle tonus.

An active sympathetic attitude and treatment which consists of 'fondling' the patient's muscles, may of course lead to the patient becoming strongly attached to the therapist, or to countertransference on the part of the therapist. It is essential that the therapist should be aware of these possibilities, particularly when giving treatment to hypotonic musculature with its varied underlying content. The therapist's attitude can be perceptive and sensitive without the engagement involving her identifying with the individual's needs which emerge during the treatment. All the same, the therapist can concentrate actively upon observing and directing the muscular-emotional process taking place in the patient. The purpose of this approach is to provide security at all levels, conforming with the basic analytic law that 'not orders, but security, relaxation and time release spontaneity'. The margin between identification and an approach giving maximum faith and security, is narrow and yet very great. Identification has a restrictive effect on the patient's level of spontaneity, the other approach brings release. (When treating tense muscles, the therapist often during treatment brings out her own affects in relation to the patient.)

One could easily be led to deduce a constant ratio between hypotonic and hypertonic musculature. In practice one will seldom find this constant ratio in the overall picture of muscles. Anomalies of posture and impaired sight or hearing can, according to my experience, represent muscular compensation in the form of tensions in the same way as ordinary muscular tensions, which are more easily observed. A marked difference in the consistency of the right and left side represents emotional disharmony. Conjointly with other symptoms, these findings denote identification disorders as primary causal factors in reduced or weakened ego-strength.

Furthermore a 'strained intellect' and similar characteristics may be found to be present at the cost of resolution of emotional conflicts. These factors serve to upset the constant ratio between tensions and hypotonia. The tensions (the defence), is no longer related to the weakness (the surrender), but is part and parcel of a more or less complicated overall picture.

It is, however, my opinion that the state of consistency in the underdeveloped muscular qualities represents the real emotional status, despite the multiplicity of defensive veils. This has no consequence for the method of treatment, as it has to be considered in each individual case whether tensions will gradually yield as the prefunctional, hypotonic qualities acquire meaning. One might say that the hypotonic condition represents the content one wishes to arouse in the patient, and that it is this inadequate content which maintains the stagnation and the neurotic status of the patient's personality. This implies that extra importance should be attached to the hypotonic conditions in the planning and applying of treatment. The hypotonic muscles are at the centre of the aim of muscular approach, and not irrelevant to it.

By starting with the central factors, respiration and hypotonic musculature, as a base for the understanding of blocking and of mobilization, the deep awakening of spontaneity will be represented by vegetative visceral responses such as sounds and rumbling. These responses are functionally deep-reaching reactions. They amount to a 'yes' for something personally meaningful and appear when personality changes take place. The genuine, adequate form of behaviour is beginning to take the place of its substitute. The treatment influences basic psychosomatic conditions, so that the vegetative visceral functions assume more adequate proportion in the body. These responses are awakened when the segments concerned acquire adequate muscular consistency, and to the patient this brings a sensation of relief in that region. That the response represents levels of experience can be heard, because at first the sound will be high-pitched, becoming gradually deeper in tone as the adequate muscle consistency develops. While this is taking place, there will simultaneously be an alteration in the patient's use of his voice. (It has previously been said that if the internal organs could be influenced through muscles and sinews, one would truly be able to cure neurosis.)

As previously mentioned, the relationship between the patient and the therapist must be one of trust, not of identification. It is also important that the therapist's intuition is sound. It is essential that these two basic factors are present with the therapist. It is therefore important that the therapist should be conscious of earlier blockings or existing conflicts in her own personality. The therapist will scarcely be able to apply the correct degree of strength when working on muscular segments in the patient, unless her own relationship to such musculature is free from restraint. If there are such underdeveloped segments in her own body (stages in a psychological sense), the therapist will usually refrain from treating, give only approximate treatment, or apply hesitant grips to the corresponding segments in the patient. Consequently psychoanalysis should be desirable. Errors lie most often in the manifold manifestations of human spirit. Our influence on the patient is great but our impact can be harmful as well as helpful. Similar conditions are also often encountered with regard to the therapist's attitude in verbal perceptive therapy.

When judging indications for muscular therapy, experience shows that they are most in keeping with the indications for orthodox analytic therapy — with modifications, however, since through bodily approach the resources held in check are awakened without the patient's associations being connected very strongly with the deep-seated affliction. Starting with the deep-rooted affliction, the associations show the way onward, with a parallel in a creative contemporary situation. This again emphasizes the necessity on the part of the muscular therapist to understand the methods and problems of the verbally communicating therapist, and vice versa. In an analysis, the memory image is often a substitute for the experience. In muscular therapy, the expressive form is promoted through physical experience which is then integrated through memory. Furthermore dream material gives depth of meaning when muscle-correlatives with expressive tendencies and placed in segments with equal muscular qualities are being stimulated. Dreams will promote insight by being especially abundant and by giving progressively more unmasked symbolic material. The patient may be surprised at how dreams now have a specific meaning to him. Instead of experiencing the dream from the outside, like a cinema story, it is living in him all day as something personally significant, leading him towards insight into his inner life.

Also, the patient will frequently, in discussing his shortcomings, make use of verbal expressions which clearly formulate the connection between his physical condition and his personality make-up, expressions like 'stiff-legged', 'stiff-necked' and others, most of them being rather untranslatable, with their double meaning. The use of such words and expressions from general conversation, denoting a specific connection between mental and somatic factors, usually signifies that the patient has won significant insights, and therefore most often take place during important stages in the development of therapy.

Depths of Personal Resources

For my own part I was confirmed in what I previously had sensed through the dreams of my patients, that we are involved in the patient's emotional life to a far greater extent than being a mere listener with intuitive understanding. I may add, there is surely a right way of listening. The art of listening is to find out what the patient is trying to convey, which is the only essential value. The furthering of creative activity in the patient demands a questioning self-dialogue, a manifestation of symbolic language in the patient. This has nothing to do with any theory or learning, particular philosophy or code of ethics. The drive is centred around the self, the language in 'me' to bring about the transformation which is essential.

The questioning appeal to the prefunctional/preconscious material in body and mind makes the furthering of creative activity in the individual possible. However, for this development to take place, it is important that everything between them is based on a living, creative atmosphere of mutual trust and confidence.

In the last stage of therapy, in particular, it is of vital importance that the patient should have a profound and secure belief in the therapist's integrity and honesty. This will enable him to use his own 'personal' language, and this, in its turn, is one of the patient's greatest experiences during the treatment, viz. the deeply felt opinions and emotions with all of himself. He feels free when he has gained the certainty that he is no longer under any obligation to give emotional expressions in a rational way. He now realizes that he no longer thinks, feels or listens only with his intellect, but with the whole of his body and his being. And this is, it is now clear to him, as it should be. Now, when all this is 'living' in him, the reverse is also true, namely that he will be able to use his intellect, and only that, when the situation so requires.

One of my clients described this thinking of his whole body as a fundamental change. He had given up his ambitions which had been felt as a destructive force: 'My rational thinking has changed to wisdom, a feeling you cannot put into words'.

If integrated respiration therapy is to prove meaningful, it must bring forward a development that enables us to reach deep into the personality structure of the individual. Through the richness of associative material on this basis, the patient will easily undergo perceivable changes in behaviour and in general outlook, as well as changes concerning ethics.

The dream-dynamics give the patient this possibility. The atmosphere, pictures and dynamics of dreams are based on a corrective emotional experience in the patient and he will detect his true self by means of a metaphorical language and the intensively personal atmosphere of his dreams. The patient forms a personal language of his own, thus expressing in a better way than before his inner activity and life. The metaphorical language thus spoken of is a penetrating reflection of the inner life of the patient.

This true-to-oneself activity makes it possible for the therapist to avoid the pitfalls inherent in the use of ordinary language, when pointing to the many aspects of severe neurosis. Thus seen, the metaphorical language makes deep reflection in a symbolic language possible.

The dynamics of bodily structure found through the diagnostic of muscular consistencies in my experience forms a key in the furthering of an adequate, constructive therapy. The integrated respiration therapy represents a possibility for an understanding of the great difference between strictly intellectual thinking and the flexibility in individuals thinking and acting with their body and mind as a whole.

On deeper levels integrated respiration therapy brings forth body-and-mind qualities correlating with respiration. The free function of the glabella* gives the possibility of a nuanced expression of face, hands, and feet, when simultaneously the roof of the mouth and the diaphragm are free from strain. The experience of these deep-rooted good feelings are emotions which encourage the manifestation of the individual's genuine values.

The inhibition of these deep-seated expressions of good feelings is mostly to be found in the ligaments of the small muscles of the chest, sacrum and shoulder-neck regions.

Psychologically speaking: If we do not find the content of the many ego-frustrations hidden in mind and body, through behaviour, thoughts and action, how to revive the good emotions?

The experience of the nuanced emotional manifestation of eyes-face, hands-fingers, feet-toes is a fundamental experience, a certainty of genuine quality, which is a spiritual experience beyond the function of the mind. In a way you may say that the eyes are the mirror of the soul.

Perhaps the reader may believe here that there is an idea of therapeutic completeness. You may wonder: Who can say in therapy that a real change has taken place? My experience has convinced me that integrated respiration therapy can bring about fundamental changes in patients with severe neurotic disturbances. I am one of those who have tried various approaches in learning, worshipped authorities, and pursued patterns of thought. But is the fundamental change to be found in the pursuit of pattern of thoughts?

However, I have the hope that the fundamental change in therapy, the tremendous feeling of something entirely new, which you cannot put a name on, is possible. The nameless source in itself is within reach in therapy. This internal character/quality in mind and body may find its manifestation in respiration, the breathing in 'me'.

---

*The centre between the eyes.

The Divided Body

by David Boadella

Paper given at the University of Manchester, 8th March, 1975.

David Boadella took his first degree in English at the University of London, and an M.Ed at Nottingham University. He has been actively involved with the work of Reich since 1952. He learned vegetotherapy with Dr. Doris Howard, who trained with Od Havrevold, one of Reich's co-workers in Oslo; and from Paul Ritter. He founded and edits Energy and Character: the Journal of Bio-energetic Research, *and is the author of* Wilhelm Reich: The Evolution of his Work. *He works now as the head teacher of Abbotsbury School in Dorset, and as a therapist at the Centre for Bio-energy in London, at weekends. The paper 'The Divided Body' first appeared in* Energy and Character, *Vol.3, No.2; and also in* Quaderni Reichiani *(edited by Luciano Rispoli) in Naples, No.2, 1973.*

The man described in this case-history was treated by me for a total of about 250 sessions. Since the therapy ended, nearly nine years ago, I have remained in touch with him on a basis of friendship, and this case-history will include an account of developments in his life in that period.

At the time the treatment started James was in his mid-twenties and was earning his living in a local government office. He was of medium height, wore spectacles for short-sightedness, and gave as his reason for wanting therapy that he felt generally inadequate, and had done so since adolescence. He mentioned in passing that he often had homosexual feelings, but that his social contacts with either sex were very limited. As an adolescent he had had an attack of suicidal depression, and had seriously contemplated taking his own life at one stage.

In the first session he complained of a sense of pressure in his head, which he said was there all the time. Not a pain, but just a sense of pressure. Often he felt his head was not part of his body, and that his brains were all tangled up and needed to be scooped clean. He related these feelings about his head in an unemotional manner, but shortly after he began to chuckle. Often, he said, when he lay down to relax, he found that he began to chuckle. The chuckling was rather violent, and involved a lot of convulsive movements, but I experienced it as very strange because there was nothing it seemed to relate to. Later he added that when he smiled he felt more knit together. On the other hand when he stopped smiling, he felt more serious.

He told me in the same session, as though to reassure me, that he did not always smile, that he found it very easy to cry, whenever he became aware of all the things that he lacked, particularly a girl-friend. He described an evening when he had walked through the streets of the industrial town near where he lived, feeling an urge to smash all the windows in, and crying at the same time. He felt horrible. His body had cried, but his head had only looked on.

He also told me that he often got into tempers at home, and at work. His anger, he said, was always with things, never against people. But people always misunderstood, and were afraid of his tempers.

He told me that it was his custom to masturbate very frequently, and usually with little pleasure. The fantasies were commonly of other men being treated sadistically, i.e. having their genitals beaten or branded, or being castrated.

Before the end of the first session I began to interpret his smile as a defence, and this brought from him the comment: 'I think my smile goes along with feeling I could bash your head in'.

One of the most characteristic features of schizoid people is the relative accessibility of material, and the eagerness with which they work on this. Conventional character-analysis, as I learnt fairly early on in this treatment, is of little use in treating such people. There is no character armour to break down in the sense of the rigid structure of defences which one meets in the compulsive characters. Rather, the schizoid person threatens at any time to break out of the very frail system of defences which only just contain him. Whereas the problem in many therapies is one of mobilising energy, the schizoid energy is already in a potentially dangerous state of flood. Removing too soon what defences there are to contain this flood would be a reasonably sure way to precipitate a psychotic breakdown, as Dr. Nic Waal pointed out, in a private communication (1).

So one of the first things which I learned in treating James was to discard the textbook and to follow the patient, pacing the therapy carefully so that a mutual understanding could eventually grow between us of exactly what was going on in his body and mind. The treatment was scarcely at all analytic therapy; it soon became contact therapy. What the schizoid person needs most of all is a person who can open his mind to make room for all the bizarre forms of behaviour of which the schizoid person is capable; who can open his heart so that genuine affection can be felt for the sufferings of a patient who is one of the first to relapse into illness in the face of any cold intellectual attempt to help him; and who can open his arms, often literally, so that the patient can experience the sense of bodily warmth and energetic skin contact of which he is so deprived, and which is so basic to his condition.

All of this I did not realise immediately; but in the account which follows will be found chiefly descriptions of what the patient did or said, or how he behaved. My role, as therapist, was predominantly a passive one, in Braatøy's sense of a midwife who provides encouragement and support so that the mother can deliver her own child (2). Throughout this treatment my main support in being prepared to let the neurosis unfold in its own way, driven by its own internal energy, and to work itself out upon me, has been the understanding of the schizoid disturbance which I gained from Alexander Lowen. He it was who, by his clear and sympathetic diagnosis of the schizoid predicament, helped me to overcome my own fear of madness, and to learn to trust my schizoid patient.

The Basic Disturbance
The remainder of this account will not attempt to follow the

The divided body

therapy through session by session, but to deal with the general pattern of developments.

The central problem of the disturbance in James was the relationship of his head to his body. Moshe Feldenkrais has drawn attention to how crucial the alignment of the head with the trunk is, in determining a person's total posture:

> 'A coherent picture of the whole course of adaptation to gravity is obtained if the head is regarded as the support of the teleceptors, i.e. the instruments through which our relation with the outside world is extended beyond our body. Thus the anatomy of the head determines the conditioning of response to sound, and the reflective response to gravity. Next the motility of the eyes is integrated into the already existing basic movements of the head. The first manifestations of consciousness will appear with the control of the head which allows the child to follow and direct itself towards moving objects or sources of sound' (3).

In the schizoid person there is a specific disjointedness in the neck area which involves tension in the deep muscles at the base of the skull. My patient felt this tension in the form of a noose drawn round his neck, and pulled tight, with the threat that he would have his head cut off from his body if he did not do what was expected of him. When his head felt all right, his body was wrong. When his body felt all right, his head felt wrong. His head was literally cut off, that is, dissociated from his body by the tensions. Whereas the compulsive character is stiff-necked, and it is possible to mobilise aggression by working on the muscles at the nape of the neck, the schizoid neck tensions are not so readily accessible.

Lowen has described the longitudinal swing of energy in the healthy organism as being pendular in character. Energy moves to the head-end, as it does to the genitals and the musculature. The pattern of energy movement which seemed to explain James best was as follows: the normal pendular swing had been grossly disturbed in the direction of over-charging the head end. The constant movement of energy upwards into his head James described as 'surging'. But instead of swinging downwards again, and flowing back into the body to be discharged normally in co-ordinated movements or pleasurable sexuality, the energy became stored, held back by the tensions at the base of the skull. He showed a perversion of the normal reservoir function of the head cavity. 'One cannot comprehend the reality principle if one ignores the fact that the brain, and in fact the whole head, can contain the most powerful impulses', Lowen writes. 'The brain, too, functions like a condenser, equal in capacity to the condenser-like function of the genital apparatus. The actual amount of energy which can be held and focused in the human brain is tremendous. In very healthy organisms it creates a glow about the head' (4).

In this schizoid head, however, the energy is caught in a bottle-neck. It is constricted from beneath, and it is also blocked from being expressed outwardly in the form of mobile facial expression and warm lively eyes. The schizoid person does not have the furrowed, worried forehead of the average neurotic. Rather he has a flat, dull, forehead, which my patient experienced like an iron curtain. Energy is frozen in the front of the head and face, just as it is frozen in the top of the neck. This block in the forehead is deeply connected with the typical expression in the schizoid eyes.

Wilhelm Reich, in his brilliant pioneering study of the schizophrenic split, in which bio-energetic principles were applied for the first time to this condition, gives a full description of the remote schizophrenic expression in the eyes. It occurred to him that this expression has a focal significance in understanding the nature of the split:

> 'One thought stuck in my mind and did not budge: is it possible that the schizophrenic attack or process is locally anchored just as are other disease symptoms such as anorexia or a headache or cardiac anxiety? Is it the base of the brain, the region of the crossing of the optic nerve? Would it be reasonable to assume that schizophrenia is a true 'brain disease' induced by some specific type of emotional upheaval, with a local contraction of special parts of the brain, due to severe anxiety?' (5).

The divided body

There were three kinds of expression I learned to expect from James' eyes. The first was a cold, glassy, rather impersonal look, which I experienced as fish-like. He looked at me like a cold fish. The second expression was an intense burning look, which had a quality of desperation about it. The third expression was when his eyes 'went off' that is to say all focusing went, and the eyes began to go 'swimmy'.

The meaning of these three expressions as they were explored during the treatment was as follows. The glassy, fish-like expression was the normal frozen look, which he felt as a 'clouding over'. Maurice Nicoll, writing not of the schizoid person, but of the dissociated state of the average neurotic, once wrote:

> 'We would like the power of feeling meaning in all the experiences we have had. As a rule we are not there. We are never at home. We are nearly always out. If a person lives in the imagination and its meanings, he is then always out. He is not at home. Such a person does not see you. He sees his dream of you, his imagination of you, his illusion of you' (6).

The other appearance of being out, not with it, was experienced inwardly also as a feeling of not being there. The basis of this feeling is the withdrawal of energy from the body as a whole towards the head, and from the outside of the head (the face) to the interior. The high central head tension of the schizoid person has indeed little contact with the outside world, and the feeling of islolation and unreality corresponds exactly to the energetic state.

The second expression in the eyes, the intense burning look, was always associated with a sense of strain. He willed himself, as it were, to overcome the difficulty in meeting the world, and forced his eyes to make contact with someone. This was one reaction to the sense of clouding over, the attempt to snap out of it, and drill a hole in the clouds with his eyes. The trouble was that maintaining this strained sense of focusing meant forcing even more energy up to the head, and the usual effect was to increase the sense of pressure. So he suffered for years from frequent very painful headaches, and a sensation of bursting in the head. This is how he once described the sensation, in a letter to me between sessions:

'The pressure in my head at the moment is definitely pulsatile. Pressure mounts and mounts, and I feel desperate, and then, snap, for a while there is relief. I almost heave a sigh of contentment, and then the pressure starts mounting even more, and inwardly I cry out "Oh no, not any more, not again". And so on, ad infinitum. Sometimes my scalp itches, at other times I feel a fierce pain in my head. I feel I'm constantly shutting something out with my eyes. When I first thought about it, I thought it might have something to do with the glare of the sun, but my forehead is still contracted in the dim light of this room. Raising my eye-brows affords temporary relief, but only serves to aggravate the sensation in my forehead not being open and clear. Makes me feel like cutting a slit in the middle of it.'

What happens to all this energy piling up into the head end? It cannot stay there for ever. What manifestations does it give rise to, and what happens to it eventually? On the one hand it helps to explain the particularly vivid dreams, nightmares, and hallucinations which the schizoid person is prone to. It undoubtedly colours the fantasy-life. It was certainly no accident that fantasies of hanging, or decapitation, had an obsessional interest for my patient. Related to these fantasies was the idea he had that it would be wonderful if he could take off his alien head, and replace it with a good one, namely mine. At other times when he was particularly desperate, feeling the pressure would make him feel like banging his head against a wall 'so hard that all my grey matter would come oozing out. I actually slapped my face, once, until it was sore. I was also filled with the desire to shave my hair off.'

Since the energy does not discharge normally and rhythmically it must discharge abnormally and unrhythmically. If this discharge, in movement, and sexual behaviour takes place in bits and pieces by a process of leak-back, it explains the familiar unco-ordinated nature of schizoid body movements. If on the other hand the energy rushes back into the body (and we must remember that it is under pressure) the effect is explosive and disturbing.

Such sudden breakthroughs of energy from the compressed

area of the head, with its overcharged reservoir, into the rest of the body, were experienced by James as very frightening. It is in such circumstances that the third characteristic expression of the eyes could be seen: the swimmy look. Usually James fought against giving in to this expression, and tried to maintain his eye-contact in the intensely focused way. I learned however that this swimmy expression was the prelude to more energy coming through to the surface of his body, in muscles and facial expression, and he was, after a time, deliberately encouraged to yield to this expression whenever he felt it coming on during a session.

This swimmy expression, which always went with a rolling upwards of the eyes, and a marked change in the breathing rhythm, was first described clearly by Reich:

> 'Her eyes would become veiled, the expression would become one of looking into the far distance, and in addition the eyeballs would turn sharply upwards when the melting organ sensations became very strong.' (5).

One schizoid person once said to me: 'My body does not keep my head up. Rather my head keeps my body up.' James similarly felt his head as his 'stronghold'. Whenever energy went surging upwards he felt (for a time) strong, superior, inflated, and omnipotent. He felt as though he was no longer tied to the ground. It was an ethereal, spiritual, heavenly feeling of soaring. Not out-going, but up-going. He related a dream he remembered from adolescence in which he was in a building like a cathedral, of immeasurable proportions. He was in contact with everyone inside it, and had a sense of peace and one-ness. Since he had difficulty in moving outwards to meet the world, he wanted to expand sufficiently to invite the world into himself, to share it on his terms. Unfortunately this dream of heaven soon turns into a nightmare: the upsurging energy does not find immeasurable space to expand into. Sooner or later it meets the vault of the human skull, which he dreamed of recurrently in the form of an underground cellar in which he was imprisoned, and the lid of which he could not raise. To let the energy swing back was difficult for him, as for all schizoid people. He was confident only while the upsurging lasted. The downward flow of energy, tending to lower the pressure in his head, was experienced as collapse. Any strong spontaneous flow downwards, in the direction of the body and discharge, was felt as a loss and as an even greater disorientation. Hence the lost, swimmy expression in the eyes, as though drowning.

Collapse of the body is what is feared as the energy moves downwards and outwards strongly. This feeling of loss of self and disintegration is rationally based, since it is precisely in this way that the schizoid disturbance can be removed. Only the convulsive body movements which the schizoid fears can bring the integration and co-ordination which he lacks. At the same time, to give in to expressive movements of the body, including the head is tantamount to the collapse of the special schizoid way of life.

The schizoid person hangs on to his head in the same way that the homosexual character hangs on to his penis. Lowen (7) suggested that the homosexual is afraid of the 'little death' of orgasm because all his feeling of life is concentrated on the genitals, so that the loss of genital feeling after intercourse is felt as a reduction of personality. The homosexual is afraid to lose his genitals (castration anxiety); but the schizoid person is afraid to lose his head (capitation anxiety). It can also be said that James was constantly trying to maintain his head in a state of erection.

At first I did not understand this process properly, and tended to avoid situations which induced strong streaming and the swimmy look, with the collapse feeling. To bring all this on was tantamount to robbing the patient of that spurious reality sense which he had developed. I was afraid, simply, to send him mad. Perhaps it was as well that I did not rush him into too powerful sensations by pressurised treatment. At the same time he did not begin to get well until he was able to let the charge in his head collapse, and let the energy find its own pathways in his body.

I have spent some time describing the blockages in his head and eyes, as I feel these are the root of the disturbance. Indeed I would venture the term 'ocular character' as an alternative descriptive term, by analogy with the oral character.* When

---

*This article was written in August 1967 before I had read Elsworth Baker's *Man in the Trap*, where the term 'ocular character' is also introduced.

Reich developed his theory of the segmental nature of armouring, he took the view that it was desirable to resolve the tensions of different areas in segmental order, beginning with the facial expression, and in particular the expression in the eyes. Whether or not this is a generally necessary mode of procedure (and Lowen's work suggests a different approach), I believe it to be true that until some degree of resolution of the energetic problem of the expressions in the eyes, in the schizoid treatment little progress can be made (8).

Bodily Co-ordination

The lack of co-ordination in James' body was expressed in a number of ways, and these must now be described. He was unable, for example, to catch a ball, and felt inadequate because he had always failed to achieve anything in sport, swimming, etc. At the time he began therapy he was using a motor-cycle, but on two occasions he lost control of the vehicle and crashed, though it is difficult to know how far this may have been due to errors of vision and discrimination, and how much to schizoid muscle unco-ordination. On the whole in the material functions of day to day life, his body was not markedly disturbed, except in times of stress. Such times would be tantamount to an over-production of energy, to his having more energy than his head could absorb and contain, in other words. There would then be a process of flood-back into, for instance, his limbs, which he experienced as unusual and disturbing. Thus under strong emotional stress he felt weak and shaky in the knees and legs. Also there had been times when his hands had shaken while holding a knife and fork, in a restaurant situation where he had felt particularly self-conscious and embarrassed.

It was the expressive use of his body that was most defective. I shall describe this in relation to three main aspects: facial expression; sexual behaviour; and manifestations of anger.

I have already described the prominence his smile took in the first session. His lips were on the thin side, and he felt his whole mouth and chin area as alien. He felt he wanted to cut off his chin because it did not belong to him, and to bite off his lip because it was not feeling anything. He felt his face underneath the smile, to be like a skull. He was aware of the sense of dead flesh in his facial expression, and described a hallucinatory feeling he had had, which was most likely a projection of his own facial expression outwards. A man with expressionless eyes and a featureless face beckoned him through a trap-door in the floor of the house, down through the earth into a rock tomb where he was imprisoned. This rock tomb was a literal expression of the sense he had that his energy was shut in, in the vault of his skull, and kept imprisoned there by the petrification in the frontal and basal areas of his head.

He hated the sight of himself in a mirror, and felt completely cut off from what he saw. He experienced his facial appearance as revoltingly ugly. At the same time he had covered this up with a spurious vanity, and a boosted up idea of his own self-importance. The rational root of this superior feeling was his sense that his energy charge was stronger and more lively than many people's. The fund of tenderness and sensitivity and understanding was waiting within him to be harnessed. What stopped this taking place was, amongst other things, his cold frozen facial expression.

Sometimes, usually in situations where he was sexually attracted, the feeling broke through into his face and cheeks in the form of blushing. He experienced this as something disturbing and unsettling which he wanted to get rid of. Blushing was itself a kind of collapse, in the same way that any spontaneous autonomic reaction was. He had to learn during the course of the therapy to tolerate and identify with this blushing and to recognise it as one of the ways in which his body, in spite of its disturbance, still proclaimed its aliveness.

Sexually, he was strongly aroused by other men, whose bodies he felt to be more lively, and graceful and co-ordinated than his own. However, his sexual fantasies were predominantly at this time, sadistic, and left him feeling alienated from himself. It was as though he needed to punish the fantasy figures for having better bodies than his own. His behaviour, as he described it, in masturbation, involved great muscular concentration and pressure to focus the energy on the genitals. He himself expressed it that 'I deliberately use genital sensation to take away energy from my head'. Thus genital discharge was very hard work, the motive force was supplied from the over-charged head end, with its elaborate visual fantasy structure, and the result, as with all sexuality that one has flogged oneself into, was very poor satisfaction, with most of the energy still left undrained in the head. The pattern that was typical for him, was thus a series of repeated masturbations, each one increasingly dissatisfying, but the overall effect of which was to dull his energy level for a while. This would be followed by a feeling of remorse, and the need to make a 'fresh start' — basically to begin a new rhythm of surging upwards and expanding again. This was associated with a sense of 'pitching in' to work, fresh attempts to contact people, etc., until the sense of head-pressure mounted and a new round of masturbation was initiated.

Expressions of anger are always difficult for the schizoid person. What James described as losing his temper, at home or at work, involved verbal activity: shouting at someone who had done something he regarded as stupid, for example. He believed that by verbal attacks of this kind he might break down people's armour sufficiently to get soft contact and a warm response from them. This verbal attack was therefore a focusing of energy, comparable to the focusing through eye contact. It did not in itself provide a very adequate discharge. On the other hand when rage reached his musculature, where it could discharge, he went off and dissociated. He described one such occasion in a letter:

> 'My head makes me feel desperate. One evening I found myself alone in the house. I felt angry and lonely. I picked flowers off the mantelpiece, and tore them up, throwing them on the floor. I stamped on the ground, and threw a glass bottle to the floor with all my might, expecting a shattering of glass. But the bottle was tough, and in bigger bursts of anger I finally succeeded in permanently denting the kitchen sink. I grovelled on the floor and wept, and cursed you. I spewed saliva all over the floor and cushions. Finally feeling spent, I wrote a diatribe, almost incoherent, against you. I could really have murdered you. I blamed you for the state I was in'.

Having described the main ingredients of the schizoid disturbance in James, and how it unfolded itself during the therapy, it is now relevant to describe the transference situation.

The Transference Situation

According to Frieda Fromm-Reichmann, 'the thorough and sympathetic handling of the transference is the core of psychotherapy with the schizoid person.' (9).

The first emotion transferred to me, was distrust. He felt superior to me, in so many ways, and did not believe I could really help him. All he needed was love, and all he was getting was a lot of meaningless words. I did not measure up to him, I could never be strong enough to cope with his energies, etc. Now in all transference situations, but particularly when dealing with schizoid people, it is vital for the therapist to be aware of his counter-transferences. Otherwise the therapy can soon be wrecked on the rocks of the therapist's own incipient problems which the schizoid perception has an uncanny way of ferreting out. 'They can see through the therapist', Lowen comments, 'as quickly as any therapist can see through them. And who of us is not free from his neurotic problem?' (4).

The counter-transference to the feeling of distrust, is self-justification. One tells oneself really it is only the patient's illness that makes him so critical, etc.; naturally the therapist is not the withdrawn remote figure which the patient thinks he is, and so on. Fortunately I had learnt from Reich the value of taking seriously the schizoid perceptions: in doing so I learned a great deal about myself, and was able to develop in the therapy so that I really was able to help James in ways I could not have imagined. If it is true, as Lowen says, that the schizoid resistance will take the form of distrust, of fear of the therapist and fear of the therapy, it is also true that many therapists have an unrecognised fear of the patient. The schizoid patient is only too ready to overcome his distrust, if the therapist is equally ready to overcome his fear.

The transference situation is further complicated by the fact that the schizoid person is also prone to project his own states on to the therapist. For several months James complained of my coldness and remoteness from him. Sometimes he correctly perceived a guardedness on my own part which was obstructing the course of therapy; at other times he projected on to the relationship between us his own feeling of withdrawal and of being out of things. The only solution is for the therapist to be sufficiently in touch with his own feelings, and sufficiently willing to credit the patient with the likelihood of being right at least part of the time, for genuine mutual understanding and trust to grow. Wherever the relationship is blocked, and fails to be established, Frieda Fromm-Reichmann reminds us, it is due to the therapist's personality difficulties, not to the patient's psychopathology.

For a long time I was afraid of James' frozen destructiveness. In this I echoed the world he had already experienced, and it was precisely this fear which fed the destructiveness, because it bred isolation and separation, and re-inforced the split already present between murderous feelings and the undercharged muscles.

John Rosen has realised the importance of focusing the patient's aggression upon himself. 'The aim of therapy is to direct this aggression towards the therapist rather than to have the patient dissipate it amorphously in his usual fashion' (quoted by Lowen from Rosen's book, 10). In physically struggling and wrestling with a schizoid patient, much more than a tangible expression of anger is involved. The therapist begins to trust the aggressive force in the patient as the healing and restorative power which it is when it flows cleanly through charged muscles. It is far less alarming to wrestle vigorously with an enraged patient who is in contact with the context of the situation, than to meet the remark of the first session: 'I could bash your head in', in conjunction with a cold, fixed smile. Needless to say, the situation where such physical activity became possible in this form, occurred only after we had worked through to a large extent the function of the expression in his eyes which has already been described at length.

What James learned in the process of letting the energy come through into his muscles, was that he need not fear his violent emotions. The outward expression of aggression helped him to face more directly the violence of his fantasies, in the sense that these now became focused on me, as a person close to him, rather than on remote people he hardly knew. Thus by degrees he allowed his head and his body to fuse more. I believe that these sadistic fantasies did not finally begin to be resolved until he had focused them on his father, and this did eventually occur quite naturally, as he accepted and identified with these particular expressions of his energy, without struggling to keep above them, and without feeling disgusted with himself when he had given in to them. Similarly Reich's schizophrenic patient had to learn, slowly, 'to produce the expression of murderous hate in her eyes, without becoming frightened by it. This gave her some feeling of security against her fear of committing murder; she realised that one can express murderous hatred fully, and that this did not mean that one actually had to commit murder.'

Just as Rosen, and many bio-energetically orientated therapists have taken up the challenge of physical aggression on their own person, so some therapists have taken up the challenge of physical warmth in their own person. Philip Gold, in his case-history of a manic-depressive patient, describes how she went through a period of feeling the coldness of her skin. 'In later sessions she came spontaneously into my arms, nestled close to my body, nuzzled and made sucking and sighing sounds, until again she fell asleep.' (11).

The schizoid patient has a similar profound hunger for physical warmth and contact. James could not move towards this spontaneously. Rather he sought it at first compulsively, in the sense that he would have to come close to my body in a rush, and without any warning or preparatory movements. The first few times that he did so he was overcome with feelings of wretchedness for being so 'abject'. He learned gradually to accept the advantages of approaching without the rush, and with his head involved.

The turning point in the whole treatment was when it first became possible for him to reach out with his lips. As his lips became mobilised through work on his smile, and some of the tensions in his jaw were released through biting, his throat area began to thaw out. For a long time he had guarded himself against feeling this need, by his sadistic fantasies, and by the general thinness and tightness of his lips and mouth. James' mouth proved to be the gateway to the integration of his head and his body. Through it poured a torrent of feeling: by turns erotic, tender and sorrowful. For the first time his heart and his head fused in the expressive movements of his body, triggered by the energetic charge which had broken through to his lips. Whereas before whenever he had given in to crying it had been forced out violently and noisily through the bottle-neck of his throat, he now became capable for the first time of deep convulsive sobbing, which relaxed his entire body and flooded it with warmth. He re-lived particularly vividly the need to make warm contact with his mother, and the fact that as a baby this had not been possible. But now he experienced the deprivation sorrowfully, and with bitterness. Above all without freezing.

'The therapist's warmth', Lowen wrote, 'is the therapeutic agent by means of which he can bring the patient more deeply into reality ... The warmth that the patient needs is the heat produced by the energy flow in his own tissues and musculature. Few patients are more thrilled than when they find their body becoming alive, their extremities warm, their skin pink and rosey.' James had almost literally drunk his warmth in at first, using the contact with me as a bridge to his own body. Now for the first time he began to be strongly attracted by the opposite sex. The charging of his body tissues was paralleled by a spontaneous out-going-ness in social life. He established tentative relationships with one or two girls. None of this led to very much at first, and many fears and mistrusts outside the therapeutic situation still remained. Nevertheless the orientation of his life had begun to shift: from homosexual to heterosexual, from sadistic fantasies to tender fantasies; from split-off heady contact, to whole body contact; from eyes that were clouded or 'off', to eyes that could melt with feeling; and from a head that was clogged and compressed to a head that felt sweet and clear.

Basically the pattern of disturbed pendular swing of energy had been broken. Whereas before the upsurging movement of energy to the over-charged head, followed by the down-pushing movement of energy to the under-charged genitals (a perversion of the normal rhythm) had been his only way of functioning, he now fell back on this schizoid mechanism, only in times of stress. Increasingly he experienced that it was possible to masturbate with pleasure, with his head in the experience. The sense of pressure left him, as energy became able to discharge healthily, his legs became strengthened by the now strongly flowing energy, and his body lost its tendency to collapse.

The main problem remaining was a social one. In spite of his out-going attempts to establish a sexual relationship, he did not find a suitable partner. For a time he felt that he was expected to indulge compulsively in partner-hunting activities, even though he felt a reluctance for instance to go to dances, or social gatherings. After a while, his anxiety about never finding a partner reduced, and he derived considerable pleasure and satisfaction from his varied activities as a single person. Indeed it would be true to say that all the normal functions of his life became pleasurable, and most of the tensions he still felt were due to the outward strains of his professional life.

He had now been in therapy with me for a total of 250 sessions. In that time he had moved much further than I had at one time expected would be possible. I felt that all his major difficulties had been worked through. It remained for him to test out his new co-ordination in the reality of a sexual relationship. I felt there was not much more to be achieved through therapy, and we agreed mutually to bring treatment to an end.

Developments After the End of Therapy

Too many case-histories finish at this point, and leave one wondering how the patient experienced the return to life outside the therapeutic sessions. With the schizoid person, because of the disturbed reality sense, it is particularly important to make sure that gains made in therapy are maintained afterwards, if one is to gain a true picture of what has been achieved. Therefore I delayed writing anything about this therapy until a further four years had elapsed.

Fairly soon after the therapy had ended, James fell in love with a girl a few years younger than him, who seemed equally drawn to him. An intense relationship developed between them very quickly. Unfortunately the girl concerned proved to have a rather flighty, basically hysterical character, whose behaviour pattern was to warmly encourage a man she felt loving towards, but to go cold and hostile and hard to get, when she met with strong attraction in return. I knew this girl independently. Although he was strongly drawn to the girl in spite of her problems, she became afraid of the changes in her life which a serious relationship would involve, and was in addition subject to powerful pressure from her mother. Amid stormy scenes she therefore broke the relationship off after a few months.

For someone who had taken so long before gaining the confidence to reach out to a girl strongly, this was a devastating and heart-breaking rejection, which it took him a long time to recover from. Nevertheless, he reacted in a relatively healthy way, with justifiable anger, and sadness. Some time after this experience he found a new lease of life in gaining promotion in his work, which took him to a new town where he met fresh groups of people. Before too long he was again in contact with a number of women, through drama circles, and humanist groups of which he was a member. One of these, a divorced art teacher, with two children by her former marriage, felt strongly attracted to him.

There developed eventually a relationship characterised by mutual drawing together and discovery of many pleasures which could be shared; but marred by fear on both sides to commit themselves too far sexually. Once bitten twice shy applied to both. She, however, could not relax sexually in the context of the guilt of an extra-marital situation. He on the other hand was secretly terrified of having to force himself forwards to focus his life on a marriage which everyone was expecting.

This situation of approaching commitment became one of maximum stress in which all the schizoid mechanisms became temporarily reactivated. He felt caught in an expected social situation which he was in duty bound to go through with, but which he did not feel emotionally committed to, in a way which threw him into a state of total uncertainty and ambivalence in regard to his feelings. He oscillated from day to day between strong attraction for and strong repulsion from the woman he was due to marry, yet felt helpless to find out what in his behaviour was genuine, and what was neurotic and induced by fear. Feelings of surging and collapsing and other old symptoms came back with renewed force. He began to doubt his sanity, and shortly before the marriage was due, he came to me for an emergency session.

This took place purely at the level of counselling. There was only one thing provoking the relapse, and that was the intense sense of pressure surrounding the marriage, a pressure very much bound up with the social conventions that accompany marriage. The only way to overcome the relapse, and restore the state of being well and in touch with his feelings, and able to function in a basically enjoyable manner, was to remove the sense of pressure. The only advice that was appropriate was to call the marriage off indefinitely, until he felt pleasurably attracted to the idea. This simple advice, which I gave, worked wonders. Every other influence in his environment added up to saying 'grit your teeth and go through with it; you can't back out now'. He realised that to postpone the marriage might mean the risk of alienating his partner for good. At the same time he felt that if she did not have sufficient understanding to see that in the state he was in, this was the only wise course, she was probably the wrong person for him anyway. In the event, the marriage was called off, to the consternation of all friends and relatives, the wife-to-be was not alienated, but felt almost as great a sense of relief, and both felt free to explore their feelings towards each other at leisure.

Some months later, in the quietest way imaginable, and almost as an afterthought and without any sense of pressure at all, they did in fact get married, and the relationship as it exists today is a very alive one.

What is worthy of emphasis here, is that with the exception of this solitary emergency session, and a few supportive letters and discussions which took place at irregular intervals, the process of adjustment to his wife was undertaken without any therapeutic interpretations or comment from me. Many difficulties of personal adjustment remained to be sorted out, and by the account which I received of this period in due course, it was a very hectic and emotionally explosive time. Many average people who have drifted, half-aware, into a conventional marriage, have been shipwrecked on the rapids of an intimate living together which they were personally unprepared for. For a person with a previous schizoid disturbance to have worked so honestly through his difficulties and have won such a happy relationship as a result, reveals once again what powers of vitality and creative life lie buried within the divided body and the dissociated mind.

REFERENCES

1. Waal, Nic, M.D., *Private Communication.* February, 1952
2. Braatøy, Trygve, *Fundamentals of Psychoanalytic Teaching.* New York, 1954
3. Feldenkrais, Moshe, *Body and Mature Behaviour.* London, 1949
4. Lowen, Alexander, M.D., *Physical Dynamics of Character Structure.* New York and London, 1958
5. Reich, Wilhelm, M.D., The Schizophrenic Split, *Character-Analysis,* 3rd ed. New York, 1949
6. Nicoll, Maurice, *Psychological Commentaries.* London, 1954
7. Lowen, Alexander, M.D., *Love and Orgasm.* New York and London, 1965
8. Reich, Wilhelm, M.D., The Expressive Language of the Living, *Character-Analysis,* 3rd ed. New York, 1949
9. Fromm-Reichman, Frieda, Some Aspects of Psycho-Analytic Psychotherapy with Schizophrenics, *Psychotherapy with Schizophrenics,* ed. Brody and Redlich. New York, 1952
10. Rosen, John, M.D., *Direct Analysis.* New York, 1953
11. Gold, Philip, M.D., Orgonomic Functions in a Manic-Depressive Case, *Orgone Energy Bulletin,* Vol. 3. New York, 1951

The Development of the Schizoid Character and the Therapeutic Process

Part I by Robert Hilton, Th.D.

Dr. Robert M. Hilton is an associate of the Institute of Therapeutic Psychology in Santa Ana, California, where as a licensed Marriage and Family Counsellor he conducts a private practice in individual and group therapy. Prior to his coming to the Institute he served for four years as the Minister of an American Baptist Church in Los Angeles and for six years as the Professor of Counselling at the California Baptist Theological Seminary, Covina, California.

Dr. Hilton is a member of the Association for Humanistic Psychology, The American Psychological Association, The California State Psychological Association and The California State Marriage Counseling Association. He is currently on the teaching staff in the department of Psychology of the University of California Extension at Irvine and is an Associate Clinical Professor of Human Behaviour at the United States International University in San Diego, California. This paper was given at the 2nd International Conference on Bio-energetic Analysis, Aspen, Colorado, July 1973.

The original organismic self-expression is a pulsatory movement of expansion and contraction. It involves reaching out and taking in; contacting and incorporating through digestion. The microscopic study of protoplasm is an example of this primal process. Likewise, the study of an amoeba reveals this same basic rhythmic movement.

This basic life movement directs the human organism in the environment toward meeting its needs and through this contact builds a structure wherein an increasing amount of independence and self-determination are evident. A human being begins in birth with an organismic declaration of his own right to exist, proceeds to express his needs, affirm his independence, and eventually to reproduce himself through expressions of love and sexuality. The strength of these core expressions vary in keeping with the growth and expansion of the organism and to the degree to which each core need has been met by the environment. If a human being's right to existence is challenged from the beginning, he may spend the rest of his life in a struggle to affirm this basic core expression. All of the other needs become minimized or are used in an attempt to fill the pre-existing deficiency.

Parental and environmental frustration enter in and block and attempts of the organism to fulfil itself. The environmental negativity may be directed more against the expanding-contracting impulses (such as in the Oral structures), or it may be directed more against the contracting-independence needs of the organism (such as in the Masochistic structures).

When the frustration persists and is seemingly immovable, the organism, in an attempt to survive, begins to inhibit the impulses which are causing the negative reaction in the environment. This inhibition is structured in the organism in the form of muscular contraction which says NO to the impulses.

The ego, through use of the voluntary musculature, inhibits the impulses and thereby identifies with the parental or environmental prohibition. Through this process it (ego) creates a pattern of behaviour which brings about survival at the loss of spontaneous organismic aliveness. This imposition divides the unitary function of the organism and man becomes at war with himself. The environmental struggle has now become an internalized struggle between the basic needs of the organism and its attempts to survive. This survival behaviour pattern becomes an ideal of the ego, and part of a character attitude which is threatened by an alive body. To reduce the threat to survival, the body must be kept in check through reduced respiration and restricted awareness.

This survival attitude toward reality is developed according to the ideals and blocked impulses. The illusion of security is maintained through ego control. For the oral character, the block is mainly toward reaching. The block says, 'Don't reach, you will be abandoned'. So, of course, he sees the world as depriving him, and his quest is to find someone to take care of him. However, his ego ideal of independence and self-sufficiency refuses to allow him to surrender to his needs. He is thereby in a constant state of frustration. The masochist blocks his independent self-expression. He found the price of independence too costly in terms of guilt. So, he sees the world as oppressing and burdening him. At the same time, his ego ideal leads him to seek the responsibility of caring for others.

Since the security of the organism depends on the parental and environmental approval, the self-expressive function must be kept under control. The feeling is: 'If I express myself, I will lose my security'; or, 'When I let spontaneous movement through, I feel frightened and anxious'. This happens when the oral person reaches for help and says 'I need you' or when the masochist rejects someone's request for help and says 'I don't need you'.

With this structural attitude, the person continues to gravitate toward situations that perpetuate the early traumas. These situations say YES to the ego ideal and thus NO to the spontaneous impulses. The complaint is then made, 'They won't let me be'. The block is reinforced by the partner who has interest in perpetuating the ideal for his own security and thus a constant state of frustration exists in the organism between security, which is really ego ideal reinforcement, and being self-expressive.

The impulse inhibiting factor is now projected onto the partner and an attempt is made to reverse the initial self-esteem loss experienced through the rejecting environment by getting the partner to accept the repressed core needs. At the same time, these needs are not fully recognized or accepted by the person himself.

Often the reinforcement of the blocked impulse continues until the block gives away, the ideal crumbles and the underlying impulse emerges. The partner says, 'Just as I always thought'. Now anxiety rises.

Anxiety develops when a person is caught between security and self-expression. Anxiety emerges when the form of the organism cannot expand with the available energy. An impulse of aliveness is emerging and meeting a 'security' block in the organism. An organismic need is being blocked by an ego ideal or character attitude.

At this point, the therapist enters the environment. The goal and process of therapy are succinctly stated by Stanley Keleman*:

> 'The end goals in our work are to enable a person to live his energetic processes, to tolerate a higher level of energy (which means tolerating more of himself), thus giving him more freedom. Specifically, then, we work to *identify* the block, to allow the person to *experience* his block and to attempt to get him to *release* it, aiding the release through pressure or muscle release techniques, to allow the individual to experience himself, his own unity, more fully and to help him *live* that fully.'
> (Accented by the author).

Through the integration of the energy locked into the ego ideal and the repressed bodily needs, a functioning ego develops which is congruent with organismic impulses and the environment. From this view of reality, the person is able to ground himself in his body and thereby gradually melt the character attitude into spontaneous aliveness.

With the release and integration of the repressed impulse, the instinctual ground of self-expression is restored. This grounding is often accompanied with timidity and childlikeness. This new expansion of the organism may appear to the outsider as small, but it is always experienced by the person as significant.

If this expansion receives acceptance from the new environment, further self-exploration will follow which will bring about more anxiety and thus the rebirth process continues. There is always a risk involved in living out the new expansion and allowing the organism to find a new form of expression. Slowly the person seeks less situations which say 'yes' to the inhibiting blocks and 'no' to his self-expression. In this way, the life process continues to express and ground itself until the person is strong

---

*Stanley Keleman, The Body, Energy, and Groups, *Energy and Character*, Vol.3, No.1, January 1972, pp.47,48.

enough to live out his core experience in an environment that is not always accepting.

As grounding increases, so does the organism's capacity to experience instinctual movement. The more a person recovers his instinctual ground, the more he knows and experiences his own truth. He develops a sense of reality with himself and his environment. What eventually emerges as he recovers his unity is a loving impulse which is in the core of every character structure.

The Schizoid Experience

It was mentioned that in each organism there is a core expression which is frustrated by the environment. The result of the negative environmental response is to create a block toward self-expression and thereby inhibit the spontaneous movement of the body. The end result of the blocks is to create a form which expresses particular personality characteristics. These characteristics often develop into fixed character attitudes. The following is an example of how the schizoid character structure develops and the resultant behaviour of blocked impulses.

1   Core Expression
The basic core expression is 'I am' or 'I exist'. This expression is met with a negativity from the environment that says NO to this expression and threatens the organism with **annihilation**.

Core Expression   *Negative Environmental Response*
    I am --------- BLOCK --------- annihilation
   (I exist)

2   *Physical Dynamics*
The result of this block on a physical level is to **cause the person to** contract and *hold together* against the fear of *falling apart*.

3   *Interpersonal Ego Dynamics*
The result is to cause the person to attempt to get others to affirm in him, on an ego level, what was denied him on a body level.

To get a feeling of 'I am', he attempts to get other people to tell him that he exists. He gets them to say, in some way, 'you are', or to tell him that he is special, talented, understanding, etc. His way of eliciting this is to give freedom to others *to be*. Once he gets those around him to confirm his existence, the ego is reinforced and it appears as if the original loss has been recovered. However, he now has to stay in this superior, 'special' position. He must now use his energy to maintain the original block toward self-affirmation and reinforce his ego idealization. He gets ego reinforcement from the environment, but not an affirmation of his core expression. Nothing has changed — he still is not *being* his existence.

4 Dyad

This core conflict may be simulated and personally experienced by participation in the following dyad. It is important that each participant experience both parts of the dyad.

P = Parent; C = Child

The P and C sit on the floor facing each other. C closes his eyes and puts his head down in a foetal-like position. Slowly C begins to lift his head and arms, reaching toward P. He does this in slow progressive stages, each time opening a little more toward the environment. P meanwhile, takes a position of rigidity and allows a feeling of resentment and hostility toward C to come through his eyes and facial expression.

Eventually C opens his eyes, experiences his helplessness, says 'I am', and meets the rejecting eyes of P. The more he attempts to express the 'I am' of his existence, the more he receives hostility from the parent. C's fear of annihilation causes him to shrink. At this point, the body reaction of C sets the structural formation for the schizoid character.

P now needs to contact C because of guilt and C needs to contact P out of fear and desperation. They attempt to do this while maintaining their body position and tension. P and C now become aware of what they have to deny in themselves in order to make contact and what they need to do to get affirmation from the environment.

P and C also move around the room and attempt to make

contact with others from within their own structures. In this way, they will discover how they make contact on an ego level.

5 *Dynamics*

Through demonstration, the conflict between the child's 'I am' and the parent's negativity is experienced. The resulting responses give clues to the physical contractions in the schizoid experience. By acting out the experience of the child (reaching out toward the parent and meeting the acted-out negativity) the body response to the negativity gives form to the character structure. That response, physically maintained, demonstrates the dynamics of the creation of the form and how the structure, through physical tension, is maintained.

The dyad brings you in touch with the negativity of the child toward the parent as well. Where you are the rejected, you become the rejector. Emphasis is fixed on the necessity of a patient accepting his own negativity for integration to be effected. That acceptance is avoided in a number of ways, i.e. being forgiving or understanding of the parent or turning the hostility toward the self. The acknowledgement of that negative element within the self is crushing to the ego ideal.

No change takes place in the therapy until the patient integrates and accepts his own negative response toward the rejector. As a therapist, you must be aware of your own response when dealing with people who are expressing core feelings toward you; your own blocks will be stimulated. You must be aware that all these responses are in your structure as well.

Schizoid character and the therapeutic process

Part II by Renato Monaco, M.D.

Dr. Renato Monaco is a senior training therapist of the Institute of Bioenergetic Analysis. He has a private practice as a bioenergetic therapist in California and conducts many therapeutic workshops on the West coast of America.

Development

The schizoid state and schizophrenia are both a body response to terror, characterized by withdrawal of feeling and fragmentation.

The development of this character type implies the original lie: 'Somebody cares for me. Mother really loves me.' Or, 'If I could only do the right thing I could be loved.' Everything else develops upon this original fantasy. If the schizoid begins to base his whole life on this kind of lie, he will then distort his relationship to external and internal reality. He will see people the way he wants them to be, rather than the way they are, or he will see them in a way which is safer for him. Everyone he meets he views with suspicion and danger.

The fear of the schizoid personality is that he will die or fall apart if he experiences feeling. The reality of his life is that he has survivied.

Basic Delusion

The basic delusion that presupposes the splitting off of feeling in the schizoid or schizophrenic is: 'If I can get into my head, I can handle my terror. If I freeze my body I won't feel the pain of my experience — the pain of my existence. I can't trust my body. I can't trust myself to feel.' So, the schizoid withdraws. This withdrawal is on both a psychological level and a physical level.

Psychological Characteristics
The schizoid character, and to a more extreme degree, the schizophrenic, has:

1. A tenuous identity. His identity is based on roles adopted from others, i.e. 'I am a mother,' 'I am a doctor,' etc. His identity is not based on inner experience.

2. A splitting off of thought from feelings. He has a tendency to intellectualize all experiences. When asked how he feels, he will tell one what he thinks.

3. An extreme sensitivity to closeness. He has a fear of losing his identity or of being overwhelmed when he is with another person. At the same time, the schizoid craves contact, sometimes to the point of desperation. He will usually choose other people with schizoid qualities to be with or to marry.

Body Characteristics
The withdrawal of the schizoid is manifested by a twisting away from the painful feelings, which leads to an actual twisting in the body:

1. Scoliosis (or lateral twisting of the spine). Sometimes the scoliosis is not rigidified but is flexible.

2. Cocking of the head (slight lateral tilting).

3. A ring-like constriction in the body separating one part of the body from the other (head from trunk, chest from pelvis, etc.).

4. Blocking off of certain areas in the trunk. This may occur later on in life. In the blocked area sensation is diminished, skin is often cold and often has a pasty look below the waist. Above the waist the blocked areas may be hot.

    A very primitive block is seen in the eyes. This may be constant or evanescent. This occurs very early in life and is an attempt on the part of the person not to *see* the painful truth of his state of existence. Generally, the eyes seem in some way not to fit the face. There may be a quality of coldness, or sometimes frozen terror in the eyes which does not correspond

Schizoid character and the therapeutic process

to the rest of the facial expression, or to the external circumstances. There may be an evanescent, staring quality, or a blank quality. Then again, there may be the look of a caged animal.

The fragmentation of the schizoid is expressed by a freezing in the joints at several different levels of the neck and trunk as well as in the extremities. The freezing leads to a diminished capacity for feeling distal to the joint — the joint can often be felt as being cold. Levels of freezing can occur at:

1. Cervical, at the base of the skull.
2. Upper thoracic, at the base of the neck.
3. Lower thoracic, at origin of the diaphragm.
4. Lower lumbar, at base of sacrum.
5. Hip and shoulder joints.
6. Knee and elbow joints.
7. Ankle and wrist.
8. Digits of hands and feet.

The schizoid also has a physical orientation toward the head with poor contact with his legs. He may have a disturbed stereotactic sense in his feet and legs. There may also be a diminished kinesthetic sense in his legs.

There is always shallow breathing in the schizoid or schizophrenic.

Other manifestations of this character type may be disproportionment of the body:

1. Disproportionately thin arms as compared to the trunk.
2. Disproportionately small hands and feet.
3. Marked bilateral asymmetry.

Therapy

In order to deal with the extreme sensitivity to closeness in the schizoid, it is important to:

1. Gain trust. This person is looking for someone to trust. He may often test and re-test the therapist to see if he is honest and genuine and really understands him. Gaining this trust may take months, even years. The most important thing the therapist can do is show his respect for this person. The therapist shows this by not putting the person in a pigeon-hole and also listening to him.
2. Move slowly. Never try to break in with a schizoid. If the person is flooded with too much feeling he will become terrified and may leave therapy.

When the therapist sees fragmentation he can use the gradual application of touch to put the person in touch with his own body.

1. The therapist can apply his hand to the back of the neck of the person and gradually encourage feeling. Let the person feel his own level.
2. Warm the joints by covering the joints with hands.
3. May use massage or pressure on certain areas to open body feelings: base of skull, base of neck and also in the lower thoracic lumboscoral area.
4. Sit behind the person and have the person lean slowly back. Many times too much contact to the front of the body may be too terrifying to the schizoid. With the therapist behind, the schizoid may feel safer and the therapist can start leg movement to increase contact with legs and feet.

When the schizoid is having trouble with his tenuous identity the therapist may have him identify with his body (i.e. 'I am my tight chest, I am my cold hands'.) Help him discover that his sense of self is based on his thoughts and inner experiences, not on roles.

Help this person identify and experience his blocks. Release the emotion by working with the musculature (overcharging the muscles until they are forced to release), or working with the musculature to see where the body compensated.

Finally, remember that this person was frightened out of the feeling in his body, so do not try to frighten him back into it.

Part Four

Bio-energy in Health and Disease

BIO-ENERGY IN HEALTH AND DISEASE: INTRODUCTION

If the flow of aliveness in our tissues is the basis of health, then disturbance in this flow is the basis of much of our illness: this is the fundamental thesis underlying all of Reich's properly 'medical' work. When Reich, the psychiatrist, began to work in the realm of the functional illnesses — his critics said: 'so what? We know all about psycho-somatic medicine. What's new in that?' When he moved into the area of illnesses regarded as organic, and in particular, cancer, they threw their hands up in horror.

Unfortunately for his critics, Reich's uncanny insights came home to roost. Each of the fundamental claims that he made about the nature of the cancer illness have been confirmed since, but in separate areas, and without the overall sense of connectedness that he supplied.

Reich's work on cancer, as on many other physical illnesses, is difficult to understand until one grasps the nature of biological energy processes. Reich probed this problem on two fronts: the microscopic and the macroscopic. He looked at the oxidation of the tissues in relation to the blood circulation, and the overall tonicity of the body, and the disposition of the tensions in the musculature. He saw the bad breathing of the people who came to him for treatment, and he looked at the reactivity of their blood under the microscope. He found that poorly oxygenated tissue became suffocated tissue, which provided the soil on which various pathological processes could flourish. He also studied the impact of atmospheric conditions on biological energy. His 'orgone accumulator', a simple apparatus through which he claimed to concentrate atmospheric energy, seemed laughable on first reading. But those who investigated it found that there were definite biological effects, however difficult they were to explain in terms of the physics of Reich's time.

Through the work on atmospheric medicine which is now being pursued in many countries by teams of doctors, we know that Reich's insight was no illusion. There are many subtle interactions between the charged particles of the atmosphere and the biological charge of the blood and the tissues. The new technique of Kirlian photography has made some of these interactions visible for the first time. The study of what is called by more and more researchers, the 'energy field' of the body is receiving sharply increased attention, and it is now recognised that in this area also Reich was a major pioneer.

Sexual Repression and Individual Pathology

by Luigi de Marchi

Luigi de Marchi is one of Italy's most prominent sociologists. He is the author of Sex and Civilisation *and* The Sociology of Sex, *and the founder and director of the Association for Demographic Education in Italy. After many legal battles in the fight to provide better contraceptive information in Italy, he finally won from the Supreme Court in 1973, the abolition of all anti-birth control legislation in Italy. He was active in introducing the work of Reich into Italy through his lectures, his translations, and his third book* Sexual Repression and Social Oppression *[Sugar, Milan, 1965] from which this section is taken. Translated from the Italian by David Boadella.*

It was Wilhelm Reich, in my view, who provided modern medicine with a pathogenic theory capable of leading medical science from the blind alleys in which the mechanistic conceptions of traditional psychosomatics have trapped it. In place of the concept of diseased organs or diseased cells, Reich gave us the unitary concept of a *biopathy*, that is of a deterioration in the functional totality of the organism.

Reich considered pulsation (that is the alternation of expansion and contraction) to be the fundamental functional principle of every living organism: from the amoeba, to the whale, and to man. This natural pulsation of the living organism is perceived as a condition of well-being and pleasure which finds its most intense expression (in animals which are sexually differentiated) in sexual orgasm. In the orgastic pulsation, the sexually alive organism participates in a process of expansion, which at the emotional and psychic level is experienced as pleasure. Faced with any kind of threat, external or internal, each organism (once again from the smallest to the largest) reacts with a process of contraction. In the higher mammals, and in man in particular, these two fundamental functions of expansion and contraction (with all their emotional implications) find their own physiological organisation in the autonomic nervous system. In this connection, the Reichian attempt to give a systematic and unitary explanation for the complex functions (apparently contradictory) of the vagus and sympathetic nerves is extremely interesting.

A person who grows up and lives in a sexually repressive and authoritarian environment undergoes a systematic frustration of pleasurable sensations (connected with feeding, and with the stimulation of the most sensitive parts of the body: the oral and anal mucous membranes, the breasts, the stomach, the genitals, etc.). Once these frustrations take effect on the infant organism, the logical reaction is a feeling of rage, which stimulates the sympathetic system. Pretty quickly the rage becomes associated for the child with the fear of pleasure, associated by now with the expectation of punishment. All these fears similarly produce recurrent excitation of the sympathetic system. As the child grows towards adolescence with the increasing focus of pleasure (and with it anxiety) in the genital area, they take on a chronic form, which ends in a condition of chronic sympatheticotonia, which Reich considered the central pathogenic factor in all functional illnesses.

Hyperactivity of the sympathetic system, in fact, places the organism chronically in a defensive attitude (defence against punishment, primarily, and then simply defence against prohibited or guilty pleasure, particularly sexual pleasure). These defences inevitably break down the functional unity of the organism, and from this stems the origin of this or that biopathy. The fact of repression of emotional impulses connected with erotic pleasure produces, in the repressed individual, a series of emotional blockages (re-motions) which are organised into an individualised *character armour*. At the somatic level, the fact of repressing the impulses and physical sensations associated with sexual pleasure, leads to the formation of a series of blocks and spasms of the musculature (smooth and striated), which similarly are organised into a characteristic *muscular armour*. The muscular blockages produced by the over-activity of the sympathetic system increase the damage to the organism, and finally reduce even more the already restricted motility of the cells and the hampered blood supply to the tissues.

The characterological and muscular armour, as Reich constantly emphasised, must not be understood as two separate processes, but as two manifestations operating at different levels, of the same fundamental disturbance of the wholeness of functioning of the organism. The fundamental identity of the two biopathic phenomena, Reich pointed out, is shown in their interchangeability both pathologically and therapeutically. In the pathological realm, a precise correspondence can be found between a particular emotional block and a particular muscular block; whilst in the realm of therapy it can similarly be seen how a psychic resistance (that is an emotional block) which appears insurmountable, can be loosened during psychotherapy simultaneously with the loosening of the muscular blockage. It is clear that these phenomena cannot be understood — Reich concluded — except through an energetic approach to the problems of health and sickness. Both the character armour and the muscular armour have the ability to bind up and hold back the energy of the organism, the liberation of which comes to be feared. But this energy charge, expressing itself at times in the form of psychic impulses, and at others in the form of plasmatic currents, is identical, although the symptoms and the therapy of their effects may be alternatively psychic or somatic.

These clinical observations induced Reich to postulate, according to a perfectly consistent logic, the existence in the living organism of an energy previously unrecognised, which he called 'orgone', which had its most obvious and characteristic expression in orgasm. Later, Reich maintained, and sought to demonstrate, that this energy could not be exclusive to living organisms, for he succeeded in observing it in other states: in certain pre-cellular forms (which he called bions), in the atmosphere and in the cosmos. He claimed that it could be accumulated from the atmosphere and concentrated by means of special apparatus (orgone accumulators). All this last phase of

Reichian theory and research is still more controversial. There are two reasons for this: Reich was faced for decades with the resistance and the animosity of the scientific, cultural and political leadership of many diverse groups (from mechanistic scientists, to Freudian psychotherapists, Adlerians, Jungians, existentialists, neo-Freudians, Marxists and reformists, Fascist totalitarians, Stalinists, and the rest); all these had in common an identical hatred for life in general, and for sexuality in particular. The second reason is that, without doubt, the functional variability of living energetic phenomena makes experimentation and controlled observation difficult, and so hinders quantification by the traditional methods of mechanistic science.

On the other hand, whilst the negation of the existence of orgone energy and of the validity of the laws governing it that Reich has described, remains a fact, there is also the danger of acts of faith and of affirmation of the existence of orgone energy on a priori grounds without the extensive and patient experimentation and verification which must take place before orgonomy (the orgone theory) can be considered a truly scientific revolution, and not seen as a pure science fiction fantasy. Meanwhile I believe that the validity of the Reichian theory of pathology, in which we are most directly interested, does not depend on the existence or otherwise of orgone energy as a sine qua non, any more than is the case with the psychological, anthropological, sociological and political theory of Reich. The concepts of impulse, excitation, emotion, pleasure, anxiety, are already used currently with a psycho-physical ambiguity which is sufficient to legitimise the Reichian view that we are dealing with phenomena and processes which are fundamentally indistinguishable, even for those who cannot accept the existence of a vital energy which functions specifically in the organism and is variously expressed and perceived by people.

Character armour and muscular armour are realities clearly and experimentally observable in everyone who has been particularly repressed, and both can be understood easily as reaction formations of the organism against repression, and so against the pleasure anxiety (particularly sexual pleasure) instilled by methods of up-bringing and education, and by traditional modes of living. Both are in fact the results of crystallisation of the psychic and somatic attitudes of defence: the mobilisation of anxiety and aggression, first against the environment which threatens and punishes the pleasurable sensations, and then, through the internalisation of the prohibiting authority, against the pleasurable sensations themselves. This crystallisation into an attitude of anxious self-control finds, in the sympathetic contraction, its inevitable pathological existence, and at the same time, the factor which determines that it should be chronic.

One of the fundamental reasons for the distance between Reich and the Freudian analysts was his conviction that although the primary cause of neurosis, and of other functional illnesses was undoubtedly of an emotional nature, it was not sufficient to bring back to consciousness the psychic factors which had caused the pathology in order to cure the neurosis or the functional illness connected with it, because once the pleasure anxiety was established during up-bringing and at the time of the repressive experience, it created the muscular armour and chronic vegetative disturbance in most cases, which became independent largely of the originating psychic factors. These disturbances continue to nourish and maintain the existence of the frustrating customs, institutions, and moralisms, of our society, and of every authoritarian and sex-negative society.

The damage caused by sympatheticotonia is naturally not limited to the formation of the characterological and muscular armour. It is also, as Reich showed in *Die Funktion des Orgasmsus* in 1927, the origin of a whole series of maladies: gastro-intestinal, cardio-vascular, and endocrine. The dynamisms of each of these illnesses is clearly described by Reich: the state of anxiety leads to the sympatheticotonia which in its turn leads little by little to an inhibition of the digestive function (such as anorexia nervosa, cardiospasm, or spastic colitis); just as a disturbance of circulation (such as cardiac neurosis, arterial hypertension, etc.) is a consequence of the stimulating action exercised by the sympathetic system on the rhythm and elasticity of the peripheral circulation. Finally a glandular or metabolic disequilibrium (hyperthyroidism, stress states, diabetes, etc.) which is due to the increased secretion of adrenalin can lead in hyperthyroidism to an abnormal and continuous excitation of the pituitary which in turn provokes an exaggerated secretion of the hormone thyrotropin; or in diabetes, to a greater destruction of glycogen in the liver, and so to an increase in glycaemia or in glycosuria.

We must recognise, in describing this side of the Reichian pathogenic theory, that the dynamic articulation of the reactions of the organism to the anxiety of prohibited (sexual) pleasure, appears much too schematic. With its insistence on the sympatheticotonic origin of all these ailments it does not offer a satisfactory explanation for many illnesses of obvious or hidden vagotonic origin. For the understanding of the obvious vagotonia which characterises a great many morbid states (hyperkinesis of the stomach or the intestines, hypotension states, exhaustion, etc.), we can make use, with some corrections, of two dynamic hypotheses advanced in psychosomatics. The first is that vagotonia and sympatheticotonia are states which react upon each other. If we agree with Reich that the original character of sympatheticotonia is in reactions of anxiety, then the vagotonia of many illnesses can be understood as an exaggerated chronic reaction of the vagus to the constant threat of overactivity by the sympathetic. The second hypothesis is that in each situation of threat the organism can react either with a mobilisation which is defensive-aggressive (thus sympathetic); or with a withdrawal to a vegetative attitude of neo-natal or proto-infantile well-being (which leads to vagotonia, with its mobilisation of the digestive apparatus which symbolically indicates a demand for food or for maternal protection.) Once again, by accepting with Reich the fundamental sex-negative character of the threat perceived by a person, the vagotonic states can be understood as a compensatory flight or regression of the organism, towards extra-genital forms of pleasure. All the original sympathetic excitation of sex-negative nature, can thus be overcome either by a simple antagonistic reaction, or by a 'flight towards compensatory pleasure which is not prohibited, resulting in a hypertonus of the vagus. The entire field of functional maladies, whether sympathetic or vagotonic at base, becomes clearly intelligible in terms of a fundamental and unitary psychological cause (of a sexual nature in our society and in other sex-negative cultures). There is no longer any need for medicine to lose itself, as psychosomatic research has done, in the meanders of inconclusive hypotheses about 'personality profiles', or 'individual causes' of various illnesses, or to resign itself to a vision of a humanity, made sick with the conflict entailed in civilising itself against its original and omnipresent impulses of aggression and distrust. Such impulses in the light of modern anthropological research, become perfectly understandable as secondary impulses of the organism, reactions to the social prohibitions and repressions of its freedom, its pleasure, and its organismic pulsation.

This is the end of what I have to say about functional illness. Both psychosomatic medicine and the Reichian theory are not restricted exclusively to these pathological spheres when they study the repercussions of psychic or neuro-vegetative disturbance. But it is perfectly possible, in line with our theory, that each organ which is exposed to an intense and prolonged stimulation or inhibition of the neuro-vegetative centres which innervate it, will end up by undergoing deteriorations and lesions in its own structure: in this way, then, a functional illness becomes organic. The Reichian and psychosomatic schools of thought have demonstrated abundantly the validity of this thesis, with their studies of peptic ulcers (usually caused by a corrosion of the gastric wall as a result of an excessive secretion, provoked in turn by a steady neuro-vegetative stimulation of a psychogenic origin); or of ulcerative colitis (provoked by a hyper-secretion which results in an auto-digestion of the mucosa of the colon, and opens the way to the invasion of bacteria); or of rheumatoid arthritis (as a result of chronic spastic attitudes adopted by the skeletal muscles).

Reich in particular has developed a pathogenic theory which is sympatheticotonic in origin, for the cancer disease, in his book *The Cancer Biopathy*. Once again he sees as the origin of the sympatheticotonic process the sexual repressions and frustrations imposed by our society, as by every traditionally authoritarian and sex-negative society. These repressions, he shows, provoke and maintain a condition of pleasure anxiety and so a chronic mobilisation of the sympathetic system directed to prevent and repress the excitations which are sexual or associated with sexuality. (For our part, it must be pointed out once again that the hypertonus of the sympathetic is probably not only connected with pleasure anxiety, but also with the aggressive reactions, normally hidden but still operative, which spring up in the organism from the repressions and frustrations of sexual impulses and of all other vital impulses: such as rage and anger, which the psychosomatic school correctly finds present in all sympatheticotonic patients. These can be likewise understood as reactions to the frustrations of natural sexuality and as accompaniments to its conversion into sadism.

Sympatheticotonia, once established, produces both a constriction of the peripheral blood vessels, and so a reduction in the blood circulation, and (due to the prevailing attitude of inspiration with the reduced breathing typical of anxiety reactions and organismic defences) a reduced oxygenation of the blood. The result of all these reactions in the sympathetic system is that the organism is provided with a flow of blood which is impoverished in its oxygen content. Such a condition, Reich stated, implies a predisposition to cancerous degeneration of the cells, as is shown by the fact which Otto Warburg observed at the end of 1925, that all the cells of whatever kind of cancer are characterised by a form of anoxia (shortage of oxygen). Reich goes on to explain how in certain parts of the body the anoxic cells are further caused to deteriorate by the spasms and muscular blockages associated with the muscular armour. Frequently such spasms are directly and clearly related to the repression of sexuality and its associated pleasure anxiety. Thus, Reich pointed out, in women who have been constrained by traditional education, to repress more severely and to fear more anxiously their own sexual excitations, cancer arises with particular frequency in the erotic zones or in parts of the body directly concerned with the sexual function: vagina, uterine cervix, uterus, breasts. In these areas, in fact, the spasms of the smooth and striated muscles and the sympathetic tension assume extreme levels.

Sexual repression and individual pathology

For my part, I can mention some interesting data which support the Reichian thesis. The American Annual *Psychological Abstracts* in 1960 reported an example of an interesting investigation carried out by a psychological and sociological group, on a random sample of cancerous women in the USA compared with a control sample of healthy women. The result of this investigation was that the cancerous patients had all had a sexual life that was much more repressive and frustrated, and who presented in general a personality much more inhibited than that of the healthy women. The psychiatric literature today has shown the existence of frequent coincidence between emotional illness and neoplasms.

No less interesting is the research carried out in another school of American cancerology on the frequency of cancer in nuns. The results of this research — which has analysed the cause of death in 116,000 American catholic nuns — were communicated by Professor J.T. Nix to the last Congress of the American Cancer Prevention Society (March, 1964), and seemed to me impressive: not only were the nuns more exposed to most forms of neoplasm, but there was much greater morbidity from cancer of the female organs: vagina, uterus, breasts. One apparent exception was the lesser frequency of cancer of the cervix, but this is possibly due to a reduced association with the injuries and irritations to which the cervix of married women is exposed, as a result of abortive intervention and its sequelae, which are noticeable in almost every woman who has such experiences in western society.

The American research, finally, confirmed only what anyone consulting the Yearbook of Statistics can observe directly: nubile women from 25 to 35 years of age (and that is the age of life when the sexual frustrations obviously have their strongest effect) show a level of cancerosity in female organs which is clearly greater than that found in people of the same age who are married.

If we turn to cancer in the man, we find that two sites most frequently associated with cancer in the man are the rectum and the larynx. These are clearly related to the artificial imposition of models of virility and masculine comportment imposed by traditional education on children and on all adult males. The systematic repression of fear and of tears, establishes a chronic spasticity of the throat and the rectum, and can undoubtedly contribute to the dangerous increase of anoxia in these areas. An interest in the Reichian theory of the pathogenesis of cancer contributes to the extension of the etiology of sympatheticotonia (and thus of sex-negation) from the sphere of functional illnesses to the whole field of pathology. How far this is true became clear to me by way of a famous Russian doctor, Alexander Salmanoff, who was a doctor at the time of Lenin, and was settled in Paris where he died only a few years ago. A brilliant Italian follower of Salmanoff, Dr. Mario Mancini, has undertaken the translation of one of Salmanoff's principal books: *Secret Wisdom of the Body* (published by Bompiani, in 1963).

Salmanoff starts from the premise that the immense network of arterial and venous capillaries (100,000 kilometres long, and 63,000 square metres of membrane in an adult organism) are responsible for the health of our body. This health depends precisely on the constant renewal of the metabolites for the tissues; and illness (or the predisposition to illness) is produced by the deterioration of tissues and their intoxication (by accumulation of toxins, or invasion by bacteria or viruses). On the efficiency of the capillary circulation depends an adequate exchange in the tissues and in the organs. Similarly, proper functioning of the most vital internal organs — heart, kidneys, liver, lungs, intestines — is conditional on an efficient transfer of metabolites, and thus on well functioning capillaries.

'Pathology of the capillaries', writes Salmanoff 'is the most important chapter of pathology.' He goes on to say that the alteration in the capillaries forms the basis of all morbid processes, even those due to infectious bacteria. As we can now begin to understand: the stasis of the capillary circulation produces a progressive intoxication in the tissues which prepares the way for an invasion of bacteria. 'In most cases', writes Salmanoff, 'the infectious agents in our illnesses are the same microbes which, before the illness, have always lived on our skin, in the mouth, in the throat, in the digestive tract, in the tissues, in the blood. We live always in a state of latent infection: yet we rarely succumb to an infectious illness. The reactions of the organism to the bacteria depend chiefly on the conditions of the individual organs and tissues responding to attack. The same streptococcus can provoke an arthritis, a peritonitis, an erysipelas, a thrombophlebitis.'

These truths are almost universally recognised (and as universally forgotten) in modern medicine. But what, according to Salmanoff, is the cause of the capillary stasis, the slowing down and blockage of the capillary circulation with all its pathological consequences? It is a reduction in the diameter and elasticity of the capillaries. To sum up, it is a spastic condition in the vessels and an alteration in the membranes.

At this point we must emphasise that the primary effect of the sympatheticotonia resulting from the pleasure anxiety induced in the organism by sexual repression and the general repressive educational system, is precisely this peripheral vasoconstriction, with the resulting loss in elasticity, and the interference with their essential transport function on which the health of the body depends. Naturally, the problem does not appear to be radically different when the neurovegetative disturbance is predominantly vagotonic: in this case the capillary condition is still spastic, but in the sense of over dilation, and the capillary will have lost its natural pulsation.

Even if it is only unconsciously, but with the sure instinct of a genius, Salmanoff shows in his work the possible psychogenic origin of capillary pathology. At a certain point he makes some observations which, precisely because of their unconscious Reichian resonance, are particularly impressive to the attentive reader:

'Carrel', he writes, 'working with A. Flexner at the Rockefeller Institute, has stated that if the liquid nutrients supplied to tissues in culture are not renewed rapidly for a certain time, then the tissues perish ... Atmospheric or emotional depression provokes cytolysis (the destruction of cells) in the tissues which find themselves in difficult conditions. The cytolysis produces toxins which lead to an intoxication of the nerve centres. Then follow the capillary stasis and the invasion of germs.'

It seems to me full of interest that Salmanoff, though not interested in psychology or psychosomatics, has with all his authority underlined the importance of emotional depression (which by definition is a state created by the conditions of frustration and repression in which we live today), in the genesis of capillary pathology, and thus of all these illnesses. But even more interesting perhaps is that he had underlined the importance of atmospheric depression (and his connection of this with emotional depression is already shown by the increase of suicide on days of low pressure) in the establishment of morbid processes. The report on the two types of depression not only leads us back to the psychic factors which underlie these morbid processes, but also they can unwittingly confirm the orgone theory of Reich: in his work in orgonomy, Reich insists on the fact that there is a fall in the orgonotic level of the atmosphere during humid days and days of low pressure (the accumulator on such days also functions less intensely) and also a fall in the charge of the organism, a weakening in its orgonotic currents, and an increase in morbid states.

In different ways, and without knowledge of each other, Reich and Salmanoff have thus constructed a pathogenic theory which is essentially complementary, even though the first concentrated his energy on the removal of the social causes and the emotional and energetic conditions of illness, while the second has concentrated his attention on the first and fundamental functional effect, the capillary pathology, which stands at the root of all morbid processes.

New Techniques in Vision Improvement

by Charles R. Kelley, Ph.D.

Charles R. Kelley, Ph.D., director of the Radix Institute and its California facility, the Radix Work Shop, has been active in the field of applied experimental psychology for more than twenty years. For thirteen years chief scientist and laboratory director for Dunlap and Associates Inc., one of the country's major human factors consulting firms, he was, during the four previous years, assistant professor and director of the Division of Applied Vision Research, Department of Psychology, North Carolina State College. He subsequently served as adjunct associate professor, New York University, as NATO visiting lecturer before major scientific institutions in Europe, and in 1970 as George A. Miller visiting professor at the University of Illinois.

Outside of academia he was a student of Wilhelm Reich, and contributed to Reich's journals when Reich was alive, and to the study of his theories in the years since Reich died. He was for five years editor of The Creative Process, *at a time when it was America's only scientific journal exploring Reich's concepts. He had previously become interested in the work of the ophthalmologist, William H. Bates, became an instructor, and for two years taught the Bates method of vision improvement.*

Dr. Kelley has been elected a Fellow in both the American Psychological Association and the Human Factors Society of America. He is a biographee in American Men of Science *and a member of the board of editors of* Human Factors. *He has lectured and given workshops at universities, growth centres and scientific organizations across Europe and America. He is author of more than fifty scientific publications on vision research and training, human factors research, and 'new education' techniques. The present article on vision first appeared in an expanded form in* Energy and Character *Vol.2, No.3, and Vol.3, No.1, September 1971 and January 1972. Parts 2 and 3 were first presented as a paper at the Institute for Bio-energetic Analysis,*

New York, in May 1969, as a demonstration and lecture to the First International Conference on Bio-energetics, Isla Mujeres, Mexico, March 27 to April 3, 1971.

Most people are surprised to learn that there are techniques that can substantially improve eye conditions usually thought of as fixed and incurable, such as myopia, hyperopia, and astigmatism. This contradicts the position of the medical and optometric professions that the eyes are a fixed optical element that cannot be modified except in unusual cases. The traditional position holds that education procedures can do no more than improve the interpretation of visual information which is of inherently fixed quality. Thus the basic visual input is conceived of as being unchangeable (save in rare instances) and the value of training limited to improving the way in which this fixed 'input information' is utilized, i.e., the process of interpretation by the brain.

My experience flatly contradicts this orthodox point of view. The view is contradicted by what I have learned as a scientist engaged in vision research, by what I have observed in students as a teacher of techniques of vision improvement, and by my direct experience improving my own vision. The eye is not an unchanging element bringing information of fixed quality to the brain for interpretation. The eye is a living organ, subject, like the rest of the body, to vicissitudes and variations of all kinds, especially in the functioning of the muscles within and surrounding it, and in the quantity and quality of the circulation delivering nutrients and carrying waste products from it. The eye, like the rest of the body, possesses an enormous capacity for change, both for the better and for the worse.

Vision changes all the time, and those with marginal vision are usually acutely aware of such changes. Vision is typically better in the morning than in the afternoon, better on a relaxed holiday than during an arduous period of work or study, better when relaxed and happy than when tense or emotionally disturbed. Nor is there any good reason for believing that it is not the 'visual input,' the optical quality of the image on the retina, that changes, rather than (or in addition to) interpretive factors in the brain.

It is muscles which direct the eye's line of sight, focus its image through accommodation, and regulate retinal illumination. And it is muscles which interfere with function when they become too tense or too flaccid, either condition interfering with ocular mobility and impairing circulation. It is mobility and circulation which the eyes require above all for both function and health. It is muscles, then, that are the primary agent for visual change.

The mechanistic view of the eye as a fixed optical system is a myth, full of contradictions and inconsistencies. The same practitioner who insists that it is impossible in principle for a ten-year-old with one and a half diopters of myopia to reduce his myopia to zero in two years of training must in honesty admit that it is very possible indeed for the 1½ diopters of myopia to increase to 3 diopters in the same two-year period. The eye that is regarded as mechanically fixed with no potential for change in the direction of improvement is at the same time recognized to be flexible and subject to substantial change when it comes to getting worse.

And it is the same with other eye conditions. Muscular tension and impaired circulation can, and do, become worse, and worsen the optical performance of the eye. Can they not also, then, given the proper changes in conditions and habits, become better? They can, of course, even though they seldom do. The truth is that vision can be improved by training, but seldom is *because vision professionals do not know how*. But one can learn a little about it, if he is willing to consider the experience of unorthodox practitioners.

I began work in vision improvement techniques as a teacher of the Bates method, and, seeing the need for research, became an experimental psychologist specializing in vision. The article begins with a personal account of my experience in the field of training and research in vision improvement. I then present a new theory of myopia and hyperopia which has gradually evolved over the past twenty-five years. The final section deals with the problems of vision improvement, contrasting more orthodox approaches with that taken in the Radix Institute vision improvement programs.

*Part I: Personal Experience**

Having to wear glasses was a real blow to me as a child. I was a skinny, gangling boy of nine when I was first required to wear them, precocious and aggressive intellectually but fearful and shy emotionally. I was tall for my age, and awkward and uncoordinated, especially in comparison with my classmates, who were usually a year or two older. I felt myself to be weak, unmasculine, a sissy, 'out of it' with my peers. Glasses contributed greatly to my bad self-image. Only two decades later as a research psychologist did I discover how typical my pattern was for a myopic child, and that the myopia derives from the fearfulness and emotional withdrawal that precedes it and forms its base.

Not every nearsighted child has the determination I did to change myself, although many do. I pushed myself into athletics, and when I went into high school, into dancing classes, social events, and into dating. I became big, muscular, and more acceptable socially. Because of my intellectual aggressiveness, I was a leader of certain kinds of activities — manager of the debate team, president of the Young Unitarians. But what I felt to be the 'real me' under the muscular and verbal front remained a thin-skinned, easily embarrassed boy, hating the metal-framed glasses I was supposed to always wear but didn't, suffering agonies when a girl turned me down when I asked for a date or even a dance. And this 'real me', I know now, formed the characterological base of my vision problem.

And my eyes got steadily worse. Once or twice a year I was sent to the ophthalmologist, and after duly peering through the pupils, expanded by drops, with his retinoscope, and running me through his trial lenses, his 'remedy' was always the same — stronger glasses. One year I wasn't allowed to read or do close work, and spent my school hours in pottery, wood shop, and the

---

*A prior section discussing the Bates method has been omitted for reasons of space.

New techniques in vision improvement

like. It did nothing to keep my eyes from getting worse. In high school and after, they only got worse a little slower.

When I got out of the army at twenty-three, I was able to barely read the largest letter on the eye chart at twenty feet with my better eye. My acuity was 20/200 in the left eye, 20/400 in the right, which means that an eye chart letter had to be 10 times as high for me to see it with my better eye as for a normal-sighted person. Glasses gave me 20/20 vision, but I still hated them, and had found that using them tended to make my eyes worse.

It was then that I read Aldous Huxley's book, *The Art of Seeing*, in which he described his experience with the Bates method, and the big improvements in vision near-sighted people had obtained through it. I contacted Mrs Margaret Corbett, Huxley's Bates teacher, and the leading exponent of the method after Bates' death. Mrs Corbett referred me to an instructor trained in her school, and I started Bates lessons, at first 3 times each week, 90 minutes each, with a daily homework program. Later I was dropped to two, finally to once per week.

I worked diligently, and my vision responded. In six months, the eyes that had for a lifetime only got worse became able to read 20/20 chart letters unaided and without squinting or other tricks, in virtually every lesson. These gains were temporary, but my basic test vision improved to 20/70 in the same period, with flashes of clear (20/20) vision at increasingly frequent intervals. By the end of two years I tested 20/40 under even unfavorable test conditions. I then passed my driving test without glasses, as I have done 8 or 10 times subsequently in four different states.

My vision has remained variable, and at times normal, but for the most part I have remained somewhat myopic. My optical correction to a consistent 20/20 had reduced to -1.25 diopters in each eye, where originally it was -2.75 in my better and -3.25 in my worse eye. It is difficult to get a precise refractive error figure on me, as my refractive condition varies substantially, even under cycloplegia, the drops in the eyes used by doctors to paralyze accommodation and expand the pupils.

I became a Bates enthusiast during my first year, and enrolled in Mrs Corbett's teacher training program. After completing the course and qualifying as an instructor (which took a year of work)

I practised as a Bates teacher and worked for my degree in psychology at the University of Hawaii. For more than two years Bates teaching was my primary occupation and means of livelihood. In those years and my year of training with Mrs Corbett, I learned more about the causes and methods of improving common visual problems than even the most 'advanced' orthodox practitioners in the vision sciences ever discover. This was still not enough to satisfy a fraction of the questions my practice raised.

My students improved substantially when they worked at it. Improvement was usually gratifyingly quick at the start, but then it slowed down. The factors that brought improvement were mostly psychological, and increasingly so as we worked. Bates' simple drills for relaxing, sunning, and mobilizing the eyes became more and more preparation and groundwork for the central problem in vision improvement, which was (as both Bates and Mrs Corbett had taught) primarily psychological. I learned intuitively, by doing it, that when I could get my students' confidence, when I could get them to relax *emotionally*, when I could get them to develop freedom from apprehension, from anger or suspicion, and from emotional pain, when I could get them to imagine pleasant scenes, their vision 'turned on.' Huxley spoke of 'dynamic relaxation' as the state that allows vision to 'turn on.' What he (like Bates and Corbett) failed to emphasize sufficiently was the deep emotional roots of the tensions blocking this state of dynamic relaxation.

Because my understanding was intuitive and not yet conceptual, I struggled blindly for better techniques to bring vision to my students. The effort required with some students was prodigious. The nearsighted students (most of my students were nearsighted) were thin-skinned and vulnerable, and especially so when they opened up and their vision 'turned on.' Working with them — especially those with higher degrees of myopia — required me to 'walk tip-toed on egg shells.' When I could get myopic students to laugh, get them to trust, get them to expand, their lesson went beautifully; improvement from 20/100 to 20/20 or better during one lesson in my studio was not uncommon. But let me lift an eyebrow wrong, let the slightest trace of impatience or irritation creep into my voice, and there went my student's vision! It became a great strain to teach many of these students. When they called and cancelled a lesson, I felt such relief — even though I needed the money to pay my rent.

Had I understood fully why it was such a strain, I could have coped more effectively, but I was operating on feeling. Neither Bates nor Corbett provided an adequate conceptual base for me to understand what was going on. I did not then realize that no such base existed anywhere, and I kept reading and searching, struggling after knowledge that did not exist. I soon realized the need for research, and was drawn increasingly toward a career in research in the psychology of vision.

Perhaps the most eminent psychologist specializing in vision at that time was Professor Samuel Renshaw of Ohio State. Dr. Renshaw was the architect of the U.S. Navy's Aircraft Recognition Training Program of World War II. He was also the psychologist mainstay of the 'Optometric Extension Program,' a radical, psychologically-oriented group of optometrists. However, the most advanced thinker I could find on the emotional problems of the kind that I faced in my students was Wilhelm Reich. I resolved to learn what I could from both men.

After graduating from the University of Hawaii, I was accepted as a graduate student under Renshaw in the fall of 1949 and, after a college quarter, became a research assistant to him. I earned my master's degree under his direction the following year. Renshaw made a great deal of use of tachistiscopic techniques. Words, numbers, or patterns were employed that the student tried to reproduce from a flash (tachistiscopic) exposure of a twentieth of a second or less. This tachistiscopic training not only improved the recognition of visual form but, Renshaw observed, sometimes decreased myopia among students.

Working for Renshaw, I developed a means for generating random visual patterns of any desired level of difficulty for use in tachistiscopic training. I also learned the thoroughness, discipline and patience required of a good experimentalist, and I acquired a great amount of knowledge about the psychophysiology and the experimental psychology of visual perception. I became familiar with the optometric and medical as well as the psychological literature on vision. Nowhere was there anything that threw light on my experience with vision improvement via the Bates method. Psychology, optometry and ophthalmology did not even recognize that such improvements took place, much less investigate how and why. Everyone among the orthodox was caught up with the study of mechanisms, and the mechanism of vision is exceedingly intricate and interesting. No-one was working with the emotional functions producing visual problems.

But Wilhelm Reich and his students were into the bodily basis of such emotional functions, and were employing powerful techniques of emotional release based on Reich's discoveries. I went to New York to study Reich, and to go into therapy with a doctor he had trained, while I worked for my Ph.D. In New York I took my first professional job as an applied experimental psychologist, and I enrolled as a doctoral student in the New School for Social Research.

My major professor at the New School was Dr. Hans Wallach, a fine experimental psychologist working in the area of visual perception. My doctoral dissertation under Dr. Wallach was entitled 'Psychological factors in myopia.' I investigated the medical and optometric theories of myopia, to be discussed later, and I studied research on the nature and correlates of myopia, both in the physiological and psychological realm. I went back over the improvement of vision of myopic students I had taught as a Bates teacher, on whom I had kept careful records. Most significant, I did an experimental study on the use of psychological techniques derived from the Bates method to improve myopia. Using optical instruments from the former School of Optometry at Columbia University, and working in the Optometric Center of New York, I showed conclusively that:

1 Myopia is not a fixed optical condition, but a plastic and variable one.

2 Large temporary improvements in myopia could be produced by the techniques derived from Bates.

3 The improvements were not due to improved interpretation of blur, contraction of the pupil, tears on the cornea, or to changes in shape of the lens (accommodation).

4 The changes were unaffected by cycloplegia (drops in the eyes).

There is a strong presumption from my data that the improvement in myopia of the experimental subjects was due to a change in the length of the eyeball as a result of action of the extrinsic muscles of the eye. Bates had said that myopia was due to contraction of these muscles. The implication of the study was also that permanent improvements in myopia should be possible using the techniques I had employed.

The study created a minor stir. It was awarded the Alumni prize as the finest dissertation of the university in the 1957-58 academic year. It was presented to the American Psychological Association convention, printed in a summary article in the *Journal of the American Optometric Association,* written up in *Time* magazine and the *New York Times,* recorded and broadcast over radio stations in New York and California. With that, interest died. Its effect on the vision professions has been nil. This carefully controlled research program has never had a fraction of the influence of, for example, the attack on Bates and his work by Martin Gardner in the book *Fads and Fallacies in the Name of Science.* Gardner had no educational or professional qualifications for discussing Bates, did no serious investigation of Bates' claims, and condemned out of hand Bates and those who reported deriving benefits from Bates' work. The article was full of 'authoritative' pseudo-scientific pronouncements, attacks on Bates' character, and gross and ignorant distortions of his scientific position. Gardner's attack on Bates and its widespread influence infuriated me. It is best described as an example of the pseudo-scientist urinating on his scientific betters. This practice is very safe; indeed, it is encouraged, as long as the victims are espousing an unorthodox position.

The attitude toward Bates' work generated by Gardner's attack and others like it make it possible for the optometrists and medics of New York to band together to have the Bates method outlawed in New York State. I still get letters on occasion from people in New York wanting to know where they can get Bates training. Many of these correspondents are in desperate visual condition, and I know with certainty that Bates' work could help some of them. I sometimes feel like writing them to go blind, courtesy of Martin Gardner and their local medical and optometric associations.

Despite my vindication of Bates' claims, techniques to change the underlying emotional factors in myopia and other visual disorders were still lacking. My dissertation provided no new methods of training, but only confirmed the effectiveness of some of those I had used as a Bates teacher. I could not, in my dissertation, go into the application to vision problems of the deep emotional release techniques of Wilhelm Reich. This was both because I was not ready, and because these techniques were too unorthodox and emotion-charged to be accepted then in even as open a university as the New School for Social Research.

But my experience in Reichian therapy confirmed that I was on the right track. My therapist was Dr. Wm. F. Thorburn, an osteopath trained by Reich. My vision was much affected by the Reichian emotional release techniques he used, and in a different way than had occurred in Bates lessons. For example, when I learned to cry again with Dr. Thorburn's help, it freed my eyes and changed the quality of my visual experience. I had not cried for twenty years, and it 'opened my eyes' in a very different sense than Bates lessons ever had.

On the way to and from Dr. Thorburn's office I passed the window of a large, well-arranged florist shop. After the appointment the colors and arrangements of these flowers appeared strikingly vivid, and affected me deeply. I would stop and gaze at them in a kind of wonder. The whole visual world was opened up to me in a new direct, intense form of visual perception. Other students in Reichian therapy reported experiences similar to mine. Some also reported lasting improvements in vision, and a few discarded glasses as a result of their Reichian work. The latter were exceptional cases.

What was needed was someone to put together Bates' and Reich's work in a new synthesis. I was the right person from the standpoint of knowledge, in fact, the only person who could, but I was not yet ready emotionally.

Dr. Thorburn died in 1960. I moved back to California in 1963. I was fortunate enough to find my way to Dr. Philip Curcuruto, who proved to be among the most skilled of Reichian practitioners I had met. (I had met many in a dozen years' association with the Reichian movement.) Even so, five more years of hard work were required for me to complete my Reichian analysis. This was in 1968, then, twenty years after I first grasped the potential importance of Reich's techniques as a Bates teacher and undergraduate at the University of Hawaii.

But I was quite a different person characterologically. The deep myopic fearfulness was gone. Still intellectually aggressive, I was also much more open and spontaneous emotionally, confident in personal relations.

And I was twenty years older. I had been highly successful in my work as an applied experimental psychologist, and was now internationally known, with a book and scores of papers to my credit. My scientific work on vision had been limited to such things as studying optical information gathering on the Apollo mission, heads-up displays for Naval aircraft, motor vehicle rear vision systems, etc. Much of what I did didn't involve vision at all, and none of it vision improvement, as my scientific interests had expanded into other fields. My vision training skills had only been kept alive through the years by people who knew my background, and who came to me privately to learn what they could do for their own or their children's vision problems.

In 1967 and 68 my wife Erica and I laid plans for the first group of volunteer myopes to undergo a combination of Bates, Renshaw and Reich techniques aimed at improving their vision. The techniques we developed for the group were original, rooted in my understanding of these men's work, but brought together by us in a new synthesis. Bates and Renshaw techniques were modified to reflect my understanding of the deep emotional basis of visual dysfunction. Changing the student emotionally or characterologically to free him from the factors which generated his visual problem was our first concern. The specific vision improvement techniques then became important, so that the emotional change could be translated into improved vision.

Our first group of five volunteers met in our home for twelve weeks starting in January 1969. It was techniques of emotional release rooted in the concepts of Reich to which we gave major emphasis. They worked. We reached deep levels of spontaneous emotional discharge in most sessions with most of our students, though it took up two of the three hours of each meeting, working with each student in turn, to do so. The specific vision techniques were less effective than they could have been due to lack of time. Renshaw tachistiscopic training needs at least 3 half-hour sessions per week, for example, and we had time for only 15 or 20 minutes in our 3-hour once-a-week group meetings.

Nonetheless, all of our students changed visually. The average 12 week improvement in vision was equivalent to two lines on the eye chart. But in assessing the significance of the experiment at the end of our twelve weeks of work, the student agreed that the emotional changes they went through were more significant to them than was the improved vision. (One student said they were 'equally significant.') And all agreed that the changes were deeply significant. We really didn't have to ask; we could see them happen as we worked.

Since that time, those students who continued to work have continued to improve. One originally highly myopic student has reduced her optical correction by 3/4. A less myopic student has now brought his test vision up to 20/20. Optometrists confirm our students' improvements. And so we started offering classes in this work. As of this writing, half a year later, its vision improvement program has only begun to attract students. But for those students who have come, the program is proving its power.

Our classes, workshops and individual instruction in vision improvement have the potential for becoming the most effective program for the improvement of vision that has ever been offered. The program is new, however, and there is so much to learn that we feel we are only beginning.

Part 2: Myopia and Hyperopia

Myopia (nearsightedness) is a condition in which the eyeball is too long relative to the strength of the eye's optical elements (cornea and lens). The image of distant objects is focused in front of the myope's retina, and a negative (diverging) lens, thin in the middle and thick at the edges, must be placed in front of the eye to bring the plane of focus back to the retina. Myopes of any degree suffer very poor distant vision — worse than most people realize. It is not unusual for the myope to be unable to read the largest letter on a standard eye chart at 20 feet without glasses, and many must approach to 2-6 feet of the chart to distinguish its largest letter.

Hyperopia or hypermetropia (farsightedness) is the opposite condition to myopia, for in it the eyeball is too short relative to the eye's optical elements. When the hyperopic eye relaxes, the image of distant objects is focused on a plane behind the retina. A positive (converging or magnifying) lens, thick in the middle and thin at the edges, is required to bring the plane of focus forward to the retina. It is more difficult to detect hyperopia than myopia, because the eye can increase its own focusing power by accommodation. Accommodation is the function that makes it possible for the normal eye to adjust itself to see nearby objects clearly through an increase in the thickness of the lens of the eye. (The myope cannot accommodate in reverse to see distant objects more clearly.) If the hyperopic eye accommodates an amount just equal to the amount of hyperopia, the lens thickens enough that distant objects will be focused onto the retina, and so seen clearly. Nearby objects can also be seen clearly as long as there is enough *additional* accommodation present to adjust the eye for the closeness of the objects viewed. The hyperopic lens must thus thicken more to see near objects than does the lens of the normal eye.

Whereas the typical myope is most bothered by the blurring of his distant vision, the typical hyperope is bothered by eye strain or fatigue, difficulty in concentrating for long on near-point work, problems in focusing the eyes, and by the tendency for print (and other objects viewed at near point) to blur at an earlier age than they do for others. Hyperopes are far more subject than myopes to eye headaches, crossed eyes, and reading difficulties. Small degrees of hyperopia are common, especially with young children, but among adolescents and adults, large degrees of hyperopia are not nearly as common as large degrees of myopia. Much more has therefore been written about possible causes of myopia than of hyperopia.

Perhaps the four most widely held theories of myopia causation (the first and last of which are also theories of hyperopia causation) are:

1. *Genetic theory* — myopia and hyperopia are inherited conditions.
2. *Nutritional theory* — myopia is a product of diet.
3. *Conditions of use theory* — myopia is the result of the excessive use of eyes for near-point tasks.
4. *Normal biological variation theory* — myopia and hyperopia are, in most cases, only the reflection of normal variation in the length of the eyeball and the strength of the eye's optical elements.

The evidence against each one of these theories is substantial. I have reviewed it in detail elsewhere (Kelley, 1958) and will only summarize the main points here.

Genetic Theory
The belief that myopia (and hyperopia) is inherited does not hold up to scientific examination. True, myopia tends to run in families, but this is true of a great many acquired conditions and behaviors. The best studies of human inheritance are of identical twins, since only such twins have identical inheritance. Studies of twins by Hofstetter and Rife (1953) and Meyer-Schwickerath (1949) show that identical twins don't have the closely similar degrees of myopia that the genetic theory demands. Population genetics based on correlations of refractive error and other body measurements in a study of a great many families confirm this conclusion, making it ...

> ... highly unlikely that static refractive error (myopia and hyperopia) is primarily hereditarily determined. (Young, (1958).

The best that can be said of the role of inheritance in myopia and hyperopia is that some people may be especially prone to these conditions due to constitutional factors (Henderson, 1934). It is quite possible that there are inherited constitutional differences

Nutritional Theory

The nutritional theory of myopia is that dietary deficiency or imbalance affects the eye's structure in such a way that myopic elongation occurs. The great differences in myopia incidence between cultures might be accounted for in this way, e.g., the notoriously poor diets and high myopia incidence in the orient. The fact that first generation American children of European parents have an incidence of myopia like that of other Americans rather than like that of the country of their parent (Nadell and Hirsch, 1955) is also evidence against a genetic and for a nutritional or other environmental theory. However, studies of the diets of myopes have not shown consistent dietary differences between myopes and non-myopes living in the same culture that could explain myopia. The incidence of myopia is higher among the well fed professional segment of the population than among the badly fed poor, for example.

There is one interesting fact that has emerged from research on dietary factors related to myopia. Young myopes tend to have depressed blood calcium compared with controls (Wood, 1927; Law, 1934). There is no evidence that this is due to their diets, however, nor that administration of calcium and vitamins (Knapp, 1939; Stansbury, 1948) arrests the progress of myopia.

Conditions of Use Theory

There is a close correlation of myopia incidence with the conditions of civilized life, which includes such a great increase in use of the eyes for near-point work. In civilized countries, school work alone results in an extremely large added use of the eyes at reading distance during the childhood years in which most myopia develops. The occurrence of myopia is low among pre-school children and increases tremendously in the school years. It continues to increase in association with education from grammar school through professional schools. Too, myopia has a lower incidence among peasants, farmers, and primitive people than among the highly educated professional classes.

Any adequate theory of myopia must account for these facts. Simplistic explanations quickly run aground, however. Thus while it is true that myopic children tend to read more than others (Young, 1955) it does not follow that the reading causes the myopia. More than average reading could be a result of the myopia, for example, or both myopia and the tendency to read a lot could be the consequence of a third factor. This factor could be, e.g., a type of over-all character or personality development that is associated with both myopia and a predilection for reading. In point of fact, there are dozens of studies, spread over seventy years, to show that severe curbs on reading, use of large type, strict control of lighting, etc. etc., does *nothing whatever* to reduce the incidence or slow the progress of myopia. Vision hygiene programs have failed repeatedly as myopia preventatives. Occasional positive results have been reported, but have not held up under massive and repeated investigation. The conditions of use theory of myopia, attractive as it is on many counts, has failed to prove its case (Nadell, *et al.*, 1957; Stansbury, 1948).

Biological Variation Theory
Yet another theory of myopia and hyperopia, somewhat akin to the genetic theory, holds that hyperopia and most myopia is the result of normal biological variation in the eye's structure (e.g., Sorsby, 1934). The theory holds that just as some people are much taller or shorter than others, or have longer arms and fingers, some people have longer eyeballs or shorter eyeballs relative to the strength of the eye's optical elements. In this view, if your eyeball happens to be too long, you are myopic; if it is too short, you are hyperopic.

This theory is refuted by two lines of evidence. First, the myopic eye follows an entirely different pattern of development from the normal eye. The normal-sighted child stays normal while the usual myopic child at age 8-12 becomes progressively more myopic, often changing markedly in a few years (Hofstetter, 1954). This means that something is happening in the myopic eye that is decidedly not merely normal biological development.

More technical but equally telling is a statistical point. Body dimensions that are subject to normal biological variation, such as height, leg and finger length, etc., are distributed in the population at large according to a 'normal distribution curve,' with most people at the center or average value, and decreasing numbers the further away from average one goes. The exact mathematical nature of this curve is well known, having been discovered by Gauss over a century and a half ago. Eye measurements (refractive error) conform to the normal distribution curve early in life, but their distribution becomes increasingly abnormal over time (Wibaut, 1926; Hofstetter, 1954). The adult curve of refractive error in the population bears little resemblance to the normal distribution curve.

Figure 1 shows one such curve for a large sample of adult male Americans, together with a best fitting normal curve. Two major changes have taken place to distort the shape of the actual refractive error distribution from the 'expected' normal shape:

1. Cases are stacked up in the central (normal vision) portion of the curve ('leptokurtosis'). This indicates that the eye has a means of correcting at least small errors in refraction toward normal.

2. The curve is very skewed in the negative (myopic) direction, showing that a large minority of the population has become myopic.

There is nothing in these data to support the theory that myopia is a 'normal biological variation.'

The Mechanism of Myopia and Hyperopia

Stenstrom (1948) showed that variations in adult refractive error are almost entirely the result of differences in elongation of the eye. The two tendencies distorting the original normal shape of the curve of refractive error are thus due to a factor that affects the relative length of the eyeball. Bates believed, and the evidence from my own studies of myopia confirm, that this factor is the extrinsic muscles of the eye. Bates' research indicated that the two oblique muscles belting the eye around the middle were responsible for lengthening the eye, and, if they were chronically

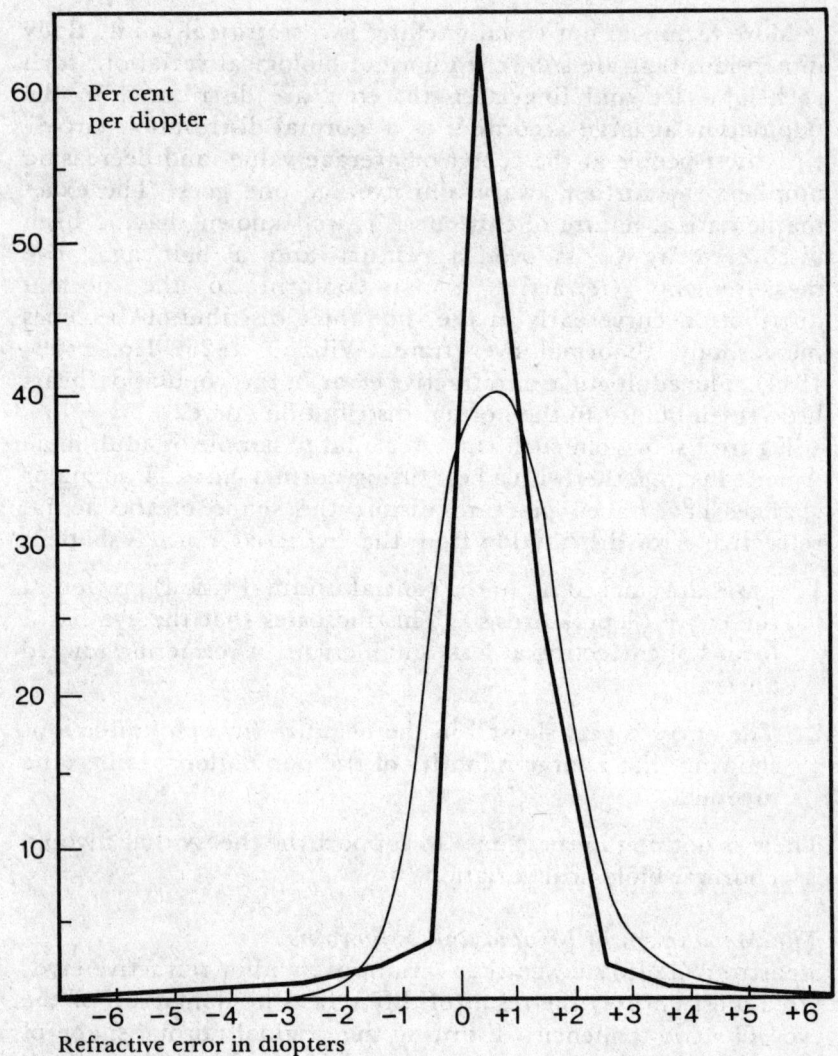

Figure 1
Frequency curve of refractive error among adult male Americans (thick line) and best fitting normal curve (thin line). (From *Stenstrom's Treatment of Original Data* by Stromberg; Stenstrom, 1948, p.31.)

tense, they produced myopia. Opposed to the action of the obliques, he held, were the four recti, extending from front to back of the eye. These, according to Bates, flattened the eye and, if chronically tense, produced hyperopia.

Bates believed that these same opposed muscle groups were responsible for accommodation of the eye, the obliques lengthening the eye for near vision, the recti flattening it for the distant view. There is substantial evidence that this is not the case and that the eye instead accommodates by action of muscles within the eye which change the shape of the lens (Helmholtz theory).

The incorrectness of Bates' theory of accommodation says nothing about the validity of his theory of refractive error. Since there appear to be two mechanisms affecting the refractive condition of the eye, one internal and one external to the eyeball, it was natural for Bates, discovering one of these mechanisms, to generalize that it also performed the second (accommodative) function. Other vision scientists have frequently made the converse error, trying to explain most myopia in terms of the accommodative mechanism within the eyeball. A special x-ray technique for measuring eyeball length had to be developed before it was established that the mechanism of myopia was, instead, eyeball elongation (Stenstrom, 1948).

Dynamics of Myopia and Hyperopia

Myopia and hyperopia are due, then, to relative elongation or flattening of the eye by the extrinsic muscles. Yet this refers only to the mechanism of refractive error, and not the underlying cause. The elongation of the eye in the direction of myopia by the oblique muscles is a kind of flexor action; the opposed direction, flattening the eye in the direction of hyperopia by the recti, is a kind of extension. This identification of a direction inward or outward is an indicator of the nature of myopia and hyperopia that is consistent with a Reichian body energy concept. In myopia the direction is inward, contractive, toward the self. Hyperopia is the reverse, i.e., outward, expansive, away from the self.

Several psychological studies of myopia and a few of hyperopia show that there are character and personality traits associated with these conditions (e.g., Young, 1967; Rosanes, 1966). Studies prior to 1958 have been reviewed elsewhere (Kelley, 1958). Table 1 summarizes important differences between myopes and hyperopes. These are generally consistent with the research literature, but go beyond it. The findings on body structure and function are (except for the first two) based on my own experience in vision improvement work.

Generalizations about the body and character dynamics of myopes and hyperopes must be made with due respect for the individual development process. The tendencies described in Table 1 refer to early, deep dynamic factors that are reacted to in many different ways. Some myopes remain shy, withdrawn, seclusive, and sedentary all their lives, for example, while others 'take themselves in hand' — often in adolescence — and force themselves to compensate. They may then go into athletics and/or social activities, for example. The myopic gymnast, weight lifter or football player, in my experience, has usually started into athletics to compensate for his deep underlying fearfulness, working to erase the suspicion that he is a 'sissy'. As a result of his compensation, his superficial appearance may contradict features of the description of Table 1. And virtually every student coming in for training has armored against, not just one basic emotion, but all of them. Thus some degree of blocked grief, rage and fear show themselves in myope and hyperope alike. Some of these blocks are later and more superficial than others. With the myope the early, deep fundamental block is of fear; it is often necessary to peel away shallower layers of armoring to reach this level. With the hyperope, however, the anger block is fundamental, and his deep rage must ultimately be reached and released, whatever surface layers may cover it.

Some of the behavioral observations that Table 1 is based on (aside from those of body structure) may help show how this understanding of myopia and hyperopia was reached. In the build-up of strong emotion that develops while using neo-Reichian techniques of emotional release, certain students develop an almost uncontrollable tendency to close their eyes, often clenching them tight despite repeated instruction to open them. It is clear from their timing and manner that this is a fear

TABLE 1
Tendencies often found in myopes versus hyperopes

Myope	Hyperope
Character and Personality	
inward, introjective, self-oriented	outward, "other" oriented
shy, withdrawn as a child	aggressive as a child
"good" in school	often a behavior problem in school
childhood "temper tantrums" rare	childhood "temper tantrums" common
stubborn, emotionally inflexible	more yielding to external pressure
more at home with self, uncomfortable with others	more at home with others, uncomfortable with self
often "off" in day dreams, subvocal thought	alert, aware of environment
comfortable with eyes closed; retreats from visual perception inward	uncomfortable with eyes closed; retreats from the self outward
Body Structure and Function	
underactive, often sedentary	hyperactive
body soft, sometimes flabby	body tense, hard, wiry
throat, high chest, jaws, back of neck, scalp — chronically tense; jaw rotated forward, forehead back; shoulder forward	eyes, side of neck, back — chronically tense; forehead rotated forward, chin back; shoulders back
disconnected from feet; "up in the head;" centered but poorly grounded	better grounded, but less well centered; "out into the muscles"
voice often breathy or husky; becomes hoarse easily	voice more often clear
chest often depressed; breathing blocks on *inspiration*	chest often expanded; breathing blocks on *expiration*
fearful; blocking terror	angry; block rage
Eyes	
usually large-looking, open; very little local armoring around eyes	usually smaller-appearing; much local armoring around eyes
squint, fusion problems not common	squint, fusion problems frequent
unusual to have pain, eye headache	pain, headache common
eyes lack sparkle, brightness	eyes bright
eyes look down or away in anger	eyes spark, look at one in anger

response, a frightened shutting off of the visual world. (The eyes will also close in grief, but the student has no trouble opening them if so instructed.) I have witnessed this fearful eye-closing reaction hundreds of times, yet it is *only myopes* who do it; I have very rarely taught a hyperope that reacted in this way.

If the hyperope is instructed to close his eyes, it rouses anxiety; his natural tendency is to keep his eyes open as his feelings build. For this reason it is often difficult to teach a hyperope to palm successfully, i.e., to close the eyes and cover them with the palms in the way Bates recommends. The instant either the student himself or his vision teacher speaks, the hyperopic student tends to take down the palms, open the eyes, and look at the teacher. — Yet I've never known a myope to do this.

In a workshop full of myopes, the teacher must continually work to keep the group in motion. When not carrying out drills or instructions, the myope tends to stop activity, to sit, lie down, or just stand, but in any event, to become inert. In a group of hyperopes, the usual problem is to get the students to shut up, be still, and pay attention enough that instruction can proceed! These facts, known, I think by every Bates teacher, were confirmed in the doctoral research of Rosanes (1966), which showed that hyperopes express anxiety by increased motor activity, myopes by decreased motor activity.

When a compensatory posture has not obscured it, the basically fearful body expression of the myope is clearly evident. The shoulders are held forward and often dropped, the chest deflated. The skull is rotated chin forward — forehead back, as if a blow were expected. The flexors at the back of the neck, a key point in the myope's body armor, are primarily responsible for the myope's typical neck posture (see Figure 2). They pull the head back and into the torso. The throat is highly energized, blocking and holding against the fear. Inner thinking with sub-vocalization is common, and helps keep the myope 'in his head.' The forehead tends to be smooth and pulled back by the tense scalp, the eyes opened wide, but with a certain deadness of expression. The eyes of the myope lack sparkle and life, and pull back from contact, even as they look at you.

New techniques in vision improvement

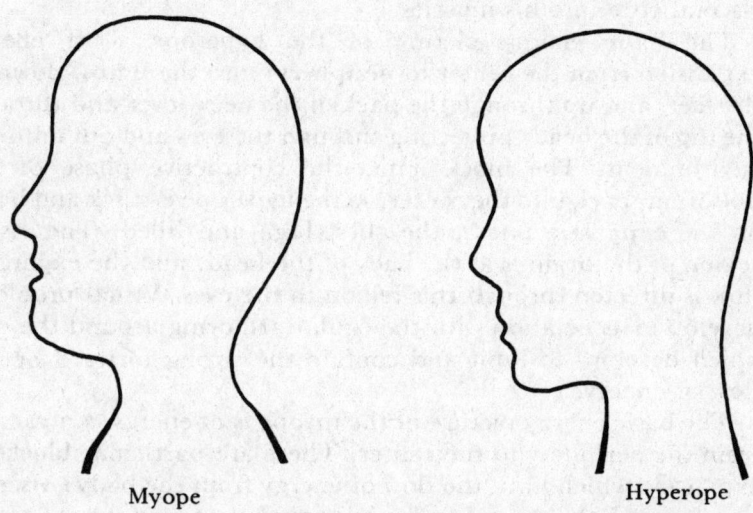

Figure 2 Typical myopic and hyperopic head posture.

The hyperopic posture is stiff, expressing the held-in anger. The shoulders are often pulled up, the chest held full and high. The skull is rotated forehead forward — chin back, making the head stiff and tall. The tense muscles at the side of the neck tilt the head forward, and also prevent the head from turning easily from side to side. There are often heavy tensions in the brows, lids and extrinsic eye muscles, and the eyes themselves may appear small because of the armoring around them. The extra-ocular muscle tension causes a tendency to stare, and interferes with coordinated binocular eye movements. For all this eye armoring, the eyes of the hyperope are usually bright and lively in expression compared with those of the myope. The eyes will flash in anger, which myopic eyes do not do, and eye contact is usually sought. There may be less energy and holding in throat, mouth and jaw than with the myope, however. The thought processes of the hyperope are frequently visual rather than sub-vocal. He is less often off 'in his head,' but is frequently scattered and away from his center, i.e., his body energy drives outward from his visceral core into his muscles.

The basic energy picture of the hyperope is of energy expansion from the center to periphery, into the limbs, down to the feet, and up through the back of the neck, over and through the top of the head, projecting through the eyes and out onto the environment. The block limits the contractive phase of the pulsation, back into the center, so the hyperope is stuck and holds on the expansive phase, the chest high and filled. The visual region of the brain is at the back of the head, and the expansive flow is directed through this region to the eyes. Visual problems develop in association with the ocular armoring around the eyes which develops to limit and contain the strong forward ocular flow of energy.

The basic energy picture of the myope is of energy contraction from the periphery to the center. There are particular blocks to expansion which limit the flow of energy from the body's visceral core through the genital and pelvic area below, and the top of the chest and neck above. The chest is usually depressed and holds against full inhalation. There is a fundamental block at the back of the neck and head, extending over the scalp. Picture the posture and expression of a child in chronic fear of a parent or teacher. The ocular flow itself is much weakened, and energy flows strongly instead into the throat and jaws, often with heavy sub-vocal thinking. In addition to the obvious head and neck posture, the pelvis is held, usually forward. The testicles are lifted in the male, the buttocks pulled in, and the genital, perineal and anal area contracted in both sexes. The basic armor of the myope, then, is not ocular, but it blocks the ocular flow of energy before it reaches the eyes, and even before it reaches the visual region of the brain at the back of the head.

Although the myopic posture is fearful, it is not often yielding or acquiescent. There is stubbornness and determination expressed in the stiff neck and tense jaw. It expresses a layer of anger present in most myopes that must be freed before the more fundamental fearfulness becomes accessible. Occasionally an 'angry' myope is found, with a high stiff chest. This anger is superficial, easily accessible compared with the deep fear underneath.

Part 3: The Improvement of Vision

The medical and optometric professions have had some success in improving the vision of myopes — more, in fact, than many of the most respected men in the field have acknowledged. This is doubtless because orthodox doctrine is that little genuine improvement in sight without glasses can occur with most people having defective vision, and doctrine is often more important to conservative practitioners than well-documented experimental results by the more venturesome members of the professions dealing with vision.

Table 2 presents example data from a few studies of myopia improvement. To make the data from all studies comparable, I have presented the results in terms of how large the smallest visual acuity test targets were which were read correctly after training, expressed as a per cent of the size (area) of the smallest read before training, both tests being made without glasses, of course. An improvement from 20/40 to 20/20 or from 20/100 to 20/50 would both be classed as 25 per cent, since the smaller targets seen 'after' have 1/4 the area of those seen 'before' in both cases. In the group training experiment of Berens and his co-authors, who employed 30 sessions of Renshaw tachistiscopic techniques, an improvement to about 35 per cent of initial target size was found, about four lines improvement on the test chart used (Berens, *et al.*, 1957). This substantial average improvement was for a group of 80 subjects, and was published in the prestigious *American Journal of Ophthalmology*. The authors are a team of four investigators of repute, three MD's and a psychologist. A control group of 60 subjects failed to improve, as would be expected without the training.

Other techniques bring even greater improvement, as the studies cited confirm. The results of extended Bates training show that the improvements in visual acuity demonstrated in relatively brief group experiments could be greatly extended by prolonged individual Bates training. Part 1 of this article showed that comparable improvements in other visual functions occur with conditions other than myopia as a result of long continued Bates training.

TABLE 2

Effectiveness of visual improvement techniques in myopia; a summary of experimental studies

Reference	Area of targets seen after training as a percentage of the smallest seen before training	Improvement ratio (approx.)
Optometric group training methods:		
Hildreth, et al., 1947	70%	1.5
Woods, 1946	50%	2.0
Tachistiscopic training:		
Berens, et al., 1957	35%	3.0
Experimental suggestion:		
Fox, 1959	25%	4.0
Kelley, 1958	20%	5.0
Extensive individual Bates training: (four subjects trained 50-200 hours each)		
Kelley, 1958	less than 2%	50.0

It is not yet possible to present data comparing the result of the Interscience Work Shop's new techniques with the results of prior studies. The techniques are too new, and as yet we lack resources necessary for properly controlled experimental research. But the results are striking. Students are improving their vision, some dramatically, and in most cases more quickly than by use of any other techniques with which I am familiar. We expect to be able to demonstrate improvements greater than are possible with the Bates method, both in rate of improvement and final level reached through training. We expect also to show some major improvements in very serious visual conditions, but we want to avoid building anyone's hopes unduly. We give training experimentally to some applicants with severe vision problems when their condition is not communicable, making certain they understand that we can promise nothing. We ask that they have their eye doctor monitor their progress. We will report our results in these cases, failures and successes alike.

Vision and Feeling
The most important changes taking place in most students are not in vision itself, however, but in the whole person, at the feeling level. When a person has been haunted unconsciously since childhood with the effects of blocked fear, rage, or grief, the release of the blocked emotion brings changes that are usually much more significant to him than the improved vision in itself.

The release of blocked fear brings a freedom and opening out of the student that changes his being profoundly. The deflated chest fills, the posture straightens, and the student faces his life with new confidence. He is better able to express anger or love, both of which were held by the fear block. The voice drops in pitch and becomes more resonant as the throat — which, like the eyes, plays a key role in the fear block — relaxes. Genital tensions relax and the sexual experience deepens. — And the vision improves! There is no experience as significant for bringing vision improvement to the myope as the release of blocked fear.

Similar things can be said about freeing the blocked rage that typifies hyperopia. There is a relaxation and often a lightening of the personality, an opening and brightening, with a new sense of freedom. Frequently there is an outpouring of joy following a particular release session. The head turns more easily as tensions in the back, shoulders and the sides of the neck give way. Perhaps most significant in the long-term view, however, is a centering of the person, a coming into himself, a focusing of his vital energy. The person blocking anger has his energy scattered in the periphery, in his muscular system. Release of the anger block permits the energy to flow back to the center, the body's visceral and plasmatic core. There is a corresponding reduction in peripheral muscle tension. The stiff expanded chest softens and drops. The eyes become softer, opening wider and moving more freely as the local armoring around them disappears. Headaches, double vision, imbalances and incoordinations in the two eyes greatly improve, especially if vision drills to take advantage of the changes are practised.

When it is grief that has been blocked, release of the block results in full and free crying, with no holding back of sound. The freeing of the high chest, throat, jaw, pharynx and eyes as well as the high chest is involved. There is frequently an admixture of fear or rage in crying, in which case the crying will be partial, and may turn into a rage or fear discharge. The 'purest' release of grief does not involve fear or rage, however, but very deep hurt or disappointment that was blocked out of awareness by the armor. Release then results in agonizing sobs and cries from the depths of the being.

The release of grief affects vision significantly. Crying is a discharge of energy through the throat, mouth, nose and the eyes. The lids typically close tight at the peak of a grief discharge, as if to contain the strong outpouring of energy through the eyes. The high chest heaves convulsively, the upper face turns red, and the tears and sounds pour out with full involuntary expirations. After the discharge the eyes are temporarily puffy and red. Emotionally, there is a relief and calm, with an integration of the deep feelings. The expression is serious and open. Eye contact is unusually intense and direct, and the visual surroundings are experienced with unusual vividness. Things of beauty affect the student deeply. He is sensitized, not only to colors and forms, but to emotional expressions. He is strongly aware of where other people are, including their blocks and inhibitions to feeling.

When the opening is sudden and new, the expressions of many people are a shock. People on the street can appear grotesque and agonized. 'To see' in our sense of the word means to become aware of what is there, be it lovely or unlovely.

The release and spontaneous discharge of fear, rage, and grief are central to our vision improvement work, as to our 'education in feeling' program. People ask about the positive emotions: Do we not free them also? — What we free is what is present within the student, of course. Most people must work through negative emotion before reaching the positive. Approaches which endeavor to create joy without first working through pain are of necessity superficial, for no deeply joyous experience is possible when deep fear, rage, or grief is blocked and held in.

And the primary positive emotions are but the 'other side of the coin,' polar opposites of the negative, i.e.,

$$\text{pain} \longleftrightarrow \text{pleasure}$$
$$\text{fear} \longleftrightarrow \text{trust, receptivity, openness}$$
$$\text{rage} \longleftrightarrow \text{joy, love}$$
$$\text{grief} \longleftrightarrow \text{mirth, humor}$$

To block a negative emotion from awareness results in blocking the positive that is its polar opposite. To free the one opens the capacity for the other.

The freeing and discharge of feeling is the ground on which our vision improvement work takes place. Opening the feelings does not in itself guarantee measurable changes in vision, though they do occur. Its main function is to make the student much more accessible to specific vision improvement techniques, such as those derived from Bates and from Renshaw.

Our vision improvement work thus includes these four classes of techniques:

1. Neo-Reichian emotional release work, including the Interscience Intensive, for freeing blocks to feeling that affect vision. This is the core of our program.

2. Lowen stress positions and other bioenergetic drills to mobilize the body's energy.

3. Bates vision improvement drills.

4. Renshaw tachistiscopic training, the flashing of visual patterns for a fraction of a second, to be observed and reproduced by the student.

In addition, we are developing some new feeling-oriented vision improvement drills, which we hope will prove of real value. The Bates drills are described by Bates (1920) and Corbett (1949), and our neo-Reichian techniques for the freeing of feeling in Kelley (1970). Our program began as a blending of these.

Our techniques will doubtless change considerably in the years ahead. It is well to remember how young our approach is. It has been less than three years since the first small group of myopes volunteered to undergo a mixture of Bates and Reichian techniques. This was the inception of our program. Our facility for teaching this work has, of this writing (September 1970) been open less than a year. It has, we believe, been a truly significant year for understanding the nature of, and developing techniques to improve, the major disorders of sight.

BIBLIOGRAPHY

Bates, W.H.: *The Cure of Imperfect Sight by Treatment without Glasses*, New York, Central Fixation Co., 1920.

Berens, C., Girard, L.J., Fonda, G. and Sells, S.B.: Effects of Tachistiscopic Training on Visual Function in Myopic Patients. *Amer.J.Ophthal.*, 1957, 44 (Part II), 25-48.

Corbett, M.D.: *Help Yourself to Better Sight*. New York, Prentice-Hall, 1949.

Fox, J.: *Functional Factors in Myopia*. Unpublished Ph.D. dissertation, UCLA Dept. of Psychology, 1959.

Fox, S.: *Your Eyes*. New York, A.A. Knopt, 1944.

Gardner, M.: *Fads and Fallacies in the Name of Science*. New York, Dover, 1957.

Henderson, T.: The Constitutional Factor in Myopia. *Trans. Ophthal. Soc. U.K.*, 1934, 54, 451-9.

Hildreth, H.R., Mainberg, W.H., Milder, B., Post, L.T. and Sanders, T.E.: The Effects of Visual Training on Existing Myopia. *Amer.J.Ophthal.*, 1947, 30, 1563-1576.

Hofstetter, H.W.: Some Interrelationships of Age, Refraction, and Rate of Refractive Change. *Amer.J.Optam*, 1954, 31, 161-9.

Hofstetter, H.W. and Rife, D.C.: Miscellaneous Optometric Data on Twins. *Amer.H.Optom.*, 1953, 30, 139-50.

Huxley, A.: *The Art of Seeing*. New York, Harper, 1942.

Kelley, C.R.: *Education in Feeling and Purpose*. Santa Monica, Calif., Interscience Work Shop, 1970. Published in *Energy and Character*, Jan. 1971, 2(1)

Kelley, C.R.: Psychological Factors in Myopia. *J.Amer.Optom. Assoc.*, 1962, 33 (11), 833-7.

Kelley, C.R.: *Psychological Factors in Myopia*. Unpublished Ph.D. dissertation, New School for Social Research, New York, 1958.

Knapp, A.A.: Vitamin-D Complex in Progressive Myopia. *Amer.J.Ophthal.* 1939, 22, 1329-37.

Law, F.W.: Calcium and Parathyroid Therapy in Progressive Myopia. *Trans. Ophthal. Soc. U.K.*, 1934, 54, 281-290.

Lowen, A.: The Eyes and Feeling, in *Self-Expression*, New York, Inst. for Bio-Energetic Analysis, 1968.

Meyer-Schwickerath, G.: Zwillingsstatistische unter suchung uber den einfluss von unwelt faktoren auf den myopie grad. *V. Graefes. Arch. Ophthal.*, 1949, *149*, 695-700.

Nadeil, M.C., Weymouth, F.W. and Hirsch, M.J.: The Relationship of Frequency of Use of the Eyes in Close Work to the Distribution of Refractive Error in a Selected Sample. *Amer.J.Optom.*, 1957, *34*, 523-537.

Nadell, M.C. and Hirsch, M.J.: The Relationship of the Birthplace of Parents and Grandparents to the Refractive State of the Child. *Amer.J. Optom.*, 1955, *32*, 137-141.

Rosanes, M.B.: *Psychological Correlates to Myopia Compared to Hyperopia and Emmetropia.* Unpublished doctoral dissertation, Yeshiva University, 1966.

Sorsby, A.: The Pre-myopic State; its Bearing on the Incidence of Myopia. *Trans. Ophthal. Soc.*, U.K., 1934, *54*, 459.

Stansbury, F.C.: Pathogenesis of Myopia; a New Classification. *Arch. Ophthal.*, 1948, *39*, 273-99.

Stenstrom, S. (trans. by D. Woolf): Investigation of the Variation and the Correlation of the Optical Elements of Human Eyes. *Amer.J.Optom.*, 1948, Monograph No.58.

Wibaut, F.: Uber die emmetropisation und dem wisprung der spharischen refraktionsanotmalien. *Arch. F. Ophthal.*, 1926, *116*, 596-612.

Wood, D.J.: Calcium Deficiency in the Blood with Reference to Spring Catarrh and Malignant Myopia. *Brit.J.Ophthal.*, 1927, *11*, 224-230.

Woods, A.C.: Report from the Wilmer Institute on the Results Obtained in the Treatment of Myopia by Visual Training. *Amer.J.Ophthal.*, 1946, *29*, 28-57.

Young, F.A.: Myopia and Personality. *Amer. J. Optom. and Arch. Amer. Acad. of Optom.*, 1967, *44*(3), 192-201.

Young, F.A.: Reading, Measures of Intelligence and Refractive Errors. *Amer. J. Optom.*, 1963, *40*(5), 257-264.

Young, F.A.: An Estimate of the Hereditary Component of Myopia. *Amer. J. Optom*, 1958, *35*, 337-345.

Young, F.A.: Myopes versus Non-myopes — a Comparison. *Amer. J. Optom.*, 1955, *32*, 180-91.

Bio-energy and Cancer Formation

by Professor Giorgio Chiurco, F.I.C.S.

Director of the International Centre for the Study of Pre-cancer Conditions, Rome
Formerly head of Department of Surgical Pathology, University of Rome

and Dr. Bruno Bizzi

Vice-Director of 'L. Lolli' Psychiatric Hospital, Imola, Italy
Hon. Member of the Institute of Advanced Studies, University of Rome

Giorgio Chiurco is Head of the Department of Surgical Pathology at the University of Rome, and Director of the Centre for the Study of Pre-cancer conditions, in Rome. In the latter role he co-ordinated and directed two International Seminars on cancer prevention and prophylaxis which were the outcome of some twenty years uninterrupted study of the background to cancer development. He is the author of a three-volume study of this subject, and recognised to be one of the world's leading authorities in this area.

Bruno Bizzi is the Vice-Director of the 'L. Lolli' hospital in Imola, near Bologna, Italy. He took his medical qualification with a specialism in psychiatry at the University of Bologna and worked at the Neuro-Psychiatric clinic there. He is keenly interested in acupuncture, in the work of Wilhelm Reich, and the connections between them. He participates in many congresses, both national and international, and is the author of more than fifty scientific papers. He has worked closely both with Professor Chiurco; and with Dr. Walter Hoppe, the Director of the Orgone

Research Laboratories in Israel. Dr. Bizzi has been using orgone accumulators in his hospital for a period of several years. He is an Honorary Member of the Institute of Advanced Studies, at the University of Rome.

Introductory note: The following contribution falls into two parts. Part I is taken from a paper entitled 'From Galvanism to Orgonomy' which was presented by Professor Chiurco and by Dr. Bizzi jointly at the First Italian Symposium of Acupuncture, in June 1970, at San Remo, Italy. Part II is taken from Dr. Bizzi's paper 'Orgone Energy: Life-force (Galvani) and Morbid States' which was first presented at the Second International Seminar on Cancer Prophylaxis and Prevention, in Rome, October 1968. The full text of Dr. Bizzi's paper was published in English (translated from the Italian by Jenny James) in *Energy and Character*, Vol.1, No.1, January 1970.

Part I

Orgone Energy: Vital Force in Individuals and in the Atmosphere

'Ever since a time far back in the history of the world, particles of extraordinary energy and with a power of penetration which defies all imagination, have been bombarding our planet. They fall as a continuous hail, with implacable constancy; an imperturbable hail which has no regard either for time or for the seasons, for the position of the sun and moon, or even of the Milky Way; a hail which surrounds everything, which ever since we were born has been penetrating our bodies at the rate of several million corpuscles a day, without in general causing any harm, though on rare occasions it also causes unexpected and complex atomic phenomena.' (Louis Leprince-Ringuet: *Cosmic Rays,* ed. Einaudi, 1954).

This observation of the French writer recalls many points in the work of Newton where the founder of modern physics describes the cosmic energy which he defined in terms of the ether, although unaware of its precise bio-energetic activity.

We do not know very precisely how far Galvani was familiar with the work of Newton; however, his animal experiments and his theoretical elaborations constitute a demonstration of the validity, in the same field, of these theories of Newton.

Galvani is the first, in the history of studies of life-energy, to put the concept on an experimental basis in a laboratory.

The term 'life energy' is an intuitive term which is not associated solely with the possibility of laboratory experimentation though it is certain that this is the right way to make it secure. It is clear that many surprises and novelties can be expected, for we find ourselves at the beginning of a vast topic which is infinitely complex, if we do not close our eyes to it.

Galvani is recognised as the founder of electro-physiology; in reality he founded and expressed the theory of vital force in modern scientific terms, without realisation of its true value.

Galvani discovered a biological energy which is active in every living organism and which he defined — in accordance with the mechanistic concepts of his day — as 'animal electricity'. This denomination obviously could not stand for long, because an element from the world of physics, from a field which deals with inanimate, inorganic material, cannot, by virtue of its scientific definition, describe or define vital processes.

Continuous investigation and an unending discovery of laws governing the functioning of the life apparatus led Galvani and his pupil Aldini to modify their terms of definition: they dropped the term 'animal electricity' and adopted the expression 'galvanic fluid', and finally settled for the fitting description 'life force.'

We are witnessing here the development of a great bio-energetic concept which we can summarize in the following points, relying of course on direct study of the various experiments for a complete grasp of the subject.

Galvani mantains that the circulation of bio-energy within the organism has some kind of important and complex relationship with atmospheric electricity, whether we are dealing with the normal or the pathological. In his opinion, the skin itself provides the means of entry for the 'electricity', thus playing an important role in the maintenance of an uninterrupted, dynamic balance between the organism and the 'electric' ocean which surrounds it.

Thus Galvani accepted and adopted as his own the concept of an 'electrical fluid' almost as it had been elaborated by B. Franklin, who explained all electrostatic phenomena by the hypothesis of the existence in nature of a 'single fluid', composed of particles which repel one another, but which are attracted by those of another body. In the place of two kinds of electricity, positive and negative, conceived of as opposite and clearly divided, he postulated a single fluid, capable of two opposite functions, the contraction and expansion of its 'particles'.

On the biological level, this physical energy determines processes of actual protoplasmic expansions and contractions: expansions and contractions which we find repeated in all somatic and psychic structures: the pulsations of the cardiovascular and muscular apparatus, and of all organs in general, sympatheticotonia and vagotonia, excitations and inhibitions in the nervous structures, as can readily be seen, for example, from the examination of encephalograms in the succession of waves which are of just such a pulsating nature (Gozzano-Colomboti).

'Life-force' in Recent Scientific Thought

The concept of a 'life force' permeates the thought of many researchers and philosophers, just as it constitutes the central nucleus of therapies and of millenarian medical techniques such as acupuncture and moxibustion.

U. Lanza has reaffirmed this concept, with regard to acupuncture, in his recent volume *Modern Acupuncture: Reflexology*.

'This is not', he writes, 'a metaphysical physiological entity, but a force which results on the one hand from the activity of the sex cells (pre-natal energy) and on the other is reinforced, maintained and reintegrated by the absorption of energy obtained from air breathed in and from the ingestion of food.' (op.cit. p.138).

On the more philosophical plane, the most complete and systematic elaboration of this concept we certainly owe to E.

Kant. His whole work *Opus Postumum* is a concise study of the concept of ether — the main preoccupation of the mechanistic physics of the time. It is surprising that in Kant this ether also assumes the name of 'calory', or 'luminous material', and had the characteristics of expanding bodies in all three dimensions, of rendering material fluid and swelling it, and of filling the whole cosmos. Kant mentions this 'ether' as an element which forms the 'flux of the sensations' and he speaks quite simply at one point (p.388) of the galvanism of reason and of reasoning.

If we turn now to the group of American, English, Norwegian and Israeli researchers who were headed by W. Reich and Theodore P. Wolfe, we find ourselves face to face with an experimental investigation into the concept of 'life energy' which in the first place confirms and extends in a truly amazing manner all the basic Galvani-Aldini theories. A more refined laboratory technique, the development of philosophical thought and more up-to-date ideas on astrophysics and meteorology of course make for the formulation of deeper, more elaborate concepts.

'Orgone energy' is the name W. Reich uses for 'life energy', asserting that 'orgone energy' represents the primordial energy of nature. Reich also had the merit of having invented an apparatus for accumulating the life energy, an apparatus which recalls the Leyden jar, the 'square' of Franklin, and the arrangement of glass and metal used by Galvani to increase the contractions of the muscular preparations of his frogs in the laboratory.

It is quite clear that the possibility — now recognised to be a valid one — of concentrating the vital atmospheric energy creates an important premise for the deeper study of the characteristics of the external surroundings of the organism, in the atmosphere and in the cosmos, and opens the way to a more intimate comprehension of its particular mode of action in the interior of the living organism, and to a better quantitative and qualitative analysis. It was the same with the study of oxygen: first in the atmosphere, and secondly within the living organism.

Part II

Orgone Energy and Morbid States

For three years now we have been using orgone accumulators in our Psychiatric Hospital, with the approval of the Director, Professor Telatin; of course we are far from being in possession of adequate space or equipment, though we have obtained good results when dealing with pain of rheumatic origin, with some kinds of neuralgia, constipation and insomnia. In the psychiatric field, its use has proved helpful in treating anxiety and neurasthenia. Good results in such a variety of phenomena should not be cause for surprise: the radiation has in fact a precise vagotonic effect which relaxes the muscles and treats the sympatheticotonia which is an essential basic component of various morbid states on the symptomatological level. Constipation, for example, can be of a sympatheticotonic nature, just as anxiety has a marked cardiovascular component.

It is important in the majority of morbid cases that treatment should be prolonged and very regular; we have never witnessed miracles, and we have recorded failures in chronic cases which had already resisted other treatment. An increase in the generation of energy is evident in quite a high percentage of cases: resistance to fatigue is improved through deeper sleep and so is the capacity to work and study.

As far as therapeutic and laboratory research is concerned, which is, I think, even more important and demanding, our Hospital is certainly not the most suitable place as it lacks the necessary guarantees of environment and control.

I can, however, affirm that the positive results of our first therapeutic experiments have convinced me that there is a firm basis for everything expounded by Reich; and precisely for this reason I have managed to interest the University of Rome and Professor Chiurco himself, with regard to his own particular field of medical pathology and the clinic. G.A. Chiurco has accurately defined 'the present mechanistic impasse'.

Bio-energy and precancerogenesis

A few words on the central theme of our Second International Seminar on anti-cancer prophylaxis and precancerogenesis.

The cancerous tumour is no more than a symptom of the underlying cancerous condition. Local treatment of the tumour — surgical intervention, X-ray, radiation or radium treatment — does not influence the cancerous condition as such, but only one of its visible symptoms. On the other hand, from this point of view, the term 'predisposition to cancer' is misleading and devoid of any real meaning as it is abstract.

The expression 'precancerogenesis' has, on the other hand, a precise meaning, because it draws attention to all those concrete facts which precede an actual cancerous formation on the psychic and somatic level and which get to the root of the carcinomatous disease. Modern medicine cannot and ought not to be only curative, but should aim, as Bonadies affirms, towards prevention.

Nicola Pende — quoted by Chiurco — affirmed at the International Symposium in Rome in 1959 and 1965 that: 'medicine should deal with the whole human being, that is, a synthesis of an individual body and mind plus a synthesis of an individual life and a collective social life.' This is the real point: it is not enough for the doctor to use a microscope; he must be able to relate what he sees with the help of the microscope to the functioning of the autonomous life of the organism as a whole. Local medical practice, with its continual contact with the person in his living unity, leads towards this total vision.

My first observations concerning this relationship between character structure, psychic and somatic disturbances, and carcinoma took place about five years ago when I treated a woman of thirty-five who was suffering from anxiety crises, extreme reserve in her general behaviour, extreme timidity, lack of initiative, and resignation. During the course of the analysis, really aggressive feelings towards the opposite sex emerged and total frigidity (vaginal anaesthesia) was discovered.

Her emotional difficulties were such that the patient had never been able to get married. After about eight months of treatment, disturbances in the sexual organs appeared and got worse, leading to a diagnosis of carcinoma of the neck of the womb and subsequent surgical intervention.

I was not able at the time to see a relationship between the character structure and cancer, between somatic disturbances and disturbances in the emotional-psychic sphere; but today frigidity is precisely and obviously identifiable as precancerogenous terrain, just as is real shrinking. By what mechanisms, by way of what processes?

I was able to carry out research on thousands of women suffering from various neurotic and somatic disturbances, and I discovered that in this group, frigidity (vaginal anaesthesia) is present in the very high percentage of 92 to 94 per cent! Today it is possible to affirm that this mass disturbance is the ground on which the malignant flower of cancer flourishes, affecting one or another part of the feminine genital apparatus (uterus, vagina, ovaries, breasts).

In this group of people, alongside anxiety and constriction, we find thick fibroids and growths in the womb, lumbago, rigidity of the sacral lumbar tract of the spine and pathological curvature of the spine. Spasm of the uterus usually extends to some part or other of the small pelvis and to the adductor muscles of the thighs; and finally an ever-present disturbance is always the inhibition of expiration with a chronic inspiratory attitude and diaphragm block.

Today a coherent comprehension of these various disturbances is possible from the bio-energetic point of view. We have referred to pulsation as a fundamental characteristic of bio-energy; all organs and apparatuses are subject to this law. The physiological concomitants of the joy of living are: a state of bio-energetic expansion, general vagotonia, complete vascularization, perfect and calm pulsation of the cardiovascular apparatus and thorax. Anxiety on the other hand is accompanied by bio-energetic contraction, a concentration of fluid in the centre of the organism, sympatheticotonia, with hypertonia of the cardiovascular apparatus, spasms, divers contractions in this or that organ, of varying intensity and localization.

Breathing is always reduced with inhibition in particular of expiration: and poor external respiration must go hand in hand with reduced internal respiration.

The connection between respiratory inhibition in the neurotic character of sympatheticotonic type and the discovery by O. Warburg of respiratory disturbance in cancerous organs throws light on the whole pathological process. In cases of extreme sympatheticotonia, uterine spasms suffocate the tissue; reduced blood supply leads on the one hand to an accumulation of CO_2; and on the other to an insufficient supply of nutritional material, oxygen and proper biological energy.

The problem of isolating all the social and biological causal phenomena remains — and it is a matter of life or death for millions of women. 'Some day', writes W. Reich, 'psychosomatic medicine, which is at present the domain of a few specialists, will become what it should be: the general framework of the medicine of the future. It is obvious that we cannot reach such a stage as long as the normal sexual functions of the living organism continue to be confused with the pathological manifestations of neurotics and with the products of the pornographic industry.'

BIBLIOGRAPHY

Leprince-Ringuet, L., *I raggi cosmici*. Einaudi, 1954.
Chiurco, G.A., *Precancerogenesi e Tumori Professionali*. Ed. INAIL (3 Vol.), 1955-62-63.
Galvani, L., *Opere Scelte*. Utet, 1967.
Kant, E., *Opus Postumum*. Zanichelli Bo. 1963.
Lanza, U., *Agopuntura Moderna-Reflexologia*. Minerva Medica, Torino, 1966.
Newton, I., *Principi Matematici della filosofia naturale*. Utet, Torino.
Reich, W., *La Funzione dell 'Orgasmo*. Sugar, 1969.

The Treatment of a Malignant Melanoma with Orgone Energy

by Walter Hoppe, M.D.

Orgone Therapist, Tel Aviv, Israel

Dr. Walter Hoppe was trained in psychiatry at the University of Berlin, and has had a private practice in Israel for the past forty years. When Reich discovered the orgone accumulator, he was one of the earliest physicians to confirm its effectiveness, and he has extended its application to a wide range of physical illnesses over the past thirty years. He was director of the Orgone Institute Research Laboratories in Tel Aviv, and the editor of the Internationale Zeitschrift für Orgonomie. *He has published many papers in orgonomic periodicals on his clinical findings. In November 1969, he was nominated a member of the Sybaris Magna Graecia Accademia, in Sibari, Italy, in recognition of his work in cancer research. The paper published below is one of two papers that Dr. Hoppe delivered at the Second International Seminar on Cancer Prophylaxis and Prevention, held in Rome in October 1968. It first appeared in the* Proceedings *of that Seminar, published by CESPRE, Rome, and is reproduced by kind permission of Professor G.A. Chiurco, the director of CESPRE and organiser of the Seminar. Translated from German, by David Boadella.*

When the first orgone accumulator was built in Tel Aviv twenty-six years ago, I had some doubts. I asked myself whether the orgone accumulator could really have the results that were described by Reich. It is true that I could follow Reich scientifically to a great extent. I knew many of his publications in the psychiatric field, and I was very impressed by his clear scientific thinking.

When Wilhelm Reich, in a number of experiments between

1935 and 1939, tried to comprehend the physical basis of the sexual energy, Freud's libido concept, I was reminded, as I studied his 'bion' experiments, of Freud's *Three Contributions to a Theory of Sexuality* which he had published at the turn of the century: 'The unsatisfactory conclusion, however, that emerges from these investigations of the disturbances of sexual life, is that we know far too little of the biological processes constituting the essence of sexuality, to be able to construct from our fragmentary information a theory adequate to the understanding alike of normal and of pathological conditions'.

With the bion experiments, Reich entered deeply into the field of biological processes. His work led him finally to discover the life energy in 1939, in small pulsating energy vesicles, the *Sapa* bions, which were produced from ocean sand. He named this energy 'orgone'. This name was used for its association with the biological charging effect of the energy in the living organism, and with the 'orgasm formula' that Reich had established before his discovery — a four-beat which described the process of biological tension-charge-discharge-relaxation. This four-beat was of fundamental scientific significance for the later development of orgonomy.

In the year 1940, Reich was able to discover that orgone energy existed also in the atmosphere. Orgone-physical laws were discovered that made it possible for Reich to accumulate the atmospheric orgone energy; and in the year 1941, the first orgone accumulator was built.

Two years later, in 1943, I learned of the first publications on the orgone energy discovered by Reich, and I felt driven to test the truth of his findings with my own observations. Reich had found that metallic material, particularly iron, first attracted orgone energy and then repelled it again, whereas all material which gave good insulation against electricity had the capacity to absorb orgone energy. Reich found, in addition, that orgone was better absorbed at great heights than on level plains, and that the absorption was also more effective the nearer one approached the equator; so that in Israel, for example, the accumulator is more effective than in Holland. The effectiveness of the accumulator is also dependent upon atmospheric conditions: it works better in fine weather than in conditions of wind and rain. The accumulator can be strengthened by increasing the number of layers used, a layer consisting for this purpose of organic material on the outside and iron on the inside. There is a variety of other problems concerning the effectiveness of the accumulator, such as the condition and arrangement of the materials, the thermical and electroscopic measurements inside the accumulator, and so on.

Whereas radium and X-rays are body-alien radiations, the atmospheric energy is natural to the body. Two orgonotic systems, the living organism and the orgone accumulator, have a functional relationship with each other. Reich has experimentally proved that when this functional relationship is established, the two orgonotic systems exert a mutually attractive and excitatory effect on each other. The biological centre of the orgonotic system begins to radiate more intensely. Reich considered that cell-radiation was the essential therapeutic factor in the treatment with the accumulator.

I began my observations using a two-layer accumulator for a variety of illnesses. I was able to establish, in this way, that one cannot treat patients unselectively in the accumulator, and that in certain cases there exist contra-indications. Nevertheless, I could claim a whole range of important successes. Gradually I proceeded to use stronger accumulators in treatment, and I worked therapeutically with a twenty-layer accumulator. However, one must be governed by caution when using stronger accumulators, especially as over-radiation can in many cases cause harm.

I will not enter here into an account of the full range of my experiences, but will report on an unusually dramatic development in a cancer patient who undertook an accumulator treatment. It was a case of a malignant melanoma of the skin on the right cheek of a fifty-two year old patient. A change in the skin had set in about ten years before the accumulator treatment, in the form of a 'concentration of freckles' which in the course of time covered two square centimetres. Half a year before the treatment this had developed into a hard-consistency tumour which projected several millimetres above the skin surface, and was about ¾ of a centimetre long when the patient began the accumulator treatment. The tumour had a dark brown colouring and looked to me like a melanoma. Before the patient came to me she had been for a long time under the observation of a dermatologist, of a surgeon, and of a radiologist, as her submaxillary gland was swollen. All three were very well-known specialists. They were united in a diagnosis of cancer. The surgeon felt that a surgical intervention was contra-indicated, and three deep radiation treatments were proposed at intervals of four hours. The patient herself, and her husband, were informed of the diagnosis. Both hesitated to undertake the orgone accumulator treatment, for fear of missing the radium treatment. The patient's wish to irradiate with orgone and with radium at the same time was refused by me on the grounds of Reich's 'Oranur experiment' in which the combination of orgone and radium in an orgone accumulator had produced effects harmful to life in a few hours, over a wide area. When I first drew the attention of the patient and her husband to the fact that with the help of the orgone accumulator the whole organism would be irradiated, and not just the local tumour, and that for this reason the glandular swelling could also be expected to disappear, they agreed to the accumulator treatment. Moreover I gave them my view that within fourteen days the first visible results could make an appearance. They decided, therefore, to follow the orgone treatment for these fourteen days, and to postpone the radium treatment until the end of this time.

Before I began the accumulator treatment, I carried out the 'Reich blood-test', which is described in Reich's book *The Cancer Biopathy*. According to Reich's view each single red blood cell is an energy vesicle charged with orgone. Reich conceived the cancer process not as a local manifestation — the simple tumour formation, but as a general process of sickening. The illness began with a fundamental disturbance of the living pulsation. Alternate expansion and contraction led to a healthy equilibrium, but a disturbance in this pulsation resulted in a chronic preponderance of contraction, and an inhibition of expansion. In this way, a biological shrinking process gradually developed. We then have to deal with a sympatheticotonia in the vegetative nervous system which can encompass the whole organ system and also the blood system.

We take from our patient a small drop of blood and transfer it to a concavity slide containing physiological saline, in order to establish whether, on microscopic examination, the red blood corpuscles disintegrate slowly or quickly. Reich has pointed out that the disintegration of biologically healthy blood takes about twenty minutes, while in the case of the shrinking process the length of time before the disintegration sets in can drop to between one and three minutes. In our patient we found a period of nine minutes — already a significant sign that a shrinking process existed even though it was not, it is true, advancing. A sample of vaginal secretion gave, on microscopic examination, isolated spindle-cells, with the suggestion of disintegrating epithelial tissue, which according to Reich is similarly a symptom of the shrinking process.

The patient was treated in a twenty-layer accumulator. She sat in it in the first three weeks three times daily for half an hour at a time. Moreover, in addition to the general irradiation of the whole body within the accumulator, the tumour was also treated locally. An arrangement was set up within the accumulator, whereby orgone energy was led through flexible pipes from a small accumulator which was also made of metal on the inside and organic material on the outside, and could then be brought to the organism locally. The local irradiation lasted each time for five minutes.

The accumulator has a vagotonic effect, that is to say, the accumulator opposes the sympatheticotonic contraction. The plasma system gives up its chronic contraction and begins to expand. It is to be expected that the red blood corpuscles, after such a period of treatment within the accumulator will be re-energised, and that the disintegration process as seen under the microscope will also be correspondingly delayed. This was the case after some weeks, just as the disintegration of the epithelial cells in the vaginal secretion was arrested, and no more spindle-cells were traceable.

Furthermore, the disintegration of the tumour began. The first results were already recognisable after one week, as the tumour clearly grew lighter in colour. However, this was not accepted by the patient and her husband as a change. On the twelfth day the tumour split into two parts. This splitting was observed by several people without any doubt. By now the patient and her husband were agreed on continuing the treatment after they could see clearly visible changes. In the third week, the treatment was reduced to twice daily, and the tumour grew smaller and smaller from day to day, as could easily be seen. It could be observed that sometimes small pieces of tumour simply broke off. At the end of a month, almost nine-tenths of the projecting tumour had disappeared. It was obvious that within a short time the tumour would fully disappear. Also the swelling of the submaxillary gland was for the most part no longer there.

In the meantime the patient had gone, with my agreement, to her dermatologist who was so surprised that he withdrew his original diagnosis of cancer at once, and characterised the symptoms now as only those of an 'inflamed naevus'. He conceded that her treatment with the orgone accumulator had been successful, and advised her to continue with it. The patient went similarly to her radiologist to inform him. He explained to her immediately that it would be on her own head if she did not get well, and that he could not understand why she had not begun the radium treatment at once. After he had examined the tumour, however, he was so nonplussed that he proposed she should continue with the accumulator treatment for a further fourteen days, and then come back to him; and this she also did. Now it was no longer a question of her pursuing this treatment off her own bat, but the diagnosis of cancer was withdrawn by the radiologist as well.

Meanwhile I was disturbed by a renewed growth of the tumour, even though this took place very slowly. At this time, I heard a report that Wilhelm Reich had found a means not only of charging the organism with orgone energy, but also of drawing the energy from the organism, and in this way inducing streaming movements. He named the device invented by him a 'Medical dor-buster', whose history and construction I shall omit here.*

---

*Reich's discoveries both of 'dor' and of 'melanor' are described in Chapter 12 of *Wilhelm Reich: The Evolution of his Work* by David Boadella (Vision Press, 1973).

I remembered a later significant discovery that Reich had made a few years before. When the granite of his observatory in some places showed symptoms of disintegration, it led Reich to discover a material in the disintegrating black substance, which was later analysed chemically and which he called 'melanor'. Perhaps this 'melanor' was contained in the melanoma? Could it be that melanor was the cause of the fact that the charging with orgone energy was not able to succeed in fully eliminating the tumour? So I wondered if possibly Reich's medical dor-buster could draw out the black substance, together with the orgone energy. In any case, I would try the experiment, and I began now daily to draw with the medical dor-buster on the tumour for several minutes.

A further problem was the superficial breathing of the patient. I was familiar with the concept of Professor Otto Warburg that the cancer cell is a badly breathing cell; and Wilhelm Reich had also described in detail the relationship between superficial breathing and the cancer process in general. The oxygen supply and the elimination of carbon-dioxide were both severely disturbed because of this. Our patient had what Reich termed an 'inspiratory attitude', in which the expiration was shallower than the inspiration. I found she had a spastic respiratory musculature. She began to relax and to deepen her breathing at the same time, but soon she became anxious on doing this, and began to develop a resistance against it, which also she maintained against the treatment with the medical dor-buster.

In this phase of resistance she sought her dermatologist again, who emphasised once again that she should feel no concern, that a malignant illness was out of the question, and that he would now treat her with penicillin. Whereupon she broke off the treatment with me before a further result could be expected.

However, her trouble returned nine months later with the further growth of her tumour. She asked for a treatment solely with the orgone accumulator, but turned against the breathing therapy and the medical dor-buster. Accordingly, with her agreement, I had a meeting with the dermatologist who explained to me at once that fortunately the cancer diagnosis had not been confirmed. Yet after a short explanation from me he was uncertain, and confessed that my interpretation could be correct. He was also in agreement with me that first of all a combined therapy with the accumulator and the medical dor-buster should be carried out, and that this should be pursued for a month. The patient now consented to this as well. At the end of this month the tumour had not grown any more, but had at the same time not become obviously any smaller; however, it was clearly lighter in colour. Moreover, it happened that the tumour burst open shortly before the end of the month, after which a dirty yellow-green thick-flowing mass oozed out. After some days the tumour dried up again.

The dermatologist was now disturbed, and advised operative removal of the tumour. I agreed not to wait for the end of my treatment, and to accept the operation, which would also make it possible for a microscopic examination to be carried out, and for a definitive diagnosis to be ascertained.

Before the beginning of the accumulator treatment, the surgeon, we will remember, had advised against an operation and had recommended only the radium treatment. But after the complete reduction of the submaxillary gland and of a swelling which, now it had gone, showed little connection with the original tumour, the operative removal could be undertaken without hesitation.

The operation, at the University Clinic in Jerusalem, was postponed for several weeks for technical reasons, and I used the interval to proceed with my combined treatment. Now we saw that the tumour burst open again at the same place, with the release of dirty greenish-yellow matter, and again closed up. In addition the tumour was somewhat smaller now. Although I believed that a full reduction of the tumour was possible by my continued treatment, I had no objection against an operation, since now not only the dermatologist but the examining doctor at the University Clinic as well, advised pressing on with the operation.

From the operation, the surgeon was of the definite opinion that the fat under the skin looked as if the patient had been irradiated. The histological examination of the tumour provided him with a diagnosis of 'malignant melanoma'. Some days after the operation, the right submaxillary gland was also removed operatively. The histological examination of the gland gave no pathological findings. The patient today, thirteen years after the operative interference, is free of cancerous symptoms.

In conclusion, we can say that the orgone accumulator had without doubt a strongly healing effect on the melanoma, even though in the end a new tumourous development set in. The possibility of a complete healing of tumours through a supplementary treatment with the medical dor-buster cannot be ruled out of the question.

The rumour has repeatedly been spread abroad that, in the orgone accumulator, Reich had found a universal treatment against the cancer illness; and similar claims have been made in different press media. In reality, in *The Cancer Biopathy*, Reich made clear that it was of the utmost importance to prevent the view that he had found a way to heal cancer with the help of the orgone accumulator, under all conditions. He has published his disappointments, as well as the positive results obtained with the help of this treatment, and has described in detail the difficulties that occur, even after the removal of the cancer tumour, in fighting the general cancer condition. At the same time, Reich has opened up a completely new approach to the cancer problem.

The accumulator can and will have a great prophylactic significance against cancer. For this purpose, everyone who wishes to protect himself in this manner against the cancer sickness, should try to use the accumulator regularly and over a very long period of time. Not a single case of cancer has been registered, as far as I know, among those who have done this for years.

The Case of the Broken Heart

by John C. Pierrakos, M.D.

After his formal training in psychiatry, John Pierrakos came in contact with Wilhelm Reich in 1947, and continued his association with him until 1955, when, with Dr. Alexander Lowen he created the Institute for Bio-energetic Analysis. He resigned as the Director from the Institute in the Fall of 1974, after a long association, to devote his time to the creation of the Institute of the New Age of Man. This New Institute represents further developments and new concepts in the healing process by integrating the domains of the body, mind and spirit, and transforms therapy into a process of evolution according to the consciousness of the New Age. This paper was given at the 2nd International Conference on Bio-energetic Analysis, Aspen, Colorado, July 1973. It was first published in Energy and Character, *Vol.5, No.3, September 1974.*

Introduction

Heart disease in the United States has reached appalling proportions. It kills four times as many people today as in 1900 and more than twice the number that cancer does. It took the lives of slightly more than 361 people per 100,000 in 1972, accounting for three-fourths of the deaths from all cardio-vascular-renal causes and 38.3 per cent of all fatalities of every kind, deaths from accidents included.
WHY?
This is a question that preoccupies virtually every definable sector of American society, from the federal government to the general practitioner in a village of 700 souls. It has crucial meaning for the successful business or professional man in his 40s to early 50s, because actuarial profiles show that this person is the prime target for any of the acute coronary incidents known popularly as heart attacks.

Just recently, I was called in by two cardiologists at Montefiore Hospital of the Albert Einstein Medical School in New York City to evaluate ten patients under their care. The cases were all men, their ages in the critical range: eight had had one or more coronaries, and two had angina. The purpose of the consultation was for me to see whether the auras of these patients — the energy fields surrounding their bodies — gave specific indications of their disease. While my findings are preliminary, and many more evaluations are needed before they can be utilized confidently, the observations were fascinating to me; and I will present them in some detail toward the end of this article as well as in an independent study at a future date, which will include further findings related to the medical workups by the referring physicians.

To place these observations in physiological and psychiatric perspective, I will summarize some of the principles of my work in bioenergetic analysis as they relate to the human heart and circulatory system. The foundation of these principles is our knowledge of the phenomenon of energy in man. The functioning of energetic life is a relatively new discovery in the history of medicine — it was first explored by Wilhelm Reich, who died nearly twenty years ago — and understanding it requires us to open ourselves to new concepts and new relationships as guideposts for our perceptual processes.

It is a demanding but exhilarating thing to reach beyond known experience. We can consider ourselves like astronauts, catapulting into outer space. As they pull out of the gravitational field of the earth, they leave behind the three-dimensional physical reality they have always known: motion, time, and space. These dimensions capture man, so that his body — his organs, his energies, his whole physical being — and thus his framework of thought are bound by their laws.

Time is a concept that exists only if there is a mind to perceive it. Suppose you want to traverse space from one point to another through a vehicle of motion, such as a plane. As the motion accelerates, the time becomes shorter and shorter. For example, it takes about five hours to fly from New York to London, whereas astronauts, propelled by a rocket that moves with much greater energy, circumnavigate the earth in about an hour and forty minutes. Thus, as motion accelerates, time (as well as space) contracts further until theoretically it is totally eclipsed, and we arrive at a timeless existence.

We can compress time radically through our minds. For example, you can transport yourself to the beaches of Mexico right now in a fraction of a millisecond, and part of you will truly be there instantaneously. Many of the people who have so-called out-of-body experiences report that they can actually dispatch a segment of their energetic body through space. The phenomena of mediumship and mental telepathy relate closely to this potential of the human energy systems.

As space travelers accept new perceptual categories to encompass the momentously different realities of extra-terrestrial existence, so students of the human organism surpass traditional formulations to contemplate the inner realities of man's energetic nature. Life, as we perceive it in our three-dimensional reality, is movement that makes itself known through the pulse — the beat of the heart. Most of us have at some time gathered up a bird lying motionless on the ground and listened for its heartbeat to find out whether it was alive. But this movement is composed of a far more essential substance than the physiological elements of blood, chemical secretions, neurological impulses, and the like. It is composed of energy. Man lives by the movement of his energy — energy received from within and outside himself. And the unique organ for transmitting this movement, for regulating and protecting life throughout the organism, is the heart.

Heart disease, then, needs to be conceived of not only as a failure of tissues or an invasion of the organ by hostile microbes or an effect of strain due to another illness or abuse of the body. It needs to be seen as a pathological implication of energetic dysfunction.

In the pages that follow, I will develop this perspective through a review and interpretation of several very large studies on heart disease as well as my own small sample. In discussing these cases, I will present three aspects of cardiovascular illnesses: some of their psychological manifestations, the body structure of the sufferers, and my observations of the energy fields of the aura corresponding with the physical pathologies. Let me begin with the heart itself and its action.

The Heart and its Pulsatory Movement

If we look at the development of the human being or any animal in the upper evolutionary scale, we see that a few cells of the protoplasmic mass, which divides itself at the inception of life, differentiate and assume the special function of maintaining the essential movement that later becomes the pulsatory activity of the whole organism. These cells come from the ectoderm, or outer layer, of the tiny new creature, but they form what will be an interior organ, the embryonic heart. They involute in their growth to shape a spiral, wound mostly counter-clockwise, and to create two subdivided sections, so that the fully formed heart has four chambers encased in a muscular membrane of fibers — the pericardium — that expands and contracts. The organ is also equipped with doors, or flaps (valves), that open and close by the contracting and releasing of the heartstrings (tendons called chordae).

The heart's pulsation is regulated by a specific grouping of cells called the bundle of His, which originate within the right chambers and spread throughout the organ. These have nuclei that fire like batteries, making a fusillade that permeates the whole musculature of the heart and creates its rhythmic movement inward (the systole) and outward (the diastole). If the pulsation is charted on an electrocardiograph, we can see that it is composed of many different rhythms, which come from the different parts of the heart to make up the whole organ's rhythm of about sixty beats a minute. And this exceptional organ never ceases its pulsatory movement until the entity it serves leaves the three-dimensional reality.

The physiological function of the heart is to propel the liquid substance of man, the blood, through the arteries to the ends of the body and back again through the veins. In its course around the circulatory system, the blood picks up and distributes countless particles of energy — biological energies, electrical, chemical — to the very small channels of the vascular tree, the arterioles. These minute blood vessels pulsate too, operating on signals from the autonomic nervous system, which not only controls the body's involuntary functions but is also involved in primal emotional activity. Therefore, when people experience emotion, it is translated all the way down to the arterioles as well as to the heart through the bundle of His. The cardiovascular network, then, bears the strain both of pumping and channeling nourishment to the entire organism and of coping with emotion-related impulses that can, as we will see, literally break the heart.

The heartbeat itself replicates the pulsation observable in the whole of nature, from the rhythmic movement in the single-cell animal to the cyclical patterns of vast meteorological phenomena. While the pulse-and-rest timings of the myriad life forms differ, rhythm as such is an innate characteristic of life. Birds in their flights follow the rhythms of nature to find the routes of migration. There are many theories about just how they do this. One is that they trace the pulsatory movements of the magnetic lines of the earth; another holds that they are responding to the rhythmic changes in the atmosphere.

Other massive biological clocks in nature, repeating rhythms continuously and perpetually, ally with the generative activity of living organisms. In Mexico, for instance, there is a small, gopher-like animal that is drawn to the sands when what is called the paint-brush tide is at its fullest. The animals stay for a day, procreate, and then go away again; they do not visit the shore at any other time. And of course the most important rhythmical event in human biology is the menstrual cycle in the woman.

Reich has pointed out that the common function principle in a process repeats itself from the highest to the lowest unit. A tree, for example, replicates its shape from its largest to its smallest limbs. The major branches have the same structure as the trunk; so do the thinner branches and the littlest twigs. In the same way, the heart, which specializes in transmitting the pulsatory movements of life throughout the organism, represents the common functioning principle in man. Rhythmic pulsation can be found not only in the arterioles and in every cell but also in the basic building blocks of organic matter, such as deoxyribonucleic acid — DNA — which, moreover, has a helix shape, as does the heart. Thus the heart is the organized ensemble of pulsatory movements that flow through the smallest components of the physical body.

Pulsatory movement pervades the energy bodies of the person as well. Every living thing consists of more than just the physical form that we ordinarily perceive and touch. In a sense, the physical organism is the solidified element of an entity composed of energy, an unsolid and dynamic substance that surrounds the physical body and both interpenetrates and extends beyond it. I can see the energy field in a halo, or aura, outside the skin that various observers have described in different ways (see Figure 1). I often use the analogy of water as ice, liquid, and vapor. If you put water in a basin and freeze it, it takes the shape of the basin. Return it to a larger container of water that is exposed to hot air. There will then be the solid ice, which is the physical body; the fluid water, which is the densest energetic body; and envelopes of vapor, or increasingly thin energetic bodies. I use this analogy because I can see three energetic bodies — the water and two densities of vapor. People who are transcendentally or spiritually adept have perceived as many as seven.

When I view the aura, the energy field appears as a pulsatory wave that forms an ovoid or egg shape around the physical body of a healthy person. The energy field glows, like a light-bulb, and it pulsates between fifteen and twenty-five times a minute. This aura has three layers. The one closest to the skin is dark, the second one is somewhat less dark, and the outermost is light.

The rhythmic pulsation of the energy field, the heart, and all other living unities have two phases, which may be called the assertion and reception phases. The first spans the process of activation, and the second the process of repose, or distension. Every component of the body has this dual function. The heart contracts to send blood through the body and then relaxes to let blood into its chambers. The hand can reach out to take or lie open to be given to. Sexual movement can thrust forward and then pull back to allow the pelvis to fill with energy.

In voluntary movement, to assert means that we act: we set in motion, move toward, determine, and use purposefully the forces

Figure 1
The Aura of the Healthy Organism

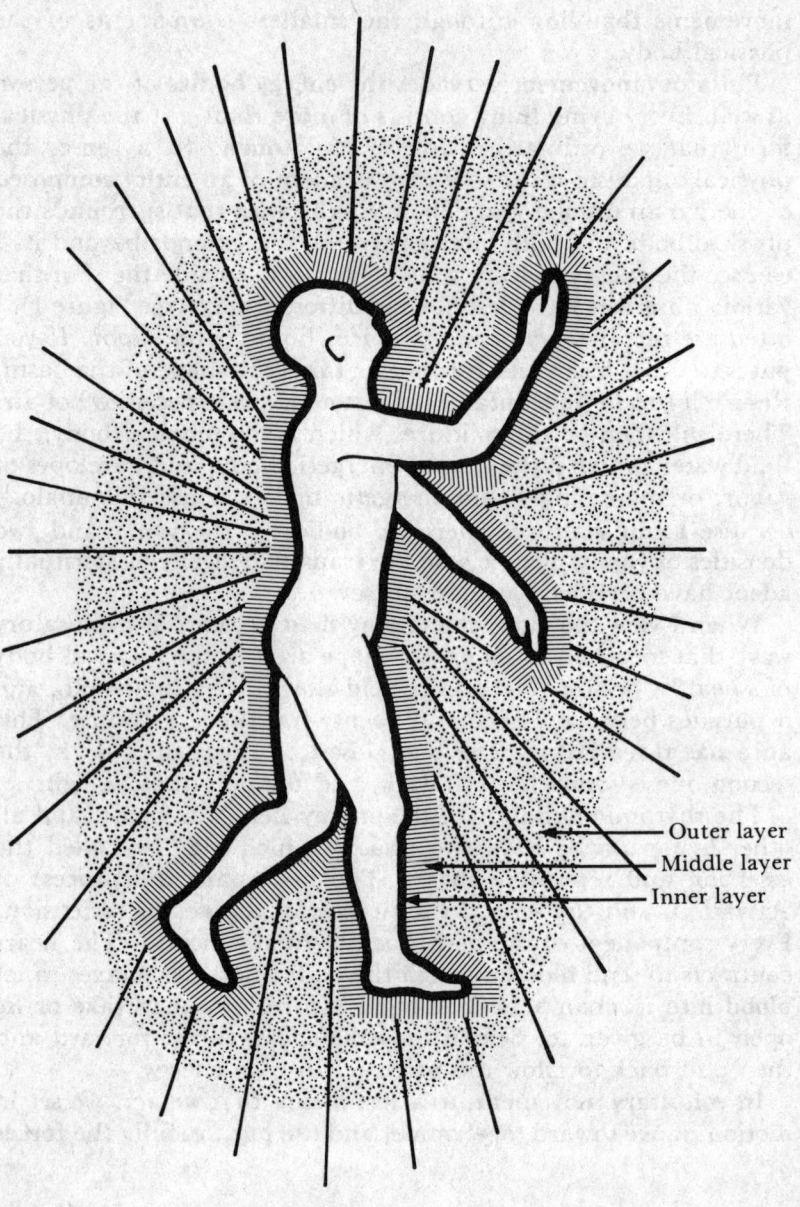

at our disposal. To receive means that we are acted upon, from within or without: we accept motion, wait for it, allow it to determine us, and incorporate the forces that pulsate in or into us.

Each principle can be intensified, and each can be pathologically exaggerated. So the hand can hit or cringe; the sexual movement can thrust aggressively or withdraw coldly. We will see some effects or distortions of the rhythmic phases a little later. Here, let me comment that in the healthy organism, the assertive and receptive principles are balanced in beautiful reciprocity.

Within the physical body of man, the most comprehensive units of the two-phase pulsatory movement correspond with the energy flow in the torso, which forms a figure 8 pivoting around the solar plexus, the center of the vital organs. Thus the upper and lower parts of the trunk each have an overall assertive and receptive expression. Energy circulates upward and downward, crossing the body at the solar plexus, in a continuous stream whose two segments are about equal in the normal person.

Nature provides a preponderant psychosomatic activity in each part of the figure 8: in the upper torso, there are the heart feelings, the various dimensions of love; and in the lower torso, there are the sexual feelings. The intermovement between the heart and sex feelings is very much affected by eros, by romance. Eros is like a little weight on the scale that a person shifts back and forth, making the sexual experience, for example, more heartfelt or more passionate. Eros does not of itself distort the equilibrium between the heart and the sexual feelings, but attitudes of denial and negation will, because the balance is very delicate. If the movement of energy in the figure 8 is cut off from the heart, then the expression of the assertion phase can become hard, pornographic, pushy; if it is cut off from the sex, the assertive expression can become wholly romantic, sentimentalized, stilted.

In healthy functioning, however, the balance can be shifted to accommodate the realities of a relationship and to take advantage of the particular kind of enrichment each human communion may offer. A man was telling me recently, for example, that bringing up his baby has increased his heart feelings tremendously. This is because a little baby is in a sense all heart; his whole being calls to adult love. That is, infants perceive their energy movements without these being focused in the genital area. So the intense pulsatory movement of their organism resonates, vibrates, and fuses with the adult heart.

I have written elsewhere that the assertive and receptive phases of movement represent respectively the masculine and feminine principles of creation, terms that of course reflect the male and female roles in procreation. But the two principles operate in both women and men, shaping every physiological action, every creative endeavor, every response to external stimulus. Harmony and balance between them signal as well as sustain the wholeness of the human person, which is health.

Cardiovascular Disease and Energetic Dysfunction

The person is disunified, the health disrupted, when the harmony between the assertive and the receptive principles is disturbed. In bioenergetics, we can see the disturbance physiologically in blocks that indicate the site of energetic dysfunction. This imbalance is apparent in all illnesses, including those of the heart and circulatory system.

In terms of organic medicine, cardiovascular ailments can be divided broadly into four categories. One consists of diseases of the flaps, or doors (the valves), and the strings (the chordae). Heart murmur is such an illness. Another, which often comes early in life, is rheumatic heart disease. The valves (as well as the pericardium) become inflamed from infection, which damages their ability to close tightly and breaks down the heartstrings.

A second category comprises diseases of the substance of the heart, in other words, the muscle. These are due to degenerative changes, inflammations, or acute vascular accidents such as coronary occlusion.

A third set of diseases afflicts the heart's rhythm. These frequently accompany and may endure beyond the term of the ailments in the first two classifications, especially those of the heart muscle.

The last category includes ailments of the circulatory system, such as high blood pressure, a condition that permeates the whole vascular tree and that can begin in the early years. At the outset, high blood pressure fluctuates; later in life, it becomes chronic. The immediate cause, as explained in medical books, is the constriction of the arterioles, the tiny end tubes that take care of the outflow of the blood. Sometimes the arterioles have vascular lesions, but not necessarily so. Most high blood pressure is technically known as essential, or idiopathic, hypertension — both modifiers meaning simply 'of its own nature' and being fancy ways of saying that the causes of the disease are unknown. Actually, the causes are known, as we shall see.

The dread that people have of cardiovascular diseases of all kinds revolves naturally around the high incidence of abrupt deaths that they provoke. Circulatory illnesses and heart cripplers such as rheumatic fever can issue in a fatal and relatively unpredictable attack on the heart, just as can a single big affront like a coronary occlusion. According to medical understanding, the mechanism of sudden heart failure can operate in one of several ways. The parasympathetic nervous system (a subdivision of the autonomic), which slows down the heart, becomes dominant. This produces a state of bradycardia, or very slow heartbeat, shown by a very wide interval between peaks on an electrocardiogram, and ultimately the beat ceases. Or a blood vessel may break or a clot hit the heart, stunning it and stopping its pulsation. But these and other physiological explanations are basically descriptive. The question remains of *why* the arterioles are constricted, *why* the parasympathetic impulses come to dominate, *why* the blood vessel bursts, *why* a clot forms. Not until the advent of psychosomatic medicine did the fundamental causes of most cardiovascular disease begin to be unearthed.

After the advent of scientific medicine, a development of the eighteenth-century Enlightenment, human pathology came to be considered as strictly physical in origin. About the turn of the twentieth century, and thanks in part to the insights of Sigmund Freud, rigorous investigators began to see that the human being is a psychosomatic unity. Among the pioneers in the work to formulate this approach was William Osler, a great clinician who was studying angina pectoris. Osler established from observing numerous cases that these patients were reacting directly to causes outside their bodies, causes in their life situations.

In American medicine, the physiologist Walter Cannon did a now-famous study on fear and rage in the late 1910s, proving that the blood pressure of animals in these states changed. He explained that the sympathetic nervous system (the other subdivision of the autonomic) responds in two opposite ways under the impact of such intense emotions: by expanding or contracting the whole organism. This activity in turn produces one of two reactions: the flight or capitulation syndrome, expressed in fleeing or in freezing and holding; or the fight syndrome.

In 1932, Franz Alexander inaugurated further groundbreaking work in psychosomatic medicine at the Chicago Psychoanalytic Institute. After studying many people with heart conditions, he and his colleagues found that they persistently uncovered abounding hostility in these patients, a neurotic complex that expressed itself in aggression, the desire to dominate, and an overweening ambition to 'achieve.' Simultaneously, Flanders Dunbar was making extensive observations that demonstrated the relation between emotions and specific pathologies such as heart disease. Her findings led her to describe 'the coronary personality' as well as 'the ulcer personality,' 'the arthritic personality,' and others. In that period and since, the Menninger brothers, William and Karl, have furnished overwhelming evidence connecting cardiovascular disease with emotional causes.

From this expanse of research, a picture has emerged of the cardiovascular patient as a person caught in a vice between unremitting hostility and fear. Each emotion breeds the other in a vicious cycle that traps the organism and ultimately simply exhausts the heart or irreparably damages the arterioles through constrictive pressure.

To visualize how this cycle works, take the example of a slave, such as one from old Africa in centuries past. Terrorized at the beginning of his captivity, he will freeze, thinking of nothing but how to survive. Later, as he grows familiar with his bondage and feels safer, he can allow himself to feel anger against his captivity and to look for ways of undermining his master. But as he develops these feelings, which range from a sense of friction to murderous rage, his fear surfaces again because he is afraid his hostility will be discovered by his master and that he will be punished for it. Thus, in sequence, fear for survival begets hostility against captivity, which in turn begets fear of discovery (in fact, a survival fear) and hostility against dependency (a form of captivity) — or, to put it in bioenergetic perspective, submission begets aggression and so on.

The slave is of course an extreme example. The elements of the chain reaction can be far subtler, deriving from a family configuration that implants precisely the same cycle. We may in fact voluntarily strengthen this dangerous pattern. Take any one of us who knowingly maintains a feeling of superiority over others and indulges persistently in small, critical judgments. We may think these habits are meaningless and unimportant. They are not. As they gain strength, they feed a state of hostility as a behavior, which then leads back to chronic anxiety. And the person is caught in the mechanism that can produce cardiovascular disease. He is in effect digging his own grave until he severs that chain, until he breaks free of that vicious cycle.

Bioenergetically, breaking the fear-hostility circuit means opening blockages of the energy flow that hobble the organism both characterologically and physiologically. The trained practitioner, as I said, can see the operation of the blocking throughout the energy manifestations of the person, from the set of the bones and muscles to the qualities of the aura — rate of pulsation, extension outward from the body, color, and other aspects. What happens is that when the organism's energy, which cannot stop moving, meets a barrier in one segment of its figure-8 flow, it will back up into the other section, swelling it and exaggerating its functioning. This inevitably causes an imbalance in the normally rhythmic reciprocity of the assertive and receptive phases, and one principle will come to dominate the character expression of the organism.

Suppose, for instance, that the two halves of the 8 pulsate twenty-five times a minute and that the movement is impeded in the pelvis. The blockage will decrease the pulsation in the lower part of the 8 to perhaps only ten times a minute. Therefore, while the energy will still take something of a figure 8 form, the lower section of the movement will be smaller, and the organism will be feeding its energy into the upper part of the 8, which will enlarge.

Now, let us say that the receptive principle predominates. For a number of reasons, some of them cultural, this often occurs with women who are blocked in the pelvic region. The fear-hostility cycle will express itself in extreme submissiveness, the organism will perceive the humiliation of this state, and a hostile reaction will set in. Energy blockage is the foundation of emotional illness, which, as we have seen, can and often does trigger organic pathology. With this character formation, dysfunction may afflict the biologically receptive organ of the uterus. The majority of the diseases take the form of deep tissue changes, such as uterine lesions or possibly tumors, or of functional disturbances in the menstrual cycle.

On the other hand, when the assertive principle is overdeveloped at the expense of the receptive, it becomes aggressivity and brutality. Many men identify destructive aggression with manhood, mistaking it for independence from parents and for personal creativity. This distortion issues in various ways, again depending on other factors. It may make the man's sex expression hard and pornographic, as I mentioned earlier. It may turn him into a bar-room brawler. Or it may trigger cardiovascular disease, which is an affliction mainly of men, as two of the studies to be described in the next section show.

In bioenergetic terms, the causality of these ailments is the same as that of uterine disorders in women: the arrest of the healthy, open movement of energy in the organism. The blockage is, once again, in the pelvis, and the excess energy dammed in the upper torso blows up the ego, a conceptual faculty based in the head. The inflated ego propels its host into aggressive behavior aimed at 'achieving,' at 'accomplishing,' at elevating his status in life, at appearing admirable — indeed, superior to others. This is the man who drives for success, equated in our culture with power and money. And this is the prime target for cardiovascular disease.

Obviously, not all physical pathologies follow the gender pattern that shows men sustaining heart attacks and women suffering illnesses of the sexual organs. I have seen many cases of rheumatic heart among women, for example. Generally the onset of the disease came in puberty, right after the young girl's heart had received the shock of rejection by the father. The parent abruptly cut off the tremendous movement of love back and forth between him and the child, probably because he could not deal with the signs that the flow of her energy was now focusing not only in her heart but in her sex as well. So, to protect his own lopsided equilibrium, he withdrew his affection and tenderness from her — breaking her heart-strings. The damage did not always stop with the heart, moreover. Several of these patients had succumbed to tuberculosis soon after developing the rheumatic heart, meaning that the whole chest had become involved in the unresolved longing for the father.

A second possible departure from the rule is a type of patient whom I have described at some length in an article titled 'The Problems and Position of the Modern Woman'.* She is a professional woman, usually gifted in the arts or sciences, who has entered the competitive realm of career making. Like her male counterpart, she amplifies the assertive principle at the expense of the receptive; she is unable to open her heart feelings. Her behavior is predominantly aggressive, a mask that lifts in therapy to show her ricocheting from fear to anger to fear to anger ... the wearying rat race again. I do not have enough evidence to demonstrate persuasively that this character configuration makes a woman prone to heart and circulatory affliction. But I have learned recently that a comparison of actuarial tables over about the last decade provides some disturbing testimony: the number of women with cardiovascular disorders is rising rapidly — and so is the number of women in the work-force.

There are other exceptions to the gender pattern, of course, such as men who develop cancer of the testes or other diseases of

---

*Energy and Character, Vol.3, No.2, May 1972.

the sex organs. But, in general, the blockage complex that breaks a man's heart breaks a woman's uterus instead.

Profiles of Cardiovascular Cases

The early findings on the psychogenesis of cardiovascular disease have been confirmed and expanded by study after study in the intervening decades. But two recent sets of research stand out for their innovations in classification. One, a project initiated by Meyer Friedman and Ray H. Rosenman in 1960-1961 and carried forward since, originally comprised 3,500 male corporate employees aged 39 to 59.* The second, reported by George L. Engel, analyzes 170 cases of sudden death from mainly cardiovascular failure among people of all ages and both sexes.**

Drs. Friedman and Rosenman have categorized their subjects according to two broad behavior patterns that they call Type A and Type B. Type A is characteristic of the action-and-motion man who struggles excessively to obtain the greatest possible possessions and power in the shortest possible time. He will drive himself hard; he will grapple with any challenge; he will grasp for any advantage; he will rarely be introspective or sensitive to the needs of others. In a word, he is aggressive. Type B takes it easier. He is less addicted to a self-image of 'success' and lives a generally less pressured life. The authors' seminal finding in their study of these two groups is that Type A people are two to five times more prone to developing various cardiovascular disturbances than Type Bs. And one follow-up of the original sample, done in 1967, showed that twenty-two of twenty-five deaths — or 88 per cent — from coronary heart disease occurred among Type As.

The medical assessments of Type As show an anomalous

---

*See Ray H. Rosenman, M.D. and Meyer Friedman, M.D., *Neurogenic Factors in Pathogenesis of Coronary Heart Disease,* monograph (Xerox), San Francisco, n.d. (1972?), 33 pp.; and see also Friedman and Rosenman's *Type A Behavior and Your Heart,* New York, Alfred A. Knopf Inc., 1974.

**George L. Engel, M.D., Sudden and Rapid Death during Psychological Stress, *Annals of Internal Medicine,* Vol.74, No.5 (May 1971), pp.771-782.

biochemical picture, including increased cholesterol and increased insulin in the blood and an excess of norepinephrine — an adrenal secretion — in the urine. As in Cannon's animals, then, the hormone balance needed for proper heart functioning has been thrown out of whack, so that these people labor their heart in the struggle against the tremendous swing between the fight and flight syndromes.

Reviewing my own patients from the standpoint of the Type A and B classifications, I find the Type As showing a very similar profile in their work lives and social settings. This is contrary to the lack of correlation between status and behavior type observed by Rosenman and Friedman, a difference due probably to the specific sociometric traits that define the psychiatric patient population. Type As whom I have treated have been accomplished people who held important jobs and were financially well off and socially well respected. They have tended to dominate others, using speech as a means to this end, and they have disliked sharing authority.

Their behavior toward women, though, has been generally less aggressive, and they have been exemplary husbands — superficially, at least. How much they enjoyed sex relations with their wives is debatable: all have had secret affairs, which gave them intense overt anxiety. This part of the pattern corresponds with the family constellation of the Type As, who generally retained a lot of hostility toward their father and a fearful attitude toward their mother. The mother had been the authority figure and a smothering sort, and the father had shown the child hostility, either by withdrawing from him or by abusing him. Type A's wife has tended to become the boss in her own household, so that the marital relationship has perpetuated both the dependency needs and the hostile reaction to them that the man has carried forward from his early years. There is truth in the classic cartoon that shows the big corporation executive in the office giving orders to everybody and then entering his own front door timid as a mouse. In common with Rosenman and Friedman's comprehensive sample, these Type As have thus had an aggressive and a submissive element in their behavior, revealing them to be gripped between a chronic free-floating anxiety and tremendous repressed hostile impulses.

Dr. Engel's study concentrates on people who have died abruptly under the impact of an intense emotional experience. His age division, by decades from birth to 60, confirms the gender pattern of cardiovascular disease: the ratio of males to females is 18 to 1 for the age group 41 to 50, and 26 to 6 for those 51 to 60; and the peak periods occurred among men aged 45 to 55 but among women 70 to 75.

Opening his article with a long view backward into the history of medicine, Dr. Engel cites instances from sources as disparate as the Bible and military annals to show the different emotions traditionally thought to cause sudden death. When Peter the Apostle accused Ananias, 'You have not lied to man but to God,' Ananias fell dead. So did his wife, Shapphira, on learning of his death (5 Acts 3:6). The Roman Emperor Valentinian is said to have collapsed and died '"while reproaching with great passion" the deputies of a German tribe.' Chilon, King of the Spartans, supposedly dropped dead from joy 'while embracing his son who had borne away the prize at the Olympic games.' So did a doorkeeper of Congress in American Revolutionary days, according to the American physician and patriot Benjamin Rush of those times, on hearing of the capture of Lord Cornwallis' troops. Pope Innocent IV and Spain's Philip V number among many figures in history who have died on learning that their army had been defeated.

Current cases in the practice of Dr. Engel and his colleages as well as press reports led him to classify the causes of death into eight categories. Four relate to the loss or threat of loss of a close person. The relationship may be only symbolic; for example, the 27-year-old army captain who commanded the ceremonial divisions at President John F. Kennedy's funeral died ten days later of a 'cardiac irregularity and acute congestion.' Three causes concern a present or even a past danger to the person himself. Dr. Engel tells of numerous people who have walked away unhurt from train and car accidents only to collapse with fatal heart attacks within a few hours. The threat may weigh against status or self-esteem rather than physical safety, as is perhaps the explanation for Wilhelm Reich's death. A matter of days after the announcement of his release on parole from prison, he died of a coronary.

Dr. Engel's eighth category covers the puzzling phenomenon of sudden death at a time of reunion with a loved one, success, or triumph. There is the case of a 55-year-old man, for instance, who died on meeting his father for the first time in twenty years — and whose father then dropped dead himself.

On the bioenergetic plane, it is not hard to understand how a tragedy or acute danger can break the heart: the shock of the event produces such a severe blockage that the energy whips back on the organism with fatal violence. I discuss this causality at greater length in the article 'The Core of Man.' But why would joy or pleasure emulate the lethal potential of grief or terror?

It is not the expansive emotion itself that kills — it is not the positive surge of energy. It is a blockage, and a powerful one, against any feeling, even good feeling. That is, the joy or the pleasure is not accepted; it meets with an immovable negation. This denial may arise from guilt, an overwhelming conviction that one does not deserve the joy. Who knows, for instance, what Chilon, King of the Spartans, had done to his son in the past?

The inability to accept feeling, and specifically heart feeling, was a common denominator of the ten patients whom I was asked to evaluate by the two cardiologists at Montefiore Hospital as well as of other cardiovascular sufferers among my cases. As I said at the beginning of this article, my task was to report what their auras testified about their condition. After some interdisciplinary wrestling, which I will report on further in my future article, the referring physicians circumscribed the scope of the sample so that a correlation could be established between the bioenergetic symptomology and the physical pathology; and I accepted the assignment. Here, in summary, is what I found:

The first trait I noticed in all ten patients was an atypical body structure — a passive, feminine aspect showing a masochistic lower half, energy-charged and holding, and a rigid-hysterical upper part. Some had immature chest configurations, denoting orality; all had a driving head, making a lot of contact with the eyes. Second, regarding their psychological pattern, the behavior of all ten men was passive-aggressive. Aggression characterized their work — they were highly accomplished people — while passivity marked their relationships with their wives.

The third level of observations encompassed the auras of the patients. Here again, as in body structure, there were marked similarities. All ten subjects had a very severe block at the root of the neck, where energy was flying out in a winglike protrusion. In that area, I saw a strong reddish-brown color, which clinically denotes repressed hatred and held-back anger. Almost everyone will manifest some of this tint at the root of the neck periodically; what distinguished these patients was its intensity and continuousness. A major block showed as well in the small of their back.

The most striking aural distortion came out in the front of the chest, just over the sternum. Here, in most of the coronary cases, I saw a very dark emanation shot with some purple and yellow, cylindrical in shape and measuring 1½ to 2 inches wide at its base. This is shown, slightly enlarged, in Figure 2. On the other hand, patients whose attacks had occurred more recently — less than a year previously — exhibited a spiral blockage, shown in Figure 3. This was brownish-yellow in color and graduated from ½ inch to width nearest the chest to 2 inches at its outer edge, and it consisted of strings with grape-like formations in the middle. I do not yet know the meaning of this difference in configurations. The angina sufferers, like others I have treated, exhibited a shape resembling a honeycombed and many-pointed star, as in Figure 4.

These various formations all contained the backed-up and stagnated energy that was being prevented from flowing normally through the torso. And they demonstrated visibly how blockage damages the organism. The enormous excess energy within the chest bombards the heart, overcharges it, and bursts this most vital of man's vital organs.

Figure 2
The Aura with Coronary Heart Disease: Configuration 1

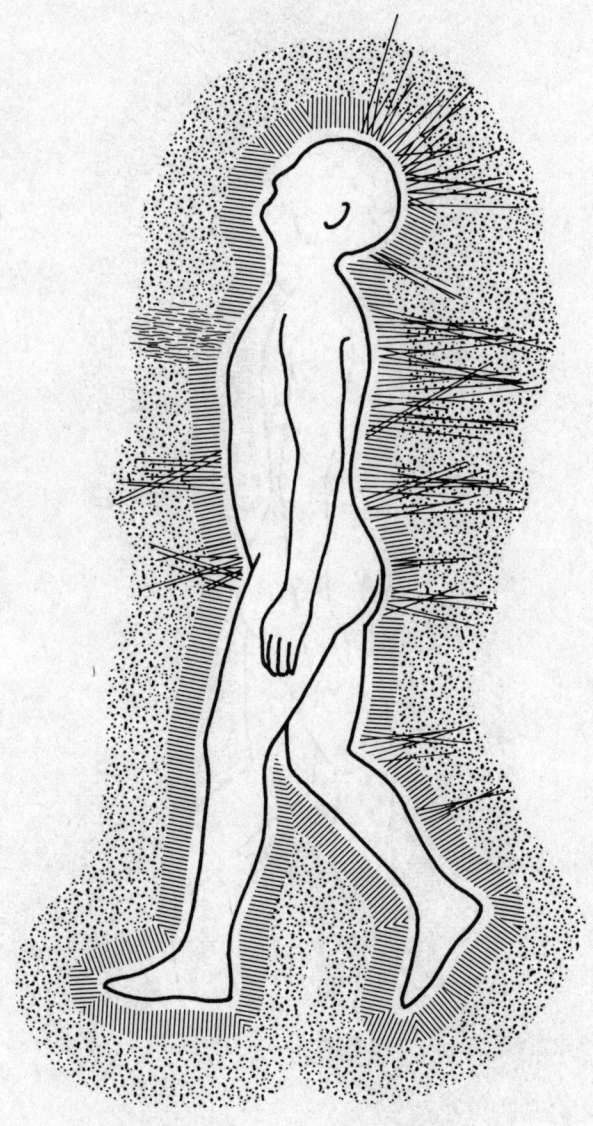

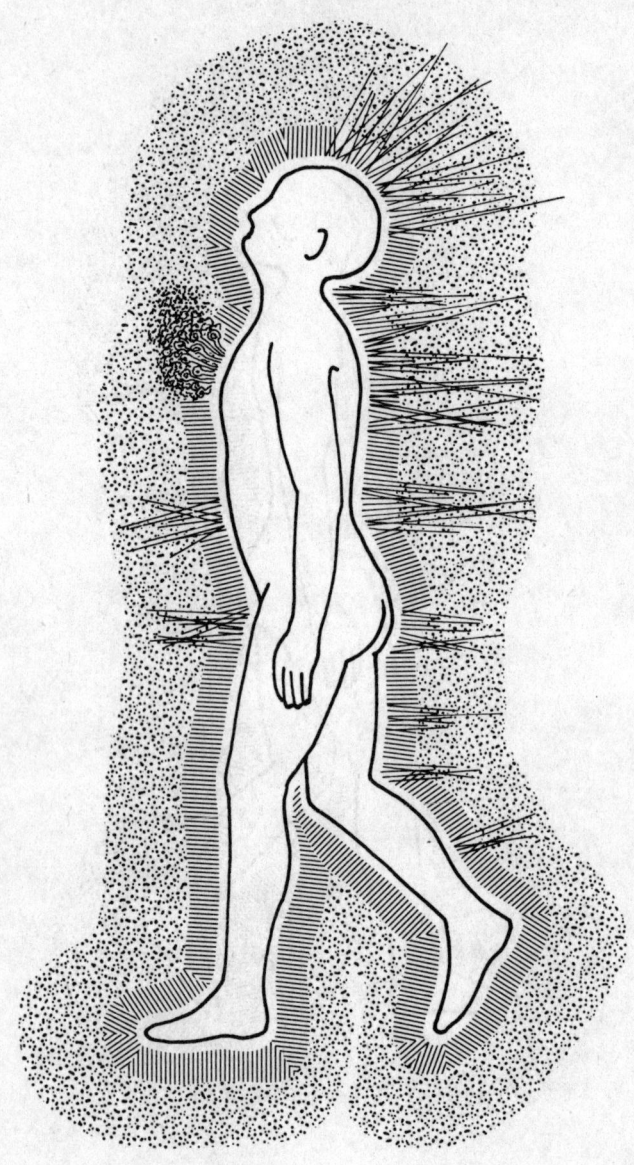

Figure 3
The Aura with Coronary Heart Disease: Configuration 2

Figure 4
The Aura with Angina Pectoris

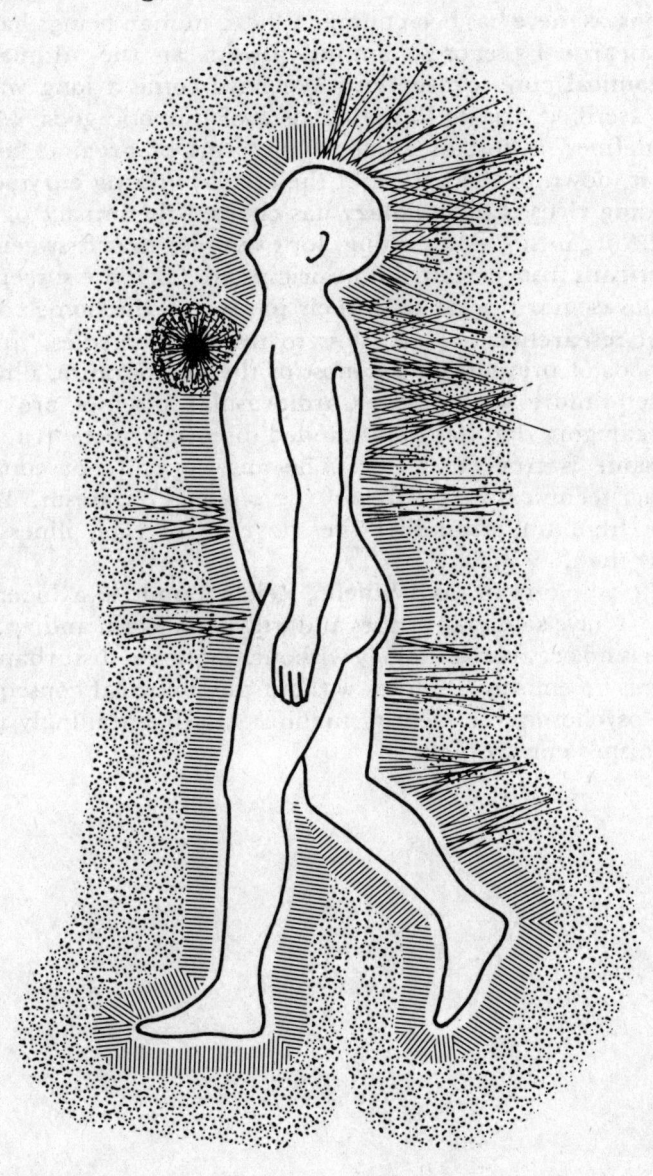

Conclusion

As long as there has been human illness, human beings have tried to unearth its causes, aiming always at the ultimate and economical cure: prevention. We have come a long way since men ascribed disease to the egotism of quixotic gods. Medicine has defined a host of ailments in terms of organic failure or defeat, down to the nature of the crucial missing enzyme or the invading virus. Epidemiology has charted the impact of culture on the organism, establishing, for example, that first-generation Americans from certain ethnic origins are far more susceptible to cardiovascular disease than their parents in the home country.

Yet researchers are at a loss to provide remedies, much less methods of prevention, for most of the deteriorating illnesses or sudden-failure syndromes. Cardiovasular diseases are not the only category that has so far eluded discovery of the true causes; the same is true of cancer. The answers will not come from further technical knowledge of the physical organism. They will come from understanding the meaning of each illness to the whole man.

The whole man, as Wilhelm Reich found, is a bioenergetic unity. I have said many times and will stress again and again that there is no organic pathology without emotional disturbance, and there is no emotional illness without physiological consequences. This psychosomatic identity manifests itself unfailingly in every organism's energy field.

CENTRES AND INSTITUTES

A number of organisations, some formal, some informal, have grown up with an interest in developing some part of Reich's work. The principal ones are given below, so that anyone interested to learn more about bio-energetic therapy or research in their part of the world may do so.

USA
1. *The American College of Orgonomy*, 515 East 88th St, New York. Directed by Elsworth Baker, M.D., the therapist to whom Reich delegated prime responsibility for teaching and training. Publishes journal: *The Journal of Orgonomy* (twice yearly).

2. *The Wilhelm Reich Institute for Orgonomic Studies*, 84-87 Daniels St, Jamaica. New York. Directed by Chester Raphael, M.D.

3. *The Institute of Bio-energetic Analysis*, 114 East 36th St, New York. Directed by Alexander Lowen, M.D.

4. *The Institute for the New Age of Man*. Directed by John Pierrakos, M.D.

5. *The Centre for Energetic Studies*, 1645 Virginia, Berkeley, California. Directed by Stanley Keleman.

6. *The Radix Institute*, PO Box 3218, Santa Monica, California. Directed by Charles Kelley, Ph.D.

7. *The Wilhelm Reich Seminar Group*, 18 Duncklee St, Newton Highlands, Massachusetts. Coordinated by Myron Sharaf, Ph.D.

CANADA Enquiries to Professor W. Edward Mann, Department of Sociology, York University, 4700 Keele St, Downsview, Ontario.

MEXICO *Instituto Wilhelm Reich,* Asturias 43, Col Insurgentes Mixcoac DF. Directed by Dr. Estrada Villa.

ENGLAND *Centre for Bio-energy*, c/o David Boadella, Abbotsbury Publications, Abbotsbury, Weymouth, Dorset. Directed by Gerda Boyesen. Publishes journal: *Energy and Character*, £3 per year ($7.50).

FRANCE 1 *Centre d'Evolution*, 14 Rue St. Pierre, Paris. Enquiries to Ebba Boyesen.

2 *Laboratoire d'Orgonomie Generale*, BP 83, 75923, Paris, Cedex 19.

GERMANY *Wilhelm Reich Study Group*, 8571 Spies, Nr 48. Coordinated by Bernd Laska. Publishes: *WR Blätter* (bi-monthly).

HOLLAND *Institute for Bio-dynamic Psychology*, Ewyckshoeve, Soestdykseneg 12, Lage Vuursche, near Utrecht, Holland. Directed by Jay Stattman and Mona Lisa Boyesen.

ITALY 1 *Instituto de Bio-energetico*, Via Andrea Doria 48, Rome. Directed by Luigi de Marchi. Publishes journal: *Revista Bio-energetica* (quarterly).

2 *Centro Studi Wilhelm Reich*, Cupa Caiafa 36, 80122, Napoli. President: Dr. Federico Navarro. Publishes journal: *Quaderni Reichiani* (twice yearly).

NORWAY 1 *Forum for Character-analytic Vegetotherapy*, Inkognitogt 32, Oslo 2. Coordinated by Bjorn Blumenthal.

2 *Nic Waal Institute*, Spangbergveien 25, Oslo 8. Directed by Berit Waal.

SWITZERLAND Enquiries to Robert Hacco, 27c Chemin Boissier, 1223 Cologny, Geneva.

ISRAEL Enquiries to Moshe Caspi, POB 8706, Jerusalem.

AUSTRALIA 1 *Department of Bio-energetic Research*. Enquiries to: David Lancaster.

2 *The PEER Institute*, 76 Brookton Highway, Kelmscott, W. Australia. Directed by Paul Ritter.

NO LONGER THE PROPERTY
OF THE
UNIVERSITY OF R. I. LIBRARY